1988

Voice
and
Diction

Voice and Diction

A Program for Improvement

fifth edition

Jon Eisenson
Former Distinguished Professor,
San Francisco State University

With the assistance of
Arthur M. Eisenson

Macmillan Publishing Company
New York
Collier Macmillan Publishers
London

Earlier editions entitled *The Improvement of Voice and Diction*, copyright © 1958
by Macmillan Publishing Company; copyright © 1965 by Jon Eisenson; and
copyright © 1974 and 1979 by Macmillan Publishing Company.

Macmillan Publishing Company
866 Third Avenue, New York, New York 10022

Collier Macmillan Canada, Inc.

Library of Congress Cataloging in Publication Data

Eisenson, Jon,
  Voice and diction.

  Includes bibliographies and index.
  1. Voice culture—Exercises. 2. English language—
United States—Pronunciation. I. Eisenson, Arthur M.
II. Title.
PN4197.E46   1985   808.5   83-19951
ISBN 0–02–331960–7

Printing: 1 2 3 4 5 6 7 8   Year: 5 6 7 8 9 1 2 3

ISBN   0-02-331960-7

To Eileen
  and
To Rosanne and Jamie
  and
Their parents

preface

The fifth edition of *Voice and Diction: A Program for Improvement* has been updated to provide contemporary information about voice production and diction (articulation, pronunciation, and intonation) to persons who wish to apply this body of knowledge to the improvement of their own speech. Such improvement is in the interest of increasing their effectiveness as communicators. As in the previous editions, the information includes relevant materials from the related disciplines of speech and hearing science, linguistics, and phonetics.

This edition has been reorganized along the following lines: Part One is concerned with basic considerations and now includes an expanded chapter on "Our Changing Speech Patterns." In this chapter, I review the origins of American English with emphasis on ever-changing and ongoing influences, such as black English and "special" dialects, that may briefly affect the way we talk or must learn to listen and that occasionally have long-term effects. Part Two deals with voice and Part Three with diction. All three appendixes have been revised and somewhat expanded.

As in the earlier editions, I have avoided the temptation to be prescriptive, that is, to recommend any one standard of what is desirable and appropriate for effective oral communication. Instead, I have continued to be descriptive and to present "functional" standards that relate to regions and to specific situations. The final decision to employ pronunciations in keeping with one regional dialect or another, or in one or another speaking situation, as well as choosing "how to turn a phrase," is a matter of individual choice that is made on the basis of individual motivation and objectives, tempered by knowledge. When we speak, we use a complex set of habits. Most of the time, these habits are appropriate to the speaking situation; sometimes they are not. When they are not, they can be changed, but not without major effort and a strong, persistent drive. In some instances, external imposition may bring about a change, but only with the cooperation of a speaker who will accept the imposition. Usually, identification and emulation are more effective motivators for change.

If this book is used in an academic course, it is likely that the students will fall into one of two groups. The first group will probably include persons who are self-motivated to use their voices effectively and to improve their diction, either as a goal worthwhile in itself or as a vocational asset. The four preceding editions of this book have, in fact, been used in courses for students who are preparing to teach, to practice law, to enter the ministry, or to work in the mass media, as well as by persons already in these professions.

A second group is composed of students who may not have been initially self-motivated but who were advised by a teacher, a counselor, or a friend to "take a course" in voice and/or diction. Even though the advice may have been accepted reluctantly, and the motivation may be "external," mature students will avail themselves of the opportunity to learn more than they may know of the mechanism for the human behavior called *speech* and to learn, as well, how to use the mechanisms for voice and speech proficiently and effectively.

This book has also been used by persons who, without specific professional goals, were nevertheless interested in improving their voice and diction. Such persons, through the use of recordings on tapes and cassettes, were their own teachers. Often, I have learned that these motivated speakers used the practice materials in the book to record their friends whose speech they admired as models for emulation. Their own recordings were then compared with those of their models. Though speech is a human endowment, how well we speak is an individual achievement. I hope that the fifth edition of *Voice and Diction* will help to make the effort and the achievement pleasant, if not enjoyable.

For this edition of *Voice and Diction,* I have incurred several debts. I am deeply indebted to the reviewers and the instructors who have offered positive and constructive suggestions for updating materials and making them relevant. I am indebted to the readers who have sent me thoughtful notes about what they liked in the book and what they might like even more if their suggestions were followed. Many of these suggestions have been accepted with gratitude. I wish also to acknowledge my appreciation to Arthur Eisenson for insights and research, and to Sara Krane for several creative dialogues that should make for interesting practice material.

J. E.

contents

Voice
and
Diction

part one

Basic Considerations

Speech is the mirror of the soul: as a man speaks,
so is he.
—PUBLIUS SYRUS, *Maxims*

Speech is civilization itself. The word, even the most
contradictory word, preserves contact. It is
silence which isolates.
—THOMAS MANN, *The Magic Mountain*

What Do I Sound Like?

Why Do I Speak as I Do?

What needs Improvement—
How can I Improve it?

Voice, Diction, and Effective Communication

Although this book is not concerned with communication in its broadest sense, it is concerned with the effective use of the voice and with diction, and therefore with oral (speech) communication. Whatever the speaker's purpose may be, whether it is to share ideas or feelings, to provide information, or to provoke thinking or emotions, the achievement of the purpose or purposes will be enhanced with the effective use of the voice and readily intelligible articulation. We do not pretend that it is not possible for a person to be a potent communicator despite negative qualities of voice, or despite diction that suggests either a narrow regional influence or a strong foreign background. We have, and in a democratic society will continue to have, speakers whose messages may be of such importance that we, as listeners, will expend whatever effort is necessary to adjust to the differences in speech. But such speakers are the exceptions. Few of our outstanding communicators make such demands on us. It is true that among recent effective communicators, including ones we may consider truly great—Winston Churchill, Franklin Delano Roosevelt, John F. Kennedy, and Martin Luther King, Jr.— some had speech that was "nonstandard" or expressive of regional or local dialect influence. However, what identified each of these speakers was a positive and attractive use of the voice, a clear diction, and a felicitous use of language. Each of these communicators conveyed thoughts and feelings with voice, words, and diction appropriate to the occasion and with particular attention to the listeners.

However, most of us may have neither the aspiration or the occasion to become "great communicators." Still, we probably do wish to be effective in our communicative efforts, even if they are limited to conversation or to the few times when we are engaged as public speakers and wish to say a few words particularly well. Those of us who teach, or who plan to become teachers, will find that the occasions for saying a few words well occur every day. We believe that to be able to use the voice easily and

3

effectively, and to articulate intelligibly with a minimum of dialectal influence, will help toward this end.

Part One of this book is intended to provide information that should help the student to become aware of what constitutes an effective voice and what and how the voice expresses the speaker and is perceived by the listeners as suggesting personality and states of health. One of the objectives in Part One is to provide information about the mechanisms of the voice and of articulation on the assumption that intelligent persons wish to understand the functioning of the "specialized equipment" that makes human beings unique in both the manner in which they communicate and the content they are able to communicate.

We will begin with some preliminary considerations relative to vocalization and articulation.

Effective Vocalization

Responsiveness

Above all else, an effective voice is responsive to the intentions of the speaker. Through such responsiveness, the speaker shares attitudes and feelings as well as nuances of thought. Thus, a listener knows not only what the speaker thinks, but also how the speaker feels about the thoughts that are part of the communicative effort.

Appropriateness of Attributes

An effective voice is intimately associated with what the speaker is saying and attracts no attention to itself; it therefore does not distract from what the speaker is trying to communicate. Distraction may result from either the attributes of the voice or the manner in which the voice is produced. If the duration, quality, pitch, loudness, or any combination of these vocal characteristics is faulty or in some way not consonant with the contents of the speech, an element of distraction is introduced. For example, matters of importance are usually spoken slowly rather than hurriedly. Unless secrecy is to be suggested, important content is uttered more loudly than content of lesser importance. Solemn utterances are usually associated with relatively low pitch, and lighter remarks with relatively higher pitch. A reversal of these pitch-contents relationships is likely to be either distracting or misleading. Excessive nasality, huskiness, or any other vocal characteristic that is striking and culturally undesirable may serve as a distraction. In contrast, a very fine voice may also be momentarily distracting if it directs the listener's attention to its unusual qualities. Most listeners, however, soon accept the fine voice and respond to the contents of the speech. On the other hand, a voice that includes a constant element of irritation may continue to distract and may thus impair the speaker's ability to communicate.

We respond negatively to a speaker who, with loud voice and flashing eyes, insists, "I am not angry." We respond both negatively and with disbelief to a speaker whose voice level is just above that of a whisper, seeming by manner to suggest that he or she is about to share a secret, but who says something of little value, even if not a secret.

Manner of Production

A voice may have acceptable characteristics and still be ineffective if the speaker's manner of producing the voice attracts attention. If the speaker is obviously straining to be heard, or if the external throat muscles appear tense or the jaw tight, the listeners may be distracted by what they observe. If listeners must force themselves to be attentive, the effort may be unpleasant. Some listeners may also become tense as a result of what they may see and, through empathy, feel. On the other hand, overly relaxed speakers who seem to be too tired to vocalize and articulate with enough energy to be heard may fatigue their listener-observers.

Appropriateness Related to Sex, Age, and Physique

Another area of vocal appropriateness is related to the sex, age, and physical build of the speaker. We expect men's voices to be different from those of women. We expect the voice of a mature person to sound different from that of a child, and we expect big persons to have "big" voices. A high-pitched, "thin" voice may be acceptable from a small, delicate child, but it is not likely to be acceptable from either a man, a physically mature-looking woman, or a large boy.

Listeners' Criteria of Effectiveness

From the viewpoint of the listener, an effective voice is one that can be heard without conscious effort or strain. It is consistent with the speaker's message and helps to make the message readily audible and intelligible. An effective voice is pleasant to hear, but the pleasure should be unconscious and should not dominate the listeners' reactions, as it might if they were listening to a good singer. To be effective, the voice should be as loud as the specific speaking situation demands. If the speaker is talking to a group, the voice should be heard with ease by every listener, but none should be disturbed because of its loudness. In a conversational situation, the listener with normal hearing and a normal power of concentration should not have to ask a speaker to repeat because of a failure to hear, nor should anyone wish to move away to avoid discomfort from overloudness. In summary, the listener, if inclined to be analytic, should be able to conclude that the speaker's voice, as well as her or his actions, suits the words, the overall situation, and the speaker as an individual. However, a word of caution is in order. Just as speakers should adjust their vocal efforts to the occasion, listeners should adjust their expectations and demands. The public orator may be an autocrat at the breakfast table, but he or she should refrain from orating not only at breakfast with the family but also when dining with friends. His or her companions should make clear their demands; that they prefer conversational speaking to orating.

Objective Self-listening

Although it is not always easy to see ourselves as others see us, the mechanics for hearing ourselves as others hear us are readily available to most of us. Tape or cassette recordings of reasonable fidelity can be made at low cost at home, in speech clinics, or by agencies specializing in recording equipment. Most academic speech departments have adequate equipment for recording and playing back samples of speech. Although the most useful recording is one made when the speaker is not aware that he or she is being recorded and so is least self-conscious, "candid" recordings are not always possible. If the recording is staged rather than candid, we recommend that it include conversational speaking as well as material read in a conversational voice and material spoken as if for a small audience. If the speaker frequently makes public addresses, he or she should also include material spoken as if for a public address. The speaker should then play back the recordings on an instrument that has a fidelity at least equal to that of the recording instrument. While listening, the speaker should respond to these questions:

1. Is my voice pleasant to hear?

2. Does my voice have any characteristics that I would consider undesirable in another speaker?

3. Does my voice reflect what I intended to convey in thought and in feeling?

4. Were the changes in pitch, loudness, duration, and quality appropriate to the changes of thought and/or feeling that I was trying to convey?[1]

5. Would I listen to this voice if I were not the speaker?

6. Does the voice reflect me as a personality?

7. Is it the personality I want to express?

8. Is my articulation (diction) up to the standard of my own expectations? Are there any sounds or sound combinations that need improvement?

If as a speaker-listener you are completely satisfied with all of the answers to the questions just posed, then you are among the fortunate persons who are making the most of the gift of a good, effective voice. If you are not entirely satisfied and you recognize the need for improvement, then you should also be ready and willing to do whatever is necessary to bring about the required changes. An important step in this direction is to learn to hear yourself as others hear you.

Normally, the voice and the articulatory productions you hear when you speak—what you hear if you try to tune into yourself while you are speaking—is different from what other listeners hear. If you wish to hear yourself as if you were a listener, make a high-fidelity voice recording of something you might read aloud to a friend to emphasize a point, or record about a hundred words of conversation with a friend. Both of you may be in for an interesting experience. Each of you will probably recognize the other's voice more readily than your own. Because you are so close to the source of your own voice, you cannot hear it as does a listener who is at even a small distance from you. You hear your voice through the tissues of your body, especially the bones of the head, as these tissues directly conduct the sounds you produce to your hearing mechanism. You also hear yourself by way of the sound waves you produce in the air,

[1] Quality will be considered in the next chapter in some detail. For the present, let us regard quality as the complex of voice features that enable us to identify an individual speaker. Voice quality may also be characterized as nasal, harsh, and orotund (full, "rounded," resonant). The last—orotund—may make a speaker sound pompous if the quality is not appropriate to the occasion. On the positive side, we may use such terms as pleasant, clean, flexible, responsive, smooth, rich, mature, and strong. These terms are obviously subjective. The inventory of words that we use to describe vocal quality is limited only by the lexicon of the listener.

which simultaneously stimulate the hearing apparatus. The listener hears you only through these sound waves.

You can appreciate some of the differences between the two avenues of stimulation if you plug up your ears while you talk. You then hear more nearly through bone conduction than you do with your ears "open." Your voice sounds different and somewhat strange. For immediate contrast, repeat what you have said with your ears unstopped. If at all possible, you should then immediately listen to a high-fidelity recording of your voice. Only then, making allowance for subjective reactions, will you be able to hear yourself as others hear you. Among the important differences resulting from our multiple-conduction feedback system of listening to ourselves is that we may misjudge the pitch, range, loudness, and quality, and possibly the rate, of our speech. Because we cannot hear ourselves as others hear us, we must accept the evaluation of others, especially if they are objective and professionally trained voice teachers or therapists. Fortunately, despite the limitations of our self-monitoring system, we have considerable evidence to show that learning to listen to our own voices is helpful in the improvement of both voice and diction.

The Process of Self-Monitoring: The Normal Feedback Loop

Although we cannot hear ourselves as others hear us, it may be of help to understand how we do hear ourselves, and how we feel when we talk and about what we are saying. If we have normal sensory mechanisms for hearing, seeing, feeling, and movement, our vocal efforts are sent back to us for *monitoring* as we speak. In the act of talking (or for any other learned behavior) we are engaged in producing and responding to the products of our ongoing productions. This is the feedback response. By virtue of these back-flow responses to sound (auditory), feeling (tactile), and articulatory movement (kinesthetic), we become the receivers (responders) to the flow of sensory information that we produce. If we are able to see ourselves in a mirror as we speak we can add the *visual*, although this is seldom possible in normal speaking situations. The feedback process is, of course, neither unique nor peculiar to speaking. Self-monitoring through feedback tells us whether we are walking as we should, throwing a ball as we would like, or swinging a racket, a bat, or a golf club according to instruction. Feedback functions in any learned activity over which we can exercise control.

When speaking, we may have control of sound, feeling, and movement if we are in a quiet environment. When talking in competition with noise, human or mechanical, we have a reduction of reliable information about the sound of our voice and articulation, and must depend more than is usually necessary on the tactile and kinesthetic. Some of us are much better at this than others. Some of us do less talking at cocktail parties because we do not have adequate feedback control of our speech.

Normally, feedback involves two ongoing, simultaneous processes and, when needed, a third. The simultaneous processes are *self inspection* and *evaluation* (comparison). Are we doing—producing—what we intended? Are we swinging the club according to intended plan? Are we vocalizing at the anticipated loudness level and within the desired pitch range? Is the articulation correct? If all is going according to plan, then we continue; if not, we may try to adjust or correct. On occasion, the decision may be not to make an obvious correction of the past effort, but to make corrections for subsequent efforts. In any event, to adjust and/or to correct, the speaker must have a model in mind, a target or goal, toward which to move.

When, after years of habitual vocal or articulatory behavior a modification is desired, no speaker should assume that target behaviors will come without considerable practice. Even after new habits are established, there may be temporary disruption under stress or high emotion. Stage fright may produce such disruption. However, as in the case of Eliza Doolittle in Shaw's *Pygmalion* (or in the musical version, *My Fair Lady*), when calm and the opportunity to practice were restored, the vocal and articulatory changes were also restored.

Listening to Others

In addition to turning the mirror on ourselves, it might help to do some directed listening to the voices that are part of our everyday living. We may find that some of our acceptances and rejections of individuals are related to their voices. The following are a few projects that should be useful.

EXERCISES FOR LISTENING TO OTHERS

Feelings

1. Tune in to a daytime television "soap opera" and listen to the voices of the performers with your eyes closed. Can you identify the hero or the heroine through the medium of voice alone? Can you detect the likely role of other characters by their initial utterances? Can you pick out the family friend? The pseudofriend? A person whom you would like to like? One whom you instantly distrust? What are the specific vocal attributes of each character that influenced your decision? Try to imitate these attributes.

2. Compare the newscaster you habitually listen to with one you seldom hear or even avoid. Do the vocal characteristics of the newscasters have anything to do with your choice? List for each of them the vocal characteristics that you like and dislike. Which of the two has a more favorable balance? Are there any television or radio personalities who intentionally use an unusual quality of voice to attract attention? Are these people whom you would accept as entertainers? Do you have the same expectations and "standards" for the voice of a newscaster and that of a commentator on the news? For a person who is regarded as an authority on a particular subject or issue? For a sportscaster or someone who gives the weather report? For a weather forecaster who is identified as a meteorologist?

3. Listen critically to two or three of your friends. Are there any characteristics of their voices that you particularly like? Are there any that you would like to have modified? Why?

4. Listen critically to some persons whom you do not particularly like. Do you hear any vocal characteristics that might account for your reactions to them? Do they remind you of anyone you disliked as a child?

5. Recall a teacher, present or past, whom you consider especially effective. Is the voice of the teacher an important factor in your judgment?

Describe the teacher's vocal attributes. Contrast this teacher with one you consider ineffective. Describe the voice of this teacher and determine whether it was a factor in your evaluation.

6. Tune in to a radio or television round-table discussion on a contro- *Melt* versial topic. Do you find yourself inclined to the point of view of any of the speakers because of the way they sound? Do you find yourself disinclined to any of them for the same reason? List as specifically as you can the attributes and their effects on you. How would the following terms suit the individual speakers: *agreeable, irritable, pompous, antagonistic, aggressive, negativistic, soft-spoken, firm, tired, energetic, pedantic, indecisive, weak, complaining, congenial, authoritative, warm, cultured, charming, indifferent, conciliatory, nonconforming, rigid?*

7. Listen to a radio or television network program on which there are a professional moderator and two or more participants. Compare the vocal tones of the moderator with those of the participants. Observe whether the moderator reveals any partiality or personal prejudices through her or his voice.

8. Listen to a group of friends or acquaintances engaged in a conversation or discussion on a controversial topic. Do the participants reveal their personalities as well as their viewpoints through their voices? What terms listed in Project 6, or terms of your own choosing, would you apply to them?

9. Do you know any public figures who have had voice training? (Many public figures have had such training, and some prepare specifically for each important address.) Can you recall any changes resulting from this training? Are there any who have changed in a direction you consider undesirable? Are there any whose voices are so obviously "trained" that they no longer seem to be themselves? Are there any who might benefit from voice training? What vocal characteristics would you like to have improved?

Listening to Diction: Articulation

Let us turn our attention to diction (articulation) in our role as listeners and evaluate the production of friends, acquaintances, and mass media personalities. Do any of the above make obvious and/or habitual articulatory errors such as lisping, lalling (substituting a *w* sound for an *r* or *l*)? Do any of them slur syllables or sounds in unstressed positions? Do any stress or accent the wrong syllable, or give equal stress to all syllables in multiple-syllable words? Do any "mouth too much" and make their articulation both effortful and unpleasant to observe? Do any articulate so rapidly as to make you uncomfortable because you prefer not to listen that fast?

Are there any politicians or mass media personalities who seem to attack the language rather than articulate it with respect? In contrast, are there any speakers you look forward to hearing because of their respect for the language; a respect they share with their listeners? What characteristics of their speech evokes this response?

What did Hamlet mean when he advised his players to "Speak the speech, I pray you, as I pronounced it to you, trippingly on the tongue; but if you mouth it, as many of your players do, I had as lief the town-crier spoke my lines"?

Physical Health

The voices of most speakers who are not especially aware of their speaking habits and who are not trained self-listeners are likely to reflect states and changes in physical health. In the absence of any specific, chronic condition affecting health or attitude, vocalization is adversely affected by such conditions as fatigue, involvements of the respiratory tract, and conditions that produce either hypertense or hypotense muscle tone.

Perhaps the single cause that most frequently affects our voices is the common cold, which, because it directly involves the nose and throat, impairs normal vocal reinforcement. In addition, if the larynx is involved, the vibrators (vocal bands) may be temporarily thickened and so may produce tones that are not adequately reinforced. If there is a significant amount of inflammation, we tend to avoid laryngeal pain by keeping our vocal bands apart, and as a result, we produce breathy and husky tones.

Similar to the effects of the common cold are those produced by allergies that involve the respiratory tract. These may include nasal congestion, irritation of the throat and larynx, and coughing. If the coughing is persistent and severe, the vocal bands may become involved. We may begin to appreciate the effects of persistent coughing from the following:

> When you cough you force air through the windpipe at a speed approaching or exceeding that of sound, which is 723 miles an hour at sea level. . . . By the time the air reaches the level of the Adam's apple, its speed has dwindled to hurricane velocity of about 100 miles per hour. When it blows out of the mouth the air is moving at fifteen miles per hour, a mere zephyr.[2]

Most of us may be able to vocalize effectively despite the possible abuse to which our vocal bands are subjected when air is occasionally propelled at up to supersonic speeds. It should be no surprise, however, that many of us cannot be both chronic coughers and effective vocalizers, especially if our coughing is violent and hacking.

Figure 1–1 is a diagram that shows the vocal bands in a position too far apart for efficient vocalization. In this position, the voice becomes husky and suggests, at best, a partially voiced whisper. Swollen vocal bands, usually associated with laryngitis, may

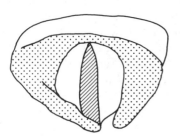

FIGURE 1–1 Diagram, adapted from a high-speed photograph, showing vocal bands not sufficiently approximated for good voice production, and too closely approximated for normal breathing. [Courtesy Bell Telephone Company Laboratories, New York.]

[2] This extract is based on the experimental findings of B. B. Ross, R. Gramiak, and R. Hahn, "Physical Dynamics of the Cough Mechanism," *Journal of Applied Physiology* **8**:264–268 (1955). They found that, depending on various external pressures and the size of the opening of the trachea, the velocity of air during a cough may range from a speed equivalent to a 15-mile-per-hour wind to that of a 100-mile-per-hour hurricane: "If . . . the tracheal lumen is compressed to one-sixth its normal cross section area, the linear velocity thus generated is 28,000 cm/sec., nearly 85% of the speed of sound."

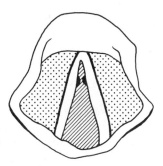

FIGURE 1–2 **Vocal nodules, often associated with high-pitched shouting. Note the typical paired formation in the upper part (middle third) of the vocal folds.**

be a temporary cause of this condition because there may be pain if the bands are brought together as in normal vocal effort. Intentional and prolonged ''whispering'' or the voluntary and habitual production of a husky voice may be associated with thickened vocal bands and so may constitute both the cause and the effect of a chronic condition.

Figure 1–2 shows nodules on the vocal bands. This condition is often associated with high-pitched shouting and may develop at any age.

Good vocal hygiene calls for either avoiding the conditions that are conducive to poor vocalization or reducing vocal efforts when such conditions cannot be avoided. Persons who must speak often have an obligation to practice good vocal hygiene. This calls for avoiding talking under conditions that involve competition with excessive noise or reducing talking to a minimum under such conditions. Otherwise, good vocal hygiene calls for doing whatever is required to keep physically healthy by observing the ''rules'' for proper rest and exercise and doing whatever else your doctor is likely to tell you if you want to stay in good health.

Personality and Mental Health

Mentally healthy persons are aware of what is going on about them and respond without violence to their own integrity to the demands of their environment. Mental health[3] and a healthy, well-adjusting personality are attained through continuous effort. Speech and voice are both the tools and the results of this process.

Young infants respond to their environment and express themselves almost entirely through the voice and reflexive body movements. Babies who cry much of their waking time may be colicky. Those who whine or are almost always on the verge of crying are probably unhappy. If they do little crying, but coo for self-amusement, as well as for the amusement of those who surround them, they may be considered happy, or at least normal, babies. Whatever the condition, whether it is temporary or chronic, babies express themselves mostly through the voice. At each successive stage of development, from infancy to maturity, a child's voice continues to express—to reveal or to betray—both personality and mental health.

Earlier in this chapter, we suggested that you become an objective self-listener and

[3] In this discussion of mental health, the reference is to conditions that suggest anxiety, mild depression (indifference), and neurotic states, rather than to psychotic conditions. Sometimes, speakers are not aware that their vocalizations express their attitudes. Occasionally, vocal habits persist even when the condition is no longer present. The voice may then be a mirror that reflects the past as well as the present.

decide whether the voice you hear reflects you as a personality. Another question to be answered is whether your voice has any characteristic that you would consider is undesirable in another speaker. Here are some further questions that we hope you can answer in the negative. Does your voice suggest a whine when no whine is intended? Do you sound as if you are complaining about something when you intend only to state a fact? Do you sound defeated? Do you sound aggressive or hostile rather than poised and secure? Do you sound chronically tired, bored, annoyed, or just too, too sophisticated for this mundane world in general and your associates in particular? If the answer is "yes" to any of these questions and you have no intention of suggesting the trait that is expressed, insight and recognition should be of help in motivating a change.

Among the more frequent vocal problems associated with maturation is the failure of the voice to drop in pitch during physiological adolescence. Occasionally, we meet chronological adolescents and postadolescents who still speak in their childhood pitch range. Sometimes, we even find the habitual pitch level raised above that of preadolescence. Although in rare instances this vocal problem may be related to disturbances in motor control or in the glands, more often the cause is emotional. The chronological adolescent, whether boy or girl, who wants to continue to be mother's or daddy's child, or who is, for other reasons, apprehensive about growing up and assuming grown-up responsibilities, may be announcing the wish or the fear through an infantile voice.

Another adolescent problem frequently associated with vocal disturbance may arise from a strong identification with an older person. As a result of such an identification, an adolescent girl, for example, may imitate the pitch and other vocal characteristics of an idolized adult. Unfortunately, the voice of the adult may be the product of a vocal mechanism unlike that of the imitator. The woman teacher on whom the high school girl has a "crush" may properly be a contralto with a pitch range too low for the vocal apparatus of the imitator. The effect may be a strained, husky voice. The problem for the boy in high school may be even more acute if he is intended by nature to be a tenor and his hero-figure is a person with a bass voice.

The author has had several male students who might have had good tenor voices, and may possibly even have been effective speakers within the upper part of their baritone range, but who wanted very much to speak like bassos. Within the bass range, unfortunately, they were constantly hoarse and could not be heard beyond the first two or three rows of a classroom. Psychological investigation strongly suggested that the young men were overanxious to be recognized as men—and fearful that they might not be so regarded. The author has also had several middle-aged male voice patients with much the same problems of voice and associated psychodynamics. He has also had a number of women voice patients who were referred to him by laryngologists because of thickened vocal bands resulting from habitual vocalization in too low a pitch range. In several instances, the women were working in professional areas that until recently had been considered the province of males. The suspicion of "masculine protest" was supported by the psychodiagnostic evaluation. Fortunately, this type of protest is now less often needed than in the past twenty years.

Sometimes, to the misfortune of the speaker, habits of voice may persist and so reveal the maladjustments, pesonality, and mental health of a past period. Voice production is a motor act, and motor acts that are repeated tend to become habitual. Thus, once-dependent persons may still sound dependent, and once-aggressive, "chip-on-the-shoulder" individuals may still sound as if they are obviously hostile. With conscious effort, vocal habits can be modified so that we reveal ourselves as we are when we speak rather than as we were during a period of past adjustment difficulties. However, if adjustment difficulties continue to be present, an effective voice may not be achieved unless therapy includes the problems of which the voice is a symptom.

The Effective Vocalizer

If we examine our reactions to individuals who have effective voices, we are likely to conclude that by and large they are also effective as persons. The voice, or any other attribute of human behavior, is not the free-floating essence of a blithe, disembodied spirit. It is, on the contrary, an essential product and aspect of human behavior. It may sometimes be possible for a mentally or physically sick individual who has had considerable professional training to produce the voice effectively for a specific purpose and for a limited time, as actors and some public speakers may be required to do. Even professional performers, however, cannot continue to vocalize effectively, act effectively, or in general pretend effectively for an indefinite period. In our discussion in subsequent chapters, we assume that we are addressing ourselves to essentially healthy persons. This assumption permits leeway for the expression of a little bit of neuroticism that is or should be the privilege of all. It also allows for occasional physical ailments—even those that may be classified as psychosomatic because the body does protest what the mind sometimes must accept.

If readers are at any time in doubt about whether their lack of an effective voice may be associated with either a temporary or a chronic state of subpar physical or mental well-being, proper medical consultation is in order. Certainly, a person who has suffered from chronic hoarseness, or who has had any disturbance centered in the larynx, should not undertake voice training without examination and clearance from a physician, preferably a laryngologist. Although voice training can improve most people's vocal efforts, such training should not be undertaken when a physician prescribes vocal rest. We would also urge that no person become his or her own physician or use as a substitute for a physician a friend who has had what may appear to be similar voice symptoms. There is danger in using a friend's prescription. The individual who would be an effective vocalizer should have a personal examination by his or her own physician.

As a general suggestion, vocal practice should be undertaken only when we are rested. If vocal fatigue sets in after a short period of practice, check with your physician, who may in turn refer you to a laryngologist. Distributed practice throughout a day is better than long periods that may produce boredom. Specific suggestions for voice practice are given in the chapters that follow.

2

The Mechanisms for Speech
(Voice and Articulation)

This chapter considers the mechanisms through which human beings achieve speech and are able to communicate their thoughts, feelings, attitudes, and intentions, according to their needs. Conversely, when it suits their needs, they may be able to conceal what under other circumstances they try to reveal. All of us know speakers who are more proficient than others at revealing and/or concealing. Essentially, this discrepancy implies differences in the degree of control that we have over our speech mechanisms, control that normally becomes more voluntary as we mature. Acting demands a high level of such proficiency.

We first consider how the voice is produced. For our purposes, *voice* may be defined as the tones that are created by the movement (pulsation) of the vocal folds (bands, cords), and that are modified and amplified by the cavities of the mouth and the throat. We use the terms *vocal bands* and *vocal folds* interchangeably; we avoid the popular and lay use of the term *cords* simply because whatever else this apparatus is, its constituents are *not* cords.

Articulation refers to the modification and interruptions of voice and breath that result in the controlled succession of sounds that we think of as speech. Speaking, of course, requires the use of a linguistic symbol system.

The human vocal mechanism deserves understanding and respect for what it is: a sensitive instrument capable of permitting us to produce a type of sound of distinct quality called *voice*. Direct comparisons with mechanical instruments tend to minimize the attributes and the potential of the vocal mechanism and its product. There are, however, several parallels between the human vocal mechanism and some musical wind instruments that may help to give us at least an intellectual appreciation of how each functions.

Voice Production

In most wind instruments, sound is produced when air is blown over a reed or through vibrating lips, as in the case of a trumpeter. The reed, or the reed substitute (the lips), is usually near the blowing end of an elongated tube. The quality of the sound produced with a wind instrument is determined partly by the size, shape, and nature of the material; partly by the length, thickness, and type of reed, and partly by the ability of the person doing the blowing. The human voice-producing mechanism permits even the average speaker to be a virtuoso. Without conscious practice, most of us become skilled in making our voice mechanisms respond to our wishes. We play our vocal apparatus through ranges of pitch, loudness, and quality not possible by many wind instruments. The extreme flexibility of the vocal mechanism is the basis for its superiority over musical wind instruments.

Some Fundamental Definitions

We have used the terms *pitch, loudness,* and *quality* with the assumption that their meaning is understood. Nevertheless, we will define the terms technically, so that their use will be clear throughout our discussions in Part One of this text.

Pitch is the result of the frequency of vibration of a sound source. In the voice, pitch is the attribute or ''dimension'' of sound that results primarily from the rapidity of movement of the vocal bands. We perceive vocal pitch as levels and ranges in speaking; in music, we perceive it as notes in the scale.

Loudness is related physically to the amplitude of the movement of the vocal bands; that is, to the amount of force or energy that is applied to the vocal bands as they are set and maintained in motion.

Quality is produced by the complexity of the sound wave and its reinforcement by the speaker's resonating cavities. From the listener's point of view, quality is the auditory impression of sound wave activity. In technical terms,

> This complexity is related to the number and strength of the partials that compose the sound, and these in turn are determined by the combination of the vibratory patterns of the sound source and the selective alterations of the sound in the resonators. (Moore, 1971, p. 2)

These definitions include both physical and subjective aspects. The physical properties are inherent in the sound wave per se, and they can be measured objectively by appropriate instruments. The subjective properties are the sensations or reactions of the listener to the physical phenomena. Our concern is largely with the subjective aspects or properties of the sounds produced by the human phonatory (vocal) mechanism.

Requisites for Sound Production

In order to produce sound, whether it be music, noise, or voice, three essential conditions must prevail: (1) There must be a body capable of being set in vibration; (2) there must be an available force that may be applied to the body to set it in vibration; and (3) there must be a medium for transmitting the results of the vibration to individuals capable of awareness and response. The first two requisites are found in the normal human mechanisms for breathing and are discussed subsequently. The third requisite is air.

When necessary, a normal person is readily able to modify and control the breathing mechanism to produce the voice while sustaining the functions of respiration. We shall be able to understand how voice production is accomplished through a study of the nature and the structure of the vocal mechanism. In our discussion, our objective is an overall view of the voice-producing mechanism rather than a detailed consideration of its component parts.

The Vocal Bands

The vocal bands, or vocal folds, are bodies capable of vibration (pulsation); thus, they meet the first requirement for sound production. Biologically, the potential vibrators function as part of a valve mechanism to prevent foreign matter from entering the windpipe (trachea) and the lungs. The vocal bands are two small, tough folds of connective, or ligamentous, tissue situated in the larynx, or voice box, at the top of the trachea (see Figures 2–1 and 2–2). The bands are continuous with folds of muscle tissue and are connected to cartilages of the larynx.

The *trachea* is a tube, or a "pipe," about four inches in length and an inch in diameter that is continuous between the pharynx and the lungs. In construction, the trachea is a series of incomplete rings of cartilage and membranous tissue (see Figures 2–1 and 2–2). This construction provides form and elasticity so that there is no danger of tube constriction or collapse when air is drawn into the lungs. The elasticity of the trachea also permits movement in swallowing and in speaking. These movements may be felt with the finger and may also be observed in a mirror. In swallowing, the top of the trachea moves upward and slightly forward toward the chin. These movements are usually more apparent in men than in women, especially in those men who have a conspicuous Adam's apple.

The trachea subdivides into two tubes known as *bronchi*. Each *bronchus* further divides and subdivides into smaller tubes within the lungs. These smaller-sized tubes are known as *bronchioles*.

If we could view the vocal bands from above, as in Figure 2–2, they would appear as flat folds of muscle that have inner edges of connective tissue. The vocal bands are attached to the inner curved walls of the thyroid cartilage at either side. At the midline, the bands are attached to the angle formed by the fusion of the two shields of the thyroid cartilage. At the back of the larynx, each band is attached to a pyramid-shaped cartilage called the *arytenoid*.

Because of their shape and their muscular connections, the arytenoid cartilages can move in several directions. In doing so, they directly influence the position and state of tension of the vocal bands. The arytenoid cartilages can pivot or rotate and tilt backward and sidewise. As a result of these movements, the vocal bands can be brought into a straight line along the midline position so that there is only a narrow opening between them (*B* in Figure 2–2), or they can be separated for quiet breathing (*A* in Figure 2–2). If the bands are brought together in a narrow V, as in the upper part of Figure 2–2, noisy whispering or possibly a breathy voice would be produced if an effort were made to vocalize.

The small, tough vocal bands, ranging in length from seven-eighths of an inch to

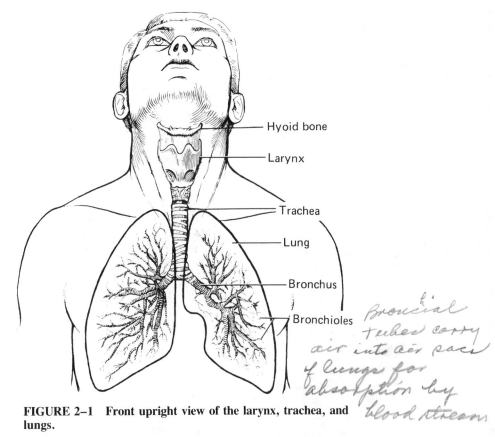

— Hyoid bone

— Larynx

— Trachea

— Lung

— Bronchus

Bronchioles

Bronchial tubes carry air into air sacs of lungs for absorption by blood stream

FIGURE 2–1   Front upright view of the larynx, trachea, and lungs.

The larynx is a structure of cartilage, muscles, and membranous tissue at the top of the trachea. The largest cartilage of the larynx is the *thyroid* cartilage, consisting of two fused shieldlike parts. The vocal bands are attached to the inner curved walls of the thyroid cartilage laterally, and in front to the angle of the two fused parts of the thyroid. At the back, the vocal bands are attached to the arytenoid cartilages.

The trachea divides into two *bronchi*. Each *bronchus* divides into tubes of decreasing size known as *bronchioles*.

one and one-fourth inches in adult males, and from less than one-half to seven-eighths of an inch in adult females, are directly responsible for the sound called *voice* that is produced by human beings.

The *frequency of vibration* of the vocal bands is determined by their length, thickness, and degree of tension when they begin to vibrate. We think of pitch as being high, medium, or low, or we use such terms as *soprano, alto, tenor, baritone,* or *bass* to designate ranges of vocal pitch.

Although the term *vibration* is used to designate the action of the vocal bands, a more accurate term might be *flutter*. When the column of breath is forced through the narrowed opening between the approximated vocal bands, they are literally blown apart and then come together in a flutterlike manner. If the breath stream is steady and con-

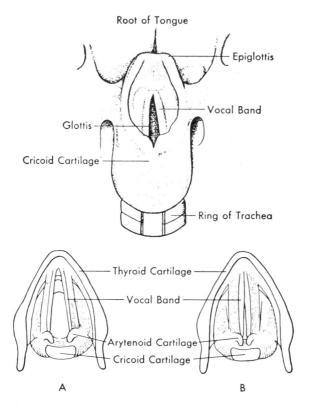

Root of Tongue

Epiglottis

Vocal Band

Glottis

Cricoid Cartilage

Ring of Trachea

Thyroid Cartilage

Vocal Band

Arytenoid Cartilage

Cricoid Cartilage

A   B

FIGURE 2–2 View and diagrammatic representation of the larynx and the vocal bands, showing attachments to cartilages and larynx.

Upper diagram: The larynx viewed from above and behind (posterior aspect).

Lower diagrams: *(A)* Vocal bands shown in position for quiet breathing; *(B)* Vocal bands in position for vocalization.

trolled, the result is a sequence of rhythmical flutters that produce in turn a rhythmical sequence of air puffs. The vocal tone is a product of the number of flutters, or "vibrations," per unit of time and the vigor with which the bands are blown apart. The greater the number of flutters, or vibrations, the higher the pitch. The greater the vigor with which the vocal bands are blown apart, the louder the tone. When the vocal bands flutter or vibrate with evenness and regularity, "smooth" or "clear" tone is produced. Irregularity of vibration, caused either by inadequate control of the breath stream (poor motive control) or by an unfavorable condition of the vocal bands, results in the production of uneven or "noisy" vocal tones.

The frequency of vibration varies directly (increases) according to the tension, and varies inversely (decreases) according to the mass and length of the vibrating bodies. Because most men have longer and thicker vocal bands than most women, male voices are on the average lower in pitch than female voices. The average fundamental frequency for male voices is 128 cycles (waves) per second; it is between 200 and 256 cycles per second[1] for adult female voices. Vocal tones are actually a complex of frequencies. Zemlin (1981, p. 253) explained that "the laryngeal tone is complex, composed of a *fundamental frequency* which is determined by the vibratory rate of the vocal folds, and a number of *overtones* that are *integral* multiples of the fundamental frequency." Thus, when the vocal folds vibrate at 100 times per second—the funda-

---

[1] The letters Hz (Hertz) are now commonly used instead of cycles (waves) in referring to frequency. Hz = cycles per second (cps).

mental frequency—the complex tone we hear includes overtones at 200, 300, 400 . . . cps. Hollien, Dew, and Phillips (1971, pp. 755–760) found that the mean frequency (pitch) range for adults exceeded three octaves, with individual ranges varying from one and a half to four and a half octaves: "Further it appears that many normal adults exhibit ranges comparable to those of singers."

Variation from our fundamental frequencies is, for the most part, a result of the changes in tension of our vocal bands. We have considerable control over their state of tension. Such control becomes evident each time we sing the musical scale or a song or raise or lower the pitch level of a sound or a word when talking. Variation also occurs as a result of involuntary changes in the vocal bands associated with overall states of bodily tension. The tensions of the vocal bands vary as other muscles voluntarily or involuntarily become tense or relaxed. If you are habitually a tense individual, you are likely to vocalize at a higher pitch level than if you are habitually a relaxed person. Immediate responses to situations produce overall changes in bodily tension that are likely to be associated with tension changes in the vocal bands and therefore in their frequency of vibration. These changes become apparent in situations conducive to excitement and elation at one extreme, and to sadness or depression at the other. (This topic is considered in some detail in Chapter 8, "Pitch and Effective Vocalization.")

The Motive Force

The second requisite for sound production, the force that vibrates the vocal bands, is the column of air or expired breath stream. In ordinary breathing, the vocal bands are open in a wide-shaped V so that the stream of breath meets no resistance as it is exhaled. For purposes of vocalization, we recall, the vocal bands are brought together so that there is a narrow, relatively straight opening rather than a V-shaped one. The result is that the exhaled air meets resistance. In order for the air to be expired, the air column must be more energetically exhaled than it is in ordinary breathing. The energetic exhalation "vibrates" the vocal bands and voice is produced.

As indicated, vocalization for speech requires control. Control, which normally takes place without conscious effort on our part, is usually achieved by the action of the muscles of the abdominal wall and the muscles of the chest cavity.

The *chest* (thoracic) *cavity* consists of a framework of bones and cartilages that include the collarbone, the shoulder blades, the ribs, the breastbone, and the backbone. At the floor of the chest cavity, and separating it from the abdominal cavity immediately below, is the *diaphragm*. We can locate the large, double-dome–shaped muscle called the *diaphragm* by placing our fingers just below the *sternum,* or breastplate, and moving them around the front, sides, and back of the thoracic cavity to the spinal column. In breathing, the diaphragm rises toward the chest cavity during exhalation and descends toward the abdominal cavity during inhalation. In breathing for purposes of speech, both the normal respiratory rhythm and the extent of the upward and downward excursions may be modified according to the speaker's immediate needs.

The *lungs,* which function as air reservoirs, contain much elastic tissue and consist of a mass of tiny air sacs supplied by a multiple of air tubes and blood vessels. Because the lungs contain no muscle tissue, they can neither expand nor contract directly. They play a passive role in respiration, expanding or contracting because of differences in pressure brought about by the activity of the abdominal and rib muscles that serve to expand and control the thoracic cavity. Air is drawn into the lungs as a result of outside air pressure when the chest cavity, expanded through muscle action, provides increased space for the air. Air is forced out of the lungs when the chest cavity decreases in size and the pressure of the enclosed air is increased. This sequence is normally accomplished through action in which the diaphragm is passively but importantly involved.

Diaphragmatic Action. When the volume of the chest cavity is increased, air is inhaled into the lungs by way of either the mouth or the nose and the trachea. An increase in the volume of the chest cavity may be effected through a downward, contracting movement of the diaphragm; through an upward, outward movement of the lower ribs; or through a combination of both. During inhalation, the diaphragm is active in contracting, thereby lowering the floor of the thoracic cavity. When inhalation is completed, the diaphragm becomes passive and relaxes. The abdominal organs then exert an upward pressure, and so the diaphragm is returned to its former position. When it becomes necessary to control exhalation for purposes of vocalization and speech, the muscles of the front and sides of the abdominal wall contract and press inward on the liver, the stomach, and the intestines. These abdominal organs exert an upward pressure on the undersurface of the diaphragm. This pressure, combined with the downward and inward movement of the ribs, increases the pressure within the thorax, causing the air to be expelled from the lungs. Throughout the breathing cycle, the diaphragm is roughly dome-shaped. The height of the dome is greater after exhalation than after inhalation. (See Figures 2–3 and 2–4.)

It is important to understand that the diaphragm, though passive in exhalation, does not relax all at once. If it did, breath would be expelled suddenly and in a manner that

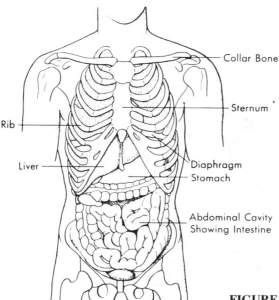

FIGURE 2–3 The chest (thoracic) and abdominal cavities.

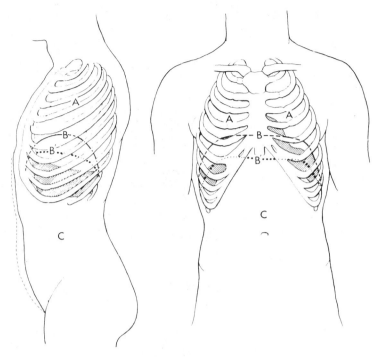

FIGURE 2–4 Diaphragmatic and abdominal activity in breathing.

A. The thorax or chest cavity.
B. The diaphragm passive and "relaxed" as at the completion of exhalation.
B′. The diaphragm contracted as in deep inhalation.
C. The abdominal cavity. Note the forward movement of the abdominal wall that accompanies the downward movement of the diaphragm during inhalation.
(The crosshatched portion of the lung represents the additional volume of the expanded lung as in deep inhalation.)

would make sustained vocalization impossible. Fortunately, the diaphragm maintains some degree of muscle tension at all times. When the diaphragm relaxes because of the pressure of the abdominal organs, it does so slowly and gradually as the air is expired. Thus, a steady stream rather than a sudden rush of breath is provided for the purposes of speech.

In regard to thoracic and diaphragmatic action, what has just been described is in effect an application of the principle of air motion to breathing. Air, regardless of its source, flows from areas of relatively high pressure to areas of relatively low pressure. The pressure of contained air may be decreased by an expansion of the container and increased by compression of the container. As applied to breathing, air (breath) is moved (breathing takes place) as a result of the muscular changes of the thoracic cavity. Specifically, when the chest cavity is enlarged (pressure is reduced), air flows in; when the chest cavity is reduced in size (pressure is increased), air flows out.

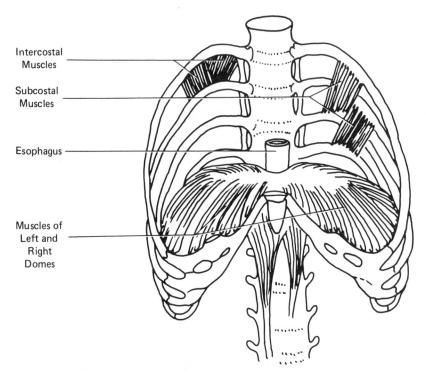

Intercostal Muscles

Subcostal Muscles

Esophagus

Muscles of Left and Right Domes

FIGURE 2–5   The thoracic (chest) cavity showing the domelike structure of the diaphragm and its attachments to the rib cage and the vertebral column.

Figure 2–5 presents a "view from above" of the diaphragm and the organs within the chest cavity. It shows the domelike structure of the diaphragm more clearly than Figure 2–4.

Breathing for Speech.   In breathing for ordinary life processes, the periods of inhalation and exhalation are approximately equal. Breathing for speech, however, usually requires that this regular rhythmic respiratory cycle be modified so that the period of exhalation exceeds that of inhalation. Normally, for speech, we inhale quickly between units of utterance and exhale slowly while speaking. This modification necessitates a degree of voluntary control not required for automatic breathing. Such control is usually achieved by abdominal activity.[2] This point is considered in greater detail in our discussion on voice improvement.

In normal nonspeech breathing, an average of about a pint of air (500 cc) is interchanged in each respiratory cycle. Conversational speech may require little or no more air; vigorous speaking may require more air. Seldom, however, do we use more than 10–20 percent of the total amount of air that our lungs are capable of holding. Control

[2] See Lieberman (1977, pp. 3–9) for a detailed consideration of the physiology of breathing for speech production.

of breath and the appropriate use of our resonators for the reinforcement of vocal tones, rather than increasing the amount of breath, are essential to adequate voice production.

Reinforcement of Sound Through Resonance

Hallow *area*   *Save*

The requisites of sound production are satisfied when a force is applied to a body capable of vibration and is transmitted or conducted through a medium to a receiver. From a strictly physical point of view, a receiver is not necessary. Psychologically, however, there can be no report or corroboration of the occurrence of a sound unless the sound is received. The receiver must be capable of auditory sensitivity within the pitch range of the vibrating body. Furthermore, the receiver's auditory sensitivity or threshold for hearing must be low enough for the intensity level of the sound. If a receiver is far away from the source of a sound (the initiating vibration body), considerable energy has to be used to create vibrations of enough amplitude to be heard. At least, this would be the situation if a body were to be set in vibration in an "open field," by which we mean under conditions in which the sound is not reinforced through resonating bodies. We are assuming, also, that the sound is not amplified through mechanical devices, such as an electrical sound system. Fortunately, the human voice does have the immediate benefit of reinforcement through resonating bodies. Later, we shall consider how reinforcement through resonance is accomplished in the human voice mechanism. For the present, we shall discuss as briefly and as simply as possible two kinds of resonance reinforcement that may be used for any sound.

Forced Resonance

Forced resonance or forced vibration occurs when a body that is set in vibration has a contact with another body that is capable of the same frequency of vibration. The result of this contact is to set the second body in vibration. In effect, a sound has been transmitted directly from one body to a second, and so the sound is reinforced. This is partly what happens when the sounding body of a piano vibrates and when a vibrating string of a violin transmits sound by way of the bridge to the body of the violin. It is also partly what happens when a tuning fork is set on a box or a board or a tabletop. The effect is the production of a sound that we perceive as louder than would be the case if there were no forced vibration or forced resonance.

Cavity Resonance

A second form of reinforcement that is common for musical instruments, and for sound enhancement in general, takes place as a result of cavity resonance. By *cavity,* we mean a partially enclosed body. Examples include the shell or the conventional stage used by an orchestra; the tubular arrangement of a wind instrument; a tumbler or drinking glass; and the "cavities" of the mouth, nose, pharynx, and larynx of the human body. Each cavity, depending on its size, shape, texture of tissue, and opening, has a natural frequency range for the sounds that it will reinforce with *optimum efficiency,* that is, for the sound range with which *the cavity is in tune.* Even a limited knowledge of musical instruments should lead us to generalize that the larger the cavity body, the lower will be its natural frequency range (that is, the more efficiently the resonating cavity will reinforce low-pitched sounds). Conversely, the smaller the cavity body, the higher will be its natural frequency range. Thus, a bass viol, with its large cavity, is tuned for the reinforcement of low-pitched ranges of sound, and a violin (fiddle), which has a smaller body, is tuned for the reinforcement of high-pitched ranges of sound. These ranges, of course, are relative to the family of string instruments. Comparable correlations between the size and the pitch range hold true for wind instruments. Thus, we can account for the differences in the range of sound for woodwind instruments that are similar in shape but different in size.

Reinforcement and Coloring of Vocal Tones

If we depended only on the energetic use of controlled breathing to make ourselves heard, we would have little "broadcast" ability without the help of mechanical (electrical) amplification. Fortunately, our vocal mechanisms are constructed so that a building up of laryngeal tones takes place through the reinforcement capacities of the resonators of our vocal apparatus. Before considering the contribution of each of our principal resonators—the cavities of the larynx, throat (pharynx), and nose, and the mouth (the oral cavity)—we shall briefly discuss the overall reinforcement of laryngeal tones.

The tones that are initiated in the larynx are modified and reinforced or "built up" in the structures beneath and above the vocal bands. The result of what takes place in these subglottal and supraglottal structures (see Figure 2–6) is production of the voice that emphasizes or brings out the potentialities of some vocal characteristics and minimizes or damps out others.

The chest, or thoracic structure, reinforces and modifies the laryngeal tone through a combination of forced (bone) and cavity resonance. When the vocal bands are set into action, with a resultant vocal tone, the tone is transmitted to the bones of the chest. We can feel this effect by placing a hand on the upper part of the chest while vocalizing an *ah*. We should also be able to note that there is considerably more bone vibration felt with the vocalization of an *ah* than with an *ee*. We may then appropriately conclude that our lower laryngeal tones are given considerably more reinforcement through the forced (bone) resonance than are the higher-pitched laryngeal tones. Except for avoiding cramped postures, there is nothing we can do to enhance this type of vocal reinforcement. There is, however, much that we can do in regard to cavity reinforcement, which we now consider.

As already indicated, the principal human vocal resonators are the cavities of the larynx, pharynx, and mouth, and the nasal passages. To a significant degree, the tracheal area just below the larynx and, to a lesser degree, the bronchi also reinforce laryngeal tones.

Each of the principal resonators, by virtue of its size, shape, and tissue texture, has special properties that enable it to make a unique contribution to the modification and reinforcement of the initial laryngeal tone and the production of the final or "finished" voice that the listener hears. We should be mindful, however, that at all times the vocal tones that emerge are the products of the contributions resulting from combined characteristics of all the resonators as well as the bony structures of the chest and head. Though some tones may have primary or predominant coloring resulting from the properties of one of the principal resonators, the others contribute to the finished voice.

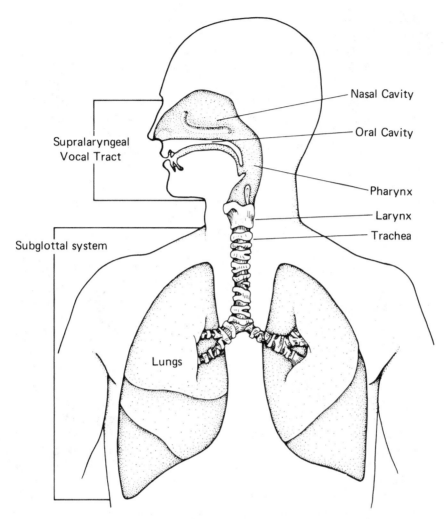

FIGURE 2–6   The three physiological components of human speech production. [After P. Lieberman, *Speech Physiology and Acoustic Phonetics* (New York: Macmillan Publishing Company, 1974), p. 4.]

The discussion that follows considers the features of each of the principal resonators and the contribution that each makes to our vocal efforts.

The Larynx As a Resonator

Vocal tones, as soon as they are initiated, are reinforced in the larynx. If the larynx is free of organic pathology and not under strain, and if the speaker initiates and maintains vocalization without abnormal tension, there is little he or she can or need consciously do about obtaining good laryngeal resonance. If the speaker has laryngitis, however, normal laryngeal reinforcement is not possible. If you suffer from laryngitis, it is best to reduce your talking to a minimum and, if possible, do no talking. If the condition is recurrent, or persistent, a visit to a physician is in order.

The extrinsic muscles of the larynx are those that connect it to the jaw and other bones and cartilages so that it will maintain its normal position when at rest and be lifted upward and forward for swallowing. Tension of the extrinsic muscles of the larynx, as indicated, interferes with the reinforcing function of the larynx. Such tension is also likely to interfere with the free action of the vocal bands for good tone production. Tension is necessary in the act of swallowing. You can feel the tension of the extrinsic muscles by placing your hand on your throat as you swallow. Such muscular tension should, however, be avoided in most speech efforts. We approximate such tension for the vowels of *see* and *sue* and, to a lesser degree, for the vowels of *hate* and *hat*.

The Pharynx

The pharynx, or throat cavity, has the necessary attributes for optimum sound reinforcement. How a cavity resonates (reinforces) a given tone or range of tones is determined by several factors. These include the size, shape, and nature (material, texture, tension, and the like) of the cavity walls and the size of its opening as related to the source of the sound (the vibrating body) and/or other connecting cavities. The pharynx, because of its size and the control we can exercise over it to modify its shape and tension, is much more important as a vocal reinforcer than is the larynx. We modify the length of the cavity each time we swallow or each time the soft palate is raised or relaxed. We change the quality of vocal tones through changes in the tension of the pharyngeal walls. Growths, such as enlarged adenoids or tonsils, may damp vocal tones and modify loudness as well as sound quality. When, because of infection or emotional tension, the pharynx is abnormally tense, the voice quality tends to become strident and metallic. Higher-pitched tones are reinforced at the expense of low tones. The result sometimes is an unpleasant voice that lacks adequate loudness and carrying power. When the pharyngeal tensions are normal, the voice is likely to be rich and mellow— at least as rich and mellow as the individual throat permits.

Our understanding of the action of the pharynx as a resonator can be enhanced by a brief review of its structure. Figure 2–7 shows us that the pharynx begins just above the larynx and extends up to the entrance to the nasal cavity. The portion near the larynx—the *laryngopharynx*—is capable of considerable modification. The diameter can be changed for the reinforcement of the fundamental tones and overtones produced in the larynx. The tones we identify as the vowels of our language are produced in part as a result of action of the laryngopharynx.

The *oropharynx* is the area just above the laryngopharynx. The oropharynx can pair either with the area below (the laryngopharynx) or above (the nasopharynx), or with the oral cavity (the mouth), or with all three to modify vocal tones. As a result, the oropharynx can act subtly or grossly to reinforce tones and to produce sounds of different qualities.

The *nasopharynx* is the uppermost part of the pharyngeal cavity. This area can in effect be separated from the mouth cavity and connected (coupled) with the nasal cavity through the act of elevating the soft palate (the velum). When the velum is lowered, the nasopharynx can be paired or coupled with the lower part of the pharynx or with the oral cavity. The nasopharynx is directly involved in the reinforcement of the nasal consonants *n, m,* and *ng.*

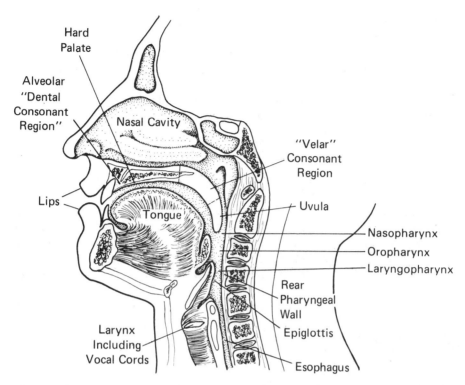

**FIGURE 2–7   Section of head showing principal resonators and organs of artic-
ulation. [Adapted from P. Lieberman, *Speech Physiology and Acoustic Phonetics*
(New York: Macmillan Publishing Company, 1977), p. 40.]**

The Oral Cavity

The mouth, or oral cavity, is the most modifiable of all the resonators of importance
for speech. Except for that part of the roof of the mouth that constitutes the hard palate, all the parts that together form or are included in the oral cavity are capable of
considerable movement. The lower jaw can move to create an oral cavity limited only
by the extent of the jaw's action. The tongue, though attached to the floor of the mouth,
can be elevated, flattened, extended out of the mouth, or drawn up and curled within
the mouth, or it can almost fill the closed mouth. The lips can close tight along a straight
line, open centrally or laterally to apertures of various sizes, or open wide as the lower
jaw drops to permit a view of the back of the throat. The velum and the uvula can be
elevated to increase the size of the back of the mouth or relaxed to make the back of
the mouth continuous with the throat. Through these many modifications, the oral cavity and the organs within it not only produce the various sounds of our language but
reinforce them as well.

The Nasal Cavity

Except when the nasopharynx is coupled with the nasal cavity, we have little direct
control over the latter. Unfortunately, the linings of the nasal cavity and the cavity

itself are considerably affected not only by physical illnesses involving the upper respiratory tract but by emotional disturbances as well. The condition of the nose, it appears, is often an excellent indicator of what is happening to us physically and emotionally. It fills up when we have a cold, when we are allergic, when we are very happy, and when we are acutely sad. When, for any one of numerous reasons, the nasal cavity is not free, adequate reinforcement of nasal sounds in particular and non-nasal sounds in general is difficult, if not impossible.

The Sinuses

The role of the sinuses as resonators has not been clearly established. We have four pairs of sinuses that drain into the nasal cavity. Most of us become aware of our sinuses when they are infected and drain the products of their infection into our respiratory tract. Short of trying to keep well so that we can avoid the unpleasant condition called *sinusitis,* there is little we can do about the sinuses to influence voice. Unlike most of the other cavities associated with the respiratory tract, we cannot control or modify the size, shape, or surface tension of the sinuses to affect the reinforcement of vocal tones.

Flexibility of the Vocal Mechanism

Earlier in the chapter, we compared the voice mechanism with that of a wind instrument. In our comparison, the point was made that the vocal mechanism was considerably more flexible and therefore superior to any wind instrument as a producer of sound. The reeds of a wind instrument are fixed in size and degree of tension. Human vocal bands, however, can be changed in length and tension so that a comparatively wide range of pitch is possible. Through muscular contraction, our resonating cavities can be modified so that the sound produced by the vocal bands can be variably reinforced. Normally, we can direct our voice through a combination of resonators so that sound emerges either orally or nasally. The manner in which we open and shape our mouths permits us to produce a variety of sounds, which are most readily exemplified in the vowels of our language. When the lips, the tongue, and the palate become more actively involved in the modification of sound, articulation, an aspect of sound production peculiar to human beings, becomes possible. This aspect of sound is considered after our discussion of the attributes of the voice and some factors that are related to vocal changes.

Characteristics of Sound—and Voice

All sounds, including those that are vocal, have four fundamental characteristics or attributes. These are *loudness, pitch, duration,* and *quality.* When we respond to a given sound, whether it be the barely audible sound of a dropped pin or a clap of thunder, we are responding to a combination of attributes. The results of our experiences enable us to recognize certain sounds as belonging to the things that make them. So, also, we are usually able to associate voices with the persons who produce them. Tom's voice is a complex of his particular vocal attributes, as are the voices of Harry and Dick. If we know Tom, Dick, and Harry well and have a fair sensitivity to the voice, we are likely to identify each by his voice. If we lack a sensitivity to vocal differences, or if the sum of Tom's vocal attributes is much like Dick's or Harry's, we may occasionally make mistakes in our identification. Usually, however, one attribute of voice is likely to be different enough so that the sum produces a voice that is sufficiently individualized to permit reliable identification.

The human voice as a sound producer is not limited to one given pitch, loudness, duration, or even quality. The human mechanism, with its subtle and complex neuromuscular controls, is capable of a range of variation for each of the sound attributes. A baritone vocalizer may produce sounds that overlap the upper range of the bass and the lower range of the tenor. A female contralto may be able to overlap the high tenor and much of the soprano ranges. No speaker produces tones at a single loudness level. As we speak, we vary the intensity of our sounds from syllable to syllable, word to word, sentence to sentence, and, of course, from occasion to occasion. We vary the duration or time given to utterance as well as the pitch and the loudness. We are usually able to speak rapidly, slowly, or at a moderate rate, according to need as well as habit. Although our vocal qualities are relatively limited by the size and the shape of our resonating cavities, these attributes can be modified. Some of us are even able to control vocal attributes well enough to imitate other speakers. Most of us who do not habitually speak nasally or harshly can do so at will. All things considered, the normal human being can do considerably more with her or his sound-making apparatus than expert musicians can do with their musical instruments.

The Individuality of the Human Voice

Although some vocal mimics can simulate the vocal production of popular or well-known personages, each of us has a voice with individual features that are almost as distinctive as our fingerprints. Our ability to hear these distinctive features may not be as keen as our ability to see differences in fingerprints, but vocal differences can be discerned when they are transformed from audible into visible forms. A device that transforms the features of the voice into visible patterns has been developed by the Bell Telephone Laboratories. Voiceprints (such as those in Figures 2–8, 2–9, and 2–10) bring out differences that reveal the individuality of the voice. The recording technique, developed by Lawrence Kersta of Bell Laboratories, indicates loudness, resonance, and pitch. In combination, these features are presumably never the same for any two persons (see Figures 2–9 and 2–10).

Correlates of Vocal Changes

Unless we consciously try to conceal our feelings as we talk, we are likely to reveal them by the way we sound. The voice, when not intentionally controlled, is a barometer of our feelings and our moods. This is so essentially because the voice is a product of muscular activity that in turn is intimately related to the emotional state of the organism. In a state of heightened emotion, as in anger or fear, we experience muscular tension. The muscles involved in voice production share in the increased total body tension. Thus, when vocalization takes place, it is on a higher pitch level than normal. Another involuntary change that accompanies heightened emotion is the addition of sugar to the blood stream. This enables us to engage in the energetic activity that is

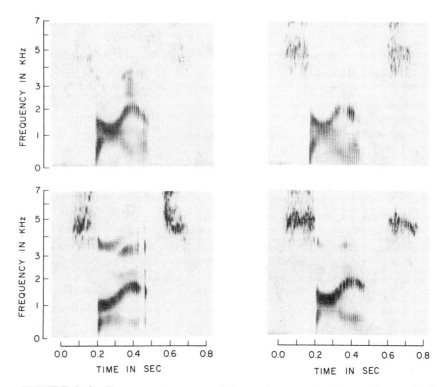

FIGURE 2–8 Four spectrograms of the spoken word *science*. The vertical scale represents frequency, the horizontal dimension is time, and the darkness represents intensity on a compressed scale. Three of the spectrograms are from three different speakers, and the remaining spectrogram is a repetition of the word by one of the speakers. The spectrograms were made on a Voiceprint Laboratories Sound Spectrograph. [From R. H. Bolt et al., "Identification of a Speaker by Speech Spectrograms," *Science*, 166:339 (1969).]

The authors of this article were of the opinion that despite the admitted individuality of the human voice, the available results of studies of speech spectrograms are not adequate to establish the reliability of voice identification by this technique. Despite this opinion, several court rulings have admitted voiceprint identification as legal evidence for identification—for example, *United States of America* v. *Albert Raymond and Roland Addison,* United States District Court, Crim. No. 800–71, February 2, 1972, and *State of Minnesota* ex. ref. *Constance L. Trimble,* Supreme Court of Minnesota, No. 43049, November 26, 1971. However, a more recent opinion was provided by the *Maryland Law Review,* **5** (39), Summer 1980, pp. 629–645. After a case review, the report indicates that testimony on voice identification based on spectrographic analysis is inadmissible because the technique has not gained general acceptance in the scientific community.

sometimes an aspect of heightened emotion. The effect on a voice is to increase its loudness. The usual overall effect of heightened feeling on utterance is that the voice becomes high-pitched, loud, and rapid.

In contrast, depressed states are associated with vocal tones that are low in pitch level and relatively weak in loudness. This is so because the muscles of the body as a whole, and the vocal bands in particular, become overrelaxed or hypotonic, and ener-

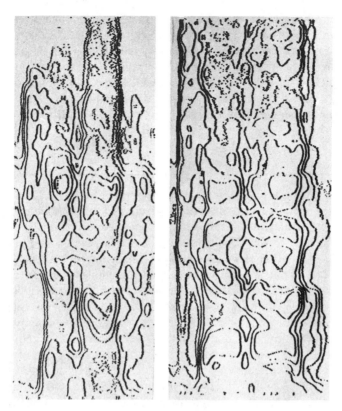

FIGURE 2–9 *(Left)*   John F. Kennedy's voiceprint, made during a talk he gave in the White House, shows Bostonian delivery in the compressed dark lines at the top. [LIFE Magazine © 1963 Time Inc. All Rights Reserved.]

FIGURE 2–10 *(Right)*   Elliott Reid used the same text and intonation as President Kennedy, but the graph that his voice made was radically different. [LIFE Magazine © 1963 Time Inc. All Rights Reserved.]

getic activity is reduced. The likely overall effect on utterance is to make it relatively low in pitch and volume, and slow in rate.

A voice that is dominated by intellect rather than emotion tends to be moderate in pitch as well as in loudness. This does not imply that intellectual efforts are devoid of feeling. It does imply that intellectual efforts accompanied by vocalization are normally not characterized by the exaggerated range and intensity of feeling that is associated with emotional behavior. Under intellectual control, we are able to simulate emotion, to suggest how we would sound if angry, afraid, ecstatically happy, or depressed. When these pretenses are not necessary, we are ourselves. If we are our normal selves, we are usually moderate not only in our behavior in general, but also in the intensity of our feelings and in the manner in which our voices reveal (or sometimes betray) how we feel and think.

Sometimes, our voices express our attitudes toward and feelings about our listeners or of the person or persons about whom we are talking. Part of the message we convey may be in what we say, but much more may be in the manner of saying it. Children may sense notes of impatience and irritation in the voices of their parents and may give expression to their own feelings in the way they respond. It does not take long to learn what comes naturally. Our voices, if not controlled, and sometimes when we intentionally pretend that they are not controlled, reflect our evaluation of the listener or a personality. Occasionally, the doubt our voices express is the doubt that we anticipate the listener will entertain if, indeed, he or she has been listening to us.

Articulated Sound

When breath that is set in vibration by the action of the vocal bands reaches the mouth as part of a speech effort, the breath stream is further modified by the action of the tongue, lips, velum, and/or cheeks to produce voiced articulate sound. If the breath stream is not set in vibration, then voiceless articulated sound may be produced. The organs of articulation serve essentially as interrupters, "filters," or modifiers of the breath stream. Some sounds—vowels and diphthongs—are produced only by an adjustment of the size and shape of the oral and adjacent cavities. These adjustments modify but do not impede or interrupt the laryngeal or vocal tone. Other sounds are produced by a stoppage or diversion of the breath or the vocal tone. Thus, we have consonants resulting from sudden interruptions, little explosions, or hissings because air is forced through narrow openings. The manner and place of interruption result in the production of articulate speech sounds. Each sound has its own characteristics or phonetic attributes. Oral speech consists of combinations of articulated sounds. When these sounds, produced according to the rules and conventions of our language, are appropriately grouped and readily audible, we speak intelligibly.

The Articulators

Most of the articulated sounds of American-English speech are produced as a result of the activity of the lips and parts of the tongue. These mobile articulators assume positions or make contact with fixed or relatively fixed parts of the upper jaw and the roof of the mouth.

The lips and the teeth enclose the oral cavity. The tongue lies within and almost completely fills the oral cavity. From the point of view of articulatory action, the tongue may be divided into the following parts: the anterior portion, or tongue tip; the blade; the midtongue; and the back. The roof of the mouth may be divided into the gum ridge, or alveolar process (directly behind the upper teeth); the hard palate; the velum; and the uvula (see Figure 2–11).

The larynx also serves an articulatory function because the presence or absence of vocalization distinguishes many pairs of sounds, such as *b* and *p* or *z* and *s*. The sound *h* is produced by a contraction within the larynx sufficient to produce audible friction.

Details of the manner in which the articulators function to produce the different sounds of our language are considered in Chapter 11. At the present time, let us consider briefly the controlling mechanism through which we are enabled to make vocal noises, to modify these noises into distinguishable sounds and intelligible words, to arrange these words into phrases and sentences in order to express our feelings, our wishes, and our needs, and to become members of a symbol-producing and symbol-responding culture.

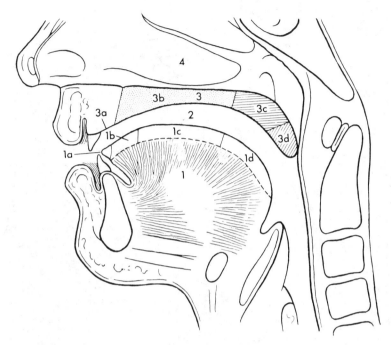

FIGURE 2–11   The oral cavity and its articulators.

1. Tongue. *1a*. Tongue tip. *1b*. Blade of tongue. *1c*. Front and mid area of tongue. *1d*. Back of tongue.
2. Mouth (oral) cavity.
3. Palate. *3a*. Gum, or alveolar, ridge. *3b*. Hard palate. *3c*. Soft palate (velum). *3d*. Uvula.
4. Nasal cavity.

The Neurological Mechanism for Speech

The achievement of speech is neurologically related to the development of the cerebrum in humans. Except for the cerebrum of the brain, the nervous system of the human being is surprisingly like that of a dog and almost completely like that of an ape. The cerebrum is significantly different in humans. It is larger in proportion to the nervous system as a whole than it is in other animals, including subhuman primates, and it includes a bulgelike frontal area of greater size than that found in animals with otherwise comparable nervous systems. The brain is a coordinator and integrator of activity. In the brain, impulses set up by sounds and movements that are received by the ear, the eye, and other sense organs are translated into images or into words that have significance and meaning.

The Cerebral Cortex

The gray outer covering of the brain is especially involved in the function of speech. The cortex contains ten to twelve billion or more nerve cells. Parts of the cortex have specialized functions that are involved in the peculiarly human ability to produce and

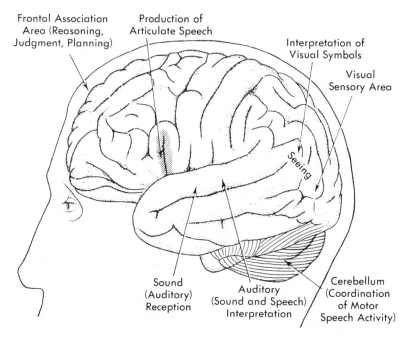

Frontal Association Area (Reasoning, Judgment, Planning)

Production of Articulate Speech

Interpretation of Visual Symbols

Visual Sensory Area

Seeing

Sound (Auditory) Reception

Auditory (Sound and Speech) Interpretation

Cerebellum (Coordination of Motor Speech Activity)

FIGURE 2-12   The cerebral cortex, the cerebellum, and some "specialized" areas related to speech.

understand oral (speech) or written symbols. These areas are indicated in Figure 2–12. The marked areas include those for *hearing, seeing,* and *speech movement.* These areas are significant because of their evident capacity to evaluate specialized experiences *for the brain as a whole.* For example, the auditory area in the lower middle part of the brain evaluates sounds, so that noises may be interpreted as *barks, wind in the trees,* or *words.* Similarly, the area in the back part of the brain (the occipital lobe) interprets impulses coming from the eye. Through this area, we are able to recognize and identify the objects that we see and to read, and so to make sense of, markings called letters and words.

Recently reported evidence (Eisenson, 1984, Chap. 2; Geschwind, 1979; Springer and Deutsch, 1981) highlights differences as well as similarities in the functions of the left and the right hemispheres, with particular reference to speech and language. Specifically, these are differences in the nature of the auditory events that are perceived and interpreted (processed) by the two temporal lobes. The perception of speech events is normally a function of the left temporal lobe, and the perception of auditory nonspeech events (e.g., environmental noises, musical melody, and animal noises) is usually perceived and processed in the right temporal lobe. Figure 2–12 features the specialized areas of the left cerebral cortex that are related to the processing of spoken and written symbols.

Similarly, the production of spoken language is normally controlled in the left cerebral hemisphere (Figure 2–12). This generalization holds for almost all right-handed persons and for a bare majority of those who are left-handed.

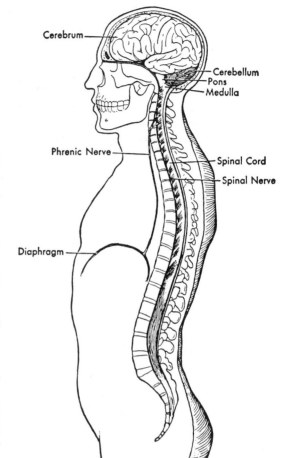

FIGURE 2–13 The central nervous system in relation to speech.

The *cerebrum* performs the integrative activity on which normal, meaningful speech is dependent.

The *cerebellum* "sorts and arranges" the muscular impulses that come to it from higher brain centers. Impulses are here correlated to make possible the precise muscular activity needed for speech.

The *pons* are a bridge of nerve fibers between the cerebral cortex and the medulla.

The *medulla* contains the respiratory and other vital reflex centers.

The *spinal cord* and its nerves control the respiratory muscles.

The *phrenic nerve* emerges from the spinal cord in the neck region and extends to the diaphragm. It supplies the impulses that cause the diaphragm to contract in breathing.

Other Parts of the Central Nervous System and Their Functions in Speech

In addition to the cerebrum, other parts of the central nervous system are essentially involved in the production of speech. These parts, which are represented in Figure 2–13, serve the following functions in the integrated speech act.

The *cerebellum*, or little brain, receives impulses from higher brain centers. The impulses are sorted, arranged, and correlated so that the coordinated and precise muscular activity needed for speech becomes possible. Damage to the cerebellum may seriously impair the flow and the control of coordinated speech activity. Damage of this sort is found in many cases of cerebral palsy.

The *medulla* contains the center essential for respiration, and damage to it may impair normal breathing. Bulbar polio involves such damage and requires the use of a mechanical respirator.

The *bulb*, the *spinal cord*, and the nerves emanating from them control the muscles involved in the coordinated act of speaking. The *phrenic* nerve, which emerges from the spinal cord in the region of the neck, extends to the diaphragm. The phrenic nerve supplies the impulse that causes the diaphragm to contract and so brings about inhalation in breathing.

Other nerves that initiate movements involved in speech are the trigeminal (face and jaw muscles), the glossopharyngeal (tongue and pharynx), the recurrent laryngeal (larynx), and the glossal (tongue).

In the absence of pathology, the central nervous system, dominated by the cerebral cortex, controls the impulses involved in the act of speaking. Through this system, we are able to be articulate about our impressions and to reveal what we think and how we feel. Sometimes, if it suits our purpose, we conceal rather than reveal either our feelings or our thoughts, or both. The degree of expertness with which the speech apparatus is used varies considerably from person to person. However, all of us who have unimpaired physical mechanisms and normal personalities should be capable of speaking adequately. How to make the most of our mechanisms so that we fully utilize our capabilities to vocalize and articulate with ease and intelligibility is considered in the chapters that follow.

References and Suggested Readings

Boone, D. R. *The Voice and Voice Therapy,* 3rd ed. Englewood Cliffs, N.J.: Prentice-Hall, Inc., 1983. (A clear, practical clinical approach to the understanding and treatment of the most common voice problems.)

Denes, P. B., and E. N. Pinson. *The Speech Chain: The Physics and Biology of Spoken Language.* Baltimore: Williams and Wilkins, 1963. (A concise and authoritative explanation of the nature and functioning of the mechanisms for speech.)

Eisenson, J., and M. Ogilvie. *Communicative Disorders in Children.* New York: Macmillan Publishing Company, 1983. (An introductory text on speech and language disorders. Chapter 5 is a basic consideration of the mechanisms for voice and speech; Chapter 12 deals with the most frequently occurring voice disturbances in children.)

Eisenson, J. *Adult Aphasia,* 2d ed. Englewood Cliffs, N.J.: Prentice-Hall, Inc., 1984. (Chapter 2 deals with the neurological correlates of language and speech impairments and the roles of the two cerebral hemispheres in the processing of language functions.)

Geschwind, N. *Specializations of the Human Brain* (A Scientific American Book). San Francisco: Freeman, 1979. (A well-illustrated discussion of the special processing areas of the human brain, with emphasis on speech and language.)

Hollien H., Dew D., Philips P. "Phonational Frequency Range of Adults," *Journal of Speech and Hearing Research,* 14:4: 755–760, 1971.

Lieberman, P. *Speech Physiology and Acoustic Phonetics.* New York: Macmillan Publishing Company, 1977. (An up-to-date, high-level, scientific treatment of the mechanisms controlling speech and how speech is perceived. Includes excellent surveys of relevant literature.)

Moore, P. *Organic Voice Disorders.* Englewood Cliffs, N.J.: Prentice-Hall, Inc., 1971. (A concise, easy-to-read, scientific consideration of common vocal problems.)

Springer, S. P., and G. Deutsch. *Left Brain, Right Brain.* San Francisco: Freeman, 1981.

Zemlin, W. R. *Speech and Hearing Science.* Englewood Cliffs, N.J.: Prentice-Hall, Inc., 1981. (A well-written, high-level treatment of the mechanisms of voice and speech.)

3

Our Changing Speech Patterns

Eng + America are two countries separated by the same language – G B Shaw

Parts of countries .

Qantas, the Australian Airline, provides its travelers with a booklet called *Understanding "Down Under"—The Australian "Language."* The booklet advises that "Visitors to Australia who may consider that they speak perfect English can often experience difficulty in talking to the locals." Further, we learn that "Australian slang is always growing and changing. Terms once frequently used are constantly falling into disuse and others are being created, or given different meanings."

It is altogether possible that Australia, comparatively young among the English-speaking countries and experiencing rapid economic and social changes, is undergoing even more rapid and dramatic linguistic changes than are speakers of American English. The following may serve as an example. A citizen of Sydney, Australia, arrives at his car to discover that a policeman (Brown Bomber) is writing a parking ticket for him. The irate citizen informs the Brown Bomber that "Some of you cacky-handed galahs would dob in your cheese and kisses—deadset!" Freely translated into American-English idiom this becomes "Some of you left-handed fools would inform (betray, tell on) your own wives, I'm absolutely certain!"

Would the Australian be any more informed than Americans living in Washington, D.C., pretend to be when they hear or read that "We haven't yet finalized the parameters of our thrust in that area"?

While we are engaged in conjecture, we may as well entertain one by Stuart Flexner, Senior Editor of the *Random House Dictionary,* who believes that "If Shakespeare were to materialize today in London or New York, he would be able to understand only five out of every nine words in our vocabulary."[1]

Although a materialized Shakespeare might have difficulty in understanding contemporary English, either in his own England or in the United States, few educated trav-

[1] Cited by Mario Pei, in H. A. Estrin and D. V. Mehus (eds.) (1974, p. 123).

elers, whether British or American, would be likely to experience a comparable amount of difficulty in understanding each other's language. To be sure, there are "far-out" dialects in all English-speaking countries. Some of these are frozen in time and less changed than others. For example, Evans and Evans in their Preface to the *Dictionary of Contemporary American Usage* (1957) recalled that as children who were brought up in the north of England, they "Spoke a dialect that was in many ways nearer to the English of Chaucer than that of the *New York Times*" (p. viii). Their analogy might be better if Evans and Evans had made their comparison with the spoken language of the writers and editors, rather than the printed words, but we do get the point.

Though Chaucerian English is not likely to be heard in the United States, a dialect that strongly suggests the English idiom of Shakespeare's time may still be heard in the Appalachian Mountain area. However, as Stewart (1972b) has reminded us, Appalachian Mountain speech is not pure Elizabethan English. "It is really not, of course, because since by the time the settlement of Appalachia had begun, English had already changed considerably from what it had been in Elizabethan times, a century and a half before" (p. 111).

American English

We do not have to accept the literal implications of George Bernard Shaw's observation that "England and America are two countries separated by the same language." Nevertheless, there is little doubt that at least from the time of the Revolutionary War to World War II, American English emerged and developed as a language with enough divergence from the "mother tongue" in pronunciation, word usage, and idiom to direct our attention to the differences, despite the continuing basic similarities in the major "standard" dialects. Though it may have been expected that the influence of improved communication, radio, television, and film would have worked in the direction of reducing differences, this has not seemed to happen. Counterforces such as sociopolitics and nationalism have worked to maintain the divergences rather than to reduce them.

American English is in a process of change because it is a living language. Classical Latin and Greek have become stabilized because they are "dead" languages that are no longer spoken by persons engaged in social or economic intercourse. As Whatmough observed, "If language could not change, it would be incapable of coping with new demands, new concepts, new inventions" (1956, p. 174).

This chapter considers some of the factors and historical influences that resulted in English becoming the language of the United States, features that characterize American English and its dialectal variations, and some psychosocial forces that are currently and dynamically influencing the sounds, the lexicon, and even the syntax of our language.

English Historical Backgrounds: A Brief Review

From the time of the ancient Romans until the eleventh century, the land masses known as the British Isles were successively conquered and occupied by peoples of many nations. Each of the conquering peoples left traces of influence on a language whose basic forms and structure were not to be determined until the sixteenth century.

The Romans under Caesar came to Britain in 55 B.C. and did not leave until about A.D. 400. The inhabitants who remained behind, other than the Romans, spoke a Celtic dialect but retained the use of Roman names for roads and many geographic locations (place names).

In the middle of the fifth century, Angles, Saxons, and Jutes began to invade Britain and drove the Celts westward into Wales and Cornwall and northward toward what is now Scotland. The term *English* is used for the Germanic speech of these groups of invaders and their descendants. It is important to appreciate, however, that the earlier inhabitants of Britain did not suddenly change their speech habits. Those who stayed behind and were not pushed to the west or to the north continued to speak a language much as they had spoken, except that new linguistic forms—those of their conquerors—were incorporated and modified into their previous linguistic habits. Essentially, despite military conquests, the language of the conquered assimilated that of the conquerors.

Christianity came to Saxon England during the first half of the seventh century. With Christianity, Latin was introduced as the spoken and written language for religious and learned purposes. This influence on the common person—on the vast majority of the population—however, was not significantly reflected in everyday speech.

Between the eighth and eleventh centuries, increasing numbers of Scandinavians came to Britain, and with them came Scandinavian influences on what was to become English. The Scandinavians—for the most part, Danes—also invaded and conquered the northeastern parts of France and ultimately became the ruling aristocracy of Normandy. During this period of achievement, the Scandinavians assumed Gallic ways, including French as a language, and their own Germanic speech was lost. Again, the language of the conquerors gave way to the language of the conquered.

In the historically critical year 1066, the descendants of the Scandinavians, who now were Normans and who had become essentially French in culture and in their linguistic habits, invaded England under William the Conqueror, and became the established power in England. Although French then became the language of the ruling class in England, the masses continued to speak a Germanic language. In time the language of the Norman conquerors was reduced in influence, and all but disappeared, at least as far as the speech of the ''common'' man and woman was concerned.

The English that most people in England speak today and the American English that most Americans speak are both derived from the speech of the inhabitants of the London area from the time of William the Conqueror through the Elizabethan period. But England throughout its history has never been free of divergent dialects. The Germanic groups—the Angles, Saxons, and Jutes—came from different parts of the continental lowlands. These groups spoke different dialects, settled in different parts of England, and left their linguistic influences where they settled. One important result is that the dialect differences among the inhabitants of England today are greater and more divergent than are the regional dialect differences in the United States.

It does not require an expert ear to discern differences between American-English and British speech, even assuming that the comparison is made between an educated Londoner and an educated Bostonian who may be a Radcliffe or Harvard graduate. These representative speakers are selected because, although the differences between American English and upper-class London English are comparatively few, differences do exist. They exist in idiom and in specific words to denote situations and events as well as in word pronunciation and stress and in manner of articulation. Differences are also found in speech melody. The Londoner and the Bostonian are not likely to express their enthusiasms or their irritations with the same choice of words or in the same vocal melody. A *bloody American mess* has different connotations from a *bloody English mess*. The Bostonian gets about in *streetcars* or *subway* trains, whereas the Londoner gets about in *trams* and by way of the *underground*. The Bostonian may live in an *apartment;* the Londoner lives in a *flat*. The Bostonian leaves his or her car in a gar*age* rather than in a *gar*age and watches *TV* rather than *telly*. The Bostonian law enforcer is a *police officer* or a *cop*, rather than a *bobby;* the Bostonian is entertained at the *movies* rather than at the *cinema*. The melody pattern of the Londoner, whether his or her utterance is intellectual or emotional, is likely to be characterized by wider inflectional changes than that of the Bostonian. Articulatory differences may also be heard. The sound *t* in an unstressed syllable, as in *pity,* is likely to be more clearly and more lightly articulated by our English representative than it is by the American. Neither speaker is likely to pronounce an *r* when it is in a final position in a word, as in *dear* or *hear,* but the *r* would be articulated differently in words such as *very*. Our English representative pronounces the word *very* in a manner that phoneticians describe as a *single flapped sound.* Americans[2] may think of it as approximating the pronunciation *veddy,* which, of course, it does not, except possibly to the prejudiced ear of an American comic-strip artist trying to get across a notion of English pronunciation to an American comic-strip reader.

Standard English Speech?

Americans living in the first quarter of this century who judged English speech by what they heard from Britishers who were visiting in the United States might well have concluded that all of them spoke pretty much alike. Americans who read Shaw's *Pygmalion* may have been puzzled by Professor Higgins's complaints. Yet both the Americans' and Professor Higgins's observations were correct. It is likely that the Americans, unless they happened to have traveled widely in England, would have been exposed only to the speech of British stage personalities, British political personages, members of the royal family, and well-to-do and well-educated English people with public (really private) secondary-school and Oxford or Cambridge backgrounds. Their speech is almost standard.

The speech of these groups is characterized by English phoneticians as *received pronunciation;* by *received* is meant "accepted in approved circles." This speech is described by the English phonetician Daniel Jones in his *Outline of English Phonetics* (1956). Individual recommended pronunciations may be found in Jones's *Pronunciation of English* (1956).

Although "received speech" was the one that Professor Higgins spoke as a matter of course and that Eliza Doolittle learned to speak after much rigorous training (although she still broke down under emotional stress), it is not the standard for the speech of all persons who are natives or long-term residents of England—not even for those

---

[2] We refer here to the standard dialects of British English and American English. *American* refers to North Americans who speak English. Much of what is said here also refers to Canadian speakers of English.

with moderate amounts of education who live in or near London. Members of the English Parliament, including those who represent the Conservatives, are today more likely to speak with the accents and pronunciations of the British Broadcasting Company than with those identified with Eton and Oxford. Labor members of Parliament are likely to assume Tory accents, or even Tory vocabularies, when they are aware that they may be on the air and that their words may be heard by constituents in the evening news broadcast. In brief, the forces of democracy in England, as well as the forces of the mass media of communicating, have worked in directions away from received pronunciation. Despite Professor Higgins, the English will go on being themselves and listening, so that they can appreciate British Broadcasting Company diction, American movies, and American television programs.

There are, of course, variances within the London area that are wide enough to require "translation" for many British as well as American citizens. Charles McCabe, an American journalist, presented the following as an example of the Cockney dialect: "A lorry pranged the banger in the boot and I hadn't the readies to get it out of the ricky, so do you fancy taking the tube to the cinema or slipping around to the pub for a pint?" This translates into "A truck smashed into the trunk of my car and I didn't have the money to fix it, so do you want to take the subway to the movies or go to the neighborhood bar for a beer?"

Despite variations in dialects "within cultures," we may conjecture with the popular linguist Mario Pei, who in 1949 predicted:

> Granted a continuation of present historical conditions, the English language of two hundred years hence will be likely to represent a merger of British and American phonetic habits, with comparatively little in the way of morphological or syntactical innovations, but with a turn-over in vocabulary and semantics that would make it difficult, not to say incomprehensible, to the English speaker of today. (p. 303)

American Beginnings

When may we say that American speech became sufficiently different from that of the English to give us the beginning of American English? What were the influences that produced and nurtured these differences? In what ways were they peculiarly the result of a new culture and the new forces related to this culture? What forces, regardless of culture, continue to exert their effects on our ever-changing speech patterns?

At the opening of the nineteenth century, the United States had its critics and deplorers, who raised the hue and cry, "What is happening to our language?" They were referring to English and were warning Americans about the need to keep their language pure and free from new vulgarisms. John Witherspoon, a Scottish clergyman who came to the United States to become the president of Princeton, suffered considerable anguish at the thought of the development of an American language. Mencken, in *The American Language* (1946), cited Witherspoon as being pained by what he heard in "public and solemn discourses." Said Witherspoon:

> I have heard in this country, in the senate, at the bar, and from the pulpit, and see daily in dissertations from the press, errors in grammar, improprieties and vulgarisms which

hardly any person of the same class in point of rank and literature would have fallen into in Great Britain. (p. 5)[3]

But persons such as Witherspoon, however great their prestige, were opposed by such Americans as John Adams and Thomas Jefferson. Perhaps more realistically, Jefferson declared:

> The new circumstances under which we are placed call for new words, new phrases, and for the transfer of old words to new objects. An American dialect will therefore be formed. (Mencken, 1946, p. 5)

While the dispute between Americans for English English and those for American English was going on, Noah Webster was busily at work on his *Grammatical Institute of the English Language* and, perhaps more important, on his *American Dictionary of the English Language.* Certainly, with the publication of the latter in 1828, American English achieved status and recognition and became established as a major variant of the English language.

Even a cursory review of the forces that established American English as an independent variant of the English language would reveal the following: The American geography and physiography presented new features, new creatures, and new ways of working for a livelihood, and with them, the need for new words. Many of the words came from the Indians and had no competition from the mother tongue. Thus, words such as *coyote, skunk, hickory, moose, opossum, persimmon, powpow, moccasin,* and *squash* came into our language. Place names, Mencken (1946, p. 105) pointed out, also came from the Indians. So did such names for articles of clothing and frequently used objects as *tomahawk, wigwam, toboggan,* and *mackinaw.*

It would, however, be erroneous to conclude that the spirit of rebellion and the influence of the Indians were the only forces that shaped American English. The early colonists, from the very outset, had linguistic influences from the languages of other colonizations. From the French came words such as *cache, portage,* and *voyageur,* as well as *prairie, bureau,* and *gopher.* From the Dutch in New Amsterdam, Mencken (1946, p. 108) tells us, came such words as *cruller, coleslaw, cookey, scow,* and *patroon,* as well as *boss* and *Santa Claus.* Many place names in the Hudson area containing *dorp, kill,* and *hook* are also directly from the Dutch. *Harlem* was originally *Haarlem.* The word *Yankee,* according to Mencken (p. 110), is possibly the most notable of all contributions of the Knickerbocker Dutch to the American language. Our own choice would be the word *dollar.*

Another source of Dutch influence on the speech of the colonists came by way of the Pilgrims. In their migration from England to the colonies, many Pilgrims first went to live in Holland, mostly in Leyden and Amsterdam (1607–1609). Dillard (1976) noted that by the time the Pilgrims arrived in Plymouth on the *Mayflower,* the ship "Carried passengers who did not represent the 'regional' dialects of England at all—much less in pure form" (p. 47).

Spanish influences came later, at a time when American English had become well

---

[3]There is little doubt that every generation has its critics and deplorers who are anxiously concerned about the deterioration of our language. Edwin Newman (1974) is a highly successful contemporary critic who, we hope with tongue-in-cheek, has asked the question, "Will America be the death of English?" Newman seems to think that perhaps it will.

established as a variant of British English. Texas, the Southwest, and California had been colonized by the Spanish and were developed by Mexico when it won its independence from Spain. Spanish and Mexican contributions to American English are readily recognizable in place names, architecture, agriculture, and animal husbandry. Some of the characteristic geographical features of the Southwest and California are known by Mexican-Spanish names such as *mesa, canyon,* and *arroyo.* The American—for the most part of Anglo-Saxon origin—who took over the Southwest not only learned how to construct buildings of mud and straw bricks but also learned to call them *adobes.*

Many of the words that we now associate with cattle raising are also of Spanish origin. These include *ranch, lasso,* and *riata. Chaps,* pant covers worn by cowboys to protect their legs, is an abbreviation of *chaparajos.* The word *rodeo* has as its English translation "roundup." It is now used as well to refer to an exhibition and competition in the skills that cowboys were and to some degree still are expected to perform in cattle raising. The word *ranch* has been extended to refer as a noun to an agricultural establishment and as a verb to farming activities. *Wrangler* comes from *caballarengo,* and *hoosegow* from *juzgado.*

Spanish, as we have indicated, has also given us a large number of place names. These include the names of six of our United States, more than two thousand names for our cities and towns, and thousands of names for our rivers, streams, mountains, valleys, and plains. Flexner (1976) provided the following sampling:

> *Alhambra, Eldorado, El Paso* (the full original name of the city was *El Paso del Norte,* the crossing of the river of the north . . .), *Hermosa Beach* (beautiful beach), *Key West, Los Angeles* (a shortening of the name the Spanish gave it in 1769, *El Pueblo de Nuestra Señora la Reina de Los Angeles de la Porciuncula,* which was a Franciscan shrine near Assisi), *Las Vegas* (originally built by the Mormons in 1855, using the Spanish word *vega,* meadow, in its name), *Monterey,* . . . *Palo Alto, Pueblo* (Spanish for town, literally "the town," when it was first established in 1842 it was the only trading post in the area), *Raton Pass, the Rio Grande, Sacramento, St. Augustine* (founded 1565), *San Antonio, San Bernardino, San Diego, San Francisco, San José* (named after San José de Guadaloupe), *San Luis Obispo* . . . (p. 323)

The American colonists and the early citizens of the United States were ready borrowers of words from other languages, but they were also ready creators of words and phrases that were "coined in English metal" (Mencken, 1946, p. 113). Some of these words were a product of the new circumstances and conditions in which the new Americans found themselves, but others reveal an underlying way that people—any uninhibited and resourceful people—have with words. For a variety of reasons, words were invented. One of the reasons is that inventing words is fun. It is a kind of pleasure in which we indulged ourselves as very young children and again as adolescents. Word inventing can be a sheer delight, and our American colonists needed to be delighted. Mencken (1946) reminds us that "the American, even in the seventeenth century, already showed many of the characteristics that were to set him off from the Englishman later on—his bold and somewhat grotesque imagination, his contempt for dignified authority, his lack of aesthetic sensitiveness, his extravagant humor" (pp. 113–114). Not restrained by grammatical awareness or a knowledge of the structure of their language, and largely illiterate, our uncouth and headstrong early colonists added words as the occasion demanded. So nouns such as *cowhide* and *logroll,* and adjectives and adverbs such as *no-account, nohow,* and *lickitty-split,* became terms to reckon with in the utterances of our seventeenth-century Americans. These speakers also introduced such compound words as *bullfrog, hogwallow,* and *hoecake.* All of these are useful terms for persons who are busy working with or against the creatures and forces of nature in a new environment.

A living language shows the effects of a busy people. Early in our history, the word *cent,* a verbal invention of Gouveneur Morris, was substituted for the two-syllable *penny.* *Dime* was a Jeffersonian invention derived from the French word *dixième.*

Later, we consider in some detail other examples of abbreviatory processes that have us riding in autos or cars rather than in automobiles, watching TV rather than television, or using the phone rather than the telephone.

Flexner (1976) summed up the status of the English language in America at the end of the eighteenth century that made American English an established linguistic achievement:

> When this new nation took its first census in 1790 there were four million Americans, 90% of them descendants of English colonists. Thus there was no question that English was the mother tongue and native language of the United States. By 1720, however, some English colonists in America had already begun to notice that their language differed seriously from that spoken back home in England. Almost without being aware of it, they had:
>
>   (1) coined some new words for themselves;
>   (2) borrowed other words from the Indians, Dutch, French, and Spanish;
>   (3) been using English dialect words in their general speech;
>   (4) continued to use some English words that had now become obsolete in England;
>   (5) evolved some peculiar uses, pronunciations, grammar and syntax.
>
> Doing these things was very natural. Many of the coinages and borrowing were for plants, animals, landscapes, living conditions, institutions, and attitudes which were seldom if ever encountered in England, so the English had no words for them. The widespread use of English dialect words was also natural: most of the Puritans came from England's southern and southeastern counties and spoke the East Anglia dialect, most of the Quakers spoke the midland dialect, and after 1720, many new colonists were Scots-Irish, speaking the Ulster dialect. The continuing use of words that had become obsolete in England, and of unusual usage, pronunciations, grammar, and syntax, was also natural for colonists isolated from the niceties of current English speech and English education. Thus, naturally, a hundred years after the Pilgrims landed, English as spoken in America differed from that spoken in England. (p. 7)

Ongoing Forces for Change

Thus far, we have traced the influences that created an American English and some of the differences in linguistic forms between British English and American English. Now we consider some of the forces that make any living language a changing language, constantly though slowly yielding to human inclinations and to changing verbal habits. To begin with, we should appreciate the effects of our contemporary ability for speed of movement and our general mobility as a nation of people on wheels or on wings. Washington and Julius Caesar traveled on state occasions in much the same kind of vehicles. Except for slight differences in styling and the addition of springs, similar vehicles were used by United States presidents up to McKinley, although out of choice rather than of necessity, to ride to their inaugurations. Recent presidents are no longer earthbound. They may now move about with supersonic speed. What influence future presidents or future English-speaking citizens, American or British, or from other parts of the English-speaking world, will have on American speech or English speech is a matter of conjecture.

Despite the efforts of some of our nineteenth- and early-twentieth-century teachers of elocution and diction who considered British English a more genteel standard than the emerging American differences, the people of the United States do not observe or aspire to a single standard of what constitutes good American speech. Differences, however, at least among educated speakers, are relatively small. The members of Congress, regardless of the states they represent, have no difficulty in understanding one another because of differences in pronunciation or idiom. Nevertheless, as McDavid (1958) pointed out, "every speaker of American English knows that other varieties exist, different from the one he speaks, empirically he has learned to distinguish several of these varieties, sometimes with amazing precision and accuracy." (p. 482).

Most of us are aware that there are differences in spoken language features in details of pronunciation, vocabulary, or grammar—that we may as individuals consider substandard and therefore undesirable. Certainly we should exercise our judgment and prerogatives and avoid such forms in our own speech. However, it is also important to appreciate that speakers may show marked differences in the pronunciation of words, word usage, and other details of *dialect* and yet may be speaking a socially accepted variant of English. McDavid (1975) reminds us that "No geographic region is without its local subtypes, and in the United States there is nothing that qualifies as a mythically uniform General American Speech" (p. xxi).

Dialect is a term used for a variety of a language with features of pronunciation, grammar, or vocabulary that distinguish it from other varieties (dialects) of the same language. Most dialects are related to an identified area, that is, a geographic region. However, with a mobile population, dialects may not be restricted to a given region.

FIGURE 3–1   Some of the dialect areas in the United States. [From R. W. Shuy, *Discovering American Dialects* (Urbana, Ill.: National Council of Teachers of English, 1967), p. 47.]

Shuy (1967) recognized nine dialect regions in the United States (Figure 3–1). Nist (Figure 3–2) recognized seven major speech variants. It is of interest to note that the western part of the United States is still "unmapped."

Regional Differences

In the continental United States, differences in pronunciation are most striking along the Atlantic Coast. As we move inland and westward, the differences become blurred. Differences are so slight that casual listeners rarely notice them at all. Although the differences are greatest along the Atlantic Coast, merchants from Maine have no anxiety that they will not be readily understood if they speak by telephone to merchants from New York, Maryland, or Florida.

Differences in the pronunciation of words are more likely to be marked by vowel variations than by consonants. For American-English speakers, the pronunciation of *Harry* and *hairy* may or may not be different, depending on region and social class. Similarly, there may or may not be differences in the vowel choice for *Mary, merry,* and *marry.* The words *class, not, hot, orange, creek, coffee, candy, nurse,* and *first* have vowel variation according to region. In regard to consonants, the major variation for "standard" dialects is in the pronunciation of words ending in *ng,* such as *being, going,* and *talking.* Speakers in some regions of the United States pronounce these words with a final *n* sound; others with an *ng.* Many speakers vary in their pronunciations

FIGURE 3–2   Map of major American-English speech varieties ca. 1965. [After J. Nist, "American Regionalisms," in E. M. Kerr (Ed.), *Aspects of American English,* **2nd ed. (New York: Harcourt Brace Jovanovich, 1971), p. 170.]**

Nist believes that "Because of the increase of population mobility and the immense impact of the mass media, at present these . . . regionalisms constitute an Emerging General American, which in time may become the accepted American Standard." At present, however, Nist recognizes seven major speech varieties of American English as indicated in the map above.

Table 3-1.   **Dialect Areas and Word Usage**

Item	Northern	Midland	Southern
Paper container	bag	sack	sack
Type of cheese (cottage cheese)	Dutch cheese pot cheese	smearcase	clabber cheese
Bread	johnnycake corn bread	corn bread	corn bread corn pone
Valve mechanism over a sink	faucet	spigot spicket	spigot spicket
Small, striped, bushy-tailed animal	skunk	skunk polecat wood pussy	polecat
Cherry seed	pit stone	seed stone	seed stone
Container	pail	bucket	bucket

Adapted from R. W. Shuy, *Discovering American Dialects* (Urbana, Ill.: National Council of Teachers of English, 1967), pp. 26–27.

according to whether they are speaking formally or informally. Others vary according to circumstances, such as speaking to impress or to identify with a particular social class according to the occasion. We will discuss differences in pronunciation (phonology) in the chapters that follow.

Probably the greatest variation in consonant pronunciation is in words that include the letter *r* in a medial or a final position. Most students of American dialects agree with Thomas (1958) that "the most striking differences between the various regional pronunciations, and the difference around which the most likely, though inconclusive, arguments have revolved, is the nature of the sounds which correspond to the letter *r*" (p. 195).

Table 3–1 indicates differences in word usage in some parts of the northern, midland, and southern dialect areas within the United States. Readers may compare their own usage of the identified items with those of their friends or associates.

Dialects and Sociocultural Class

Not all dialect differences are limited to geographic regions. Within some regions, there are dialectal differences related to social class and socioeconomic status. McDavid (1958) observed that "Social differences in language are usually more apparent in morphology [word usage] and syntax. But in some communities, particularly in the South, they manifest themselves in pronunciation as well" (p. 536). Many speakers, perhaps more so in the South than elsewhere in the United States, are bidialectal for both social and economic reasons. Certainly, many politicians—President Jimmy Carter, Senators Jesse Helms and Russell Long, and Governor George Wallace—may be cited as examples of persons who have been able to accommodate themselves to the dialect of their constituents as well as to the standards ordinarily observed in the White House and in Congress without the need to give up the southern "flavor" of their speech.

Black English[4]

A dialect, we recall, is a variety of a language that is spoken in a particular area or by a particular social group. The variants of the language are found in the lexicon (vocabulary), pronunciation, and syntax (grammar). Despite the variations that create identifiable dialects within a language system, mature speakers and listeners of different dialects have little or no difficulty in understanding one another. Speaker-listeners may need some experience to "tune in" so that they can "figure out" what is said, so that their dialects are *mutually intelligible*. So, as Wardaugh (1972), pointed out, "Cantonese and Mandarin, both of which are called Chinese, are different languages rather than different dialects of one language because they are not mutually intelligible in their spoken forms. However, Danish and Norwegian, sometimes called two different languages, are really dialects of one language in that they *have a high degree of mutual intelligibility*" (p. 191).

Black English is a sociocultural variant (dialect) of English that has no geographic boundaries within the United States. It is spoken, but not as the exclusive dialect, by a majority of black persons, especially by those who live in the "inner cities" of the major cities of the United States. According to Dillard (1972), 80 percent of American blacks speak black English. Labov, a student of dialects, prefers to use the term *black English vernacular* rather than black English. By black English vernacular, Labov (1972, p. xiii) means "the relatively uniform dialect spoken by the majority of black youth in most parts of the United States today, especially in the inner city areas of New York, Boston, Detroit, Philadelphia, Washington, Cleveland, Chicago, St. Louis, San Francisco, Los Angeles, and other urban centers." Moreover, "It is also spoken in most rural areas and used in 'the casual,' intimate conversation of many adults." If we consider black English, or black English vernacular, a dialect, it follows that many black persons are bidialectal. That is, as adults, and probably also as youths, they may on some occasions speak in black English or black English vernacular and on other occasions speak a "standard" dialect of American English.

In Chapter 11, we present some of the phonemic, morphemic, and syntactical features that have established black English as a variant or dialect of "Standard" American English. Our concern in this chapter is to highlight some of the contributions of black English to post–World War II American English as well as some of the dynamics behind these contributions.

In recent years, much American slang has been taken directly from black English. The phrase *right on* may have achieved respectability beyond its usage as slang. It is heard in political speeches and in radio and television commercials. *Rip off* is a phrase with multiple meanings. When a friend has been *ripped off*, she or he may have been robbed, cheated, overcharged, arrested, or murdered. *To rap* is to talk or to argue. So, many of us have held *rap sessions*. *Cool* is used to indicate appropriate detachment, to be able to evaluate a situation before taking action. *Bread* is for money and possibly other worthwhile commodities. *Bad*, especially when pronounced with a "stretched-out" vowel, means good. *Uptight* usually means tense and inflexible, but in black En-

---

[4] The many successful black radio and television personalities as well as actors, actresses, and political figures attest to the use of standard dialects by these speakers who are by no means the exceptions. My own impressions are that black English was a linguistic phenomenon of the post World War II era, reaching its highest incidence of usage in the 1960s and 1970s, and becoming a matter of historical interest by the 1980s. However, the influence of black English on contemporary slang is undeniable.

glish it may also have a positive and desirable implication as "ready for action." These are a few examples of borrowings from black English by American slang. However, there is a rich lexicon that is still used by speakers of black English, blacks and non-blacks included. This lexicon has not become part of the American slang. For a brief summary of the history and influence of black Americans on English and the nature of black English see Dillard (1976, Chapter 7) and Stewart (1972a, Chapters 6 and 7).[5]

There is considerable poetry in the vocabulary of black English, in that words carry values and associations beyond their immediate meanings. For example, the substitution of *fox* for *woman* implies either an evaluation of women or a description of behavior. *Stone* is a *heavy* adjective, and a *stone fox* is *something else*. A *dude* is the successor of the *hip cat* of the 1950s. However, *dude* may refer to any adult male.

Readers who are interested in the features and rules of black English (vernacular) that make it distinctly different from other English and American English dialects may consult Dillard (1972) who has supplied some historical background and some features of black English in the United States and other English-speaking countries.

Spanish

The influence of Spanish on contemporary American English is ongoing. Puerto Rican, Cuban, Mexican, and other variants of Spanish associated with migrations from Spanish-speaking nations in the Western Hemisphere are adding new terms and linguistic structures to American English. Terms such as *canyon, mañana, mesa,* and *pronto* are among those used with little change in pronunciation. Americans enjoy *chili con carne* and *enchiladas* and *tortillas* in areas of the country quite remote from where these foods were first prepared. In California and the Southwest, American speakers may part company with "Hasta la vista" or use the term *vista* without being aware of its origin.

Children and adults whose first language is Spanish often have problems in learning American English that in many instances are carry-overs from their native tongue. These problems include grammatical constructions, idiom, diction, and intonation and vocal inflections. A good review of these problems may be found in Davis (1972). We shall address ourselves to some of these problems in the chapters that follow.

Who Determines Standards of Usage? The Dictionaries

Having briefly sketched some of the forces and influences that have given us American-English speech and its dialect variations, both historical and contemporary, we return to Standard American English. Who determines when new words and new usages of older words become acceptable? Who determines what are "proper" pronunciations? When does a slang term cease to be slang and become a "respectable" term? One answer is "When the educated and/or respected members of a culture use the terms." But terms and pronunciations must be recorded, and decisions must be made about what is to be recorded. Because we have no equivalent of a French Academy whose members have stated meetings to make decisions and "fix the language," the respon-

---

[5] Dillard pointed out that blacks had considerable influence on the speech of southern white persons prior to the Civil War. Words such as *goobers* for *peanuts* and *jazz* for *frenetic activity* and especially for a type of music are examples of early black contributions to American English.

sibility inevitably falls on the editors of dictionaries. Fortunately, even Samuel Johnson noted in the preface to his famous Dictionary, published in 1755, that "words are the daughters of earth." Johnson opposed the notion of an academy with the authority to determine what is correct and acceptable. Nevertheless, Johnson admitted personal bias in his lexical selection. For example, he included words that he recognized as obsolete "when they are found in authors not obsolete, or when they have any force or beauty that may deserve revival." Johnson's authorities were the English writers he respected. He recognized that "no dictionary of a living tongue ever can be perfect, since while it is hastening to publication, some words are budding, and some falling away."

The *American Heritage Dictionary* (1969) also employed a panel of more than one hundred "educated adults" to determine entries and usage. In the introduction by William Morris, the "educated adult" is described:

> The vocabulary recorded here, ranging from the language of Shakespeare to the idiom of the present day, is that of the "educated adult." The "educated adult" referred to is, of course, a kind of ideal person, for he has at his fingertips a most comprehensive lexicon, not only for the conduct and discussion of everyday affairs, but also for all of the arts and all of the sciences. (p. vi)

Noah Webster published his *Compendious Dictionary of the English Language* in 1806. It acknowledged that current usage rather than prescription should determine lexical entries and their definitions and pronunciations. The title page of his *Compendious Dictionary* indicates that five thousand words were added "to the number found in the Best English Compends," and that definitions of many words were "amended and improved."

Contemporary dictionary editors usually insist on recording what is established and current. Harrison Platt, Jr. (1964), presented what we consider a fair view of the degree of responsibility and authority the editors of a respected dictionary cannot avoid. In an appendix to *The American College Dictionary*, Platt said:

> What . . . is the rôle of a dictionary in settling questions of pronunciation or meaning or grammar? It is not a legislating authority on good English. It attempts to record what usage at any time actually is. Insofar as possible, it points out divided usage. It indicates regional variations of pronunciation or meaning wherever practical. It points out meanings and uses peculiar to a trade, profession, or special activity. It suggests the levels on which certain words or usages are appropriate. A dictionary . . . based on a realistic sampling of usage, furnishes the information necessary for a sound judgment of what is good English in a given situation. To this extent the dictionary is an authority, and beyond this authority should not go. (p. 1485)

In the light of this excerpt, we may reassess the significance of the entry on *ain't* in *Webster's Third New International Dictionary*. *Ain't*, according to the entry on page 45, is a contraction of *are not, is not, am not,* or *have not*. Further, we are told, *ain't*, "though disapproved by many, and more common in less educated speech, [is] used orally in most parts of the U.S. by many cultivated speakers esp. in the phrase *ain't I*." Some critics of this dictionary have pointedly asked what is meant by "less educated speech" and imply that somewhere and somehow a comparison seems to be missing. On page 209, we learn that the word *between* is no longer limited to an implication of two but may be used to suggest division or participation by two or more.

The entry cites such usage by *Time* magazine and by eminent scholars, including a linguist from Harvard University.

Bergen Evans, a recognized lexicographer, language specialist, and coauthor of *A Dictionary of Contemporary American Usage,* gave support to changes that were accepted by Webster's Third Edition. Professor Evans, in an informative and amusing article (1963), opened with the suggestion to "Mind your language, friend: words are changing their meaning all the time, some moving up the ladder of social acceptability and others down." In response to critics who accuse dictionary editors of condoning corruption and "low usage," Evans said, "Alas, the tendencies they deplore have been evident for as long as we have any record of language and are as indifferent to indignation or approval as the tides." As examples of changes in word meaning, Evans pointed out that the word *resentment* once could mean "gratitude"; in Samuel Johnson's time, it came to mean "a species of revenge" and now means "indignation." The word *censure* once meant simply "to pass judgment"; *censure* now implies "a judgment with negative criticism." The word *uncouth* once meant "unknown" (*couth* itself meant "known"), without any of the contemporary implications of "a lack of polish or 'good' (approved) manners." Few of us are aware that *wench* could once (as late as 1200) be used to refer to "a child of either sex" or that *counterfeit* once had no implication of illegal reproduction but meant "to imitate" or "to model," even with a worthy ideal.

Sumner Ives (1961), in an article reviewing as well as anticipating the controversy that followed the publication of *Webster's Third New International Dictionary,* made a number of points relative to diction and grammatical usage that are decidedly worthy of our consideration. Several of these points may be summarized as follows:

1. English has changed more during the past fifty years than during any similar period in the past.

2. Language, any language, is a system of human conventions rather than a system of natural laws.

3. A dictionary is reliable only insofar as it comprehensively and accurately describes current practices in a language, including community opinion, as to the social and regional associations of each practice described.

4. ". . . 'good' English is that which most effectively accomplishes the purpose of the author (or speaker) without drawing irrelevant attention from the purpose to the words or constructions by which this purpose is accomplished. Thus, for ordinary purposes, 'good' English is that which is customary and familiar in a given context and in the pursuit of a given objective."

5. Words may have more than one pronunciation. "Standards" of pronunciation must make allowances for regional variations and for differences related to specific contexts. *Webster's Third New International Dictionary* represents "the normal pronunciation of English as it is spoken by cultured persons in each major section of the country—the 'language of well-bred ease,' culturally determined."

Slang and Argot

Argot is the special vocabulary and idiom of a particular profession or social group. Historically, argot has been identified with the vocabulary of underworld characters, devised for "private" or ingroup communication and identification. Thus, we are informed by the *Random House Dictionary of the English Language* (1966) that *The*

Beggar's Opera by John Gay is "rich in thieves' argot." *The Random House College Dictionary* (1975) defines *slang* as "very informal usage in vocabulary and idiom that is characteristically more metaphorical, playful, elliptical, vivid, and ephemeral than ordinary language."

In his discussion of usage, dialects, and functional varieties in the preface to the *Random House College Dictionary*, McDavid (1975) made the following observation about slang and argot.

> *Slang* was once a synonym for argot, the ingroup language used by those who participate in a particular activity, especially a criminal one. In fact, much slang still derives from small, specialized groups, some of it nursed along tenderly by press agents. Popular musicians have originated many slang expressions now in general use. The word *jazz* itself is a good example: a Southern term meaning to copulate, it was used by the musicians who entertained in New Orleans brothels to describe their kinds of musical improvisations and soon came into general use despite the horror of Southerners who had previously known the word as a taboo verb. Today much slang originates with narcotic addicts, spreads to popular musicians, and then gains vogue among the young while falling into disuse among its inventors. Other argot, however, is restricted to the practitioners of a particular field: *boff*, meaning variously "a humorous line," "a belly laugh," or "a box office hit," seems restricted in its use to theatrical circles; *snow*, as it means "cocaine or heroin," is a common term only among drug addicts.
>
> The fate of slang and argot terms is unpredictable. Most of them disappear rapidly, some win their way into standard use, and still others remain what they were to begin with. *Mob*, deplored by Swift and other purists of 1700, would never be questioned today, but *moll*, meaning "a prostitute" or "the mistress of a gangster," has been in use since the early 1600's, and is still slang.
>
> Technical terms arise because it is necessary for those who share a scientific or technical interest to have a basis for discussion. The difference between scientific and popular usage may be seen most strikingly in the biological sciences. A Latin term like *Panthera leo* (lion) has a specific reference, while *cougar* may refer to any large wild American feline predator, or *partridge* may designate the bob-white quail, a kind of grouse, or some other game bird, according to local usage. Common words may be used with specific reference in a given field: *fusion* denotes one thing in politics, another in nuclear physics. As a field of inquiry becomes a matter of general interest, its technical terms will be picked up and used with less precision. Because of popular interest in Freudian psychology, such terms as *complex*, *fixation*, and *transference* are bandied about in senses Freud would never have sanctioned. (p. xxii)

Valley speech, possibly so named because of its origin and wide use among adolescents in the San Fernando Valley of California, is an example of slang and argot. According to one reporter (Demarest, *Time*, September 27, 1982), valley speech is a combination of slang with the hippie lingo of the 1960s and black street jargon. The characteristics of Valley speech include etymological reversals such as *bad* to mean *good*, *groovy* to mean *out of fashion*, and many invented terms (neologisms) that may not be readily traced to their origin. *Rolf* is used for *vomit*, *scarf-out* for *overeat*; *zod*, *spaz*, *goober*, and *geek* may all mean *weird*. *Rad* implies *excellent*, and *shanky* means the opposite. The ultimate in rejection is to be told, "I'm shurr." Demarest provided this sample of discourse: "Shopping is the funnest thing to do cause O.K. clothes. They're important. Like for your image and stuff. Like I'm sure, everything has to match. Like *everything*. And you don't want to wear stuff that people don't wear. Peopl'd look at you and just go 'Ew, she's a zod'; like get away.''

We doubt that Valley speech will have a lasting effect on American-English speech patterns. It is just too *far-out*, and we use the term in a negative sense. Nevertheless, there is little question that whether or not we are aware of it, most of us employ slang and argot in both informal and formal speaking situations without knowledge of the origin of the terms or the semantic intentions of their originators.

Argot may also come from scientists and educators. From operant learning theorists, we have such terms as *behavior shaping, conditioning, reinforcement*, and *discriminative responses*. The term *gestalt* is used for learning theory and a form—to be sure, rather nebulous—of psychotherapy. A *shrink* is almost an accepted word for a psychiatrist.

In our discussion of black English and Valley speech, we cited terms that are used by persons identified with the *counterculture* as well as by blacks. Some words and terms have a short life. One approach of dictionary editors avoids the labeling of words as either argot or slang; instead, words and phrases are listed as ones that have been in frequent usage for a stated period of time, for example, *The Barnhart Dictionary of New English Since 1963* (Barnhart *et al.*, 1973). This dictionary lists entries for the period 1963–1973. From this source we get the meanings of terms such as *alpha-helix, bad-mouth, cassette*, and *learning-curve*. A new edition may be expected to include terms of the space age as well as a few from Valley speech.

Psychological Determinants

To conclude our discussion of changing speech patterns, some psychological factors that determine the choice of words, and the effects of such choice on our patterns of verbal behavior, are reviewed. The words we use are generally selected according to our needs as speakers. The words we select to be impressive depend on the situation and the person or persons we wish to impress. Not infrequently, we may want to impress ourselves, rather than the listener. As speakers, we may have occasional need for a large mouthful of sounds, and so we speak polysyllabically and at length in a manner that would make Freudian listeners click their tongues and nod their heads with weighty surmises. More frequently, however, other factors determine the words we select. One such factor is *ease of pronunciation*. With few exceptions, short words are easier to pronounce than long words, and so, other things being equal, short words are likely to be chosen over long ones, if they can be used effectively in communicating our thoughts and feelings. It is no accident that the most frequently used words in our language are shorter than the words that are less frequently used. George K. Zipf (1949) demonstrated that frequency of word usage is related to the length (shortness) of words, and that *words become shorter as spoken words* with increased frequency of usage. Zipf wrote, '''There are copious examples of a decrease in magnitude of a word which results so far as one can judge solely from an increase in the relative frequency of its occurrence, as estimated either from the speech of an individual, in which the shortening may occur, or in the language of a minor group, or of the major speech group.''

We shorten words by *assimilation*, by *truncation*, and by *abbreviatory substitution*. All three processes, incidentally, also result in ease of pronunciation. As examples of assimilation, we have dropped the *p* from *cupboard,* and most of us drop the *d* from *handkerchief.* Even short phrases are made shorter. For example, the modification of *goodbye* to *gdby,* or just *gby.*

Truncation is exemplified by the change from *amperes* to *amps, elevator* to *el, telephone* to *phone* as either a verb or a noun, and *automobile* to *auto.* In California, the Bay Area Transportation System is briefly referred to as the *Bart. TV* for *television* is an example of truncation by abbreviation, as is *TD* for *touchdown.*

Abbreviatory substitutions are exemplified by *car* for *automobile, juice* for *electric current,* and *prexy* for *president.* The last two terms happen to be usages within special groups, but the groups are large and influential. The word *cop* for *police officer* exemplifies the processes of truncation and abbreviation: from *copper* to *cop* as truncation, and *cop* for *police officer* as abbreviatory substitution. The processes of word shortening and the substitution of abbreviations exemplify Zipf's ''principle of least effort.'' According to Zipf, the changes that are associated with word-frequency usage are expressions of a general principle of human behavior that indicates that, over a period of time, we tend to minimize or reduce our average rate of work expenditure to accomplish an objective.

Counterforces

There are a variety of counterforces that exert influence, that prevent the high-frequency use of the same word or term, and with it, the process of word shortening. The most potent, and from our point of view, the most acceptable of the counterforces is the human drive for variety of experience, including our experience with the words readily at our command. To avoid monotony, we use synonyms that may be less precise in meaning rather than reiterations of the same word. Early in our school careers, our teachers encouraged us to avoid the repeated use of a word, merely because repetition is considered undesirable. Partly because of the authority of our teachers and partly because of our drive for variety, we go out of our way to use several different words to communicate an idea that might well have been semantically more precise had a previously used word been used (employed) again.

Until recently, verbal taboos and superstitions were cultural forces that worked against the use of some words, mostly of Anglo-Saxon origin, as expletives, adjectives, and verbs. Of late, our daily metropolitan newspapers and our magazines have used, rather than abbreviated, the ''four-letter'' words. These words have lost their shock value and are no longer taboo, except to some senior citizens. We find also that there is less difference in the productive vocabularies of adolescent boys and girls and of young men and women in social situations. However, the grandparents, if not the parents, of the emancipated generation may continue to employ circumlocutions and euphemisms to suggest, rather than forcibly say, what they mean or intend. There are still some children who are *born out of wedlock* and so are *illegitimate.* People still *pass away* because speakers do not like to have them *die.* Undertakers are *morticians,* whose establishments are *mortuaries.* Verbal habits and defensive attitudes persist, in at least part of the population, to maintain and even increase the use of terms that another part of the population may aggressively avoid.

In recent years, the locutions and circumlocutions of elected and appointed government officers, politicians, and their representatives have come in for considerable criticism. Certainly, many persons in government employment, and especially those who are highly paid as spokespeople, speak a strained, if not strange, form of English. Though the pattern is by no means clear, a common element is to use many words to avoid saying anything that suggests a specific message.

We are not at all sure of the underlying dynamics of the language of politicians, government officials, and their representatives. Newman (1974) opened his book *Strictly Speaking* with a quotation from a White House press secretary. In answer to a reporter's question about the need for a four-day extension of a subpoena, the secretary "explained" that the additional time was needed so that an attorney could "evaluate and make a judgement in terms of a response." Newman suggested that a simpler answer might have been, "The attorney wanted more time to think about it." Perhaps Newman, in his crusade to save the English language from the impact of American speech, may have missed the point. The press secretary may not have wanted to make his meaning clear by direct and simple speech. Perhaps the secretary wanted to keep in practice to avoid being clear and direct, while seeming to respond to intruding and inquisitive reporters.

Newman objected to persons who prefer to say *impacted on* rather than *hit;* he does not like *at that point in time* or *that time frame* or *in point of fact.* In essence, Newman was pleading, "I speak . . . for a world from which the stilted and pompous phrase, the slogan and cliché, have not been banished—that would be too much to hope for—but which they do not dominate" (p. 32).

Russell Baker, a syndicated columnist, also objects to the pompous and clichéd terminology current among government employees in Washington. With characteristic humor, and using the technique of exaggeration (at least we hope it is exaggeration), Baker wrote the following:

> Utile. That was how Carruthers felt. Naturally he worked for the Government. It is the nation's biggest employer of the utile. This is because one of its biggest jobs is utilizing. If you have a lot of utilizing to do, it is vital to have utile people on the payroll.
>
> One day Carruthers was utilizing busily when he noticed a capability sitting in the corridor. Carruthers had just utilized the water cooler and was returning to his office to utilize the telephone, and he noted the capability watching him. Carruthers did not like that.
>
> This, he realized, might very well be the Government's investigative capability checking to see if Carruthers had become redundant. It was time to engage in the decision-making process, but there were so many processes surrounding him that he made a mistake and wound up engaged in the political process.[6]

It would be unfair to politicians and government employees to leave readers with the impression that they are the chief refugees from talking simply and directly. Postman, Weingartner, and Moran were the editors of *Language in America* (1969), a book that includes essays about persons who are members of groups that have a variety of special interests. Such groups may include blue-collar workers, farmers, and those in the sciences and the professions. A book edited by Estrin and Mehus, *The American Language in the 1970s* (1974), includes essays on the "verbal behavior" of scientists, space technologists, persons in the arts, and "Academia and its Jargon." The individuals in each group, and many are members of more than one group, have their lexicons and manner of modifying and using the language for their own purposes. These pur-

---

[6]Published in the *San Francisco Chronicle,* July 17, 1977.

poses often make the content obscure to others. In an essay in the Postman et al. book, "The Language of Self Deception," Ashley Montagu warned that in time we may become the victims of the language we use, that we may be taken in by our self-deceptions:

> the words we use as psychophysical conditioners which determine the manner in which the individual shall think, feel, and behave. . . . Hence . . . the importance of teaching language not so much as grammar but as behavior, of teaching language as a fine and delicate instrument of expression designed to put man in touch with his fellow man. (p. 95)

These, briefly, are some of the forces and counterforces that have molded our language, that have influenced our verbal habits, and that continue to modify our slow but ever-changing speech patterns. A living language is a growing language and one that changes forms, adds words and drops others, and modifies pronunciations. Some of the forces are global; others are peculiarly American.

References and Suggested Readings

American Heritage Dictionary. Boston: American Heritage Publishing Company and Houghton Mifflin, 1969.

Barnhart, C. L., S. Steinmetz, and R. K. Barnhart, *Barnhart Dictionary of New English Since 1963*. New York: Harper and Row, 1973.

Davis, A. L. "English Problems of Spanish Speakers," in D. L. Shores (Ed.), *Contemporary English*. Philadelphia: J. B. Lippincott Company, 1972, Chap. 9.

Demarest, M. "Living," in *Time*, 5(120) (September 27, 1982), 3.

Dillard, J. L. *Black English: Its History and Usage in the United States*. New York: Random House, Inc., 1972.

Dillard, J. L. *American Talk*. New York: Random House, Inc., 1976.

Estrin, H. A., and D. V. Mehus (Eds.), *The American Language in the 1970s*. Sacramento, Calif.: Boyd & Fraser Publishing Company, 1974.

Evans, B., "Couth to Uncouth and Vice Versa." *New York Times Magazine* (November 10, 1963), pp. 22 ff.

Evans, B., and C. Evans. *A Dictionary of Contemporary American Usage*. New York: Random House, Inc., 1957.

Flexner, S. B. *I Hear America Talking*. New York: Van Nostrand Reinhold, 1976.

Ives, S. "A Review of Webster's Third New International Dictionary." *Word Study* (December 1961).

Jones, D. *The Pronunciation of English*, 3rd ed. Cambridge, England: W. Hefner and Sons, 1950.

Jones, D. *An Outline of English Phonetics*, 8th ed. Cambridge, England: W. Hefner and Sons, 1956.

Labov, W. *Language in the Inner City*. Philadelphia: University of Pennsylvania Press, 1972.

McDavid, R. I., in Francis, W. N. *The Dialects of American English*. New York: The Ronald Press, 1958.

McDavid, R. I. "Usage, Dialects and Functional Varieties." *The Random House College Dictionary*, rev. ed. New York: Random House, Inc., 1975.

Mencken, H. L. *The American Language*. New York: Alfred A. Knopf, Inc., 1946.

Newman, E. *Strictly Speaking*. New York: Bobbs-Merrill, 1974.

√ Pei, M. *The Story of Language*. Philadelphia: J. B. Lippincott Co., 1949.

Pei, M. "The Language of the Election and the Watergate Years," in H. A. Estrin and D. V. Mehus (Eds.), *The American Language in the 1970s*. Sacramento, Calif.: Boyd & Fraser Publishing Company, 1974.

Platt, H. Jr. "Appendix," *The American College Dictionary*. New York: Random House, Inc., 1964.

Postman, N., C. Weingartner, and T. P. Moran (Eds.), *Language in America*. Indianapolis and New York: Pegasus (Bobbs-Merrill), 1969.

Random House College Dictionary, rev. ed. New York: Random House, Inc., 1975.

Shores, D. L. (Ed.), *Contemporary English*. Philadelphia: J. B. Lippincott Company, 1972.

Shuy, R. W., *Discovering American Dialects*. Urbana, Ill.: National Council of Teachers of English, 1967.

Stewart, W. A. "Language and Communication Problems in Southern Appalachia," in D. L. Shores, *Contemporary English*. Philadelphia: J. B. Lippincott Company, 1972a.

——— "Sociolinguistic Factors in the History of Negro Dialects" and "Continuity and Change in American Negro Dialects," in D. L. Shores, *Contemporary English*. Philadelphia: J. B. Lippincott Company, 1972b.

Thomas, C. K. *An Introduction to the Phonetics of American English*, 2nd ed. New York: The Ronald Press, 1958.

Wardaugh, R. *Introduction to Linguistics*. New York: McGraw-Hill Book Company, 1972.

Whatmough, J. *Language*. New York: St. Martin's Press, 1956.

Zipf, G. K. *Psycho-Biology of Language*. Boston: Houghton Mifflin Company, 1935.

Zipf, G. K. *Human Behavior and the Principle of Least Effort*. Reading, Mass.: Addison-Wesley, 1949.

part two

Voice Improvement

He is made one with Nature: there is heard
His voice in all her music, from the moan
Of thunder to the song of the night's sweet bird.
　　　　　—PERCY B. SHELLEY, *Adonais*

'Tis the voice of the sluggard; I heard him complain
"You have waked me too soon, I must slumber again."
　　　　　—ISAAC WATTS, *The Sluggard*

The voice of the intellect is a soft one, but it does not rest
　　　until it has gained a hearing.
　　　　　—SIGMUND FREUD, *Future of an Illusion*

4

Breathing for Effective Vocalization

Physicians who specialize in the treatment of disorders of the throat and larynx—and those few, such as Brodnitz (1973), who treat vocal disorders as well as diseases of the throat—recognize that most voice disorders are a result of the use of *inappropriate force, wrong pitch, incorrect breathing, or a combination of these faults.*

Although our experience does not show that most speakers necessarily breath incorrectly, use force inappropriately, or pitch their voices at wrong levels, a knowledge of what can be done to improve the voice may be helpful to all of us. Certainly, speakers who want a better-than-ordinary voice or who need to use the voice in their vocations have an obligation to themselves as well as to their listeners to know what students in the field of voice recommend about the use of force, pitch, and breathing. We begin with a consideration of breathing.[1]

Earlier, in our discussion of the mechanism of speech, we pointed out that breathing for speech calls for a modification of the normal respiratory cycle so that (1) the inspiration–expiration ratio is changed to provide a much longer period of exhalation than of inspiration, and (2) a steady stream of air is initiated and controlled by the speaker to ensure good tone. These modifications, we have found, are usually achieved most easily by the type of breathing that emphasizes abdominal activity.

At the outset, we would like to point out that good breathing for speech production is by no means synonymous with exaggerated, deep breathing. Many good speakers use no more breath for vigorous speaking, or public speaking, than they do for con-

---

[1] The basic physiology of respiration for speech is considered in Lieberman (1977, Chapters 2 and 6). Lieberman stressed the point that during respiration the elastic recoil of the lungs is normally sufficient to provide the force necessary to push the inspired air out of the lungs.

Boone (1983, Chapter 1), has reviewed some of the physical causes of voice defects (vocal abuse and misuse).

versational speech. Seldom is it necessary for any person to employ more than one fifth of his breath capacity for any ordinary vocal effort.

This is not to suggest that we have any objection to the practice of deep breathing. Most of us breathe (inspire and exhale) between 12 and 14 times per minute. Some persons who practice deep breathing as part of meditation or voluntary relaxation can reduce the breath cycles by deep inhalations and controlled, slow exhalations to as few as four or five per minute. Though this cycle of breathing may be excellent for bio-genics and for physical health in general, it is not a necessary procedure for breathing as far as most vocal needs are concerned. In keeping with this position, our emphasis is on control of the supply of breath rather than on deep breathing.

Breathing for speech should meet the following objectives:

1. It should afford the speaker an adequate and comfortable supply of breath with the least awareness and expenditure of effort.

2. The respiratory cycle—inhalation and exhalation—should be accomplished easily, quickly, and without interference with the flow of utterance.

3. The second objective implies ease of control over the outgoing breath so that breathing and phrasing—the grouping of ideas—can be correlated functions.

If these objectives are not established and are not habitual accomplishments, they can be most readily achieved through establishing abdominal control of breathing.

Abdominal Breathing

If we observe the breathing of a person or an animal that is sleeping on its back or side, we should be able to note that during inhalation the abdominal area moves up-ward or forward, whereas during exhalation the abdominal area recedes. Figure 2–4, (p. 21) visualizes what we can see in the way of abdominal activity, as well as what we cannot see in the way of diaphragmatic activity, for breathing that emphasizes ab-dominal control.

The essential point for us to appreciate is that, in breathing that is characterized by the action of the abdominal muscles, the muscles of the abdomen relax in inhalation and contract in exhalation. When we learn how to contract or pull in the abdominal walls consciously, and how much and how fast to control such contraction, breathing for speech becomes *voluntary if needed*. If the reader is now exercising such control unconsciously, the suggested exercises that follow are not particularly important. For persons who cannot easily sustain a hum or a gentle whisper for from twenty to thirty seconds, these exercises should be followed. The exercises are designed to create awareness and conscious control of abdominal action in breathing.

EXERCISES FOR AWARENESS AND CONTROL OF ABDOMINAL ACTIVITY IN BREATHING

1. Lie on a couch or on a bed with a firm mattress. Spread your hands on the abdominal area immediately below the ribs so that your thumbs point away from it (toward the ribs) and your fingers point downward. Inhale as you would for normal, nonspeaking breathing. Your hands should rise dur-ing inhalation and fall with the abdomen during exhalation. If the action is reversed, then your breathing is incorrect and should be changed to bring about the suggested activity. Repeat until the suggested action is accomplished easily. Be sure that you are not wearing a tight belt or a confining article of clothing while doing this and the following exercises.

2. Sit in a relaxed position in a comfortable chair with a firm seat. Your feet should be flat on the floor. Place your hands as in Exercise 1. Now the abdominal walls should push forward during inhalation and pull in during exhalation.

3. Repeat Exercise 2. Then inhale gently for about five seconds and exhale slowly, sustaining the exhalation for ten seconds. If you find yourself out of breath before the end of the ten-second period, then you have probably exhaled too quickly. Try the exercise again, intentionally slowing down the exhalation.

4. Inhale fully and then breathe out slowly and completely. Your hands should still be following the movement of the abdominal walls. Repeat, but this time press gently but firmly with your hands to force the expulsion of air from your lungs. Repeat, counting to yourself while exhaling. At this point you should be able to count for about thirty seconds before becoming uncomfortable.

5. Repeat, but this time vocalize a clear *ah* while exhaling. *Start your vocalization the moment you begin to exhale.* Stop before becoming uncomfortable. Repeat, vocalizing a sustained *hum* while exhaling. The *ah* and *hum* should be sustained longer than a nonvocalized exhalation.

6. Inhale deeply and then count out evenly and slowly until you feel the need for a second breath. *Maintain even pitch and loudness levels.* Repeat, but this time keep your hands at your sides and concentrate on a gradual pulling in of the abdominal wall during the counting. You should be able to count to at least twenty on a sustained exhalation. In any event, continue to practice until a count of at least fifteen is attained. With continued practice, a count of twenty to thirty (at the rate of two numbers per second) should become possible after a normal inhalation, and a full thirty-second count after a deep inhalation.

7. With hands at your sides, repeat this exercise on two successive breaths. Be certain that you do not exhale to a point of discomfort. Nor should you inhale so deeply that some air has to be exhaled for the sake of comfort.

8. Repeat, reciting the alphabet instead of counting. Avoid wasting breath between utterance of the letters. Note how far you are able to go on a single normal breath and on a single deep breath.

9. Repeat, whispering the alphabet. Note the letter you reach before requiring a second breath. Depending on the degree of whisper, this might be only a third or a half of the number of letters of your vocalized effort. This is normal. A whisper is wasteful of breath.

10. Count, with vocalization, in groups of three. Avoid exhalation during pauses. Did you come close to the number you reached in counting without grouping? If you did not, then you probably exhaled between groups of numbers. Try it again until the two counts are about even.

11. Repeat Exercise 10, using the alphabet instead of counting.

12. Recite the months of the year with pauses after March, June, and September. You should have no difficulty reciting all twelve months even with "seasonal" pauses.

13. Try to say each of the following sentences on a single breath.

    a. Stephen's voice expressed his humility.
    b. Spain is in the southwest corner of Europe.
    c. The night was cooled by a gentle breeze.
    d. Those who learn nothing have nothing to forget.
    e. When we persuade others, we often convince ourselves.
    f. There is little that is new except that which is forgotten.

14. If you had no difficulty with the single sentences, then try to produce these longer sentences and couplets, each on a single, sustained breath. Do not, however, force the expulsion of breath beyond a point of comfort.

    a. Adlai Stevenson advised that a wise man does not try to hurry history.
    b. Plato held that rhetoric was the art of ruling the minds of men.
    c. An Englishman thinks he is moral when he is only uncomfortable.
                —GEORGE BERNARD SHAW, *Man and Superman*
    d. In *The Devil's Disciple,* Shaw observed that indifference rather than hate was the essence of inhumanity.
    e. For he who fights and runs away
       May live to fight another day;
                 —OLIVER GOLDSMITH, *The Art of Poetry*
    f. Upon what meat doth this our Caesar feed,
       That he is grown so great?
              —WILLIAM SHAKESPEARE, *Julius Caesar,* Act I
    g. Party is the madness of the many for the gain of the few.
              —ALEXANDER POPE, *Thoughts on Various Subjects*

The following exercises involve the use of speech sounds that have an aspirate quality. They are normally more wasteful of breath than most of the previous exercises. They are, however, important in establishing breath control because much of what we say includes nonvocalized (voiceless) sounds as well as those that have a definite whispered, or fricative, quality.

EXERCISES FOR ESTABLISHING BREATH CONTROL

✓ **1.** Inhale normally and then release the breath while producing the sound *s.* Be sure the sound is evenly maintained. Try to sustain the *s* for ten seconds. Repeat with the sound *sh,* then *th* as in *think,* and *f* as in *fall.*

✓ **2.** Inhale deeply, but avoid discomfort. Repeat Exercise 1. Compare these efforts with the length of time for a sustained *m* or *ah.* You are not likely to sustain any of these breathy sounds as long as *m* or *ah,* but you should come fairly close.

  3. Try saying each of the following sentences on a single breath. If you do not succeed the first time, try a deeper inhalation on successive trials. Do not intentionally whisper.

    a. According to an ancient Arab proverb, no one is likely to complain of being tired on a day of victory.

   b. A Chinese proverb reminds us that a single picture is worth more than ten thousand words.

   c. Is it true that though you can always tell a Harvard man, you can't tell him much?

   d. The sun sank slowly and was followed by darkness and an enveloping, foggy chill.

   e. Caspar Smith had a reputation as an excellent conversationalist because he practiced listening in respectful silence.

   f. Some cynical literary critics profess that several of Shakespeare's plays were written by another author with the same name.

4. If you have been successful with all of the sentences, then try these couplets, each on a single breath. If you pause at the end of the line, try not to exhale at the pause.

   a. ''Home is the place where, when you have to
     go there,
   They have to take you in.''
               —ROBERT FROST, *The Death of the Hired Man*

   b. A moral, sensible, and well-bred man
   Will not affront me,—and no other can.
               —WILLIAM COWPER, *Conversation*

   c. My life is like a stroll upon the beach,
   As near the ocean's edge as I can go.
               —HENRY DAVID THOREAU, *The Fisher's Boy*

   d. Words are like leaves; and where they most abound,
   Much fruit of sense beneath is rarely found.
               —ALEXANDER POPE, *An Essay On Criticism*

   e. Thunder is good, thunder is impressive; but it is lightning that does the work.   —MARK TWAIN, *Letter to an Unidentified Person*

5. Try uttering the following longer sentences and triplets, if possible, on a single breath. However, if you do not succeed, be sure you pause for breath between phrases (breath groups).

   a. He who would distinguish the true from the false must have an adequate idea of what is true and false.
               —BENEDICT SPINOZA, *Ethics*

   b. We must think of our whole economics in terms of a preventive pathology instead of a curative pathology. Don't oppose forces; use them.   —BUCKMINSTER FULLER, *No More Secondhand God.*

   c. Grow old along with me!
   The best is yet to be,
   The last of life, for which
     the first was made.
               —ROBERT BROWNING, *Rabbi Ben Ezra*

   d. Music resembles poetry; in each
   Are nameless graces which no methods teach,
   And which a master-hand alone can reach.
               —ALEXANDER POPE, *Essay on Criticism*

      e. My object all sublime
         I shall achieve in time—
         To make the punishment fit the crime.

                  —W. S. GILBERT, *The Mikado*

Clavicular Breathing

As a basic principle, assuming that a speaker has enough breath for speaking, it is not the amount but the evenness of the control of the breath stream that is important. Therefore, any technique that emphasizes the quantity of air for its own sake is not held in high regard. Even if the quantity of air were important, it could be more easily increased through deep breathing with abdominal and lower-rib-cage activity that with clavicular breathing, which, at best, merely evalates the chest as a whole. In fact, clavicular breathing tends to be shallow rather than deep and requires more frequent inhalation than does abdominal breathing. Beyond this, clavicular breathing has definite disadvantages in that it has been found to be associated with a marked tendency of the muscles of the larynx and throat to become too tense for proper vocalization and reinforcement of tone.

To check on any tendency toward clavicular breathing, stand before a full-length mirror and breathe in deeply. Relax, then exhale fully. Repeat twice. Note, and correct, any tendency of the shoulders to be appreciably elevated or of the chest as a whole to be raised. Abdominal breathing, which we recommend, would call for little or no movement of the shoulders or the upper chest. Movement, if it is to be discerned, would be of the lower-chest and abdominal areas. Usually, this procedure will require a profile rather than a full-front view.

An added check, as well as an exercise to correct the tendency toward clavicular breathing, is the following: Place your hands on your chest with your fingers spread and the thumbs pointing toward the collarbone. Take a deep breath, then say the days of the week. Observe—and, if necessary, use the pressure of your hands to prevent—any appreciable upward movement of the upper chest and shoulders. For variety, the exercise might be done with counting from one through ten or reciting the alphabet in sequences from *a* through *l* and *m* through *z*. If upper chest movement is inhibited, the normal compensatory action will bring about the desired movement of the abdominal and the lower-chest muscles. Be certain that the movement is forward during inhalation and inward during exhalation.

Breathing and Phrasing

In the exercises to establish abdominal breathing and an awareness of breath control, our emphasis was on sustaining a sound, a series of words, or a sentence on a single breath. For ordinary conversational speech, and for most public speaking purposes, the length of uninterrupted utterance is not as important as the interruption of a unit of thought because of the need for additional breath. The occasions are infrequent when a speaker needs to utter more than twelve to fifteen syllables on a single breath. The speaker must learn to anticipate inhalation, and to stop at an appropriate point to inhale. Speakers who learn this will avoid having to stop at an inappropriate point because they cannot continue speaking without another breath. The appropriate or natural stopping places are at the ends of units of thought, *between phrases or sentences*. Unless the speaker is reading or reciting verse with regular meter, the units of thought are likely to be of varying lengths. Breathing must therefore be adjusted to anticipated needs. For example, if the speaker cannot comfortably quote Emerson on a single breath to the effect that "His heart was as great as the world, but there was no room in it to hold the memory of a wrong," he or she has a choice of at least two stopping places. The speaker may, without doing violence to the thought, stop at the places indicated by the vertical lines: "His heart was as great as the world ‖ but there was no room in it ‖ to hold the memory of a wrong." Similarly, the sentence "Christopher Morley held that the three ingredients in the good life are learning, earning, and yearning" can be spoken with pauses for phrasing as "Christopher Morley held ‖ that the three ingredients in the good life ‖ are learning, earning, and yearning." Incidentally, we may note that some, but not all of the units of thought (breath-phrase units) are marked off for us by punctuation. Some units of thought have no punctuation marks. The reader must, on the basis of meaning, decide where and whether to phrase. The good vocal phraser uses punctuation as a guide but is not a slave to it.

A speaker with a fair breath capacity and good breath control might easily go as far as the second vertical line before stopping for a breath. Unless he or she feels equal to the entire sentence, however, he or she should not try to go beyond the second vertical line because to do so would mean interrupting a unit of thought in order to inhale.

In Exercises 1–5 that immediately follow, possible stops for inhalation are indicated by vertical lines. In terms of your own breath capacity, mark off the places at which you plan to inhale. Inhale briefly at these places so that there is no suggestion of awkward pausing. Try to inhale as infrequently as possible so that the reading does not become jerky. Maintain abdominal control of breathing. If necessary, place your hands on the abdominal wall to feel the pushing away at the inhalations and the pulling in at the exhalations while reading aloud.

EXERCISES FOR ABDOMINAL BREATHING AND PHRASING

1. Breathe in as you would for inhalation during casual conversation; then count at the rate of two numbers per second, pausing—and if necessary, inhaling—at the marked places.

1-2-3-4-5-6-7-8-9-10-11 ‖ 12-13-14-15-16-17-18-19-20-21

The first grouping should have been produced easily on a single breath; the second would be somewhat more difficult because of the additional syllables.

2. Repeat Exercise 1, but this time pause and renew your breath supply after fourteen; then count from fifteen through twenty-one.

3. Count as long as you can on a single deep breath, but avoid becoming uncomfortable either because of too deep an inhalation or too exhaustive an exhalation. Note the point at which you pause for breath. Then count again, but this time intentionally pause and inhale two numbers earlier in the sequence than where you needed to pause the first time. Count again to the same number.

4. Recite the alphabet, pausing—and inhaling, if necessary—only at the marked places. Be sure to pause even though you do not need to inhale.

a-b-c-d-e-f-g-h ‖ i-j-k-l-m-n-o-p-q ‖ r-s-t-u-v-w-x-y-z

Were you able to go beyond the first group? With practice, the entire alphabet should be recited easily after a single moderate inhalation.

5. Read the following sentences aloud, pausing—and breathing, if necessary—at the marked places. In addition to the initial breath, it should not be necessary to inhale more than once for each sentence.

> **a.** Sheridan advised that conscience ‖ has no more to do with gallantry ‖ than it has to do with politics.
>
> **b.** A classic is something that everybody wants to have read ‖ and nobody wants to read.
> > ——MARK TWAIN, *The Disappearance of Literature*
>
> **c.** The more things a man is ashamed of ‖ the more respectable he is.
> > ——GEORGE BERNARD SHAW, *Man and Superman*
>
> **d.** Fear cannot be without hope ‖ nor hope without fear.
> > —BENEDICT SPINOZA, *Ethics*

6. In the following exercises, read the material aloud to determine where you need to stop for breath. Pause to indicate phrasing, but inhale only when you cannot go on comfortably to the next phrase on the remaining breath.

> **a.** The philosopher-poet Kahill Gibran advised us to allow for space in our togetherness.
>
> **b.** The realistic cynic Aldo Selfridge observed that things are not as good as they used to be and probably never were.
>
> **c.** I am in the habit of looking not so much to the nature of a gift as to the spirit in which it is offered.
> > —ROBERT LOUIS STEVENSON, *New Arabian Nights*
>
> **d.** Democracy is the recurrent suspicion that more than half of the people are right more than half of the time.
> > —E. B. WHITE, *World Government and Peace*
>
> **e.** As citizens of this democracy, you are the rulers and the ruled, the law-givers and the law-abiding, the beginning and the end.
> > —ADALI STEVENSON, Speech, Chicago, 1952
>
> **f.** Adam was but human—this explains it all. He did not want the apple for the apple's sake, he wanted it only because it was forbidden.   —MARK TWAIN, *Pudd'nhead Wilson*
>
> **g.** One will rarely err if extreme actions be ascribed to vanity, ordinary actions to habit, and mean actions to fear.
> > —FRIEDRICH NIETZSCHE, *Human, All Too Human*
>
> **h.** Harlequin without his mask is known to present a very sober countenance, and was himself, the story goes, the melancholy patient whom the Doctor advised to go and see Harlequin.
> > —WILLIAM M. THACKERAY, *The English Humorists*

Avoiding Waste of Breath   ✓

If while executing the exercises earlier in the chapter you had difficulty in counting up to fifteen on a single breath, you may have wasted too much breath in the vocal effort. The most likely cause of wasted breath is a failure to bring the vocal bands close enough together to prevent leakage of air during vocalized speech efforts. Whispered or semi-whispered speech is necessarily wasteful of breath because the vocal bands are kept fully or partially open. This effect may be noted in Figure 4–1, which shows the positions of the voice bands in quiet breathing, whispering, and vocalized speaking. In order to overcome breathiness, it will help first to become aware of a speech effort, which, by the nature of the sounds employed, is necessarily breathy. The sentences that follow include a number of voiceless fricative and breath-stop sounds that are normally and appropriately produced with a breathy quality. Hold your hand, palm turned toward your face, about six inches in front of your mouth as you say:

1. The ship set sail in the chill of the morning fog.
2. Paula and Fred liked to watch football.
3. Few of us can resist listening to short and simple scandals.
4. Timothy complained that he had no more privacy than a fish in a glass bowl.

In contrast with these sentences, those that follow contain only voiced sounds and few that have a plosive quality. Say the following, again holding your hand in front of your mouth to feel the difference in breathiness.

1. Lou will do all a man may do.
2. Belle was never ill.
3. The boys and girls ran around the bend.
4. None knew the old woman.
5. We were all willing and ready.

The following sentences contain a few sounds that are normally breathy. Try to say them with as little waste of breath as possible. Shorten all *f, v, th, s, z,* and *sh* sounds to reduce the length of these normally breathy consonants.[2] With good breath control, each sentence should require only a single inhalation.

1. Henry Thoreau had three chairs in his house; one was for solitude; two were for friendship; three were for society.
2. Sometimes the spin-offs of inventions are worth more than the initially invented products.
3. The siren warned us that a house was on fire.
4. Despite the fierce storm, the ship set out to sea.
5. In his essay "The Square Egg," H. H. Munro advised, "In baiting a mouse-trap with cheese, always leave room for the mouse."

Excessive breathiness may be a result of carrying over the aspirate quality of a sound to the succeeding vowel. You may avoid this effect, or reduce it, by taking care not to prolong the aspirate sounds and to emphasize the full vocalization of the vowels and diphthongs. Special caution is necessary when the initial sound is an *h,* as it is a par-

---

[2] See Chapter 12 for a discussion of the types of consonants, vowels, and diphthongs.

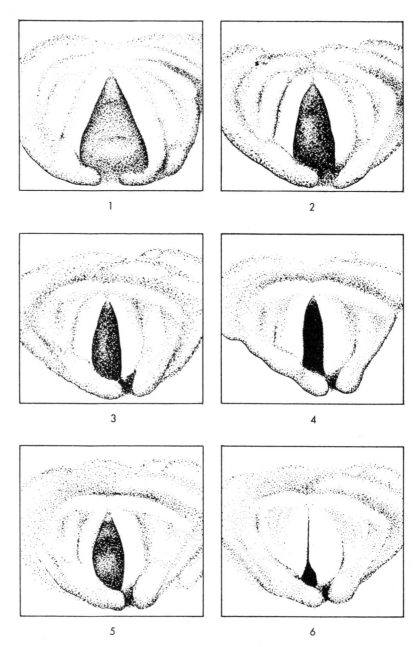

FIGURE 4–1 **Diagrams based on high-speed photos showing changes in positions of vocal bands from quiet breathing *(1, 2)* to whispering *(3, 4, 5)* to vocalization *(6)*.**

ticularly breath-consuming sound. With these thoughts in mind, try to say the following pairs of words so that there is no more aspiration on the vowel or diphthong of the second word of the pair than there is on those of the first. There should, of course, be no aspirate quality in the first word of each pair.

I	high	arm	farm
ale	pale	own	shown
oar	core	arc	park
air	fair	eel	feel
ear	tear	mold	hold
add	fad	end	send
am	ham	will	fill
awe	saw	aid	shade

In each of the following sentences, emphasize the production of the vowel or diphthong sounds. Despite the temptation provided by initial aspirate sounds, avoid an excessive carry-over of breathiness to the succeeding sounds.

1. Harry wished his friends health and happiness.

2. Hoping against hope is hoping still.

3. Paul hiked four miles through the forest.

4. People need not be poets to be impressed by the coming of spring.

5. George Eliot wrote that because a woman's hopes are woven of sunbeams, a shadow can quickly disperse them.

6. Goldsmith pointed out that people seldom improve when they simulate themselves.

7. In one of his campaign speeches, Adlai Stevenson asserted that "A hungry man is not a free man."

8. You do not have to shout. But if you whisper . . . the whisper had better be good.   —ROBERT K. LEAVITT, *Voyages and Discovery*

9. The test of a first-rate intelligence is the ability to hold two opposed ideas in the mind at the same time, and still retain the ability to function.

—F. SCOTT FITZGERALD, *The Crack-up*

10. In *The Course of Empire*, Bernard De Voto observed: "History abhors determinism but cannot tolerate chance."

Affected or Imitative Breathiness

Many persons vocalize with a breathy quality out of habit or choice. The choice is not always a conscious one. It may have had its beginning in the imitation born of admiration of a popular figure. For adolescents and young adults, the figure is often a performer, a star of radio, screen, or television. So-called "sultry-voiced" singers influence the vocal efforts of many high school and college adolescents who want to be sultry-voiced whether or not they can sing. Many young children have husky and breathy voices because of unconscious imitation of their mothers, and a few, perhaps, of their fathers. Unfortunately, excessive breathiness frequently has an adverse effect on the laryngeal mechanism as well as on the ability of the speaker to maintain as long a series of phrases or sentences as the nonbreathy speaker. The overall result is a vocal habit that loses its attractiveness in the postadolescent period. Breathy vocalizers then find themselves fatigued speakers and occasionally ones with thickened vocal bands. If this becomes the case, then considerable vocal reeducation is in order. Good voice production is achieved with good breath control in an appropriate pitch range. With such control, a clear rather than a breathy quality should be established throughout the normal pitch range. Clear tones are then produced with a minimum use of air for an efficient and maximum vocal effort.

The following exercises are intended as a general review opportunity for the practice of breath control. In doing them, make certain (1) that there is no evidence of clavicular breathing; (2) that abdominal activity and lower-chest activity characterize the breathing for vocalizations; (3) that inhalations are correlated with units of meaning; and (4) that there is no waste of breath at pauses for phrasing when there is no need for inhalation, or because of excessive aspiration on specific speech sounds, or as a characteristic of the vocal effort as a whole.

EXERCISES FOR PRACTICE OF BREATH CONTROL

1. The most beautiful thing we can experience is the mysterious. It is the source of all true art and science.

—ALBERT EINSTEIN, *What I Believe*

2. Man consists of body, mind, and imagination. His body is faulty, his mind untrustworthy, but his imagination has made him remarkable.

—JOHN MASEFIELD, *Shakespeare and Spiritual Life*

3. Speech is civilization itself. The word, even the most contradictory word, preserves contact—it is silence which isolates.

—THOMAS MANN, *The Magic Mountain*

4. Training is everything. The peach was once a bitter almond; cauliflower is nothing but cabbage with a college education.

—MARK TWAIN, *Pudd'nhead Wilson*

5. Laughter is not at all a bad beginning for a friendship, and it is far the best ending for one.

—OSCAR WILDE, *The Picture of Dorian Gray*

6. Horace Mann considered the telling of truth a serious responsibility. He advised, "You need not tell all the truth, unless to those who have a right to know it all. But let all you tell be truth."

7. The time which we have at our disposal every day is elastic; the passions that we feel every day expand it; those that we inspire contract it; and habit fills up what remains.

—MARCEL PROUST, *Within a Budding Grove*

8. Strange, when you come to think of it, that of all the countless folk who have lived before our time on this planet not one is known in history or in legend as having died of laughter.

—MAX BEERBOHM, *Laughter*

9. A good society is a means to a good life for those who compose it; not something having a kind of excellence on its own account.

—BERTRAND RUSSELL, *Authority and the Individual*

10. Optimism is a mania for maintaining that all is well when things are going badly.   —VOLTAIRE, *Candide*

References and Suggested Readings

Boone, D. R. *The Voice and Voice Therapy*, 3rd. ed. Englewood Cliffs, N.J.: Prentice-Hall, Inc., 1983. (In Chapter 1, the author reviews some of the physical causes of vocal defects and discusses appropriate breathing for speech.)

Brodnitz, F. S. *Keep Your Voice Healthy.* Springfield, Ill.: Charles C. Thomas, 1973. (The author, a physician with a special interest in voice, advises on vocal hygiene.)

Greene, M. C. *The Voice and Its Disorders.* Baltimore: Williams and Wilkins, 1980. (This is the fourth edition of a concise and clearly written book on voice and vocal disorders.)

Laver, J. *The Phonetic Description of Voice Quality.* Cambridge, England: Cambridge University Press, 1980. (Laver applies principles of phonetics to the description of vocal qualities. The treatment is technical, detailed, and generously illustrated.)

Lieberman, P. *Speech Perception and Acoustic Phonetics.* New York: Macmillan Publishing Company, 1977.

Moore, G. P. *Organic Voice Disorders.* Englewood Cliffs, N.J.: Prentice-Hall, Inc., 1971. (With authority and brevity, the author considers the more frequent causes of vocal disorders.)

Moses, P. J. *The Voice of Neurosis.* New York: Grune and Stratton, Inc., 1954. (The author, a physician and psychoanalyst, applies both fields of his expertise to his explanation of the neurotic personality and its expression in voice.)

Wilson, D. K. *Voice Problems of Children,* 2nd ed. Baltimore: Williams and Wilkins, 1979. (Although the book is about children's voice problems, the causes of these problems and the author's advice hold for adolescents and adults.)

5

Production of Clear Tones

✓ The voice, we now realize, is a product of integrated muscular activity. The combination of tendinous tissue and muscles that constitute the vocal bands is set in vibration as a result of integrated activity of the muscles of respiration and those controlling laryngeal action. When the integration is right and the vocal bands are brought together (approximated) closely enough so that there is sufficient resistance to the column of air being forced up from the lungs, voice is produced. If the vocal bands are not sufficiently approximated to create adequate resistance to the column of air, the result is either a semivocalized effort or unvocalized breathing, depending on the degree of approximation (see Figure 4–1). Our immediate concern is to establish the concept and
√ technique for the initiation of good, clear tones.

Tone, or *vocal tone,* as we will use these terms, is the vocal product considered with reference to its attributes: quality, pitch, loudness, and duration.

Good tones are free from the effects of tension or strain. Good tones are initiated with ease, appropriately reinforced by the resonating cavities, and sustained with ease. Tonal (vocal) impurities result most frequently from tensions of the muscles of the throat and neck that interfere with the free action of the muscles of the larynx, and so of the vocal bands. Tonal impurities may arise indirectly from incorrect breathing habits that may be associated with laryngeal tension. They may also be caused by inappropriate resonance.

In the absence of any structural defect of the voice-producing mechanism, of a defect of hearing that makes vocal monitoring difficult, or of any emotional disturbance associated with either excessive or inadequate muscular tonicity, reasonably good vocal tones should be possible for all speakers. Some speakers, we realize, have mechanisms whose parts are so well combined that they have excellent voices without effort or training. Others may not be so fortunate in the structure of their vocal mechanisms. For them, effort and training are necessary to make the most of their vocal instruments.

Our concern is to suggest how speakers can use what they have so that, without too much effort, most of them will be able to initiate and sustain good vocal tones.

Initiation of Tone

To initiate and maintain good tone, the vocal mechanism must be *ready for vocalization*. Readiness implies anticipation and preparation. For voice production, this means that the vocal bands must be aligned (approximated) a moment before the column of air is forced up from the lungs to set them into action. If the column of air precedes the approximation of the vocal bands, then the vocal product will begin with a whisper or an unvocalized breath. The vocal bands must be tense enough to set up resistance to the column of air, but not so tense as to be fully successful in their resistance. With excessive tension (hypertension), the vocal bands may not be able to vibrate. With a lack of sufficient tension (hypotension), vibration may take place, but with an accompanying air leakage or breathiness. What is needed is sufficient tension to require a forceful, sustained column of air to set and maintain the vocal bands in action. In brief, the tension should be just enough to permit the sustained column of air to produce an even fluttering of the vocal bands (see the discussion in Chapter 2). Although the voice can be produced even though the laryngeal tensions become excessive, the vocal tones become strained and generally unpleasant.

The exercises that follow will help to establish awareness of *proper laryngeal tension* as well as *readiness for vocalization*.

Before undertaking these exercises, review the discussion on the avoidance of breathiness in Chapter 4.

EXERCISES FOR ESTABLISHING READINESS TO VOCALIZE

1. Contract the throat muscles as you would to swallow some food or water. Note the sensation of the contracted muscles. Now open your mouth as if to produce a gentle *ah* sound. Do your throat muscles feel more or less tense than they did when you pretended to swallow? Unless they are more relaxed than for swallowing, they are likely to be too tense for the initiation of a good tone. Note the sensation of the contracted muscles so that you will know what to avoid. Be sure that your *ah* production is gentle and sustained.

2. *Yawn gently* with your mouth half open. Breathe in and out through your mouth. Note the feeling of air in the back of the throat. Now swallow, and contrast the easy breathing sensations with those in swallowing. If the yawning is gentle and the breathing easy, your throat muscles should be relaxed. This is the state of muscle tonus needed for vocalization.

3. Sit comfortably in a chair with your feet flat on the floor. Permit your head to drop to your chest as if your head were a dead weight. Yawn gently and then breathe in and out three or four times through your mouth. Note the sensation. Now swallow, and again contrast the tonus of the throat muscles in swallowing with that in gentle yawning. Repeat the gentle yawning and the easy mouth breathing until the sensation of relaxed throat muscles is fixed in your mind.

4. Stand erect but at ease. Repeat Exercise 3 in a standing position.

5. In a standing position, with the throat muscles relaxed, say the *vowels* only of the following words, each to a slow count of from one to three: *alms, all, Alps, ooze, eel.* Now vocalize from one vowel to the next, without interruption. You should be able to note somewhat increased throat and laryngeal tension for the vowels of *ooze* and *eel* as compared with those of *alms, all,* and *Alps.* This change in tension is proper if the different vowel values are to be produced. Try, however, to avoid excessive tension.

6. Open your mouth as though for a gentle yawn, but instead of yawning say *ha, how, ho, ha, haw, ho.* Next, try the sentence *Who am I?* These efforts should begin with some breathiness on the words that begin with an *h* sound, but the breath should not be noticeably carried over to the vowel that follows. Be sure that you maintain a relaxed throat throughout the exercise.

7. With a relaxed throat, count from one to ten, emphasizing the activity of the lips and the tongue. Try to become aware of oral activity in the *front of your mouth.* Now, count from one to twenty. Do not force your exhalation beyond a point of comfort. If you note any tendency to tighten the throat muscles, it may be because you are attempting too much speech on a single exhalation. Pause to inhale before excessive tension sets in.

8. Say the alphabet while emphasizing activity in the front of the mouth. Do not attempt to go beyond the letter *k* on your first attempt. On successive attempts, go as far as you can in the alphabet up to the point of laryngeal or throat tension. You may note a feeling of lip fatigue. If so, it is likely that you do not habitually articulate with sufficient activity at the front of the mouth. With practice, the feeling of fatigue should disappear.

9. Read the following materials aloud, always maintaining a relaxed throat. Make certain that you are *set for vocalization* before you begin to speak. If at any time your throat muscles become tense, or you become aware of laryngeal tension, return to Exercises 1–7.

a. In his *Institute of Oratory,* Quintilian observed, "The voice of a person is as easily distinguished by the ear as the face by the eye."

b. James Abbott McNeill Whistler, an American etcher and painter, spent much of his active life as an artist in England.

c. All progress is based upon a universal innate desire on the part of every organism to live beyond its income.

—SAMUEL BUTLER, *What Is Man?*

d. A handful of sand is an anthology of the universe.

—DAVID McCORD, *Once and for All*

e. Andrew was unfortunately not inclined to let facts get in the way of his opinions.

f.   But what am I?
An infant crying in the night:
An infant crying for the light:
And with no language but a cry

—ALFRED, LORD TENNYSON, *In Memoriam*

g. James Thurber philosophized that humor was often emotional chaos remembered in tranquility.

h. There are not enough *bon mots* in existence to provide any industrious conversationalist with a new stock for every social occasion.
—ALDOUS HUXLEY, *Point Counter Point*

i. I have had playmates, I have had companions,
In my days of childhood, in my joyful schooldays,
All, all are gone, the old familiar faces.
—CHARLES LAMB, *The Old Familiar Faces*

j. In his essay on "Civil Disobedience," Henry Thoreau advised "Any man more right than his neighbor constitutes a majority of one."

Avoidance of Glottal Initiation

In the opening paragraph of this chapter, we observed that the voice is a product of integrated muscular activity. Integration, of course, implies synchronization—timing necessary to produce the desired vocal result. The "glottal attack," or "glottal catch," unless intentionally produced, is a manifestation and product of poor synchronization. Basically, phonation characterized by a glottal catch results from excessive tension of the laryngeal muscles that in turn requires more than the normal amount of energy to provide the breath pressure to set the vocal bands in motion. The result of this combination of factors is that the vocal bands are violently blown apart, producing the "catch" or "click" instead of the even phonation that is associated with "flutter" action. Van Riper and Irwin (1958) described glottal initiation as follows:

> In this, the "glottal" catch (glottal stroke, coupe de glotte), the vocal folds (and often the ventricular folds) are brought together and strongly tightened *prior* to the starting of the chest pulse of air pressure. The normal synchrony of timing is thus disturbed . . . , and the vocal cords are very suddenly blown widely apart. Phonation occurs more abruptly than ever . . . and strident voices may result. (p. 303)

From this description it should be clear that unless the vocal bands are somewhat relaxed, or at least not excessively tense, and unless phonation is initiated in time to set the bands into flutter activity, vocal efforts may start with a click or a coughlike blast. Except when glottalization is an accepted characteristic of the speech of a national or cultural group—as it is among the Scots—voice accompanied by glottal clicks strongly suggests that the speaker's throat and larynx are hypertense and under strain. Added evidence of this condition is the presence of a high, narrow pitch range.

Glottal attacks are most likely to occur at the beginning of sentences or phrases with initial vowels. Some speakers, however, glottalize on almost all initial voiced sounds. The overall result tends to be detrimental to the speaker and unpleasant to listeners for whom glottalization is not an accepted speech characteristic.

For readers who are still uncertain about their tendency to initiate vocalization with a glottal attack, the following added explanation illustrates what should generally be avoided. A glottal stop noise is normally and appropriately produced when you clear your throat with a light, unvocalized cough. You can feel this stroke, click, or flapping of the vocal bands by gently placing your thumb and index finger just below the Adam's apple as you cough. If voice is added to the light cough, the result is likely to be the production of an *ugh* sound.

Vocal Fry

Another type of "glottal voice," one characterized by a low pitch, glottal clicking, and "pulsating," (Perkins, 1977, p. 84), has been designated by voice scientists as *vocal fry*. Moore (1971) presented a succinct description of vocal fry:

> This voice quality is distinctive for its repetitive popping or ticking sound. The vocal pitch is always extremely low and the frequency of the pulses that produce the popping characteristic may become slow enough to be heard as separate vocal pops or ticks. Breath noises are weak or absent with this type of voice, and it usually cannot be produced loudly or with the normal phonatory breath flow. The characteristic low frequency range of vocal fry sound and its presence in most voices at the extended low portion of the total vocal range has [*sic*] caused it to be considered by some as a vocal register. If an individual uses this type of voice frequently, it can be classified as functionally deviant in the same sense that persistent use of the falsetto is so classified. (pp. 8–9)

The exercises to establish proper laryngeal tension, readiness for vocalization, and easy initiation of tones should be reviewed by readers who have a tendency to initiate the voice with a glottal attack, or to fade out, usually at the end of a phrase, with vocal fry. In addition, the following exercises should be of help.

EXERCISES FOR OVERCOMING GLOTTAL PHONATION

1. Produce the sound *aw* as in *awful* with intentional breathiness (in a semiwhisper). Repeat, prolonging the *aw* for the equivalent of a count of six. Decrease the breathiness so that on the final two counts the *aw* is fully vocalized. Maintain a relaxed throat so that there is neither glottal initiation nor tension as vocalization increases.

2. Repeat Exercise 1, using the vowels of *alms, ooze, ohms, any,* and *ease*. Be especially careful that on the last vowel there is no excessive strain or glottal "explosion."

3. Try to say each of the following words without initial glottalization. If you note a glottal attack, prefix a lengthened *h* before each of the words, and move from the *h* to the word without increasing the laryngeal tension and without glottalization.

each	eager	I'll	even	eke	eon
inch	arm	ohm	ale	eat	easy
instant	ant	own	at	am	east
only	all	ill	ace	amp	aster

4. Repeat Exercise 3, prefixing the sound *m* if there is any tendency to a glottal attack. Repeat with an initial *n*.

5. Try each of the following sentences, being especially careful to avoid glottalization on the initial vowels. Words that begin with vowels *within a phrase* should be pronounced as though they were actually linked, or blended, to the last sound of the preceding word. The sounds that are most likely to be glottalized are in italics.

> **a.** Andrew and *Eve enjoyed all a*ctive sports.
> **b.** *All* of us must *at* one time *i*nhabit *our own i*sland.
> **c.** *E*dward *enjoyed cakes and a*le.
> **d.** *An ohm is a u*nit *of e*lectrical resistance.
> **e.** *It is e*asy to grow *a*sters *in* the *e*ast.

6. The following phrases may be somewhat more difficult because they contain many normally tense vowels in initial positions and so provide opportunities for glottal initiation. If you initiate the vocalization with just enough tension for the proper articulation of the vowel, but with no more than that much tension, the glottal shock should be avoided.

eerie images	eat an eel
easy access	apt and alert
up and over	apprehensive attitudes
every opportunity	insistent inclination
each event	esoteric antics
in every instance	anxious acts
any avenue	alien enemy

7. The following selections offer opportunity for additional practice.

> **a.** There is a feeling of Eternity in youth, which makes us amends for everything. To be young is to be as one of the Immortal Gods.
> —WILLIAM HAZLITT, *The Feeling of Eternity in Youth*
> **b.** Inconsistencies of opinion, arising from changes of circumstances, are often justifiable.
> —DANIEL WEBSTER, Speech, July 25, 1846
> **c.** History is the essence of innumerable biographies.
> —THOMAS CARLYLE, *On History*
> **d.** I am in earnest. I will not equivocate; I will not excuse; I will not retreat a single inch; and I will be heard.
> —WILLIAM LLOYD GARRISON, Speech, January 1831
> **e.** A hen is only an egg's way of making another egg.
> —SAMUEL BUTLER, *The Way of All Flesh*
> **f.** The actual enemy is the unknown.
> —THOMAS MANN, *The Magic Mountain*

The Glottal Stop As an Articulatory Fault

Although many persons initiate voice without a glottal attack, they may have a glottal quality in their speech because of an articulatory habit. The habit or fault is one of substituting a glottal grunt or click for a *t* or a *d* in words in which either of these sounds is followed by an *l* or an *n*. This sound substitution is considered in somewhat greater detail in our discussion of specific sound improvement. For the present, test yourself on the list of words and materials that follow. If you can feel or hear yourself produce a glottal explosive for the *t* or *d* on more than one or two of the words, make a special effort to articulate a clear but light and not exaggerated *t* or *d* and so to avoid giving your speech an overall glottal quality.

bottle	fettle	button	ladle
kettle	rattle	mutton	paddle
settle	written	patent	saddle
metal	bitten	mountain	hidden
little	subtle	kitten	nettle

Tender-handed stroke a nettle,
    And it stings you for your pains:
Grasp it like a man of mettle,
    And it soft as silk remains.
                    —AARON HILL, *Verses Written on a Window in Scotland*

Benton was in fine fettle because he was awarded a little metal button to place on his saddle.

However little the applause, Fenton was ready for a curtain call.

References and Suggested Readings

Boone, D. *The Voice and Voice Therapy,* 3rd ed., Englewood Cliffs, N.J.: Prentice-Hall, Inc. 1983. (Chapter 2 is on "The Normal Voice." Excellent diagrams and photographs highlight the discussion of the laryngeal apparatus.)

Fisher, H. *Improving Voice and Articulation,* 2nd ed. Boston: Houghton Mifflin, 1975. (Pages 73–75 describe "vocal fry" and glottal attack. They provide exercises for dealing with these vocal features.)

Lieberman, P. *Speech Physiology and Acoustic Phonetics.* New York: Macmillan Publishing Company, 1977. (A description of the production of vocal fry is presented on p. 82.)

Moore, G. P. *Organic Voice Disorders.* Englewood Cliffs, N.J.: Prentice-Hall, Inc. 1971. (Pages 8–9 deal with the problem of glottal initiation and vocal fry.)

Perkins, W. H. *Speech Pathology,* 2nd ed. St. Louis: Mosby, 1977. (Chapter 3 deals with the processes of speech, including a discussion of voice production. Chapter 13 is on the disorders of voice production.)

Van Riper, C. and Irwin, J. V. *Voice and Articulation.* Englewood Cliffs, N.J.: Prentice-Hall, Inc. 1954. (Includes a good but brief discussion [Chapter 8] of glottal initiation.)

Zemlin, W. R. *Speech and Hearing Science,* 2nd ed. Englewood Cliffs, N.J.: 1981. (Chapter 3, "Phonation" is a technical and detailed consideration of the vocal mechanism. The chapter includes excellent photographs and diagrams of the vocal apparatus and reviews theories of voice production.)

6

Making Yourself Heard

Do your listeners have any difficulty in hearing you? Can you be readily heard without strain? Are you easily able to adjust the loudness level and range of your voice to meet the needs of specific situations? Are you sometimes accused of yelling when an ordinary conversational level of vocalization is sufficient for the circumstances? On the other hand, are you occasionally accused of talking as if you were sharing a secret with a person close to you while ignoring other members in a conversational group who are farther away from you?

Adequate loudness, as was previously pointed out, is an essential attribute of an effective voice. For most of us, adequate loudness usually means being easily heard in conversational situations. Sometimes it means competing with environmental noises, both human and mechanical. Occasionally, however, we must speak to a group in a physical setting that demands a louder-than-normal conversational voice. Sometimes we must speak under conditions that demand more loudness than is ordinarily needed. We may, for example, have to yell a warning, issue a command, or address a large group without the assistance of electronic amplification, or we may suddenly have to rise to the demands of the occasion when electronic amplification fails.

Control of Loudness

Loudness is best regulated through breathing control. One way to speak loudly is to increase the energy with which the breath sets the vocal bands in vibration. The greater the amplitude (the more extensive the swing of the vocal bands), the louder the vocal tone will be. In addition, loudness is related to the way our resonating cavities reinforce our vocal tones. When we vocalize, the fundamental frequency—the tone produced by the basic rate of vibration of the vocal bands—is amplified throughout the

81

vocal tract. The tones that we identify as vowels and diphthongs are a result of the particular resonating cavity or coupling of cavities most actively involved in the vocal effort. (See the discussion of vowel sounds in Chapter 12 for an expansion of this point.) Because of the phenomenon of the reinforcement of vocal tones through resonance, vocalizing loudly enough to be readily heard usually requires less energy than might otherwise be needed.

If we recognize that the vocal attribute we think of as loudness is a result of the amplitude or swing of the vocal bands and the amount of reinforcement afforded the initiated tone by the resonating cavities acting as reinforcers, we will not overstress the amount of force or energy it takes to speak as loudly as the occasion requires. The danger in using added energetic action to produce loud tones is that pharyngeal and laryngeal strain may result. The effect of such strain is to reduce the efficiency of the cavities of the pharynx and the larynx as reinforcing cavities. As a result, the vocal tones are less loud than they might otherwise be. In carrying out the suggestions for increasing loudness, avoid increasing tension of the larynx or of the throat. In addition to the physical feeling of strain, listen for elevation of pitch. If your vocal tones are higher in pitch than normal, the muscles (walls) of your resonating cavities are probably excessively tense.

To understand the change in action of the abdominal wall in loud vocalization, place your hands on the abdomen and shout aloud, "Ready, go!" You will (or should be able to) note that there is a sudden pulling in of the abdominal muscles and that the pulling in is greater than for normal conversation. If this does not occur, and you are not readily able to speak as loudly as you would like to and should reasonably expect to, then the following exercise should be of help in establishing adequate loudness, that is, a voice that can project easily and effectively.

For the exercises that follow, as well as for all vocal exercises, the use of an area such as a music practice room where you can vocalize freely and without undue self-consciousness is of considerable help.

EXERCISES FOR DEVELOPING ADEQUATE LOUDNESS

1. Review the exercises for proper breath control (see Chapter 4). This review should create an awareness of the abdominal action established for conversation voice needs.

2. Place your hands on your abdomen and say *ah* as you might for a throat examination. Then take a moderately deep but comfortable breath and again begin to say *ah*. This time apply pressure suddenly with your hands. The tone should increase in loudness. If you have not caught yourself by surprise, and exhaled without vocalization, the *ah* should have become appreciably louder. Whether or not you have caught yourself by surprise, repeat the exercise and produce a loud *ah*.

3. Repeat Exercise 2, producing three loud *ah*'s without straining. Breathe in if necessary after each *ah*. Loud voice production requires more breath than normal conversation, so that more frequent inhalation becomes necessary to maintain a loud voice without strain. Try again, this time with *aw*.

4. Repeat, except this time exert direct control over the abdominal muscles as you produce your loud *ah*'s and *aw*'s.

5. Say the following short commands, each on a single breath, without strain and without an elevation of pitch level toward the end of the phrase.

 a. Let's go!
 b. Do it now!
 c. We're ready!
 d. Stop him!
 e. Look lively!
 f. Give him a hand.
 g. Lower away!
 h. Throw them out.
 i. Turn around.
 j. Silence, please!

6. Try the following sentences on a single breath, if possible. Speak as if there were a need to use a loud voice to assert yourself.

 a. No, this will not do.
 b. Let's waste no more time.
 c. Certainly, I meant what I said.
 d. Old fellow, just pack up and go.
 e. We'll talk about this matter later.

The following exercises are intended to help in the building up and control of degrees of loudness rather than in the sudden production of a loud voice. Such practice is closer to the normal use of loudness for emphasis and vocal variety in speaking.

EXERCISES FOR CONTROLLING LOUDNESS

1. Initiate an *ah* in a tone that is barely audible; gradually increase the loudness of the *ah* until it is louder than your usual conversational voice, and then reduce the loudness until the tone is again barely audible. Do not change the pitch or force the length of exhalation beyond a point of comfort.

2. Count from one to five, increasing the loudness on each number. Begin with a barely audible *one* and end with a *five* that can be easily heard across a forty-foot room.

3. Count to seven, increasing the loudness up to *four* and then decreasing in loudness from *five* through *seven*. Maintain the same pitch level throughout the count.

4. Say each of the following phrases or sentences three times, increasing in loudness from a normal conversational level to one that can be easily heard across a forty-foot room.

 a. He's gone.
 b. Come back!
 c. Please!
 d. No! Not now.
 e. I will not.
 f. Enough is enough.
 g. Who's there?

5. Lengthen the vowel in each of the following words and maintain uniform loudness throughout the lengthened production of the vowel. Do not, however, distort the vowel by excessive lengthening.

fawn	brawn
alms	gnaw
bomb	thaw
father	walk
pause	tall
awe	mall

6. Lengthen and maintain the force of the vowels or diphthongs of the stressed syllables in the following phrases. Again, avoid distorting the vowel or diphthong to the point where a listener would not be certain of the words you are saying.

high hills	stand aside
go away	stark madness
loud laughter	hearty applause
come on time	honest and true
almost always	large house
bounce the ball	ardent author
worthy cause	gone astray

7. Read each of the following sentences, first in an ordinary conversational tone and then as if you were trying to address a person in the tenth row of a crowded room.

a. Are you alone, Tom?
b. I'll go in a few minutes.
c. The hour has come.
d. I'll say this for the last time.
e. If you wish to understand, then listen.
f. Are you Jan Jones?
g. Who are they?

Strengthening the Voice

Thus far, our discussion of loudness has been based on the assumption that you can make yourself heard under normal conditions, but might need assistance in making yourself heard under more difficult conditions. Occasionally, however, we find persons whose habitual loudness levels are too weak for easy listening even in relatively good speaking situations. A few such persons may need help in being heard even in quiet conversations.

In some instances, the cause of a weak voice is physical and may be attributed to a structural disturbance or an anomaly of the vocal mechanism. Such instances are comparatively rare and require specialized treatment rather than self-help to improve the voice as much as possible. Sometimes, a weak voice may be a carry-over from a physical state that had its beginnings during a period of illness or a subsequent period of convalescence. Some persons, when ill, may not have the energy to make themselves heard. In the early stages of recovery, they may not care whether they are heard.

When well enough to care, some persons may decide that making others strain to listen is not without advantage. So, a habit of weak vocalization may persist. There is also a possibility that the speaker was brought up as a child in a home with an ill relative, or one who believe that children should be seen, if necessary, but were not ordinarily worthy of being heard. The barely audible voice may then have become the safer one, the one that did not bring isolation or a scolding.

Occasionally, the weak or barely audible voice characterizes the individual who feels that what he or she has to say is unworthy of a listener or that as a speaker he or she lacks value. Weak vocalization may be interpreted as apologetic noises or noises that are produced because one has a social need to say something and, at the same time, fears that, if heard, he or she may be held responsible for what is said. We associate these traits with shyness.

Such physical and mental conditions, however, are not the usual causes of a weak voice. Much more frequently, a weak voice is the result of poor vocal habits, such as poor breath control, habitual breathiness, excessive tension of the vocal mechanism, inappropriate pitch, or improper use of the resonating cavities to reinforce vocal tones. If our readers have no reason to believe that there is anything physically wrong with their vocal apparatus, if they are not longing for the advantages and immunities of the sickbed or the attentions associated with convalescence, and if they are reasonably well-adjusted people, audible voice should be no problem.

The earlier discussion on how to control loudness through breath control obviously holds for the person with a weak voice. In addition, the following exercises should be of help.

EXERCISES FOR STRENGTHENING A WEAK VOICE

1. Drop your jaw for a gentle but open-mouthed yawn. Inhale with your mouth open, and then pull in slowly but firmly on the abdominal muscles. Now permit a yawn to escape as you exhale as a "by-product" of the position of your mouth and of your controlled breathing.

2. Repeat Exercise 1 five times, making the yawn louder each time but maintaining the same pitch.

3. Now, instead of yawning, prepare to say *aw* as in *awful*. Maintain an even pitch. Repeat five times.

4. Repeat Exercise 3, but this time with the sound *oh*.

5. Say *oh* as follows: (a) as if surprise; (b) as if horrified; (c) as if pleased; and (d) as if you are shouting a warning.

6. Pretend you are imitating a siren on a fire truck, increasing and decreasing the loudness of your voice on the sound *oh*. Repeat, using the sound *aw*. Avoid any feeling of tension of the throat or larynx, and do not extend the length of vocalization to a point of discomfort.

7. Imagine that you are speaking to an audience of five hundred people. Suddenly you discover that the amplifying system has failed. You wish to accomplish the following:

   a. Notify the audience that you and they will have to get along without the benefit of mechanical amplification.

  b. Get the members in the rear rows and the side sections to fill in
  the empty seats in the front and center sections.
  c. Determine whether you are speaking loudly enough by asking,
  ''How many of you are right-handed?''
  d. Instruct your listeners to raise the right hand whenever they cannot
  hear you.

8. Count from one through five, increasing the loudness on each count
but maintaining the same pitch level. Repeat three times.

9. Practice each of the following in a voice loud enough to be readily
heard across the length of your living room.

  a. A great nose indicates a great man—
  Genial, courteous, intellectual,
  Virile, courageous.
  —EDMOND ROSTAND, *Cyrano de Bergerac*
  b. The greatest task before civilization at present is to make machines
  what they ought to be, the slaves instead of the masters of men.
  —HAVELOCK ELLIS, *Little Essays of Love and Virtue*
  c. Let's talk sense to the American people. Let's tell them the truth,
  that there are no gains without pains.
  —ADLAI STEVENSON, Speech, Chicago, 1952.
  d. The policy of repression of ideas cannot work and never has worked.
  —ROBERT HUTCHINS, Testimony before a congressional committee
  e.   And we are here as on a darkling plain
  Swept with confused alarms of struggle and flight,
  Where ignorant armies clash by night.
  —MATTHEW ARNOLD, *Dover Beach*
  f. Ah, Faustus
  Now hast thou but one bare hour to live,
  And then thou must be damn'd perpetually!
  —CHRISTOPHER MARLOWE, *Faustus*
  g. Are you through? Are you finally and completely through?
  h. Let the great world spin forever down the ringing grooves of change.
  —ALFRED, LORD TENNYSON, *Locksley Hall*
  i. He flung himself from the room, flung himself upon his horse and
  rode madly off in all directions.
  —STEPHEN LEACOCK, *Gertrude the Governess*
  j. Shrill and high, newsboys cry
  The worst of the city's infamy
  —WILLIAM VAUGHN MOODY, *In New York*
  k. Lay on, Macduff
  And damn'd be him, that first cries,
  ''Hold, enough!''
  ——WILLIAM SHAKESPEARE, *Macbeth*
  l. Pour the sweet milk of concord into hell,
  Uproar the universal peace, confound
  All unity on earth.
  —WILLIAM SHAKESPEARE, *Macbeth*

10. If you have no difficulty making yourself heard across your living room, try the same selections again, but this time pretend that your room is forty feet long and as many feet wide. If you are successful in this exercise, then repeat the selections as if you were addressing an audience from the stage of a moderate-sized theater.

11. Read the following as if you were addressing four hundred persons waiting for your announcements in an auditorium that has no public address system.

> **a.** The meeting is adjourned for the day. We will resume at 9 A.M. tomorrow.
> **b.** Our first coffee break will be at 10 A.M.
> **c.** Lunch will be served in the dining hall.
> **d.** Lenore Brown is the winner.
> **e.** Please leave promptly by the exit nearest to you.

12. Assume that you are in an auditorium about to address a large audience and are informed that there is no amplifying system. You are, however, determined that you will be heard through your own efforts. Our subject is crime. Read the following aloud:

> The first trial in history for crimes against the peace of the world imposes a grave responsibility. The wrongs which we seek to condemn and punish have been so calculated, so malignant, and so devastating that civilization cannot tolerate their being ignored because it cannot survive their being repeated.
> —ROBERT H. JACKSON, Opening address before the International
> Military Tribunal, 1945

Force, Stress, and Vocal Variety

At this point, we assume that your control of loudness for the purpose of being heard is no problem. You can be heard! Our present concern is with the subtle use of vocal force to provide color and shades of meaning in what you have to say.

Syllable Stress

Differential syllable stress is a feature of English speech. We use differential stress or accent in the pronunciation of polysyllabic words so that "normally" a word such as *rainy* or *beautiful* would be uttered with the primary stress, or accent, on the first syllable. In the word *beautiful,* a secondary stress may be heard on the final syllable. In a word such as *unkind,* the "normal" syllable stress is on the second syllable. In some contexts, however, a speaker may intentionally stress the first syllable of the word *unkind* to communicate his meaning, for example, "Yes, he certainly is an *un*kind man." Syllable stress in polysyllabic words is characterized by an increased force or loudness associated with relatively longer duration and higher pitch than for the unstressed syllables of the words.

Some words differ in parts of speech, and so in meaning, according to their syllable stress. What are the differences in meaning of the following words when the accent or syllable stress is shifted from the first to the second syllable?

ap*pro*priate	appropri*ate*
*con*duct	con*duct*
*con*vert	con*vert*
*con*vict	con*vict*
*di*gest	di*gest*
*dis*charge	dis*charge*
*ex*tract	ex*tract*
*fre*quent	fre*quent*
*ob*ject	ob*ject*
*per*mit	per*mit*
*pro*gress	pro*gress*
*pro*duce	pro*duce*
*re*bel	re*bel*
*sur*vey	sur*vey*
*sus*pect	sus*pect*

Apply the differential stress to the appropriate syllable:

1. Conduct the convert to the place of discharge.

2. Joe made rapid progress when his object was a shop that sold his favorite grape extract.

3. I will not object to your buying this art object.

4. The farmer produced a bumper crop of produce.

5. We had reason to suspect that Barton was the prime suspect.

Stress in Compound Words

In general, compound words differ from polysyllabic words in stress. For compounds, the stress is ''normally'' equal or almost so for each of the components. Compounds are similarly distinguished in stress from the components of the compound by relatively equal stress for the two parts of the former. Thus, we may distinguish the meaning of ''Jack is in the green house'' from ''Jack is in the greenhouse,'' or ''After a half hour of fishing, I hauled in a weak fish'' from ''After a half hour of fishing, I hauled in a weakfish.''

Through the use of differential syllable stress, indicate the differences in meaning of the words in the previous list and the paired words that follow by incorporating them into sentences, such as ''Bill made progress in his field'' and ''Bill was determined to progress in his field.'' In addition to changes in syllable stress, what other vocal features do you detect in the production of the compound words as distinguished?

birthday	birth day
blackbird	black bird
blowout	blow out
bluebell	blue bell
breakthrough	break through
campground	camp ground
greenhouse	green house

hideout	hide out
Irishman	Irish man
lightmeter	light meter
paperback	paper back
sometime	some time

How do you determine the meaning of the following pairs of sentences?

Since childhood, she had had her eye on the White House.
Since childhood, she had had her eye on the white house.

Please, may I have my paper back?
Please, may I have my paperback?

Hilary was a lighthouse keeper.
Hilary was a light housekeeper.

Sue spent considerable time in the greenhouse.
Sue spent considerable time in the green house.

Variety

Except for public speaking situations in which the speaker does not have the help of amplification, large differences in force are rarely necessary. A change in the use of loudness rather than in the degree of loudness is the factor of variety that permits a speaker to give importance to one idea and to subordinate other related ideas. A desired effect in giving special meaning is sometimes better achieved when the significant words are spoken with reduced rather than increased loudness, as in the sentence, "Please, my love, be still." If the words *be still* are spoken so that they are barely audible, they are given more complete meaning than might otherwise be possible.

A change in loudness may be used to achieve dramatic as well as subtle, intellectual effects. A deliberate, degree-by-degree increase in loudness from a low to a high level helps to produce a dramatic effect. A reduction from a moderately high to a low level may also be dramatic as well as sophisticated, providing *the content is worthy of the technique.*

EXERCISES FOR SUBTLE CHANGES IN LOUDNESS

1. Read the following lines with both "ascending" and "descending" changes in loudness.

    a. I believe that man will not merely endure: he will prevail.
    —WILLIAM FAULKNER, Speech upon receiving the Nobel Prize in
        Literature, 1950
    b. All animals are equal, but some animals are more equal than
        others.   —GEORGE ORWELL, *Animal Farm*

2. Read the following sentences, changing the stress from the first word of the sentence to each succeeding word. Do not, however, stress articles, conjunctions, or prepositions. How does the meaning of each sentence change with the differences in word stress?

   a. Ellie said that only she and I will go.
   b. Bob was poor but honest to the core.
   c. Either you or I must leave.
   d. Janet is quite fond of Jim.
   e. Is she the one you said you like?
   f. Well, what is your answer now?
   g. At last, this is your just reward.
   h. Joe is indeed a brilliant fellow.
   i. We thought he had returned.
   j. He will not be long for this world.
   k. Thursday was the day of reckoning.
   l. She and she alone can do anything.
   m. Fred was almost run down.
   n. Are you sure that this is the truth?

3. Read sentences a, b, and c of Exercise 2 stressing the conjunction. What are the changes in meaning?

4. Use controlled and moderate changes in stress to bring out the flavor and meaning of the wit and wisdom of the following items from Benjamin Franklin's *Poor Richard's Almanac*.

   a. The worst wheel of the cart makes the most noise.
   b. Genius without education is like silver in the mine.
   c. He that would live in peace and at ease, must not speak all he knows, nor judge all he sees.
   d. A man in a passion rides a mad horse.
   e. None but the well-bred man knows how to confess a fault, or acknowledge himself in an error.

5. The same approach—the use of controlled and moderate changes in stress—should be used in bringing out the essential meanings of the following passages.

   a. What I must do is all that concerns me, not what the people think. This rule, equally arduous in actual and intellectual life, may serve for the whole distinction between greatness and meanness. It is the harder because you will always find those who think they know what is your duty better than you know it. It is easy in the world to live after the world's opinion; it is easy in solitude to live after our own; but the great man is he who in the midst of the crowd keeps with perfect sweetness the independence of solitude.

          —RALPH WALDO EMERSON, *Self-Reliance*

   b. He may as well concern himself with his shadow on the wall. Speak what you think now in hard words and tomorrow speak what tomorrow thinks in hard words again, though it contradict everything you said today—"Ah, so you shall be sure to be misunderstood."—Is it so bad, then, to be misunderstood? Pythagoras was misunderstood, and Socrates, and Jesus, and Luther, and Copernicus, and Galileo, and Newton, and every pure and wise spirit that ever took flesh. To be great is to be misunderstood.

          —RALPH WALDO EMERSON, *Essays*

c. More important than winning the election, is governing the nation. That is the test of a political party—the acid, final test.

> —ADLAI STEVENSON, Speech accepting presidential nomination, July 20, 1952.

d. Man, unlike any other thing organic or inorganic in the universe, grows beyond his work, walks up the stairs of his concepts, emerges ahead of his accomplishments.

> —JOHN STEINBECK, *The Grapes of Wrath*

6. Use more marked changes in stress to communicate the meanings of the following passages.

a. Four freedoms: The first is freedom of speech and expression—everything in the world. The second is freedom of every person to worship God in his own way—everywhere in the world. The third is freedom from want—everywhere in the world. The fourth is freedom from fear—anywhere in the world.

> —FRANKLIN D. ROOSEVELT, Message to Congress, January 1941.

b. We, too, born to freedom, and believing in freedom, are willing to fight to maintain freedom. We, and all others who believe as deeply as we do, would rather die on our feet than live on our knees.

> —FRANKLIN D. ROOSEVELT, Speech, Harvard University, 1941.

c. The fact that man knows right from wrong proves his *intellectual* superiority to the other creatures; but the fact that he can *do* wrong proves his *moral* inferiority to any creature that *cannot*.

> —MARK TWAIN, *What Is Man?*

d. John Milton asked, "What is strength without a double share of wisdom? Vast, unwieldy, burdensome, proudly secure, yet liable to fall by weakest subtleties; strength's not made to rule, but to subserve, where wisdom bears command."

e. Two and two continue to make four, in spite of the whine of the amateur for three, or the cry of the critic for five.

> —JAMES M. WHISTLER, *Whistler v. Ruskin*

f. Read the following stanza with increased but controlled force up to the next to the last line; try reading the last line with a marked reduction in force to achieve dramatic contrast.

> O masters, lords and rulers in all lands,
> How will the future reckon with this man?
> How answer his brute question in that hour
> When whirlwinds of rebellion shake all shores?
> How will it be with kingdoms and with kings—
> With those who shaped him to the thing he is—
> When this dumb terror shall rise to judge the world,
> After the silence of the centuries?
>
> —EDWIN MARKHAM, *The Man with the Hoe*

7

Reinforcement of Vocal Tones Through Resonance

Most of us learned as children that a string with ends tied to paper cups or cereal boxes permitted us to talk at moderate loudness levels and yet be heard at distances considerably beyond the normal vocal range. What we were doing with this primitive telephone system was employing a resonating cavity—the cup or box—to reinforce the voice. Later, with more sophistication, we were able to realize that a plucked string or rubber band makes a noise that can just barely be heard if the listener is close to it. The same plucked string is more easily heard if it is attached to or is close to some cavity opening. So we learned that most musical instruments depend on resonators. Resonators build up or reinforce the sounds that are produced by applying energy to a body capable of vibration—through plucking strings; rubbing strings against strings; striking a skin or a wooden, metallic or stringlike substance; or blowing air across a vibrator into tubes of varying lengths, widths, and shapes.[1]

In Chapters 4 and 5, we emphasized the application of appropriate breathing and, when necessary, the energetic and controlled use of the breath in situations where more than a conversational level of loudness is required. In Chapter 6, we indicated that vocal tones, when well controlled, can be used to communicate subtleties and nuances of meaning that go beyond the ordinary implications of words. Now we shall turn our attention to matters of resonance, to the effortless reinforcement of the voice, and to the structures that lend quality and color to our vocal efforts. We shall emphasize the positive vocal qualities and also consider some negative aspects and how to avoid or overcome them.

---

[1] Another form of reinforcement for musical instruments is the forced vibration of sounding-board resonance. Such reinforcement is exemplified by the sounding board of a piano, as well as by the bridge of a violin and other "related" string instruments.

Improvement of Resonance

The manner in which the combination of our resonators reinforces our vocal tones produces the attributes by which the quality, or timbre, of the individual voice is identified. Unless we try to be deceptive and to sound like someone else and we are good at vocal deception, our voices can usually be recognized.

Our present concern is to create an awareness of resonance as one of the objectives for an effective voice. As we continue our discussion of resonance, we must bear in mind that none of our resonating cavities acts independently of the others. Changes in the oral cavity are likely to affect the pharynx, and changes in the pharynx are likely to affect the oral cavity, the larynx, and/or the nasal cavity. Despite this interdependence (coupling), specific modifications in one of the resonating cavities can result in vocal qualities that may be described by such terms as *oral, guttural,* and *nasal.*

The chief resonators, we recall, are the cavities of the larynx, the pharynx (throat), the mouth, and the nose. If these cavities are not temporarily irritated or inflamed by a respiratory ailment or obstructed by an organic growth such as enlarged tonsils or adenoids, good reinforcement of tone should be possible. Muscular tension may also impair the effective production of vocal tones, but unless such tension is chronic or regularly associated with some speech efforts, the effect of tension is likely to be transitory. For the sake of convenience, we are repeating a diagram (Figure 7–1) that originally appeared in Chapter 2.

Pharyngeal Resonance

In Chapter 2, we described the pharynx and its characteristics as a cavity resonator. We pointed out that this large resonating structure may enable the voice to sound full and rich if it is open and relaxed, or strident and metallic when the walls of the pharynx are tense. The implications of abnormal tissue growth or of infection relative to the damping of tone were also suggested. We now expand on this discussion.

Because the pharynx is a large resonator, it is best suited to the reinforcement of vocal tones in the lower pitch range. Normally, also, the relatively "soft" or relaxed tissue of the pharynx damps out the higher-pitched tones and reinforces the lower, or fundamental, vocal tones. If, therefore, the pharynx is relaxed and "open," the full potentialities of the pharynx are exercised for the reinforcement and coloring of the low vocal tones. If, however, as a result of tension or pathology the pharyngeal walls are tense, the potentialities of the pharynx as a resonator are not realized. The tense or "hardened" surface reinforces the higher pitches and the vocal overtones.

A "tight" pharynx, often resulting from a speaker's wish to talk "deep down in the throat," is likely to produce an unpleasant, "throaty" voice. A "throaty" voice quality sometimes follows an episode of sore throat (laryngitis and/or pharyngitis), and the speaker's voice continues to be characteristically "heavy" and narrow in pitch range. Often, however, the vocal quality we respond to as "heavy" and "throaty" is associated with a habit on the part of the speaker of keeping the tongue in a retracted and humped position while speaking. Such a tongue position modifies the shape of the oral cavity and produces an effect that suggests a muffled, "thick and heavy" voice—a vocal quality that is frequently accompanied by indistinct articulation, which is a likely result of the restricted mobility of the tongue.

Unless there is a medical basis for throatiness—a condition that should be evaluated

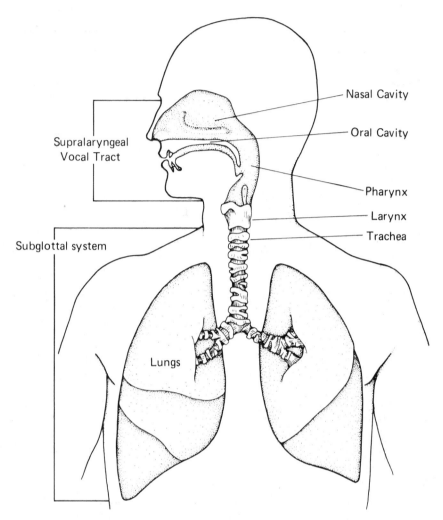

FIGURE 7–1   Diagrammatic representation of the human speech production mechanism featuring the principal resonating cavities. [After P. Lieberman, *Speech Physiology and Acoustic Phonetics* (New York: Macmillan Publishing Company, 1974), p. 4.]

by a physician and, if at all possible, by a laryngologist—the exercises that follow should help to improve this undesirable vocal quality.

Because of the relationship between the continuous and coupled oral and pharyngeal cavities, suggestions and exercises for optimal pharyngeal resonance are presented following the discussion of oral resonance.

Oral Resonance

Oral resonance is likely to be improved if the speaker makes a conscious effort to emphasize lip and tongue activity while speaking. Such activity helps to accomplish the objective of the singing teacher who directs students to "place their tones forward in the mouth.'' In our attempt to achieve oral resonance, however, we must not so exaggerate articulatory activity as to make it obvious to our listener-observer, and so to make us self-conscious. Nor should we create a condition of excessive articulatory tension that will carry over to the muscles of the throat.

Optimum oral resonance can be obtained only when the back of the oral cavity is open and relaxed so that we are able to initiate and maintain vocalization with an open throat. The following exercises should be of help for this purpose. In practice, think of your mouth as a megaphone. What is the effect when you extend this ''megaphone'' with your hands?

EXERCISES FOR ORAL AND PHARYNGEAL RESONANCE

1. The optimal use of the pharynx as a resonator presupposes proper breath control and the avoidance of any tension that might result from forced breathing or vocalization with residual air. The first step, therefore, is a review of the exposition and the exercises for breathing in effective vocalization (see Chapter 3).

2. Establish a feeling of overall bodily relaxation, as follows: (a) Slowly clench your hands to make tight fists. Note the related tension in the arms as well as in the fingers. Note also the associated tension of the jaw as your fingers are clenched into fists. (b) Relax slowly and gently until your fingers are extended. Do not, however, extend your fingers so that they become tense. Now note the associated relaxation of your arms and the muscles that control the jaw. Note also the easing of the muscles of the throat.

3. Establish your overall relaxation. Now, intentionally tense the biceps of your arms while you make tight fists. Relax slowly as you undo your fists and note the associated relaxation of your throat.

4. Breathe in gently and then exhale with a ''soft'' sigh. Note the relaxed feeling in your throat. If your throat is not relaxed, it is likely that either your inhalation or your exhalation was not sufficiently gentle. Try again until you achieve a gentle, sustained, vocalized sigh. Your tongue should lie almost completely flat at the bottom of the mouth, with a minimum of back-of-the-tongue elevation.

5. Inhale deeply, but not to a point of discomfort, and then yawn as if you were sleepy. Open your mouth wide, but avoid any feeling of tension in the muscles of your face or jaw. Your throat should feel relaxed if the yawn was convincingly but not energetically produced.

6. Optimum pharyngeal resonance is inconsistent with excessive back-of-the-tongue tension. Were you aware of an inclination toward such tension in any of the preceding exercises? Recall that the mouth and the throat are continuous, coupled resonating cavities. If the back of the tongue is buckled or humped, the result is a narrowing of the coupling passage. The effect is a narrowed resonator, constriction, and a loss of reinforcement of the low-pitched tones. So, produce a free, open, and sustained *ah*. Note the state and feeling of the back of the tongue. The back of the tongue should be elevated slightly, but not enough to block the view of the pharynx. Use a mirror, preferably a hand mirror, so that you can see the position and the feeling of an almost flattened tongue and an open, easy-to-view throat.

7. Drop your head to your chest, and vocalize an easy, sustained *aw*. Now roll your head gently and smoothly from shoulder to shoulder while sustaining the *aw*. Repeat with a long *ah*.

8. Begin as in Exercise 6, but this time add an *m* to the *ah* so that the result is *ahm*. Repeat five times.

9. With an open throat and a relaxed lower jaw, say each of the following three times. Say each slowly, and stop for a breath between vocalizations.

lah, mah, bah, dah, nah, hah, pah, fah, thah, shah, yah

In the immediately succeeding exercises, it will not be possible to keep your throat as relaxed as for Exercises 1–5. Make certain, however, that your throat and mouth muscles are as relaxed as they can be while you are producing the indicated sounds. The exercises will emphasize oral activity and articulation in the front of the mouth.

10. Observe your mouth in a mirror as you say the following words in pairs. Note the changes in lip and jaw position.

he	who	elf	off	halt
it	hook	am	ought	yawn
ate	oat	alp	alm	loom
high	hoe	higher	hear	ode

11. Observe your lip and tongue activity as you say each of the following.

entertaining trips	ship to shore
tiny tidbits	precious prize
twisted and turned	balmy breeze
do or die	petty person
tense times	polished pewter
twice-told tales	pretty polly
tip to toe	winsome wiles

12. Say the following with proper regard for tongue and lip activity.

a. The need to seek an answer to the questions "Who and what am I?" is not unique to persons who are identified as philosophers.

b. Twice-told tales may still be well told; three times told, they begin to sound stale and old.

c. Dan was persistent in his request for a game of tiddlywinks.

d. Jeanie tiptoed up the hill.

e. The wind whistled a tune in the trees.

f. The silvery moon shed its light on the lake.

g. A wag once defined an American college as a football stadium with a few associated academic buildings.

h. Is basketball replacing baseball as the most popular American sport?

> **i.** The release of atomic energy constitutes a new force too revolutionary to consider in the framework of old ideas.
> —HARRY S. TRUMAN, Message to Congress on Atomic Energy, October 3, 1945

13. The following selections should be read with emphasis on articulatory action in the front of the mouth.

> **a.** According to a Chinese proverb, two barrels of tears do not heal a bruise.
> **b.** In *The Magic Mountain*, Thomas Mann observed, "Order and simplification are the first steps toward the mastery of a subject— the actual enemy is the unknown."
> **c.** The essayist and critic George Hazlitt held that the only persons who truly deserve a monument are those who do not need one.
> **d.** Robert Louis Stevenson advised that to travel hopefully may be a better thing than to arrive.
> **e.** Stevenson also said that, in the last resort, every person is her or his own doctor of divinity.
> **f.** I speak severely to my boy,
> I beat him when he sneezes,
> For he can thoroughly enjoy
> The pepper when he pleases.
> —LEWIS CARROLL, *Alice's Adventures in Wonderland*

Nasal Resonance

We have already suggested that the importance of the nasal cavities in vocal reinforcement can be appreciated when we are suffering from a head cold. This condition not only deprives us of the ability to produce proper nasal sounds but also generally and adversely affects all our vocal efforts. We become especially aware of the need for nasal reinforcement when we try to produce the nasal sounds *n*, *m*, and *ng* /ŋ/. These nasal consonants are articulated orally, but they are reinforced in the nasal cavities and emitted through the nose. In order for the sound to enter the nasal cavities, the soft palate must be relaxed and lowered. Lowering the soft palate produces a large opening at the posterior entrance of the nasal cavities (the nares) and a narrow avenue through the nares for the sound to be resonated as it emerges from the nostrils. The characteristic differences in the three nasal consonants result from modification in the oral cavity. For the sound *m*, the entire cavity is used because the tongue lies comparatively flat at the floor of the mouth; for *n*, the tongue is raised so that a smaller part of the mouth is used; for the *ng*, only a narrow area at the back of the mouth behind the raised tongue is used as a supplemental reinforcer.

Although there are only three English sounds that are characteristically (predominantly) nasal, there is little doubt that, in connected speech, sounds in close proximity to the nasals are also partly reinforced, nasally. It is virtually impossible to avoid some degree of nasality in the vowels of words such as *nine, mine,* and *ring*. How to avoid inappropriate and excessive nasalization of vowels is considered later. At the present time, we prefer to make a case for proper nasal reinforcement, rather than to create anxiety about excessive nasality as a defect of vocal production.

Appropriate nasal reinforcement provides both roundness and carrying power to the voice. It permits us to be heard with relatively little expenditure of energy. We can become aware of these effects by sustained, easy humming. To hum easily, make certain that the throat muscles, the tongue, and the soft palate are relaxed. The jaws should be almost but not quite together. The lips should barely touch so that a slight tickling sensation is experienced when humming. An easy, properly produced hum should be felt as well as heard. You should be able to feel it not only on the lips, but also at the sides of the nostrils if your thumb and index finger are placed gently at these areas.

The fullness of tone and vibrating effects associated with proper nasal reinforcement can be appreciated when we contrast a phrase or sentence with many nasal sounds with another containing no nasals, such as the following:

1. Mary meanders. Sue walks briskly.
2. Malcolm murmured enticingly. Babs appeared to be heartless.
3. Newington enjoyed strolling in the moonlight. Peters preferred daylight jogs.
4. Norman, enough of complaining. Erase those surly looks.
5. MacDonald was the canniest member of his clan. Trusdale was the brightest of his relatives.

The following exercises should help to create an awareness of nasal resonance as well as an appreciation of the fullness of tone and carrying power that may be obtained with the careful production of nasal sounds. At first, exaggerate the length of each nasal sound, but avoid any intentional increase of effort in vocalization. Also, be certain that each exercise is performed with a relaxed throat and jaw. Sustain your tones evenly through controlled, gradual abdominal contraction on exhalation.

EXERCISES FOR AWARENESS AND IMPROVEMENT OF NASAL RESONANCE

1. Hum up and down the musical scale. Then sing the musical scale with the conventional *do—re—mi.* . . . Compare the two vocal efforts. Request a friend to do the same while you listen to his or her vocal efforts. Which sounds fuller? Was humming easier than the conventional singing? If your humming was done with your lips barely touching, the result should have been the production of a series of full, or relatively full, easy-to-produce tones.

2. Close your nostrils by pinching them and count from one through ten. Which numbers were not normally produced? Why?

3. Hum gently for the equivalent of a count of four on a sustained breath. Repeat five times.

4. Drop your jaw and bring the tip of the tongue into the position for *n*. Produce *n* for the equivalent of a count of four. Repeat five times. Repeat with the sound *m*.

5. Blend a hum with the sound *ah (mah)*. Make certain that the soft palate is raised for the *ah*. Repeat five times.

6. Blend a lengthened *n* with *ah*, then do the same for *n* and *aw*. Repeat each five times.

7. Blend a lengthened *m* and *ah* and follow with another *m (mahm)*. Do the same for *m* and *aw (mawm)*. Repeat each five times.

8. Repeat Exercise 5 with *n* before and after the sounds *ah* and *aw (nahn* and *nawn)*. Repeat each five times.

9. Exaggerate the length, but *not the loudness*, of the nasal sounds in the materials that follow:

a.
aimless movements	nominal amount
meaningful motions	ninety-nine and one
lament for humankind	monumental mansions
means to an end	mournful numbers
human inclination	nameless memories
mundane miscellany	nameless and unknown

Neanderthal Man

b. —Many Canadians speak both English and French.
—In the Northern Hemisphere, November is often a rainy month. In the Southern Hemisphere, November is a spring month.
—Mason was known for his mathematical acumen.
—Nancy was keen on digging for clams.
—A monody is a poem or a song in which one person laments the passing of another.
—Norman enjoyed meandering through winding lanes.
—Manganese is a chemical element employed in the making of steel to give it hardness and toughness.
—Milton wanted to be known as a man-about-town.
—Nicaragua and Panama are Central American nations.

c. For the common man, the best memorial is some beneficient thing or function that shall bear his name.
—CHARLES T. COPELAND, Speech, 1906.

d. In his actions, however various,
Dixon was consistently nefarious.
—J.E., *The Variable Man*

e. Of manners gentle, of affections mild,
In wit a man; simplicity a child.
—ALEXANDER POPE, *Epitaph on Gay*

f. To many Elizabethans, punning was considered a manifestation of intellectual acumen. A pun demands that the person must entertain two lines of thinking at the same moment. Why so many contemporary men and women respond to punning as a low form of humor is something of a mystery.

g. All too many physicians have an inordinate capacity to endure their patients' pains.

h. The Ming Dynasty is considered by some historians the last one of true Chinese origin. This dynasty is now renowned for its numerous contributions to scholarship and art, perhaps most notably for the making of luminous porcelain.

Nasality

Our orientation in this book is to emphasize the positive. We prefer, for example, to explain how vocal tones can be produced clearly, with adequate loudness and proper breath control, rather than to discuss how to overcome hoarseness, breathiness, or any other vocal inadequacy or defect. This was also our approach in considering resonance and the reinforcement of tone by the nasal cavities. As a precautionary measure, however, we believe it advisable at this point to discuss separately the prevalent fault of *excessive nasality*. Fortunately, when we have learned either to avoid or to overcome excessive nasality, we shall also have attained the positive objective of establishing appropriate nasal reinforcement.

Causes of Excessive Nasality

The most common cause of excessive nasality is failure of the soft palate to rise when necessary to block off the stream of breath (sound) as it enters the oral pharynx. If the soft palate is elevated, the sound is directed forward and emitted orally. A relaxed soft palate permits the sound to enter the nasal cavities, where it is reinforced to become qualitatively nasal.

If failure to elevate the soft palate has a physical basis, medical attention is in order. If the failure is caused by a general indifference to speech efforts, to listener reactions, and superficially at least to the world in general, psychotherapy may be indicated. Excessive nasality is frequently associated with articulatory sluggishness. Often the jaw, lips, and tongue as well as the soft palate move without precision and alertness. The overall result is speech that sounds slovenly and a voice that sounds tired, monotonous, and nasal.

For the most part, excessive nasality is a manner of speech that has been learned unconsciously. Even if this manner of speaking reflected at one time an attitude of thinking or of behavior, change for the better can take place if the will to change is present.

The following exercises are based on the assumption that there is no organic basis for the excessive (inappropriate) nasality and no psychological need for its persistence.

EXERCISES FOR AWARENESS OF PALATAL ACTION

1. Stand before a mirror and yawn with a wide-open mouth. Note the upward movement of the soft palate and the uvula while the yawn is maintained. Stop the yawn and relax. Repeat and note the feeling as well as the action of the elevated palate.

2. Hum gently; then think but do not vocalize a lengthy *ah*. Be certain that your mouth is open and your tongue almost flat. Observe the action of the soft palate as it is elevated and maintained for the *ah*. Now by way of contrast, permit the soft palate to relax and produce a nasalized *ah*. Again, raise the soft palate for an appropriately vocalized *nonnasal ah*. Capture the feeling of the elevated soft palate when the *ah* is properly vocalized and orally reinforced. Repeat for the vowels of *all, ooze,* and *ease.*

3. Close your nostrils by pinching them. Say *ah*. Repeat with open nostrils. Whether the nostrils are pinched or free, there should be no identifiable nasality in the sound. Repeat for the vowels of *whose, hull, home, haw, hog, harm.*

4. Say *n* while noting (feeling) the action and position of a relaxed soft palate. Then say *ah,* and again note the action and position of the elevated palate. Alternate between the two sounds until you have an immediate awareness of the difference in palatal position.

5. Place a clean, cold hand mirror under your nostrils and produce a lengthy *ah.* If the soft palate is elevated, there should be no clouding of the mirror. Practice until there is no clouding, then repeat with all the vowels of Exercise 3.

6. Repeat Exercise 5 with the vowels of *eel, if, ail, elf, hat,* and *ask.* Check with a mirror for nasalization. Be especially careful about the vowels of *elf, hat,* and *ask.*

7. Pinch your nostrils closed as you say each of the following sentences. (If you note a feeling of stuffiness in your nose, or a feeling of pressure in your ears, then you are being excessively nasal. Lift your soft palate to block off the entrance of air to the nasal cavity.)

    a. The beagle chased the fox through the fields.
    b. Bob walked his horse up the hill.
    c. The heavy fog rested atop the tall trees.
    d. What is it you wish to see?
    e. Peter helped Pat pick the flowers.
    f. Shakespeare held that brevity was the soul of wit.
    g. Paula preferred tea to coffee for supper.
    h. Ted liked to tell droll stories.
    i. All causes have effects; all effects have causes.
    j. Rita played the flute with great skill.

8. Say the following pairs of words with your attention focused on the avoidance of nasality in the second member of each pair. Make certain that your palate is elevated immediately after the nasal consonant is produced in the first member of each pair and through the production of the second member. It may also help to lessen any tendency toward nasality if you exaggerate the articulatory activity of the lips and the front part of the tongue.

neat	feat	moat	coat	nerve	verve
me	be	new	do	nest	lest
knit	lit	nook	book	knife	life
nail	dale	note	dote	meat	beat
met	wet	nought	bought	more	bore
mat	bat	not	dot	may	bay
mask	bask	man	ban	my	bye
need	bead	mare	bare	meal	keel
mud	bud	near	dear	male	bale
mile	bile	maze	daze	mike	bike
nice	dice	new	due	mob	bob
Nile	file	knob	sob	nice	dice

Associated or Assimilated Nasality

Earlier, we learned that three sounds in American and English speech appropriately require nasal reinforcement for their production. These sounds are *m, n,* and *ng* /ŋ/. In connected speech, unless there is almost anxious care taken to avoid the effect, sounds in close proximity to nasal consonants are likely to be slightly nasalized. The nasalization is a "contamination by association" resulting from the manner of the articulation of the nasal sounds. Specifically, one of the following may happen:

1. The lowered soft palate may not be raised in time to prevent the following sound from being somewhat nasalized. Delay in raising the soft palate after the production of a nasal consonant probably accounts for the nasalization of the vowels that succeed the nasals in words such as *my, may, mate, new,* and *note.*

2. The soft palate may be lowered while the sound preceding the nasal is articulated, as in words such as *aim, and, whom, only, sing,* and *young.* Here the nasalization is in *anticipation* of required articulatory movement (the lowering of the soft palate for the appropriate reinforcement of a succeeding nasal sound).

3. The soft palate may not be sufficiently elevated because of the influence of *preceding* as well as *succeeding* nasal consonants, as in *name, man, among, number, singing, ringing,* and *longing.*

There is no reasonable objection to some traces of nasalization resulting from the assimilative influence of nasal consonants. *What needs to be avoided is an overall effect of dominant nasality* merely because some nasal sounds are present.

The exercises recommended earlier for gaining awareness and control of the soft palate are, of course, applicable to overcoming the effects of excessive nasalization resulting from the influence of nasal consonants. Here also, emphasis on front-of-the-mouth (tongue and lip) activity is important. The following additional exercises should also be helpful.

EXERCISES FOR AVOIDANCE OR REDUCTION OF ASSIMILATIVE NASALITY

1. When the nasal consonant precedes the vowel, lengthen the nasal consonant. Lengthening the consonant will afford you the extra moment of time needed to elevate the soft palate. This action should reduce the "contaminating" assimilative effect of associated nasality and permit you to give appropriate reinforcement to the nasal sound in the given context.

a. Practice on the following sound combinations. At the outset, exaggerate the length of the nasals to a marked degree. Then reduce the degree of exaggeration, but maintain the actual duration of the nasal sound for a time you consider about twice as long as normal. Finally, reduce the length of the nasals so that they are of normal duration, or as close to normal as possible, without nasalizing the succeeding sounds.

m	ee	n	ee
m	oo	n	oo
m	ay	n	ay
m	ah	n	ah
m	aw	n	aw

b. Practice saying the following words, at first exaggerating the length of the nasal sounds. Then practice with the same words, this time with as little exaggeration as possible consistent with the avoidance of assimilated nasality.

meet	mock	need	nick	mice
meal	mood	neat	noose	mole
mill	mull	nil	nook	moss
melt	mode	nail	note	moist
mate	maul	never	nought	moat
mat	mob	knave	not	must
mask	moth	nap	nock	mule
mud	mirth	nut	nerve	might

c. Practice with the following phrases, being careful at first to lengthen the nasal sounds and to avoid excessive nasality on the sounds that follow. Go over the same phrases, this time lengthening the nasals only as much as necessary to avoid assimilated nasality.

inquiring scientist	Sunday and Monday
a man of moods	not my meat
more and more	now or never
new to me	native of Norway
no news	many a moon
move the map	next-door neighbor

d. Practice with the following sentences, observing the same precautions as in the preceding exercise.

—Martha enjoyed her work as a postmistress.
—Noah Webster believed that language as well as speech are immediate gifts of God.
—Ben Franklin observed that laws that are too gentle are seldom obeyed and those that are too severe are seldom enforced.
—Seneca advised that one learns best when one teaches.
—Is the primary business of the scientist to determine truths or to uncover beguiling untruths?

2. Emphasize oral activity for the sounds that precede the nasal consonants in the following words.

am	rant	lounge	turned	chance
aim	town	lunch	joined	game
end	any	round	found	want
own	only	yearn	haunt	find
on	anger	hunger	penny	sign

3. Incorporate the words of the preceding exercise into short sentences such as the following.

a. There is nothing without an end.
b. Big Jim owned the town.

c. Jim won the town from Nasty Ned in a game of chance.

d. Neanderthal Man undoubtedly had his haunts and his mental hungers.

4. The following exercises emphasize combinations in which the nasal consonants both precede and follow vowels or diphthongs. They therefore provide an opportunity for careful control to avoid temptation and inclination to excessive assimilative nasality. Nasality of the nonnasal sounds can be minimized if you lengthen the first nasal consonant and emphasize oral activity for the succeeding vowel or diphthong. Your objective should be only as much lengthening of the nasals as is necessary to avoid assimilated nasality.

a. Practice on words such as the following.

mine	noon	innumerable	murmuring
mean	nine	rumbling	Neanderthal
nimble	meander	underneath	known
main	numerous	crowning	mentor
meant	numb	ambition	mince
moan	mournful	grinding	minnow
moon	meaningful	reminding	muttering

b. Avoid excessive assimilative nasality in these phrases.

inquiring mind	attending physician
mournful ruminations	beneficent donation
immense and imaginative	nine miles from the Nile
understanding response	management decision
magnificent mansions	unconscious manners

c. In sentence contexts, the tendency toward assimilative nasality is increased. Practice careful enunciation of the following.

—A living language is dynamic and undergoes constant change.

—Martin, in common with most persons, was more mindful of his own misfortunes than those of his next-door neighbors.

—The winter snows were followed by spring rains.

—If Benson had any inclination toward genius, it was in his ability to ignore any suggestion that he might resist temptation.

—Antonia was against any position initially taken by another. This inclination earned her the nickname of Contrary Toni.

—Samuel Johnson's famous dictionary included a number of personalized definitions. One example is for the term *pension*, which Johnson defined as ''An allowance made to anyone without an equivalent. In England it is generally understood to mean pay given to a state hireling for treason to his country.''

—''And all the days of Methuselah were nine hundred sixty and nine years,'' says Genesis IV:27.

—''One precedent creates another. They soon accumulate and constitute law''; this is a principle in *The Letters of Junius*.

5. The following provide additional combinations in which the nasal consonants both precede and follow vowels or diphthongs.

   a. American football teams consist of eleven men.

   b. Dreams furnish opportunities for persons who are meek to become strong and to crown their unconscious ambitions and strivings with neither qualms nor anxieties about consequences.

   c. Mournful sounds are often made by nonmournful, gainfully employed minstrels.

   d. According to a Persian maxim, a person endowed with a long tongue may have a shortened life.

   e. Morton's farm background did not prepare him for employment on Madison Avenue.

   f. Anne preferred a short plane trip to a long one by train.

   g. The human being is a subject of thought, of scorn, of controversy, and of near divinity. Poets and thinkers through ancient times to the present have expressed their views. Here are two of them.
   —Carlyle maintained that humankind is the miracle beyond all miracles, ''the great inscrutable mystery of God.''
   —Mark Twain, not entirely in humor, once proclaimed: ''There are times when one would like to hang the whole human race, and finish the farce.''

6. As a test of your ability to resist the temptation of assimilated nasality, use the materials of Exercises 1, 2, and 4, intentionally exaggerating the overall nasality of your speech. Then, to demonstrate your control, go over the exercise materials without yielding to the temptation of assimilated nasality. By way of variety, try the same techniques for the following.

   a. Thomas Henry Huxley insisted that Nature never overlooks a mistake or makes even the smallest allowance for ignorance.

   b. In *Thunder on the Left*, Christopher Morley noted, ''If you have to keep reminding yourself of a thing, perhaps it isn't so.''

   c. As it is an ancient truth that freedom cannot be legislated into existence, so it is no less obvious that freedom cannot be censored into existence.
        —DWIGHT D. EISENHOWER, President's Letter to American Library Association, June 1953

   d. Somewhere, behind Space and Time,
   Is wetter water, slimier slime!
        —RUPERT BROOKE, *Heaven*

   e. The morns are meeker than they were,
   The nuts are getting brown;
   The berry's cheek is plumper,
   The rose is out of town.
        —EMILY DICKINSON, *Nature*, Part II

   f. What a man needs in gardening is a cast-iron back, with a hinge in it.   —CHARLES D. WARNER, *My Summer in a Garden*

g. All that we see or seem
Is but a dream within a dream.

—EDGAR ALLAN POE, *A Dream Within a Dream*

h. Voltaire maintained that doctors are people who prescribe medicine of which they know little, to cure diseases of which they know less, in human beings of whom they know nothing.

i. If the mountain won't come to Mohammed,
Mohammed must go to the mountain.

—English proverb

j. In a wonderland they lie,
Dreaming as the day goes by,
Dreaming as the summers die.

—LEWIS CARROLL, *Through the Looking-Glass*

k. In his *Divine Songs,* published in 1715, Isaac Watts inquired:

How doth the little busy bee
Improve each shining hour,
And gather honey all the day
From every opening flower!

l. In 1865, Lewis Carroll questioned in *Alice's Adventures in Wonderland:*

How doth the little crocodile
Improve his shining tail,
And pour the waters of the Nile
On every golden scale!

How cheerfully he seems to grin,
How neatly spreads his claws,
And welcomes little fishes in
With gently smiling jaws!

8

Pitch and Effective Vocalization

In our discussion of the mechanism of voice production, we made the point that vocal pitch should be related to the properties inherent in the individual's vocal mechanism. It is not advisable to choose a habitual pitch level or a pitch range according to attitudes, tastes, or whims, or to decide to change pitch level and range according to mood or fashion. We would view with suspicion a musician who played a violin like a cello and expected both to produce the same range and quality of sound. The properties inherent in the structure and the composition of these related but still different string instruments determine the pitch range and the essential quality of sound. The proficiency of the musician determines what can be produced by the instrument. Comparably, our task as speakers is to make the best use of our vocal equipment. The best use begins with determining the pitch level and the pitch range most appropriate for each speaker.

Fortunately, most speakers normally vocalize at pitch levels and within pitch ranges that are appropriate for them. Under abnormal conditions, with or without a conscious awareness of the pitch level and range that we consider optimum, vocalization may suffer because control is impaired. A professor may vocalize quite well, except when annoyed by her students, at which time her pitch may rise beyond the range of easy vocalization. If the occasions for annoyance are frequent, so are the opportunities for inappropriate vocalization. A salesman may have no cause for thinking about his voice until he becomes anxiously concerned while talking to a sales prospect. On such occasions, he may phonate within an elevated pitch range, with accompanying strain and excessive effort. The resultant effects may be both displeasing and potentially harmful to his laryngeal mechanism. A few persons, however, may habitually vocalize at pitches that are not natural or optimum, and so their voices are less effective, less pleasant, and frequently much less comfortable than they could be. Before discussing how to

107

determine the optimum pitch level and the most suitable pitch range, we present a few working definitions.

Optimum or *natural pitch* is the level within a speaker's pitch range at which he or she can initiate vocalization with ease and effectiveness in a *given set of circumstances*. This pitch level is basically determined by the specific physical characteristics of each person's vocal mechanism. However, optimum pitch level is not fixed. It may vary, but probably not more than a level or two, according to the speaker's state of fatigue, the amount of speaking the speaker has done during a time period, the speaker's physical environment (the size and the acoustic features of the place of speaking), the number of listeners, the presence of mechanical amplification, and the degree of emotion associated with the speech content and the overall situation. Optimum pitch also varies with the amount of airflow, which is in turn associated with the loudness of the vocalization. With all the factors and circumstances considered, optimum pitch is still the level at which the individual's vocal mechanism functions with the greatest ease and efficiency. Because optimum pitch is related to the structure of the vocal apparatus, it is sometimes referred to as *structural pitch*. Moreover, because optimum pitch is usually the product of "doing what comes naturally," providing there are no negating physical, emotional, or cultural pressures, the term *natural pitch* is also used. However, nothing we have said about optimum pitch should suggest that it would be natural or desirable for a speaker to maintain a monotone vocalization even at her or his optimum level. This level is the desirable one, "other things being equal," at which to initiate vocalization, and so determines the base for the optimum range for effective voice production.

For most speakers, optimum pitch is likely to be the level that is one fourth to one third above the lowest level within the entire pitch range. If, for example, the speaker has a twelve-level pitch range (analogous to musical tones according to the scale), her or his optimum pitch would probably be the third or fourth level above the lowest. If her or his pitch range were wider and were to include fifteen levels, the optimum pitch would most likely be at about level five. For a speaker with a twenty-one-level pitch range, the optimum pitch would be at about level six.

Several approaches and techniques may be used to arrive at optimum pitch. Ultimately, the best technique is the one that works successfully for the individual; it should not be limited by any voice or speech teacher's personal prejudices. We consider here the techniques that we personally have found useful and easily demonstrable without any pretense of having a monopoly on all the workable ones. For most cases, the first of these techniques is usually sufficient to establish awareness of optimum pitch.

The reader should not interpret our explanations of optimum (natural) pitch and habitual pitch and pitch range as a suggestion that, regardless of the situation and the responses of the speaker to the circumstances, vocalization should be initiated at a given pitch level or confined to a predetermined pitch range. Vocal behavior is a natural expression of a speaker's inner responses to situations. In an imaginary interview, Eric Sander (1982) "argued" that there is no single pitch that is best for all situations. (We assume that Sander meant *pitch range* rather than *pitch*.) Sander "admitted" the possibility that singers may develop vocal calluses from singing at too high a pitch, but nevertheless he took the position that no one pitch (range) is better than another. Sander suggested that the best pitch (again, we assume that he meant *range of pitch*) is the one that may be most pleasant, or the one that permits the speaker to communicate most effectively, or the one that is least tiring to the vocalizer's larynx. Sander also made a positive suggestion that the best pitch (range) is determined by testing ''How well the voice holds up when it is pitched in different ways.'' With due recognition that Sander was engaging in irony if not in satire, we have no reason to take issue with him. The danger in Sander's position is that one may decide that anything goes. What may in effect happen is that, in some instances, *the voice will go!*

We suggest that for speakers who do suffer from vocal fatigue, or who do have difficulty with easy and effective vocalization, there is considerable value in determining initial optimum pitch and, even more important, optimum pitch range. Deviations according to circumstances—vocalizing beyond (above or below) the range—are natural and so are not to be avoided unless such vocal behavior produces strain or discomfort and/or interferes with communication. The discussion that follows is intended to help to prevent vocal difficulties or to correct inappropriate vocal behavior in those who may experience difficulty in vocalization.

Determining Optimum Pitch and Pitch Range

As implied in our review of Sander's critical position, the concept of optimum pitch as a strict scientific phenomenon is subject to challenge. However, it is a useful clinical notion. Boone (1983) pointed out that the concept of an ''easy, natural pitch level is useful in voice therapy. . . . If the patient can produce good voice easily, such a voice can become an immediate therapy goal'' (p. 98). Our goal is to prevent the speaker from becoming a patient by providing techniques for recognizing and producing a voice that is both easy and effective in communication. We begin with the previously stated assumption that each person does have a pitch level that, as Boone emphasized, can be produced ''With an economy of physical effort and energy. This relatively effortless voice production is known as *optimum pitch*'' (p. 97).

We recommend that optimum pitch range should be ''built'' around an individual's optimum pitch.

Pitch range may be defined as the ''distance'' between the lowest pitch, including low falsetto (vocal fry), and the highest pitch, including falsetto or vocal fry.

Habitual pitch is the pitch level at which an individual most often initiates vocalization. *Habitual range* refers to the pitch levels that are most frequently employed in speaking. *Range* itself refers to the pitch levels that a speaker is capable of producing below and above habitual pitch level. It is obviously desirable that the speaker's optimum pitch and optimum range be the ones that are habitually used. If this is not the case, then changes need to be directed toward (1) becoming aware of optimum pitch and learning to produce this pitch level at will; (2) establishing the optimum pitch as a habit; and (3) developing a pitch range with optimum pitch as the basic level for initiating vocalization.

TECHNIQUES FOR ACHIEVING OPTIMUM PITCH

1. Relax the throat muscles. Take a moderately deep breath and vocalize an evenly sustained *ah* at whatever pitch comes out naturally. Do not think of the pitch until after you hear yourself produce it. Do not attempt to modify the tone once it has been initiated.

2. Relax, and vocalize, but this time intentionally do so at a level lower than in Exercise 1.

3. Continue, going down the scale, until you have produced the lowest-pitched tone you are capable of vocalizing. It may help to think of a descending musical scale in going from your initial pitch level to your lowest. Do not strain for an abnormally low pitch. Stop at the level at which your voice becomes a low-pitched whisper.

4. Return to the initial pitch you produced in Exercise 1. Now produce tones on an upward scale until you reach the highest-pitched falsetto. If you started vocalization at your natural pitch, you should be able to go up in pitch about twice the number of tones you were able to descend below your initial level. If this is the situation, then you are probably initiating vocalization at or very close to your optimum or natural pitch.

An alternate technique for determining optimum pitch is through the matching of vocal and piano tones throughout the pitch range, including the first low and the first high falsetto tones.

1. Sing or chant from your lowest to your highest tone, matching each tone with a corresponding one on a well-tuned piano. If your own sense of pitch discrimination is not reliable, obtain the help of a friend with a reliable ear to establish your vocal range.

2. Repeat the singing or chanting several times so that you are certain that you have established your entire range. Your optimum or natural pitch is likely to be between one-fourth and one third above the lowest tone you can produce.

3. Reproduce this tone until it is firmly fixed in your mind and you can initiate it without the help of the piano.

This approach should be repeated at different times during a day and on several different days. Pitch range may vary somewhat under conditions of fatigue or tension, but unless the variation is great, the optimum pitch level should not deviate by more than a single level.

Habitual Pitch

In order to know whether there is any need to make a conscious effort to initiate the voice at the optimum pitch level, it is necessary to compare your habitual pitch with your optimum pitch. If the two are the same, or no more than a single pitch level (a half or a full tone) apart, then there is no need to think about your initial pitch. For most persons who have had no physical ailment or emotional trauma, the likelihood is that habitual pitch and optimum pitch are close enough so that no special concern is necessary. Just to be certain, however, all who are interested in producing the voice according to their maximum capabilities might observe the suggestions that follow for determining habitual pitch and comparing it with optimum pitch.

Look over several easy prose passages and select one containing material that is neutral in emotional content and not particularly challenging in intellectual content. (Three such selections are provided under ''Reading Selections to Determine Habitual Pitch,'' which follows.) Make sure also that the selected passage includes no words that cause you uncertainty about their pronunciation. First, read the selection aloud in as natural and conversational a manner as you can. On the second and third readings, when the thought content has been reduced to insignificance because of repetition, level off toward a monotone in pitch. You can accomplish this by intentionally avoiding inflectional changes. The final reading—fourth or fifth—will begin to sound like a chant. When this happens, you have probably arrived at a single level, or at least a narrow pitch range, at or close to your habitual pitch. At the conclusion of the chanted passage, vocalize a sustained *ah* at the same pitch level.

Locate this last level on a piano. Then say a series of *ah*'s, matching your voice with the piano note. Count from one to ten at this level. Then say the alphabet at this level. If possible, have a companion listen to you to help you locate the level.

Compare your optimum pitch with your habitual pitch. Are the two nearly the same or no more than a tone or two apart? If they are, then you need not be further concerned about the matter of initial pitch. If not, then work to bring your habitual pitch closer to your optimum pitch. This accomplishment will pay large dividends if you are interested in good voice production. The most generous permissible margin of error between habitual and optimum pitch should not exceed two levels for persons with a narrow pitch range. This may be extended to one third of an octave for individuals with a wide pitch range (two or more octaves). In general, the closer habitual pitch is to optimum pitch, the better the voice is likely to be.

READING SELECTIONS TO DETERMINE HABITUAL PITCH

The following selections are essentially of an intellectual nature and so would normally be read aloud with relatively "neutral" feeling. The pitch range is likely to be fairly narrow.

1. Statistics is the branch of mathematics that describes how things are on the average. The idea of statistics is that a single observation may not be reliable, and that if the observation is repeated many times the result may not always be the same. In such cases it is necessary to talk about the likelihood rather than the certainty that some particular event will occur.
—GEORGE MILLER, *Language and Communication*

2. Physiology is the science that deals with the function of biological systems. An anatomist . . . could describe the bones and muscles of the human foot without considering how these elements work together in activities like bipedal locomotion. A physiologist would have to consider these same bones and muscles in terms of their functional value in locomotion and other activities.
—PHILIP LIEBERMAN, *Speech Physiology and Acoustic Phonetics*

3. An index is a listing, almost always in alphabetical order, of the topics treated in a book or periodical. In most books, the index is in the back. The purpose of a book index is to help the reader to locate the pages on which information is provided about the indexed names and topics. The subject and the number or numbers of the pages on which the information is found is called the *entry*. A good indexer is able to anticipate where, in the listing of topics, a reader is likely to look for an item of information or a subject treated in the book. Some books have one index for proper names and another for other entries.

Widening the Pitch Range

How wide a pitch range should we have? Practically, the answer is *wide enough to be effective as a speaker*, but not at the expense of strain or discomfort. Some persons with a demonstrably wide pitch range tend to speak habitually only at the lower end of their range. Others, especially when they are under emotional stress, may confine their vocalizations to the higher end of their range. The result for both types of speakers may be inefficient vocalization. For the listeners, the result may be unpleasant exposure to monotonous or strained vocal efforts. Although, the experimental evidence is not consistent, some studies have shown that effective speakers, and those who are regarded as having good voices, tend to use both greater variability and a wider range of pitch than do less effective speakers. Better speakers, by and large, make greater use of the upper part of their pitch ranges, and their pitch ranges generally cover at least an octave and a half. Poor speakers, in contrast, tend to have pitch ranges limited to about half an octave.

Extending Pitch Range Upward

As one's optimum pitch level is at the lower end of the pitch range, it follows that the direction for extending the pitch range for most persons is likely to be up rather than down. With this in mind, undertake the following exercises.

EXERCISES FOR EXTENDING PITCH RANGE UPWARD

1. Review the discussion of optimum pitch. Check your optimum pitch and your total pitch range.

2. Count from one through ten at your optimum pitch level. Now count to ten in a monotone three tones above your optimum pitch. Raise the pitch level three more tones above your optimum pitch. Raise the pitch level three more tones, and repeat the count. Finally, count to ten at the very top of your normal pitch range. Repeat with the letters of the alphabet, *a* through *j*.

3. Say the sentence "We're going for a walk" at your optimum pitch. Practice the same sentence, initiating the first word on successively lower levels until you reach the lowest comfortable pitch level. Start again from your optimum pitch, and now initiate the first word of the sentence at successively higher pitch levels until you have reached the top of your range.

4. First, read the following sentences and paragraphs in a manner that is natural or habitual for you, and then intentionally extend your pitch range upward.

> **a.** In his *Dialogues*, Alfred North Whitehead held that intelligence is quickness to apprehend—to perceive and to understand. Whitehead distinguished between intelligence and ability, defining the latter as "the capacity to act wisely on the thing apprehended."

b. Nature is neutral. Man has wrested from nature the power to make the world a desert or to make the deserts bloom. There is no evil in the atom; only in men's souls.

> —ADLAI STEVENSON, Speech, Hartford, Connecticut, September 18, 1952

c. Ennui, felt on the proper occasions, is a sign of intelligence.

> —CLIFTON FADIMAN, *Reading I've Liked*

d. Among animals, *one* has a sense of humor. Humor saves a few steps, it saves years. —MARIANNE MOORE, *The Pangolin*

e. Benjamin Franklin held that "There are two ways of being happy: we may either diminish our wants or augment our means. Either will do, the result is the same. And it is for each man to decide for himself and do that which happens to be the easiest."

f. Young men are fitter to invent than to judge; fitter for execution than for counsel; and fitter for new projects than for settled business. —FRANCIS BACON, *Of Youth and Age*

Extending Pitch Range Downward

Except for persons with a very narrow pitch range, all of us have more levels from the optimum range toward the top of the pitch range than toward the bottom. However, there is "room" (pitch range) toward the bottom level that can be used effectively for expressing feeling and communicating meaning through vocal variety that is appropriate to the speech content. Thus, if after determining your optimum pitch and your habitual pitch range, it becomes apparent that you are making little use of your lower pitch levels, some practice is in order. Do not, however, go so low in your range that your voice becomes throaty, excessively breathy, or barely audible. Avoid strain or any low tone that seems to be lacking in substance or that is difficult to sustain or that results in the production of a low-pitched falsetto (vocal fry). In general, try to incorporate tones into your pitch range that are one or two levels above your lowest tone within your pitch range. The following exercises, which present material on sober matters, should provide you with the opportunity to emphasize tones at the lower end of your pitch range.

EXERCISES FOR EXTENDING PITCH RANGE DOWNWARD

1. Sorrow and sadness and how human beings experience these emotions are a recurring theme of philosophers and poets. Following are some versions of sorrow through the ages.

a. In every adversity of fortune, to have been happy is the most unhappy kind of misfortune.

> —BOETHIUS, *De Consolatione Philosphiae*

b. The deeper the sorrow, the less tongue it hath.

> — *The Talmud*

c. Weep no more, nor sigh, nor groan,
Sorrow calls no time that's gone—

> —JOHN FLETCHER, *The Honest Man's Fortune*

d.   'Tis better to be lowly born,
And range with humble livers in content,
Than to be perked up in a glistering grief
And wear a golden sorrow.

—WILLIAM SHAKESPEARE, *King Henry VIII*

e.   This is truth the poet sings,
That a sorrow's crown of sorrow is remembering
happier things.

—ALFRED, LORD TENNYSON, *Locksley Hall*

2. Loneliness and lonesomeness are two related themes of poets and philosophers. However, the choice of being alone, often expressed in the writings of Henry David Thoreau, should not be confused with either loneliness or lonesomeness. Following are some observations on these states.

a. James Russell Lowell advised, "The nurse of full-grown souls is solitude."

b. Mark Twain warned, "Be good and you will be lonesome."

c. Edwin Markham wrote that Lincoln's death left "a lonesome place against the sky."

d. Robert Nathan, in *A Cedar Box,* philosophically observed, "Joy has its friends, but grief its loneliness."

e. On a happier note, Rudyard Kipling believed that "He travels the fastest who travels alone."

f. Thoreau, a lone man if not a lonely one, seemed to enjoy solitude. He wrote, in *Solitude,* "I never found the companion that was so companionable as solitude. . . . A man thinking or writing is always alone, let him be where he will.

3. Alfred North Whitehead, the English mathematician and philosopher, warned us that "There are no whole truths; all truths are half-truths. It is trying to treat them as whole truths that plays the devil.

4. Man is his own star; and that soul that can
Be honest is the only perfect man.

—JOHN FLETCHER, *Upon an "Honest Man's Fortune"*

5. People who make no noise are dangerous.

—JEAN DE LA FONTAINE, *Fables*

6. Time does not become sacred to us until we have lived it.

—JOHN BURROUGHS, *The Spell of the Past*

7. A man in armor is his armor's slave.

—ROBERT BROWNING, *Herakles*

Speech Melody (Intonation)

Speaking and Singing

All of us, including those who are resigned to being classed among the nonsingers because of the violence we do to the melody of a song, use melody in our speech. The music of speech, however, is usually subtle, and the changes in pitch may not be as wide or as distinct as they are in singing. In speaking, our voices glide from sound to sound with an almost continuous change in pitch. In singing, changes in pitch are usually more clear-cut and usually take place in discrete steps equivalent to musical tones.[1] Some of us, without intention, somehow manage to sing between the tones, and our voices fall "flat" into the cracks between the piano keys. A few singers have earned a reputation by doing intentionally and under control what seems to come naturally, accidentally, and inconsistently for others.

Intonation

Intonation, or patterned vocal variation, is an inherent feature of spoken utterance. Interestingly, despite phonological (speech sound system) and morphemic[2] variations in natural languages, intonation contours, especially in declarative sentences, are essentially alike. On the basis of data provided by Lieberman (1968, chap. 4), we may generalize that short declarative sentences are likely to end with a falling pitch contour.

In some languages, the changes in vocal tones are relatively slight, whereas in others, such as Chinese, the changes are marked. Languages such as Norwegian, Swedish, and Lithuanian have relatively fixed patterns of pitch changes. English pitch variation is relatively free. The melody of English speech is determined in part by conventions of sentence formation and in part by the mood and the subjective responses of the speaker to the content of her or his speech and the overall speech situation. Despite this highly individual determinant of American-English speech melody, there are several features that characterize the direction of inflectional changes (pitch changes that occur without interruption of phonation) for sounds of words. There are also characteristic pitch changes within word groups that constitute recognizable intonation patterns in our language.

Figures 8–1 and 8–2 (adapted from Lieberman, 1968) present spectrograms for a short declarative sentence. The variations in contour according to the word stressed should be noted.

Figure 8–3 shows several other "representative" simplified and generalized intonation contour patterns of American English. These patterns illustrate the basic downward inflection of the simple declarative sentence and the pitch elevation of the stressed word within the sentence or within the breath group (phrase) in multiple-phrase sentences. In contrast, note the difference in contour of the question sentence. So-called *wh* questions end with falling inflections, whereas questions that ordinarily may be answered by a "yes" or "no" end with rising inflections.

Figure 8–4 is a graphic representation of a somewhat more complex sentence than most of the others.

Types of Pitch Changes

Two categories of pitch changes together constitute the overall pitch variation, or *intonation,* of American-English speech. These are inflections and shifts, or steps. *Inflections* are modulations of pitch that occur during phonation. *Shifts* are changes of pitch that occur between phonations. Inflections may be subclassified according to con-

---

[1] Some singers depart from the musical score and do produce glides and vibrato effects as individual expressions in their renditions of a song. This, however, is the exception rather than the rule in singing.

[2] A morpheme is a word or a minimal part of a word that carries meaning. The words *the, to,* and *for* are single-syllable word morphemes, as are *jump* and *like.* Adding *ed* to the word *jump (jumped)* or *s* to *like (likes)* provides tense ending changes of meaning. The morpheme *s* in *likes* could also signify a plural, as in *cakes.* Root-word syllables, prefixes, and suffixes are morphemes. In general, a morpheme is the minimal grammatical unit of a language that carries meaning.

FIGURE 8-1 Spectrogram of a speaker reading the declarative sentence *"Joe* ate his soup." [Adapted from P. Lieberman, *Intonation, Perception, and Language,* M.I.T. Research Monograph No. 38 (Cambridge, Mass.: M.I.T. Press, 1968), p. 69.]

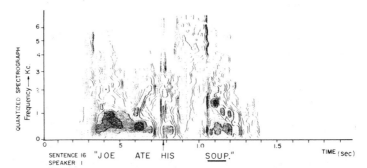

FIGURE 8-2 Spectrogram of a speaker reading the declarative sentence "Joe ate his *soup."* [Adapted from P. Lieberman, *Intonation, Perception, and Language,* M.I.T. Research Monograph No. 38 (Cambridge, Mass.: M.I.T. Press, 1968), p. 70.]

tour, or "direction" of change, as downward, upward, and circumflex. For any but very short, uninterrupted phonatory efforts or flows of utterance we are likely to have several inflectional changes. Because shifts properly occur only between subunits of utterances when the speaker takes a moment to pause to indicate a unit of thought or a "phrase," inflectional changes almost always outnumber shifts. The uses and implications of pitch changes are considered in the discussions that follow.

Shifts

Shifts, steps, or "intervals" in pitch, indicate the importance we we give to a unit of thought within an utterance or a phonatory effort. If we regard a phonatory effort as a sentence, even a two-word sentence may have two related subunits of thought, each appropriately uttered at a different pitch level. Thus, sentences such as "Go now" or "Come here" may be uttered for effect with a momentary pause at the end of the first word and a shift in level of pitch from the first to the second word. In both of the examples given, the "normal" shift in level of pitch would be upward, so that we might represent the sentences as:

$$\overrightarrow{Go} \parallel \overrightarrow{now}$$
$$\overrightarrow{Come} \parallel \overrightarrow{here}$$

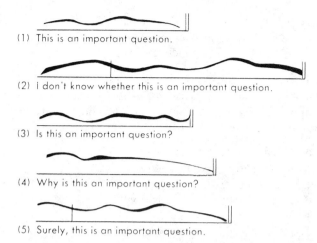

(1) This is an important question.

(2) I don't know whether this is an important question.

(3) Is this an important question?

(4) Why is this an important question?

(5) Surely, this is an important question.

FIGURE 8–3   Generalized, representative contour (intonation) patterns of American English.

Not   one   but many men will suffer the results of this action

FIGURE 8–4   A graphic representation of a relatively complex American-English intonation contour.

EXERCISES FOR CHANGE IN PITCH LEVEL

1. Practice the following short sentences using a higher initial pitch level on the second word than on the first. However, end the second word with a downward inflection.

It's over.	Please, don't.
Don't rush.	Go quickly.
That's enough.	We're late.
You're out.	Mary shouted.
They left.	Bob listened.
Jack fell.	Bill hurried.
We're ready.	Jane winced.

2. What would be the effect on the meaning of the statement if the second words were produced on a lower pitch level than the first?

3. Practice these longer sentences, changing the level of pitch as indicated by the direction of the arrow.

a. Winter came— | ↑ | wind, freeze, and snow.
b. He stopped suddenly, | ↑ | then turned to the right.
c. Why Tom did it, | ↓ | he could not tell.
d. Our team lost, | ↓ | but the game was close.
e. Will you | ↓ | or won't you?

f. It can't be done, | ↑ | no matter how you beg.
g. Come now, | ↓ | that's enough.
h. We're tired, | ↑ | much too tired.

4. How would you be inclined to shift the pitch for the following sentences after the indicated places for pause? What changes in meaning would you imply by reversing the direction of the pitch change? By using the same general level on the second part of the sentence as on the first?

a. It's late, ‖ perhaps too late.
b. Come early, ‖ come often.
c. Did you care ‖ or just pretend?
d. It can be done ‖ if you really try.
e. Waste not, ‖ want not.
f. He spoke quietly ‖ but with certainty.
g. He stopped ‖ just in time.
h. Don't write, ‖ phone him.
i. He sped away ‖ out of sight.
j. Look out, ‖ look out!

Downward or *falling inflections* (↘) are generally used to indicate the completion of a thought, and to give emphasis to an idea. The sample sentences that follow would end with falling inflections. The second sentence would probably have falling inflections on both italicized words. In the examples that immediately follow, the italicized words are those on which inflectional changes are "normally" anticipated. A change in the emphasis of a key word within the sentence would, however, alter the pitch contour.

1. This is your *pen*.
2. *Certainly*, this is your *pen*.

Command statements also end with falling inflections.

3. Stop *now!*

A question that begins with an interrogative word—*when, where, who, why, how,* or *whom*—for which an answer other than the single word "yes" or "no" is anticipated, also ends with a falling inflection.

4. When will Jane *go?*
5. Why did he do *it?*

Upward or *rising inflections* (↗) are generally used to suggest doubt, uncertainty, or incompleteness. They are also used for questions that call for a simple "yes" or "no" answer. And we are likely to use rising inflections in statements that enumerate a series of items, until the last item is stated. The last item is spoken with a falling inflection.

6. It apparently didn't occur to *us* that this was your *book*.
7. Is this your *book?*
8. We bought *groceries, meat,* and *fruit* at the supermarket.

Circumflex Inflections

We would get into great difficulty if we attempted to illustrate how irony, innuendo, sarcasm, cynicism, skepticism, or surprise combined with disbelief or incredulity is expressed in pitch. These intellectual states and attitudes all have marked degrees of feeling. Most native Americans would probably employ some form of circumflex (down-up, up-down, or down-up-and-down) inflection to express them. If, for example, surprise and ''I can't believe it'' were to be expressed at the choice of a candidate through the use of the single word *Him!*, the inflection might be:

Him!

A longer statement, such as ''Of all persons, to choose—him!''—in which a related sentiment is expressed relative to the same person—might employ a series of circumflex inflections. The specific form of inflection is likely to be even more individualized than in the illustrations previously presented.

Generalizations Relative to Intonation and Inflectional Changes

The examples presented and the generalizations we are about to make might serve as guides for a speaker who has somehow not been able to get the melody of American-English speech. Once the basic melody is learned, the speaker should feel free to indulge in variations from the fundamental melodic theme or pattern.

1. Some degree of pitch change is almost continuous in normal conversational speech.
2. Major pitch changes occur at the ends of phrases and sentences and on the most significant words within the phrase or sentence.
3. Falling or downward inflections are used when we make definite or positive assertions and when we wish to indicate the completion of a thought (Examples 1, 2, and 3 on page 118). A falling inflection is also used on the final word of a question that begins with an interrogative word (Examples 4 and 5, page 118).
4. A rising inflection is used to suggest incomplete or dependent thoughts and to express doubt or uncertainty. The rising inflection is also used in questions that may logically be answered by the words ''yes'' or ''no'' (Examples 6, 7, and 8, page 118).
5. The Pitch level of the most important word within a phrase or a unit of thought is likely to be at a level different from that of the other words of the unit. Most frequently, it is higher in level, but occasionally the emphasized word is uttered at a distinctively lower level than the other words of the unit.
6. The stressed syllable of a word is usually spoken on a higher pitch level than the unstressed syllable or syllables of the word.

The exercises that follow afford an opportunity for the application of the generalizations relative to inflectional changes and intonation patterns of American-English speech.

The first group of sentences would ordinarily end with falling inflections unless special meanings are read into them. For the present, avoid special meanings and read the sentences ''straight'' to indicate assertions and completed thoughts. Avoid any inclination for your voice to fade out at the end of the sentence so that you cannot be easily heard.

EXERCISES FOR FALLING INFLECTIONS

1. William is prompt.
2. Joe is always late.
3. Ellen is a dedicated jogger.
4. That finishes that.
5. Bob will eat anything.
6. Susan is an avid reader.
7. This is the only way.
8. It's good to be through.
9. Good lawns require care.
10. Not all roses are red.
11. Joe is always hungry.
12. Ned is a good golfer.
13. Ted is a fast reader.
14. Come when you're ready.
15. This is the way to go.
16. That's not so!
17. It's time for tea.
18. Now we're done.
19. Take your time.
20. Dan solved the puzzle.

Many of the items in the next group, if read straight, would normally employ falling inflections on the last words. If they are read to suggest doubt or uncertainty or to express an incomplete thought, rising inflections are employed. The questions ordinarily answered by a "yes" or "no" also end with rising inflections.

EXERCISES FOR RISING INFLECTIONS

1. I'm just not sure.
2. Well, perhaps.
3. You're going to ski?
4. I guess that's right.
5. Well, we'll see.
6. Is Tom going?
7. Do you meditate?
8. Shall we start?
9. Is this a rose?
10. Do you enjoy football?
11. Does Frances speak Spanish?
12. Is Bill on time?

All questions, as we recall, do not end with rising inflections. Those that begin with interrogative words usually end with falling inflections when the questions are intended to elicit information. When a rising inflection is used for questions beginning with interrogative words, some special implication or meaning is intended other than a request for information. Read the following sentences first with the expected falling inflection and then with a final rising inflection and note the change in meaning.

1. What is today's date?
2. What's your name?
3. Who came late?
4. Where are we going?
5. When shall we leave?
6. Why should we go?
7. Who knows his lines?
8. What does this cost?
9. How long is the road?
10. What is the right time?
11. How did Sue find out?
12. What makes this correct?

EXERCISES FOR PRACTICE OF INFLECTIONAL CHANGES

1. Say the word *yes* to indicate (a) certainty, (b) doubt, (c) indecision, or (d) sarcasm.
2. Say the word *no* and, by changes of inflection, indicate the following.

a. "Definitely not."
b. "Well, maybe."
c. "I'm surprised to learn that."
d. "I'm annoyed to learn that."
e. "I'm pleased and surprised to learn that."

3. Say the sentence "I shall come" so that the following attitudes are implied.

a. Determination.
b. Pleasant agreement.
c. Surprise.
d. Annoyance.

4. Say the sentence "He's really somebody" to bring out the following meanings.

a. You admire the person about whom you're talking.
b. You dislike the person.
c. You can't decide whether you like or dislike the person.
d. You have a begrudging admiration for the person.
e. You are surprised at the newly discovered qualities of the person.

5. Speak the sentence "I like Bill" to bring out the following.

a. A direct statement of fact. (You mean literally what the words say.)
b. A contradiction of the literal meaning of the words. (You definitely do not like Bill.)
c. Irritation and surprise that anyone could conceivably accuse you of liking Bill.

    d. Indecision as to your feelings about Bill.

    e. A specific indication that your liking is for Bill and not for anyone else who may be present.

    f. Your answer to the question "Who likes Bill?"

    g. An aggressive, emphatic answer to the question, "Who could possibly care for a fellow like Bill?"

Avoidance of Monotony

In discussing the differences in pitch variation between singing and speaking, we pointed out that most pitch changes in song melody are discrete and take place in distinct steps. Each song syllable is likely to be maintained on a recognizable pitch level (note) longer than is likely to be the case in either conversational or public speech. Variation in speaking is almost continuous. Distinctive changes, however, should be noted when pitch is used for purposes of emphasis. For emphasis, pitch change is likely to be on a higher rather than on a lower level than the preceding or following words. When the pitch change is to a lower level, the speaker must maintain or increase the volume of his or her voice to give the word or phrase the desired emphasis.

Repetition of pattern in singing constitutes melody. This is considered a desirable characteristic of classical song. In speaking, where verbal content rather than pitch pattern is usually important, the repetition of pitch pattern should be avoided. In American and English speech, subtleties of ideational content are expressed through pitch change. If pitch changes become patterned and repeated, shades of meaning cannot readily be communicated. In addition, pitch changes, if they can be anticipated, no longer command attention and tend to work against rather than for the maintenance of interest. For these reasons, effective speakers not only use as wide a range of pitch as they can within their normal pitch range but are also careful to avoid pitch patterning and its consequent monotony.

Although our present discussion is concerned with pitch changes, the unmodified production of voice quality, loudness, or rate can all be monotonous. We have all heard radio or television commercials, usually presented by nonprofessionals—the owners of a business who somehow think that they can do a better job of announcing than the studio announcer—literally shout their messages "at the tops of their voices." The effect is that nothing in the announcement comes across as important. At the extreme other end are the ministerial voices, by no means limited to the clergy, who vocalize every syllable in orotund if not in profound tones. In effect, such vocalization minimizes the possible effect of most of the message. In a critique of the voices of public figures, one of my students observed of his senator, "His voice reserves nothing for God."

Pitch Variation in Content Characterized by Strong Feeling

Speech content that is characterized by strong and heightened feelings such as anger, rage, and fear—feelings that are more significant for their emotional rather than for their intellectual messages—tend to use more pitch variation than in most conversational speech. These states are usually expressed with wide pitch changes at the upper end of the speaker's range. In contrast, grief and sorrow are usually expressed with

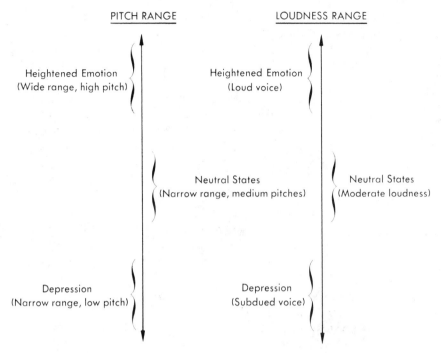

FIGURE 8–5   The relationship between changes in pitch and loudness and the states of feeling.

few pitch changes and variations, at the low end of the individual's range. Sometimes, when we wish to establish a dominant mood, or to share a strong feeling with a listener, we begin to approximate the melody of song or the relatively sustained pitch of lyrical poetry. A passage from the Bible should not be read as one reads an item from the day's news. Neither should it be read with an unvarying cadence and stereotyped intonations.

In general, the pitch changes in an effective reading of poetry or emotional prose are individually more extensive but collectively less varied and longer sustained than in an effective reading of intellectual material. The exception is content of heightened feeling when lightness rather than loftiness is to be expressed. Then, the changes in pitch are likely to be more sweeping and to occur as often as or more often than in predominantly intellectual material. Anger is also likely to be expressed with relatively wide pitch changes and in the upper pitch range. With these points in mind, read the following passages. Use pitch variation to emphasize changes in thought and feeling. Sober and solemn moods are probably best expressed through the use of relatively low, sustained pitch levels. Figure 8–5 summarizes the changes in pitch and in loudness associated with states of feeling and emotion.

EXERCISES FOR PRACTICE OF PITCH VARIATION

1. Blessed are the forgetful: for they get the better even of their blunders.   —FREDERICK NIETZSCHE, *Beyond Good and Evil*

2. The optimist proclaims that we live in the best of all possible worlds; and the pessimist fears this is true.

—JAMES BRANCH CABELL, *The Silver Stallion*

3. A tale without love is like beef without mustard: an insipid dish.

—ANATOLE FRANCE, *The Revolt of the Angels*

4. People don't ask for facts in making up their minds. They would rather have one good, soul-satisfying emotion than a dozen facts.

—ROBERT K. LEAVITT, *Voyages and Discoveries*

5. If you forgive people enough you belong to them, and they to you, whether either person likes it or not—squatter's rights of the heart.

—JAMES HILTON, *Time and Time Again*

6. Time goes, you say? Ah no!
Alas, Time stays, *we* go.

—HENRY AUSTIN DOBSON, *The Paradox of Time*

7. You have not converted a man because you have silenced him.

—JOHN, VISCOUNT MORLEY, *On Compromise*

8. In your reading of Psalm 23, level, sustained tones will help to establish the solemnity and reverence of your thought. Do not, however, fall into a patterned, unchanging reading.

The Lord is my shepherd, I shall not want. He maketh me to lie down in green pastures; he leadeth me beside the still waters. He restoreth my soul; he leadeth me in the paths of righteousness for his name's sake. Yea, though I walk through the valley of the shadow of death, I will fear no evil: for thou art with me; thy rod and thy staff they comfort me.

—Psalm 23

9. Golden lads and girls all must
As chimney sweepers, come to dust.

—WILLIAM SHAKESPEARE, *Cymbeline*

10. I was angry with my friend:
I told my wrath, my wrath did end.
I was angry with my foe:
I told it not, my wrath did grow.

—WILLIAM BLAKE, *A Poison Tree*

11. Modesty and unselfishness—these are virtues which men praise—and pass by.   —ANDRÉ MAUROIS, *Ariel*

12. The perversion of the mind is only possible when those who should be heard in its defense are silent.

—ARCHIBALD MACLEISH, *The Irresponsibles*

13. In a real dark night of the soul it is always three o'clock in the morning.   —F. SCOTT FITZGERALD, *The Crack-up*

14. Man must evolve for all human conflict a method which rejects revenge, aggression and retaliation. The foundation of such a method is love.

—MARTIN LUTHER KING, JR., Speech accepting the
Nobel Prize, 1964

15. Thinking is a momentary dismissal of irrelevancies.

—R. BUCKMINSTER FULLER, *Utopia or Oblivion*

References

Boone, D. R. *The Voice and Voice Therapy,* 3rd ed. Englewood Cliffs, N.J.: Prentice-Hall, Inc., 1983.

Lieberman, P. *Intonation, Perception, and Language.* M.I.T. Research Monographs, No. 38. Cambridge, Mass.: M.I.T. Press, 1968.

Sander, E. K. ''Optimum Vocal Behavior,'' *ASHA,* **24**(1) (1982), 35.

9

Rate and Duration (Timing)

Changes in duration, the time given to the production of an utterance and the time intervals between phrases, permit us to express feelings and to emphasize and subordinate meanings. On the emotional side, a markedly slow rate of utterance is associated with solemnity, depressed moods, and sadness or sorrow. A marked increase of rate is associated with happier states, lightheartedness, and heightened feelings. The heightened feelings, however, need not always be pleasant. Anger is usually expressed through an increased rate of utterance.

Changes in rate of behavior are related to our physiological states and associated muscular activity. We behave more slowly when our thoughts are solemn and more quickly when our mood is light or when we are excited. The muscles of our vocal and articulatory mechanism normally reflect these changes in our vocal tones and in our articulatory activity.

Changes in rate of utterance are correlated with variation in pitch and force. As we indicated in the last chapter, heightened feelings are accompanied by increases in range and higher levels of pitch and force; depressed feelings by a reduction in range, lowered pitch level, and a decrease in force. Figure 8–5 summarizes these variations. Figure 9–1 includes rate of utterance in the voice and articulation variations associated with states of feeling.

As indicated earlier, changes in duration are achieved through variation in the rate of articulation or the use of pauses between groups of articulated sounds, or both. In general, content that is articulated slowly is considered more important—intellectually more significant—than rapidly articulated content. If we listen to what is spoken slowly and are able to maintain attention while listening, we assume that what we have heard is more important than more quickly spoken content.

Some speech sounds—vowels and vowel-like consonants—lend themselves to a varied and controlled rate of articulation. Words such as *lonely, awesome, home, gone,*

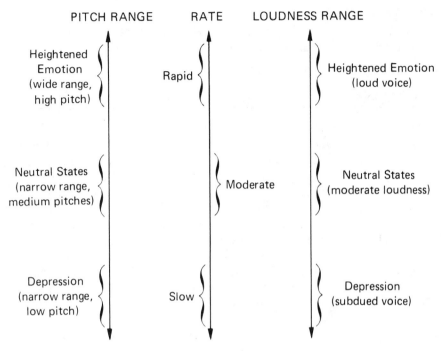

FIGURE 9–1   The relationship between changes in pitch and loudness and the states of feeling.

away, loom, always, and *evermore* contain these sounds. They can be uttered quickly or slowly according to the will of the speaker. On the other hand, words such as *pit, tip, bit, stop, quick,* and *put* are usually articulated rapidly. In lyric prose and poetry, dominant moods can be established through language that incorporates "slow" sounds and "rapid" sounds. Compare, for example, Poe's lines.

> Sorrow for the lost Lenore—
> For the rare and radiant maiden whom the angels name Lenore—
> Nameless *here* for evermore.

with Gilbert's:

> Life's a pudding
>   full of plums;
> Care's a canker
>   that benumbs,
> Wherefore waste our
>   elocution
> On impossible
>   solution?
> Life's a pleasant
>   institution,
> Let us take it as
>   it comes!

The difference in mood becomes immediately apparent. Poe's lines lend themselves to a slow rate of articulation, whereas the lines from Gilbert's *The Gondoliers* need to be articulated quickly to achieve the intended mood and meaning.

Rate and Meaning

We must, of course, appreciate that when the rate of utterance is conspicuously changed to be either relatively rapid or relatively slow, the most significant word within the phrase, or the most significant phrase within the sentence, is usually spoken more slowly than the rest of the phrase or sentence. Any sustained, unvarying rate may become monotonous. Nothing of any considerable content that we say or read aloud should be uttered at the same rate, regardless of the feeling or mood.

The *use of pause* as a technique for varying rate is perhaps the best single indication of control and sophistication in speech. When a speaker pauses at the end of a phrase, the listeners wait. While waiting, they tend to fill in the time gaps with the last bit of content they heard. The inner listener repetition of what the speaker has last said reinforces this content. A pause before and after a word or a phrase sets either off from the rest of the context and so becomes a technique for the vocal underlining of an idea or a unit of thought.

A pause may also be used to indicate transition of thought in a larger context. This is the case when a speaker pauses after the evident completion of a thought. A short pause may separate sentences, a moderate pause may separate paragraphs, and a longer pause may prepare the listeners for a new line of thought.

Dramatic effects may be achieved by the combination of a pause with a rising inflection. If the phrase before the pause ends with an upward inflection, the result is the "suspension" of a thought. The thought is then completed in the content that follows. A similar effect may be achieved with a pause before and after a presented idea. In general, a pause before the beginning of a new phrase tends to create a feeling of suspense to be satisfied by what follows in the speaker's utterance.

When an intentional pause is used, the speaker has an obligation to satisfy the expectations of the listeners. If the content that follows the pause turns out to be of no greater importance or significance than what preceded it, the speaker has failed to meet the implied obligation, and the listeners are likely to become disappointed and distrusting.

We all use pauses as one device to separate or group our phrases. In conversational speech such word groupings come naturally with the flow of thought. When our thoughts do not flow as freely as we might like, when we search for words to communicate our thoughts, we reveal this hesitation in our unintentional pauses. Under the pressure of a large or formal audience, we may become fearful and anxious about pausing, and we may fill in the gaps with *uh–uh*'s or their equivalent in nonverbal sounds to avoid moments of silence. Speakers who are poised enough to wait, who pause with intent and without fear, and who do not resort to repetitious fillers to avoid the void of silence will gain the respect of their listeners if what they have to say is worthy of the waiting and the listening. With these points in mind, the reader should find the exercises that follow of help in the practice of some of the uses of duration for vocal variety and as a technique for revealing feeling and communicating thought.

EXERCISES FOR PRACTICE OF CONTROLLED RATE

1. Read the following sentences so that full value is given to the italicized words. The sentences as a whole are to be spoken slowly, and the italicized words more slowly than the others.

    a. *Innocence* is *inconsistent* with the *acquisition* of *riches.*
    b. The *air* was *still*, the sea was *calm.*
    c. *All* rivers *find* their *way* to the *sea.*
    d. In *solitude* we may be *least alone.*
    e. *Life* is what the *living make it.*
    f. The *snow* fell and *silently* concealed the *earth.*
    g. *Freedom* can *survive only* when it is *shared.*
    h. *Tomorrow* will *come* and pass into *yesterday.*
    i. Man's *inhumanity* to *man* makes *countless* thousands *mourn.*
    j. Through *memory* we can *recreate* a *yesterday* and project a *tomorrow.*
    k. *Are* we *now* at a *time* when *knowledge* has *outrun wisdom?*
    l. *Novelists,* whatever else they may be besides, are *also children talking* to *children—in the dark.*
             —BERNARD DE VOTO, *The World of Fiction*
    m. A *handful* of *sand* is an *anthology* of the *universe.*
             —DAVID McCORD, *Once and for All*
    n. *Fanaticism* consists in *redoubling* your *efforts* when you have forgotten *your aim.*
             —GEORGE SANTAYANA, *The Life of Reason*
    o. You *can't hold* a *man down* without *staying down* with him.
             —Attributed to BOOKER T. WASHINGTON
    p. I *strove* with *none*, for none was *worth* my *strife;*
    Nature I *loved*, and next to Nature, *Art;*
    I *warmed* both *hands* before the *fire* of *life;*
    It *sinks*, and *I* am *ready* to *depart.*
             —WALTER LANDOR, *On His Seventy-fifth Birthday*

2. The next group of sentences should be spoken at a moderate rate, but the italicized words should be spoken somewhat more slowly for emphasis.

    a. *More* than an *end to war*, we want an *end* to the *beginnings* of *all wars.*   —FRANKLIN D. ROOSEVELT, Address, April 13, 1945
    b. I don't know why it is we are in such a hurry to get up when we fall down. You *might think* we would *lie there* and *rest* a *while.*
             —MAX EASTMAN, The Enjoyment of Laughter
    c. "In two words: *im-possible.*"
             —ALVA JOHNSON, *The Great Goldwyn*
    d. A *good listener* often achieves a *reputation* for being a good *conversationalist.*
    e. President *Coolidge* held that *one with the law* constituted a *majority.*
    f. *Cynics* hold that a *majority* is *almost always wrong.*

g. To *study humankind* we must study *individual* humans.

h. It might be said of *Thoreau* that he loved not *humankind* the *less* but *nature more.*

i. *Muscles,* like *iron,* wear out *faster* with *disuse* than with *use.*

j. Was it *Mark Twain* who held that *cauliflower* was *nothing* but *cabbage* with an *education?*

k. It is *rare* for a man to be a *husband and hero* to his *own* wife.

l. *Coughing* and *clearing* one's *throat* in a *theater* is *more likely* to be an *expression* of *criticism* than a *reaction* to an *irritated throat.*

m. Montaigne observed that people are most apt to believe *what they least understand.*

n. Cervantes advised that a *closed* mouth *catches no flies.*

o. Francis Bacon cautioned that *books must follow science,* and *not science books.*

RATE AND SUBORDINATION

When a sentence has several clauses, though each clause may carry significant meaning one is likely to be subordinate to the others(s). Sometimes the subordinate clause is almost parenthetic and could be dropped without serious impairment to the message of the sentence as a whole. For example, in the sentence "Joe Smith, a native of Texas, won the mile race," which is rather simple in terms of content, the phrase "a native of Texas" could be omitted without a change in the essential meaning of the sentence, except perhaps to a Texan. Changes in rate (duration) direct attention to what the speaker considers the most important part of a sentence, and within a paragraph, to the sentence and its relatively important part or parts. In general, directing attention for emphasis is achieved by a slower rate for the main clause compared with the rate of utterance for the subordinate phrases and clauses.

3. The following materials provide opportunities for practicing changes in rate to emphasize main ideas and to subordinate the other idea(s) within a sentence or paragraph.

a. Nonviolence, the first article of my faith, is also the last article of my creed.

    —Adapted from MAHATMA GHANDI, Defense against charge of sedition, 1922

b. B. F. Skinner, a behavioral psychologist, regards the real problem as not whether machines think but whether people do.

c. Equality and justice, the two great distinguishing characteristics of democracy, follow inevitably from conception of men, all men, as rational and spiritual beings.

    —ROBERT M. HUTCHINS, *Democracy and Human Nature*

d. Lawyers soon learn that, however valuable their opinion may be it becomes even more valuable in proportion to the fees they charge.

e. Heraclitus, a Greek philosopher who lived from about 535 to to 475 B.C., held that there was no permanent reality except the reality of change. Thus, Heraclitus argued, one cannot step into the same river twice. Wendell Johnson, a contemporary General Semanticist, enlarged on this contention. Johnson, in keeping with his philosophy, pointed out that "One may not step in the same river twice not only because the river flows and changes, but also because the one who steps into it changes too, and so is never at any two moments identical."

—Adapted from WENDELL JOHNSON, *People in Quandaries*

RATE AND ITS CORRELATES USED TO EMPHASIZE MEANING

4. A study of Figure 9–1 should properly lead to the conclusion that we are not likely to use a single factor—pitch, loudness, or duration—to highlight meaning within a phrase or a sentence. We are more likely to change all three of these vocal attributes together. However, a subtle and controlled change in rate with pitch and loudness "taking care of themselves" is often a sophisticated way of bringing out a desired meaning.

Practice the following materials to control the rate according to the meaning or meanings you consider important. Note the "reflective" (associated) changes that occur when any one of the vocal factors is intentionally emphasized.

    a. That's his? I thought it was mine.
    b. He's a mean man of considerable means.
    c. It was said of Lincoln that he was a homely man, beautiful in his homeliness.
    d. In biblical times, fresh water was more precious than oil.
    e. Individual culture is the residual of learning; culture is expressed in the tastes and attitudes of persons, more than in the specifics of what they may have learned.
    f. Glenda called Tom, but what she called him when she called him, Tom refused to tell.
    g. Silence can be the epitome of either tact, or aggression.
    h. Susan had a warm personality, which never overheated.
    i. When Walt Whitman sang of himself, he also sang of and for all human beings.
    j. Birdsong has been so much analyzed for its content of business communication that there seems little time left for music, but it is there. Behind the glossaries of warning call, alarms, mating messages, pronouncements of territory, calls for recruitment, and demands for dispersal, there is redundant, elegant sound that is unaccountable as part of the working day.

                  —LEWIS THOMAS, *The Lives of a Cell*

5. Read the following excerpts at appropriate basic rates but with variation to emphasize the key words and so the essential ideas. The more serious or solemn the content, the slower the basic rate should be.

    a. Tomorrow, and tomorrow, and tomorrow,
        Creeps in this petty pace from day today,
        To the last syllable of recorded time;

And all our yesterdays have lighted fools
The way to dusty death.

—WILLIAM SHAKESPEARE, *Macbeth*

b. Ah, distinctly I remember it was in the bleak December;
And each separate dying ember wrought its ghost upon the floor.

—EDGAR ALLAN POE, *The Raven*

c. The sea is calm tonight,
The tide is full, the moon lies fair
Upon the Straits.

—MATTHEW ARNOLD, *Dover Beach*

d. Alone, alone, all, all alone;
Alone on a wide, wide sea.

—SAMUEL TAYLOR COLERIDGE, *The Ancient Mariner*

e. "All right," said the Cat; and this time it vanished quite slowly, beginning with the end of the tail, and ending with the grin, which remained some time after the rest of it had gone.

—LEWIS CARROLL, *Alice's Adventures in Wonderland*

f. The only secret people keep
Is Immortality.

—EMILY DICKINSON, *Poems*, No. 1748

6. Read the following passages, using intentional pauses to set off the significant thought groups. Punctuation may help, but occasionally it may be misleading. Determine the units of thought, and pause whether or not the material is punctuated. Indicate pauses by inserting the sign ‖ at the end of thought units at which you intend to pause. Underline the words that carry the essential meanings in each selection.

a. If well enough off to be able to pay for one's travel, a vagabond at heart may be called a tourist. If rich enough, he or she may be thought of as a world traveler.

b. The secret of being a bore is to tell everything.

—VOLTAIRE, *L'Enfant Prodigue*

c. The proper study of mankind is man.

—ALEXANDER POPE, *Essays on Man*

d. Cleopatra's nose, had it been shorter, the whole aspect of the world would have been changed.   —BLAISE PASCAL, *Pensées*

e. He was a bold man that first ate an oyster.

—JONATHAN SWIFT, *Dialogue II*

f. The sky is low, the clouds are mean,
A travelling flake of snow
Across a bar or through a rut
Debates if it will go.

—EMILY DICKINSON, *Nature, Part II*

g. There is nothing more tragic in life than the utter impossibility of changing what you have done.

—JOHN GALSWORTHY, *Justice*

h. Volumes might be written upon the impiety of the pious.

—HERBERT SPENCER, *First Principles*

i. No man who has once heartily and wholly laughed can be altogether irreclaimably bad.

—THOMAS CARLYLE, *Sartor Resartus*

j. Once you have become permanently startled, as I am, by the realization that we are a social species, you tend to keep an eye out for pieces of evidence that this is, by and large, a good thing for us.   —LEWIS THOMAS, *Lives of a Cell*

7. The passages that follow call for more deliberate pauses to achieve emotional impact or to heighten dramatic meaning. In many instances, these effects may be attained by pauses before as well as after the significant words or phrases.

a. As I walked out in the streets of Laredo,
As I walked out in Laredo one day,
I spied a poor cowboy wrapped up in white linen,
Wrapped up in white linen as cold as the clay.

—ANONYMOUS, *The Cowboy's Lament*

b. The deepest thing in our nature is this dumb region of the heart in which we dwell alone with our willingnesses and our unwillingnesses, our faiths and our fears.

—WILLIAM JAMES, *The Will to Believe*

c. I will instruct my sorrow to be proud;
For grief is proud and makes its owner stoop.

—WILLIAM SHAKESPEARE, *The Merchant of Venice*

d. A little work, a little play,
To keep us going—and so, good day!
A little warmth, a little light,
Of love's bestowing—and so, good-night!

—GEORGE DU MAURIER, *Trilby*

e. Which of us has known his brother? Which of us has looked into his father's heart? Which of us has not remained prison-pent? Which of us is not forever a stranger and alone?

—THOMAS WOLFE, *Look Homeward, Angel*

f. Then darkness enveloped the whole American armada. Not a pinpoint of light showed from those hundreds of ships as they surged on through the night toward their destiny, carrying across the ageless and indifferent sea tens of thousands of young men, fighting for . . . for . . . well, at least for each other.

—ERNIE PYLE, *Brave Men*

g. I have learned silence from the talkative, toleration from the intolerant, and kindness from the unkind; yet strange, I am ungrateful to these teachers.   —KAHLIL GIBRAN, *Sand and Foam*

h. If we open a quarrel between the past and the present, we shall find that we have lost the future.

—WINSTON CHURCHILL, *Speech, House of Commons, 1940*

i. That which has always been accepted by everyone, everywhere, is almost certain to be false.   —PAUL VALERY, *Tel Quel*

10

Vocal Variety in
Speaking and Reading

Although this chapter is specifically entitled "Vocal Variety," we have been anticipating and considering aspects and implications of this subject in several of the preceding chapters. When we discussed *loudness,* we considered first the fundamental need
for the speaker to be heard if his or her intentions to communicate were to be fruitful.
Beyond this, we also considered the use of vocal force as related to word meanings,
sentence meanings, and overall communicative efforts. *Pitch* was likewise considered
a basic attribute of the voice that can be used to enhance vocalization per se. Pitch was
also discussed in relationship to linguistic melody, to word and phrase meaning, and
to the expression of states of feeling. Similarly, the vocal attribute *duration* (timing)
was viewed in relationship to the speaker's physiological state, to feeling, and to semantic implications.

This chapter is in one sense a review and reconsideration of some aspects of vocal
variety previously discussed. It also provides us with an opportunity to emphasize some
aspects that were briefly touched on in the earlier chapters that deal separately with
individual attributes of the voice.

Through the attributes of the voice—pitch, quality, loudness, and duration—we tend
as we speak to reveal our thoughts and our feelings or to express those thoughts and
feelings that we wish others to believe we entertain. The less inhibited we are, the
more the component of feeling is expressed through our voices. When we were very
young and had little or no awareness of cultural pressures, our voices faithfully and
reflexively indicated our changes in feeling and mood. As we matured, cultural pressures exerted an increasing influence on us, and we learned, almost always without
awareness, of *how* we are expected to show our feelings in our overt behavior, including the way we give voice to our utterances. Pitch changes came under our voluntary
control and conformed more and more to the pattern and the linguistic code of our
culture. By the time we were of school age, most of us spoke the sounds and the mel-

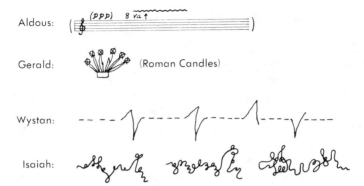

FIGURE 10–1   "Four Friends. Gerald [Herad] is a virtuoso talker, the most brilliant I have ever heard, and he *likes* to talk, just as Arthur Rubinstein *likes* to play the piano. Isaiah Berlin is even faster and funnier—an ironical gaiety underlies everything he says—but Isaiah tends to speak in spurts, like a ticker tape. Wystan Auden, by comparison, fishes, though profoundly, between words, and Aldous [Huxley] is too serenely high in tessitura, and in volume too suavely soft." (From *Dialogues and a Diary* by Igor Stravinsky and Robert Craft. Copyright © 1961, 1962, 1963 by Igor Stravinsky. Reprinted by permission of Doubleday & Company, Inc., and Faber and Faber, Ltd.)

ody (intonation) of the language or languages of our culture. We learned also that American-English speech has syllable stress within a word and word stress within a phrase. So we came to be able to emphasize ideas as we spoke. Our tendency to talk at changing rates according to mood—to talk more rapidly under heightened feelings, more slowly in the absence of heightened feelings, and quite slowly when sad or depressed—also became modified by cultural influences. Although these cultural modifications direct us toward norms of behavior, most of us still maintain and express ourselves as individuals. Sometimes, we kick over the traces, and our voices minimize the influences and effects of environmental training and pressures. But usually, we manage to conform to a sufficient degree to behave considerably as do the people with whom we identify, while still giving expression to our individual selves.

Igor Stravinsky, the noted composer, with considerably more sophistication and a much better than average ear for vocal nuances, listened carefully to how people talked. In one of his books, Stravinsky presented graphic as well as verbal descriptions of the vocal characteristics of several of his friends.[1] Stravinsky described one friend as a "virtuoso talker who *likes* to talk, just as Rubinstein *likes* to play the piano." A second friend is described as "fast and funny." A third "talks in spurts like a ticker tape." Another "fishes . . . profoundly, between words." Still another is "too serenely high in tessitura and in volume too suavely soft." (See Figure 10–1.)

[1] Igor Stravinsky and Robert Craft, *Dialogue and a Diary* (Garden City, N.Y.: Doubleday & Company, Inc., 1963).

Implications of Vocal Attributes

With the possible exception of quality, each vocal attribute, as we have noted, is capable of revealing thought as well as feeling. Within a phrase, the important word is likely to be spoken more loudly, more slowly, and at a different pitch from the other words. These changes are paralleled for the phrase–sentence relationships, as well as for the sentence–paragraph relationships, and so forth.

Through the use of vocal variety we are also able to capture attention and to maintain listener interest. In brief, through the voice, as well as through the selection of words and the construction of our sentences, we are able to reveal thought and feeling, to emphasize ideas, and to keep listeners attentive to our communicative efforts.

Quality

In our earlier discussions of quality, we considered its relationship to resonance and to the avoidance of undesirable vocal aspects such as excessive nasality and breathiness. At this time, we consider quality as it is related to feelings and moods and as an aspect of vocal variety.

Although modifications in vocal quality take place as a result of the inherent characteristics of our resonating cavities, except for those of us who tend to be either nasal or denasal there is little that we normally should do consciously to bring about these changes. Normal changes in quality are related to feelings and moods, to the emotional rather than the intellectual aspects of our behavior. Unless we are dealing with a greatly inhibited individual, the feelings we entertain will be reflected spontaneously—if we permit ourselves to be spontaneous—and expressed in our vocal efforts. Usually, we have more difficulty in concealing our feelings than in revealing them. The speaker who does not strive to conceal or inhibit inner feelings, and yet does not make a point of putting them on display, will have no difficulty with quality changes. The normally responsive speaker who initiates vocal tones properly and who uses an appropriate and flexible pitch range will do best with the quality that emerges spontaneously and naturally.

Reading Aloud to Interpret and Communicate
Another's Thoughts and Feelings

Persons who choose to read aloud to a listener or listeners have the dual responsibilities of translating (decoding) and transmitting thoughts and feelings not of their own origin. The reader-speaker who is about to speak another person's words must first determine as *faithfully as possible* what are or were the thoughts and feelings of the writer. With such an awareness of responsibility, and with such an appreciation of the task, the reader-speaker will set about to determine the dominant mood and nuances of feeling of each selection to be read aloud, as well as the underlying theme and the specific thoughts to be communicated. Even the most proficient of professional actors—*who are essentially readers because they are dealing with the verbal formulations of others*—accept the need to study their lines carefully before they read them aloud. Such study is, of course, recommended to our student-readers.

When, as a reader, you are able to understand the mood, feelings, and thoughts inherent in the selections studied-to-be-read-aloud, you should begin to do your reading aloud. If at all possible, record and play back your efforts. Listen objectively and determine whether what you thought you thought, and felt you felt, is being expressed in your speaking of another person's words. With such preparation and appreciation, the appropriate initial vocal qualities to establish the dominant mood, as well as changes in quality to suggest the particular feelings associated with particular ideas, should take place almost as spontaneously as if the words and feelings were initially your own. But because they are not quite your own (you may not even believe them), you will just have to work a bit harder to be effective in your role as a decoder and a communicator of someone else's words.

EXERCISES FOR VOCAL QUALITY: ESTABLISHING MOOD

1. Somewhere—in desolate wind-swept space—
In Twilight-land—no man's land—
Two hurrying Shapes met face to face,
And bade each other stand.

—THOMAS BAILEY ALDRICH, *Identity*

2. During the whole of a dull, dark, and resoundless day in the autumn of the year, when the clouds hung oppressively low in the heavens, I had been passing alone, on horseback, through a singularly dreary track of country, and at length found myself, as the shades of evening drew on, within view of the melancholy House of Usher. I know not how it was—but, with the first glimpse of the building, a sense of insufferable gloom pervaded my spirit.

—EDGAR ALLAN POE, *The Fall of the House of Usher*

3. All sorts of things and weather
Must be taken in together,
To make up a year
And a Sphere.

—RALPH WALDO EMERSON, *The Mountain and the Squirrel*

4. She left the web, she left the loom,
She made three paces thro' the room,
She saw the water lily bloom,
She saw the helmet and the plume,
   She look'd down to Camelot.

—ALFRED, LORD TENNYSON, *The Lady of Shalott*

5. The centipede was happy quite
   Until a toad in fun
Said, "Pray, which leg goes after which?"
That worked her mind to such a pitch,
She lay distracted in a ditch
   Considering how to run.

—MRS. EDWARD CRASTER, *Pinafore Poems*

6. Shall I, wasting in despair,
Die because a woman's fair?
Or make pale my cheeks with care
'Cause another's rosy are?
Be she fairer than the day

> Or the flowery meads in May,
>   If she be not so to me,
>   What care I how fair she be?
>
> —GEORGE WITHER, *Shall I, Wasting in Despair*

7. I remember the way we parted
      The day and the way we met;
   You hoped we were both brokenhearted
      And knew we should both forget.

> —CHARLES ALGERNON SWINBURNE, *An Interlude*

8. The sea lies all about us. The commerce of all lands must cross it. The very winds that move over the lands have been cradled on its broad expanse and seek ever to return to it. The continents themselves dissolve and pass to the sea, in grain after grain of eroded land. So the rains that rose from it return again in rivers. In its mysterious past it encompasses all the dim origins of life and receives in the end, after, it may be, many transmutations, the dead husks of that same life. For all at last returns to the sea—to Oceanus, the ocean river, like the ever flowing stream of time, the beginning and the end.

> —RACHEL L. CARSON, *The Sea Around Us*

9. It is better to lose health like a spendthrift than to waste it like a miser. It is better to live and be done with it, than to die daily in the sickroom. By all means begin your folio; even if the doctor does not give you a year, even if he hesitates about a month, make one brave push and see what can be accomplished in a week. It is not only in finished undertakings that we ought to honour useful labour. A spirit goes out of the man who means execution, which outlives the most untimely ending. All who have meant good work with their whole hearts, have done good work, although they may die before they have the time to sign it. Every heart that has beat strong and cheerfully has left a hopeful impulse behind it in the world, and bettered the tradition of mankind.

> —ROBERT LOUIS STEVENSON, *Aes Triplex*

10. I learned three things in Zurich during the war. I wrote them down. Firstly, you're either a revolutionary or you're not, and if you're not you might as well be an artist as anything else. Secondly, if you can't be an artist, you might as well be a revolutionary. . . . . I forgot the third thing.

> —TOM STOPPARD, *Travesties*

PRACTICE MATERIALS

The materials that follow will afford opportunities, some in depth, to employ knowledge and skill in the use of vocal variety. Be sure that you first read and understand the entire selection, and note the underlying, fundamental thought and mood as well as the nuances in feeling and thought. Experiment, using different techniques of emphasis (e.g., basic pitch change, force, or duration), and decide which of these is most appropriate to express the dominant meaning of each selection.

1. Future shock—the shattering stress and disorientation that we induce to individuals by subjecting them to too much change in too short a time.

> —ALVIN TOFFLER, *Future Shock*

2. "All animals are equal, but some animals are more equal than others."   —GEORGE ORWELL, *Animal Farm*

3. How sharper than a serpent's tooth it is
To have a thankless child.

—WILLIAM SHAKESPEARE, *King Lear*

4. I refuse to accept the cynical notion that nation after nation must spiral down a militaristic stairway into the hell of nuclear destruction. I believe that unarmed truth and unconditional love will have the final word in reality.   —MARTIN LUTHER KING, JR., Speech accepting the Nobel
Prize, December 1964

5. Too long did I wallow
In the cold lap of sorrow,
Knowing that each day I would mourn
The hours I feared to scorn—
Until I learned at last to see
A sadness I nurtured deep in me.

—J. E., *Delayed Confrontation*

6. Jenny kissed me when we met,
Jumping from the chair she sat in;
Time, you thief, who loves to get
Sweets into your list, put that in:

Say I'm weary, say I'm sad,
Say that health and wealth have missed me,
Say I'm growing old, but add
Jenny kissed me.

—LEIGH HUNT, *Rondeau*

7. When all the world is young, lad,
    And all the trees are green;
And every goose a swan, lad,
    And every lass a queen;
Then hey for boot and horse, lad,
    And round the world away;
Young blood must have its course, lad,
    And every dog his day.

When all the world is old, lad,
    And all the trees are brown;
And all the sport is stale, lad,
    And all the wheels run down:
Creep home, and take your place there,
    The spent and maimed among:
God grant you find one face there,
    You loved when all was young.

—CHARLES KINGSLEY, *Water Babies*

8. Remember me when I am gone away,
Gone far away into the silent land;
When you can no more hold me by the hand,

Nor I half turn to go, yet turning stay.
Remember me when no more, day by day,
You tell me of our future that you planned;
Only remember me; you understand.
It will be late to counsel then or pray.
Yet if you should forget me for a while
And afterwards remember, do not grieve:
For if the darkness and corruption leave
A vestige of the thoughts that once I had,
Better by far you should forget and smile
Than that you should remember and be sad.

—CHRISTINA ROSSETTI, *Remember*

9. In the following excerpts from the speeches and writings of John F. Kennedy, essential ideas are brought out by the balancing of phrases and by verbal contrasts resulting from positions of words within phrases. The same words often occur in contexts that are *almost but not quite the same.* Be certain that in your study of the selections you anticipate and prepare to bring out the related yet contrasting thoughts and the subtleties and nuances in feeling as well as in thought by appropriate vocal changes.

a. . . . democracy means much more than popular government and majority rule, much more than a system of political techniques to flatter or deceive powerful blocs of voters . . . the true democracy, living and growing and inspiring, puts its faith in the people—faith that the people will not simply elect men who will represent their views ably and faithfully, but also elect men who will exercise their conscientious judgment—faith that the people will not condone those whose devotion to principle leads them to unpopular causes, but reward courage, respect honor and ultimately recognize right.

—JOHN F. KENNEDY, *Profiles in Courage*

b. And thus, in the days ahead, only the very courageous will be able to take the hard and unpopular decisions necessary for our survival in the struggle with a powerful enemy—an enemy with leaders who need give little thought to the popularity of their course, who need pay little tribute to the public opinion they themselves manipulate, and who may force, without fear of retaliation at the polls, their citizens to sacrifice present laughter for future glory. And only the very courageous will be able to keep alive the spirit of individualism and dissent which gave birth to this nation, nourished it as an infant and carried it through its severest tests upon the attainment of its majority.

—JOHN F. KENNEDY, *Profiles in Courage*

c. So let us begin anew—remembering on both sides that civility is not a sign of weakness, and sincerity is always subject to proof. Let us never negotiate out of fear. But let us never fear to negotiate.

Let both sides explore what problems unite us instead of belaboring those problems which divide us.

Let both sides, for the first time, formulate serious and precise proposals for the inspection and control of arms—and bring the absolute power to destroy other nations under the absolute control of all nations.

—JOHN F. KENNEDY, Inaugural Address, 1961

10. To every thing there is a season, and a time to every purpose under the heaven: a time to be born, and a time to die; a time to plant, and a time to pluck up that which is planted; a time to kill, and a time to heal; a time to break down, and a time to build up; a time to weep, and a time to laugh; a time to mourn, and a time to dance; a time to cast away stones, and a time to gather stones together; a time to embrace, and a time to refrain from embracing; a time to seek, and a time to lose; a time to keep, and a time to cast away; a time to rend, and a time to sew; a time to keep silence, and a time to speak; a time to love, and a time to hate; a time for war, and a time for peace.   —*Ecclesiastes* 3:1–8

11. The following short selections and excerpts require careful phrasing for their full import.

> **a.** Nothing in life is so exhilarating as to be shot at without result.
> > —WINSTON CHURCHILL, *The Malakand Field Force*
>
> **b.** Dictators ride to and fro upon tigers which they dare not dismount. And the tigers are getting hungry.
> > —WINSTON CHURCHILL, *While England Slept*
>
> **c.** A truth that's told with bad intent
> Beats all the lies you can invent.
> > —WILLIAM BLAKE, *Auguries of Innocence*
>
> **d.** My only books
> Were woman's looks
> And folly's all they've taught me.
> > —THOMAS MOORE, *The Time I've Lost in Wooing*

EXERCISES FOR ROLE TAKING

Role taking, however brief, provides opportunities for vocal variety. Following are some short dialogues to be read aloud. They may be read by one reader, using some feature or features of voice to indicate a change of character (or speaker). The selections may also be read by two persons, each assuming a role. *Do not resort to falsetto* to indicate a change of role.

Apothecary. My poverty, but not my will consents.
Romeo. I pay thy poverty and not thy will.
> —WILLIAM SHAKESPEARE, *Romeo and Juliet*, Act V

Polonius. What do you read my lord?
Hamlet. Words, words, words.
> —WILLIAM SHAKESPEARE, *Hamlet*, Act II

The following conversation between Alice and Humpty Dumpty has been "adapted" as a dialogue, we hope without offense to either Lewis Carroll or the "actors."

Alice. But *glory* doesn't mean "a nice knockdown argument."

Humpty Dumpty (scornfully).   When *I* use a word it means just what I want it to mean—neither more nor less.

Alice.   The question is whether you *can* make words mean so many different things.

Humpty Dumpty.   The question is which is to be master—that's all.

The following is from the concluding act of Henrik Ibsen's *Doll's House*. Nora, the wife, rebels against her husband's treatment of her as a child, as being immature and without a sense of responsibility. Nora is no longer willing to play the expected role.

Helmer.   First and foremost, you are a wife and mother.

Nora.   That I don't believe anymore. I believe that first and foremost I am an individual, just as much as you are.

Summary

Vocal variety may be used to express feelings, to communicate meanings, to hold attention, and to make speaking and listening interesting. Any of the attributes of the voice—pitch, quality, loudness, or duration—may be used toward these ends. Rarely is a single attribute used alone. Changes in pitch and force are frequently made together. Usually, words spoken slowly are also spoken with increased force. The effective speaker achieves her or his effects by a combination of vocal factors and is able to control the factors according to the nature of what she or he has to say. Effective speakers are able to use a widened pitch range, appropriate inflection, modifications in vocal intensity, and changes in the tempo of speech to indicate how they feel about their thoughts as they talk. Furthermore, speakers can use vocal variety as a means of pointing up essential ideas and subordinating less important ones. Beyond this, Samuel Johnson reminds us, in *The Idler*, that "The joy of life is variety; the tenderest of love requires to be renewed by intervals of absence."

part three

Diction

Mend your speech a little,
Lest you may mar your fortunes.
—WILLIAM SHAKESPEARE, *King Lear*

Introduction to the Study of
American-English Speech Sounds

This part of the book has two related purposes. The first is to provide the reader with some fundamentals involved in the production of American-English speech sounds. The second is to provide specific information about the sounds of our language and practice materials for each of these sounds. Both purposes are intended to help the reader in the basic objective of becoming a more effective speaker and communicator.

Improving Diction

In this and the subsequent chapters, we make no attempt to be prescriptive or to urge any one standard of diction (pronunciation) as either more desirable than or "superior" to any other. We do, however, accept as a basic assumption that any manner of speech in a given community or environment that attracts attention to itself rather than to the intended message of its content deserves consideration as to the desirability, if not the need, of modification.

The sounds of speech, occasionally singly but usually in combination, constitute a symbol code that we use for oral and audible communication. We employ about forty-five distinctive sounds, or *phonemes,* in the symbol code of American-English speech. There are some variants in this code in different regions of the United States, as well as in virtually all parts of the English-speaking world. Major variants within the United States will be pointed out. For the most part, the variants are relatively few and are rarely so great as to prevent ready communication between educated speakers from widely separated parts of our country. Poor speakers may have difficulty in communicating in the areas in which they actually live; their difficulties tend to increase as they try to make themselves understood when they travel at distances from their homes. For the most part, however, the good speaker from New Orleans, may need a little time to "tune in" to the speech of the Bostonian, the New Yorker, or the resident of Chicago, but after a brief period all of these speakers should be able to understand one another, despite some regional differences in pronunciation and occasionally in word usage.

Dialects

A *dialect* is a linguistic system within a system that is related to a special cultural group, a community of persons, or an "identifiable" regional (geographic) area. Langacker (1967), indicated that "The basis for distinguishing various dialects of a language is that the linguistic system used by speakers of one dialect differs in certain respects from that used by speakers of others" (p. 47). The differences may be in pronunciation (diction), vocabulary (word usage or meaning for the same word forms), and/or syntactic constructions. For example, American-English speakers differ in the vowels used in words such as *roof, class, burn, after,* and *marry.* We *fetch something* in some parts of the United States that is *carried* in other areas; American-English speakers go *to the hospital* or are *in the hospital,* whereas those in England are more likely just to go *to hospital* or to be *in hospital.*

These dialectal variations are not likely to cause any difficulty in communication. However, there are dialects within the United States as well as within other parts of the English-speaking world in which the differences are so great as to constitute barriers to communication. For example, speakers from the Appalachia region might have great difficulty in communicating with speakers from rural Maine or from southern Louisiana.

Adults who wish to learn a second dialect, to change from one regional dialect to another, or to become bidialectal must be willing to immerse themselves in the effort. To a degree, it is much like learning a second language. It will not be achieved by silent study or even by careful listening, though both will help. Learning a new dialect, or modifying a dialect influence, requires a willingness to hear ourselves as others hear us, and to practice orally as well as aurally whatever needs to be practiced to modify our linguistic habits in the direction of a desired goal. It can be done!

The Sounds of American English

Sound Representation

There are two ways of representing the sounds of our language: through spelling (orthographic representation), and through a system in which there is greater consistency between the visible symbol and the sound. It is obvious that a spoken language that has only twenty-six letter symbols and more than forty different sounds cannot have sufficient consistency between letter and sound to provide a reliable guide to articulation and pronunciation. Most of our dictionaries therefore employ a system of diacritical markings and symbols to help the reader appreciate how a word should be pronounced because of or despite its spelling. Unfortunately, even the use of diacritical markings fails to provide a clear one-to-one relationship between sound and symbol. Still another system, more consistent than either of the others, employs selected symbols of the International Phonetic Alphabet (IPA). In the IPA system, one symbol is used for each distinctively different sound. Our approach emphasizes the use of the

IPA system of representation. We shall, however, indicate the dictionary equivalents of the IPA symbols. Through this approach, we hope that it will become possible for the reader (1) to become aware of the sounds (phonemes) of our language; (2) to make distinctions according to the characteristics of the different sounds, and (3) to establish a visible basis for cueing as to the manner or production for the individual sound, or for a series of sounds, in the contextual flow of speech.

The different sounds of American-English speech and their phonetic symbol and dictionary symbol representations are shown in Tables 11–1 and 11–2.[1]

The Phoneme

We approach our study of the sound of American English through a consideration of the basic unit or sound family: the *phoneme*. Phonemes are distinctive phonetic (sound) elements of words. The phonetic elements are distinctive in that they incorporate sound features that enable us to distinguish between spoken words. For example, the word *bad* has three phonemes. If we change the first, we can distinguish between *bad* and *sad*. If we change the second, we can distinguish between *bad* and *bid*; if we change the last, we can distinguish between *bad* and *ban*. These changes of phonemes included ones with several different sound features that made the differences readily apparent. However, we can bring the phoneme "closer" by changing the *b* to *p* and so have *bad* and *pad*, or by changing the vowel and so have *bad* and *bed*, or by changing the last sound and so have *bad* and *bat*. In regard to the consonants, our substitutions here are of cognate sounds, ones that differ only by the feature of voicing. In contextual speech, we might well need to depend on the overall meaning of the utterance to perceive the differences in the consonants of the key words.

Allophones

A second aspect of the phoneme concept is variation. Speech sounds vary in production according to context. The /t/ in *tell* is somewhat different from the /t/ in *its* and *plate*. Despite the variations in sound, however, they are essentially more alike than different, and we respond to all of these words as containing a /t/. These sound variations, which do not affect our understanding of what we hear, constitute the members of the phoneme or sound family. The individual variants are called *allophones*.

If our pronunciations and articulatory efforts do not show regard for possible phonemic differences, our listeners may become confused. If the vowel of *bad* begins to approximate the vowel of *bed*, we may be misunderstood if we utter a sentence such as "This will be bad for you." Similarly, if an /s/ is produced so that it begins to suggest an /ʃ/ (sh), we may not know whether something is for *sipping* or for *shipping*.

Some of the difficulty that foreign-born persons have in learning to speak English may be attributed to the fact that the phonemes in their native language are not always directly equivalent to ours. For example, we make a significant distinction between the vowels of words such as *heel* and *hill* and *seen* and *sin*. By way of television, radio,

---

[1]With minor exceptions, the dictionary symbols are those used in the *American Heritage Dictionary* (Boston: Houghton Mifflin, 1976). Essentially the same symbols are used by other leading dictionaries, including the *Random House Dictionary of the English Language* (New York: Random House, Inc., 1966), and the *Doubleday Dictionary* (New York: Doubleday and Co., 1975).

or movies, if not by direct experience, most of us know that many of our Mexican neighbors *think* with the vowel of *seen*. They may also have difficulty with the distinctions we make between *hail* and *hell*. We, of course, are not immune from these errors when we learn a foreign language. When speaking another language, we often produce the vowels and some consonants that are closest to our phonetic equivalents and so manage to sound like foreigners.

Distinctive Features

Linguists view phonemes as sounds of speech that by virtue of the particular ways in which they are produced (articulated) and their associated acoustic consequences, comprise "bundles" of features that serve to distinguish (contrast) one phoneme from another. Thus, the stoppage of breath is a distinctive feature or characteristic of /p/, /t/, /k/, /b/, /d/, and /g/. In regard to breath stoppage, these sounds differ from all other sounds in a language system without this feature. The presence or absence of voice distinguishes the last three stops from the first three in the previous series. The sounds /m/, /n/,/ŋ/ (ng) are featured by intentional nasality. In this respect these speech sounds are distinctive; that is, they differ from all other phonemes in English speech.

Table 11–1. **The Common Phonemes of American English (Consonants)**

Key Word	Most Frequent Dictionary Symbol	IPA Symbol
1. *pat*	p	p
2. *bee*	b	b
3. *tin*	t	t
4. *den*	d	d
5. *cook, key*	k	k
6. *get*	g	g
7. *fast*	f	f
8. *van*	v	v
9. *thin*	th	θ
10. *this*	th, th	ð
11. *sea*	s	s
12. *zoo*	z	z
13. *she*	sh	ʃ
14. *treasure*	zh	ʒ
15. *chick*	ch	tʃ
16. *jump*	j	dʒ
17. *me*	m	m
18. *no*	n	n
19. *sing*	ng	ŋ
20. *let*	l	l
21. *run*	r	r
22. *yell*	y	j
23. *hat*	h	h
24. *won*	w	w
25. *what*	hw	ʍ or hw

Table 11–2.   The Common Phonemes of American English (Vowels)

Key Word	Dictionary Symbol	IPA Symbol
26. f*ee*	ē	i
27. s*i*t	ĭ	ɪ
28. t*a*ke	ā	e
29. m*e*t	ĕ	ɛ
30. c*a*t	ă	æ
31. t*a*sk	ă or å	æ or a depending on regional or individual variations
32. c*a*lm	ä	ɑ
33. h*o*t	ŏ or ä	ɒ or ɑ depending on regional or individual variations
34. s*a*w	ô	ɔ
35. v*o*te	ō	o or ou
36. b*u*ll	o͡o	ʊ
37. t*oo*	o͞o	u
38. h*u*t	ŭ	ʌ
39. *a*bout	ə	ə
40. upp*er*	ər	ɚ by most Americans and ə by many others
41. b*i*rd	ûr	ɝ, ɜr by most Americans and ɜ by many others

Phonemic Diphthongs

42. ice	ī	aɪ
43. now	ou	au or ɑu
44. boy, toys	oi	ɔɪ

Linguists such as Jakobson and Halle (1956), Fant (1962), and Chomsky and Halle (1968) have "developed" distinctive feature systems that presumably permit a student of language phonology to distinguish among the phonemes of all natural languages. For our purposes, however, a more "modest" system such as that of Miller and Nicely (1955) or even the one used in this text is adequate to describe and distinguish one phoneme from the others in American-English speech. The descriptions of each of the sounds in the remaining chapters of this book may be regarded as including phonetically distinctive features.[2]

Classification of Sounds

The sounds of our language may be classified in three large groups: consonants, vowels and diphthongs. All are produced as a result of some modification of the outgoing breath by the organs of articulation.

[2]For a relatively nontechnical consideration of distinctive-feature theory and its application to the correction of articulatory defects, see Eisenson and Ogilvie (1983, pp. 126–132, 272–275).

Consonants are speech sounds that are produced by either a complete or a partial obstruction or modification of the breath channel by the organs of articulation. Aside from voice, the sound characteristics of each consonant result from the manner of vibration of the breath stream. This is determined by the way in which the breath stream is (1) modified by the closures produced by articulatory activity; (2) released by the activity of the opening of the closure; or (3) modified but not completely obstructed (stopped) by the narrowing of the breath channel.

Vowels are produced by articulatory movements of the speech organs without obstruction or interference of the vibrating breath stream in its passage through the breath channel. We determine the characteristic features of the vowels of our language by modifying the size and shape of the mouth cavity and by changing the position of the tongue within the mouth.

Diphthongs are voiced glides that are uttered in a single breath impulse within the limits or confines of one syllable as in the words *dine* and *out*. Some diphthongs are blends of two vowels. Most, however, represent an instability or "breakdown" of what at one time in the history of our language was one vowel.

A diphthong may be defined as a syllable in which two vowel resonances are clearly identified, but with *a change of resonance as an essential characteristic*. We shall discuss diphthongs in Chapter 13, where we shall also present a less technical, descriptive definition.

Voice

All vowels and diphthongs, unless intentionally whispered, are produced with vocalization accompanying the articulatory activity. Consonants, however, may be produced with or without accompanying vocalization. Those that are produced with vocalization are known as *voiced* consonants; those produced without vocalization are referred to as *voiceless*.

Manner and Place of Articulation

In the individual descriptions of the consonant sounds that are presented later, the manner and place of articulation are considered for each sound. Some consonants are described as *stops*, others as either *fricatives, glides,* or *nasals*. We anticipate some of the descriptions by defining a few terms here.

Stop sounds are produced by a stopping of the breath stream. The stop sounds are /p/, /b/, /t/, /d/, /k/, and /g/.

Fricatives are produced by a partial closure of the articulators. This action results in the creation of a constricted passage through which the stream of air must be forced. The partial closures may take place as a result of the grooving of the tongue or of having other organs of articulation come close together. The distinctively fricative sounds are /f/, /v/, /θ/ (th), /ð/ (th), /s/, /z/, /ʃ/ (sh), and /ʒ/ (zh). The sound /h/ is produced with laryngeal constriction.

Nasal sounds are reinforced and emitted nasally. The three nasals are /m/, /n/, and /ŋ/ (ng).

Glides are sounds that are produced with a continuous movement of the articulators, rather than with a fixed articulatory position. The glide consonants are /w/, /j/ (y), and most varieties of /r/.

Affricates are blends of two sounds, one a stop and the other a fricative. There are two affricates, /tʃ/ (ch), as in *chum,* and /dʒ/ (j), as in *jam.*

The sound /l/ is a *lateral* consonant. It is produced by the emission of vocalized breath at both sides of the tongue while the tip of the tongue is in contact with the gum ridge. The /l/ is designated as a *liquid* by some phoneticians and linguists.

Sounds in Context

Although our approach to the study of diction begins with a descriptive analysis of the individual sounds of our language, speech does not consist of a series of individual sounds. Speech is a sequence of sounds. In context, individual sounds are modified and produced differently from the way that they would be in isolation. If we were to speak as though our linguistic symbols were a series of sounds, we would be uttering phonetic nonsense. In context, differences in force and duration that emphasize meanings, differences according to the formality or informality of the speech situation, and differences according to the size of the listening group all result in modifications of individual sounds in the flow of speech. Some of these differences are considered here briefly.

Assimilation

If asked for the pronunciation of the words *education, mature,* and *income,* many persons would carefully pronounce these words differently from their pronunciations in contextual speech. The word *education* may regularly be pronounced [ɛdjukeʃən] (*ĕdūkāshən*) by some persons, but most of us are likely to say [ɛdʒəkeʃən] (*ĕjəkāshən*) in talking about "the education of our children" or in asserting that "education means . . . ." When we change from the careful but less usual pronunciation of words such as *educate, income,* and *handkerchief* or phrases such as *don't you* and *meet you* to the easier and more usual ones, we are yielding to and demonstrating the effects of *assimilation in connected speech.*

Assimilation refers to the phonetic changes that take place when one sound is modified by a neighboring sound or sounds in connected speech. Some of these changes become relatively fixed and therefore regularly influence the pronunciations of many words.[3] Other assimilations depend on particular verbal contexts and therefore influence the articulation and pronunciation of words only in these contexts. Examples of each are given in our brief discussions of some types of assimilative modifications.

Anticipatory Changes

Most assimilations reflect the influences of anticipatory changes. That is, the organs of articulation, in anticipation of a sound to follow, modify a preceding sound. The change tends to simplify or facilitate articulation. For example, in the word *congress,* the letter *n* is sounded as an /ŋ/ (ng) in anticipation of the sound /g/ that follows. It is easier to

---

[3] The pronunciation of /ŋ/ (ng) for the letter *n* in words such as *income, congress,* and *bank* are examples of "fixed" assimilative changes.

articulate /ŋg/ than [n + g] simply because both the /ŋ/ (ng) and the /g/ are produced with the same parts of the tongue and the palate. For the same reason, *income* is pronounced with an /ŋ/ (ng) rather than an /n/ followed by a /k/. Similarly, it is easier to say *this shoe* with a lengthened /ʃ/ (sh) than with an /s/ followed by an /ʃ/. The pronunciation of *this shoe*, incidentally, is an example of contextual, temporary assimilation.

Voicing

Changes produced in voicing by assimilation are perhaps best exemplified in words that end with a final *s* or *d*. In the words *liked, heaped, rasped,* and *guessed,* and *ropes, takes,* and *plates,* the next-to-the-last produced sound is a voiceless consonant. (The letter *e,* in each case, is silent.) As a result, the final *d* is pronounced as /t/ rather than /d/ and the final *s* as an /s/ rather than /z/.

In words such as *passes, hedges, riches,* and *roses,* the final *s* is produced as /z/ because the next-to-the-last sound is a vowel and is vocalized. Similarly, *grounded, breaded,* and *heeded* are each pronounced with a final /d/. In the words *begs, seems, togs,* and *roams,* the final sound is voiced because of the influence of the preceding voiced consonant.

As a "rule," we may generalize that when the next-to-the-last sound in a word is unvoiced, the last sound will also be unvoiced; if the next-to-the-last sound is voiced, the last sound is also voiced.

Other Assimilations

In some cases assimilations may result in the complete loss of one or more sounds which are replaced by a third sound. This happens in the assimilated pronunciation of *picture, nature,* and *feature,* where the sound /tʃ/ (ch) is heard in the second syllable of each of the words.

In both manner and content, speech is appropriate or inappropriate, correct or incorrect, according to the circumstances and the occasion. Despite possible differences in education, profession, and speaking ability, an individual's manner of communicating will or should vary according to the time, the place, and the speaking situation. The minister who feels the need to deliver a sermon to his or her family is likely to do so differently from the way he or she would speak to the congregation in church. The minister should certainly not converse at home—with family members or with visiting members of the congregation—as if talking to them from the pulpit. The lecturer speaking to a large audience on a formal occasion is likely to use more "elevated" language than the same speaker at his or her club, on a picnic, with friends, or at a home social gathering.

Informal speech employs many contractions. We use more *he's, don'ts,* and *I'ms* when speaking informally and intimately than when speaking formally. We do not, however, usually employ contracted forms when emphasis is intended. Public addresses, with the exception of the humorous afterdinner speech, are generally delivered formally unless, for special purposes (usually political), the speaker wants to establish an air of "folksiness" with the listeners.

Speech Standards

Pronunciation Variants

In going over the list of consonant and vowel sounds, some observations may be made relative to minor differences in pronunciation among Americans.

Many of us do not distinguish between the /hw/ in *what* and the /w/ of *watt* and pronounce both the way we do the first sound of *will*.

There is considered variation in the pronunciation of the vowel of the word *ask*. Most Americans use the same vowel in the words *ask* and *hat;* others broaden the vowel in *ask* to that of the /ɑ/ (ä) of *calm;* a smaller number of Americans use the vowel /a/ (à), which is phonetically between /æ/ (ă) and /ɑ/ (ä).

Most Americans use the same vowel in *hot* as they do in *calm*. A few, however, use a vowel intermediate between the vowel of *call* and the vowel of *calm*. This usage is similar to that of "standard" (London) British English.

There is considerable variation in the production of the vowel of words such as *bird* and *heard*. Some use the vowel /ɝ/, which has an *r* coloring. Others include a clear-cut *r* preceded by a vowel much like the vowel in the word *bud*.

Paralleling the variations in the vowel of words such as *bird, heard, surf,* and *mirth* are those in the final sound of words such as *after, supper,* and *thunder*. Most of us use the vowel /ɚ/, which is much like the first sound of the word *above* with the addition of *r* coloring. Others add a clear-cut /r/ sound after the same vowel, and a smaller number of people make no distinction between the first sound of the word *above* and the last sound of *after* and use /ə/ for both.

To this short list of variants in American pronunciation, we might add another relative to the articulation of the /r/ sound in words in which the spelling includes the letter *r*. We are in common agreement that an /r/ sound is produced whenever a word contains an initial *r* in its spelling, as in *rug, rice, rain,* and *runs* and in words in which the *r* is preceded by a consonant and followed by a vowel, as in *tree, grease,* and *prize*. The /r/ is also pronounced in medial positions when it is followed by a vowel, as in *forest* and *touring*. Practice differs, however, in words in which the *r* is medial in spelling and followed by a consonant, as in *farm, card,* and *sharp*, or final in the spelling, as in *car, far,* and *soar*. These differences are considered again in more detail in Chapter 18.

Assimilations and Speech Standards

Most of the examples of assimilation given earlier are considered acceptable by all except the most pedantic people. Some persons may prefer the unassimilated pronunciations of words such as *congress* and *income* and tax themselves to maintain the /n/ rather than yielding to economy in articulation and produce an /ŋ/ (ng). Not all assimilations, however, are acceptable, even to our liberal dictionary editors. For example, the word *open*, despite temptation and frequent mispronunciation by small children, should still be produced with a final /n/ rather than an /m/.[4] The word *gas* is still better

---

[4]A. J. Bronstein (1960, p. 212) recognized that an *m* may be heard in the phrase "open the door" in assimilated colloquial educated speech.

pronounced with a final /s/ than with a /z/, although the second pronunciation is frequently given by persons not habitually careless in their speech.

Criteria for Speech Standards

Speech in general and pronunciation in particular are appropriate if they are consistent with the objectives of the speaker in his or her role of a communicator of ideas. The listeners, the occasion, and the speaker as a personality are some of the factors that determine appropriateness. *What is appropriate may be accepted as standard. Speech becomes substandard if the pronunciations are such that they violate the judgments and tastes of the listeners.* We are likely to sense such violations if an official in high government office speaks to us when we are members of a large audience as he or she might to some intimate friends on a fishing trip. We might also sense some violation if a college president talking on the topic "The Need for a Liberal Arts Education" were to do so in the manner of a sports announcer at a football game.

Speech becomes distinctly substandard if it employs pronunciations that are not currently used by any persons whose backgrounds as speakers make their judgments in regard to linguistic usage worthy of respect. Even a liberal attitude toward pronunciation would still not justify pronouncing *asked* as [æst] (ăst) or *something* as [sʌmpɪm] (sŭmpĭm)—except for speakers of a dialect for whom these pronunciations are acceptable.

Pronunciations that reveal foreign language influence, such as the substitution of a sound that approximates the appropriate one in English, would also constitute substandard speech. The substitution of a /v/ for a /w/ in words such as *wife* and *went* or an /f/ for a /v/ in words such as *give* and *leave* are examples of substandard pronunciations frequently resulting from foreign language influence. Occasionally, they may reflect persistent foreign language influences in dialectal speech within this country.

Speakers who wish to improve their speech, their articulation, and their pronunciation, as well as their word usage, must be good listeners. They must listen with discrimination for what is best and current in the community in which they live. They must listen to the educated and to the respected members of the community and use them as models but should not imitate them slavishly. Above all, they should avoid trying to sound like somebody else, thus seeming to deny individuality and place of origin. This does not mean that a person should maintain what may have been nonstandard in his or her background. It does mean that the man or woman from New York should not consciously try to sound as though he or she was brought up in Atlanta, Georgia, and that a speaker from Houston, Texas, should not try to sound like a Harvard-educated Bostonian unless the speaker happens to be one. In time, if any of these speakers live long enough in an area, some of the flavor of the area's speech will naturally begin to appear. Careful listening is likely to translate itself into unconscious imitation of the speech of the immediate environment unless the speaker is negatively motivated toward the person to whom he or she is listening.

References and Suggested Readings

Bronstein, A. J. *The Pronunciation of American English.* New York: Appleton-Century-Crofts, 1960.

Burling, R. *Man's Many Voices: Language in Its Cultural Context.* New York: Holt, Rinehart and Winston, Inc., 1970

Carrell, J., and W. R. Tiffany. *Phonetics.* New York: McGraw-Hill Book Company 1960.

Chomsky, N., and M. Halle. *The Sound Pattern of English.* New York: Harper & Row, Publishers, 1968, Chap. 7.

Dillard, J. L. *American Talk.* New York: Random House, Inc., 1976.

Dillard, J. L. *Black English; Its History and Usage in the United States.* New York: Random House, Inc., 1972.

Eisenson, J., and M. Ogilvie. *Communicative Disorders in Children.* New York: Macmillan Publishing Company, 1983.

Fant, G. M. "Descriptive Analysis of the Acoustic Aspects of Speech." Logos, **5** (1962), 3–17.

Jakobson, R., and M. Halle. *Fundamentals of Language.* The Hague: Mouton, 1956.

Labov, W. *Language in the Inner City.* Philadelphia: University of Pennsylvania Press, 1972.

Langacker, R. W. *Language and Its Structure.* New York: Harcourt Brace Jovanovich, Inc., 1967.

Miller, G. A., and P. E. Nicely. "An Analysis of Perceptual Confusions Among Some English Consonants." *Journal of the Acoustical Society of America,* **27** (1955), 338–352.

Stewart W. A. "Sociolinguistic Factors in the History of Negro Dialects," in D. L. Shores, *Contemporary English.* Philadelphia: J. B. Lippincott Company, 1972.

Williams, F. (ed.), *Language and Poverty.* Chicago: Markham, 1970.

Williamson, J. V. "A Look at Black English." *Crisis* (1971) 169–173, 185.

12

Individual Study of American-English Sounds: The Vowels

Our study of American-English speech sounds is based on the assumption that knowledge of the sound (phonemic) system and the opportunity for application and practice will help toward attaining the objective of improving diction. Some sounds have been found to be more troublesome—more frequently produced in a faulty manner—than others. These sounds receive major emphasis. They are treated in more detail, and a larger amount of practice material is provided for them than for those sounds that cause relatively little difficulty for the vast majority of speakers of American English or persons who would like to speak American English.

Although we study the individual phonemes of American-English speech, we need to emphasize the point that sounds in context, in a flow of normal speech utterance, do not have all of the characteristics of the isolated phoneme. (See previous discussions in Chapter 11 of *sounds in context and assimilation*.) An utterance involves coarticulation. Both the acoustic and the physiological characteristics of a sound in context are influenced by the preceding and succeeding sounds. Thus, the [s] and [t] in *stem* are produced somewhat differently from the [s] and [t] in *so to bed* or in *it's tight* or in *hats off* or *at last*. Although it is obviously neither possible nor fruitful to consider all possible combinations of sounds in contextual utterance, we consider a number of frequently coarticulated sounds in our presentations of sound blends.

We begin our study with an analysis of the vowel sounds. Although differences in practice relative to the pronunciation of vowels are fairly wide in different parts of the country, most vowel sounds, because of their intensity and their "open" manner of production, are comparatively easy to imitate. Pronunciation habits based on regional practice may, however, result in the persistent use of one vowel in some words when most Americans use another. For example, there is considerable variation in the pronunciation of the vowel in the words *had, have, candy, bad,* and *sad,* depending on regional custom. There is also a fair amount of regional variation in the pronunciation of the vowels in words such as *word, bird, heard, dearth, earth, curdle,* and *merge.* There is also some variation in the choice of vowel for words such as *path, ask,* and *dance.* Some of the variations in practice in different parts of the country are considered in the discussion of the individual vowel sounds. The carry-over influence of a first language on the diction of persons for whom English is a second language, as in the perception and production of the vowels of *hit* and *heat, bit* and *beet,* will also be considered.

Vowel Production

All vowels share several characteristics: (1) They are all voiced sounds; (2) all are articulated in essentially the same manner in that they are continuant sounds, without interruption and without restriction of the stream of breath; and (3) although lip activity is involved, the activity of the tongue and the modifications of the resonating cavities make the essential difference in the production of the different vowel sounds.

Vowels become acoustically identifiable to the listener, including the speaker-listener, by virtue of the changes in quality that occur both because of what the articulators do and because of the modifications in the resonating cavities above the larynx—mostly in the structures of the mouth and pharynx. These cavities function as "filters" and so permit different concentrations of energy known as *formant frequencies.*[1]

Vowel Classification

Vowels may be conveniently classified according to the part of the tongue that is most actively involved in the production of the sound. If you concentrate on the vowel sounds

Table 12–1. Vowels of American-English Speech

	Front Vowels			*Central Vowels*			*Back Vowels*	
	Phonetic Symbol	*Dictionary Symbol*		*Phonetic Symbol*	*Dictionary Symbol*		*Phonetic Symbol*	*Dictionary Symbol*
m*ee*t	i	ē				b*oo*n	u	o͞o
m*i*lk	ɪ	ĭ	m*i*rth	ɜ or ɝ	ûr	b*oo*k	ʊ	o͝o
m*a*y	e	ā				b*oa*t	o	ō
m*e*n	ɛ	ĕ	*a*bout	ə	ə			
						b*a*ll	ɔ	ô
m*a*t	æ	ă	upp*er*	ɚ	ər			
						b*o*g	ɒ	ŏ
*a*sk*	a	ȧ	m*u*d	ʌ	ŭ	b*a*lm	ɑ	ä

*When the speaker compromises between the vowels of *mat* and of *balm.* This vowel is intermediate in placement as well as in sound between æ and a.

[1] A technical classification for vowels is based on the *formant frequency,* or "regions of energy concentration," for each sound. P. Lieberman provided this definition of *formant frequency:* "The formant frequencies are essentially the center frequencies of the supralaryngeal vocal tract acting as a complex filter that lets maximum sound energy through its several levels of frequency" (P. Lieberman, *Speech Physiology and Acoustic Phonetics,* New York: Macmillan, 1977, p. 34).

of the words *me* and *moo,* you should become aware that the blade of the tongue moves forward toward the hard palate for *me.* For *moo,* the back of the tongue moves toward the soft palate. Similar activity may be noted if you compare the vowels of *pet* and *paw.* For *pet,* the front of the tongue is most active, and for *paw,* the back of the tongue is most active. For neither of these vowels, however, does the tongue move as high as for the vowels of *me* and *moo.* Comparable activity may be observed for all the other *front vowels* (those produced with the front, or blade, of the tongue most active) in contrast with the corresponding *back vowels* (those produced with the back of the tongue most active). Table 12–1 presents the vowels of American-English.

The approximate differences in tongue position for the front and the back vowels are illustrated in Figures 12–1 and 12–2.

Figures 12–3 and 12–4 illustrate the position of the tongue for the central vowels, or midvowels (those produced with the middle of the tongue most active).

You may test these representative tongue positions with your own articulatory behavior relative to these vowels by incorporating them in the following key words.

Front	*Central*	*Back*
me		boot
mitt		book
made	mirth	boat
met	*above,* upp*er*	bought
mat	mud	box
mask		balm

On the basis of the production of the key vowels, a twofold basis for classification becomes possible.

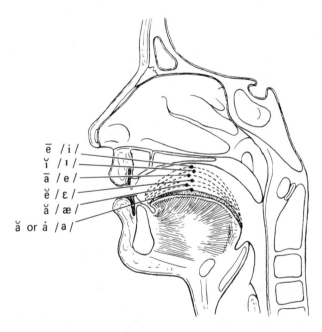

ē / i /
ĭ / ɪ /
ā / e /
ĕ / ɛ /
ă / æ /
ă or à / a /

FIGURE 12–1 **Representative tongue positions for front vowels.**

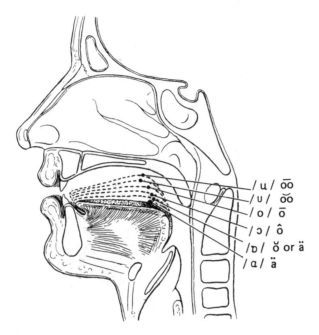

FIGURE 12–2   Representative tongue positions for back vowels.

First, vowels differ in production according to *place of articulation*—and so may be classified as *front, mid (central),* or *back* vowels according to the part of the tongue that is most actively involved in their production.

Second, vowels differ as to *height-of-tongue* position. The vowel of *me* is a high front vowel; the vowel of *moon* is a high back vowel. The vowel of *mask* is a low front vowel; that of *balm* is a low back vowel.

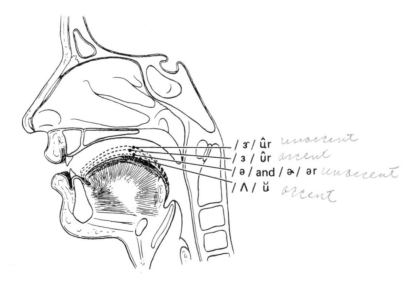

FIGURE 12–3   Representative tongue positions for the central vowels, or midvowels.

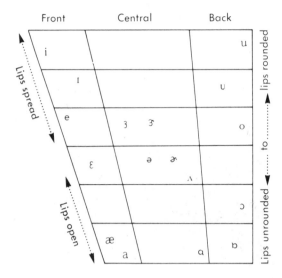

FIGURE 12–4 Tongue and lip positions of the American-English vowels. The front vowels /i/ (ē), /e/ (ā)/, and /æ/ (ă), are produced with tongue and associated articulatory tension; the vowels /ɪ/ (ĭ), /ɛ/ (ĕ), and /a/ (ȧ) are relatively lax. The back vowels /u/ (o͞o), /ʊ/ (o͝o), /o/ (ō), /ɔ/ (ô), /ɒ/ (ŏ), and /ɑ/ (ä) are produced with relatively lax tongue positions.

A *third basis* for the classification of vowels is *muscle tension*. If we compare the vowel of *peek* with that of *pick*, we should feel that the tongue is more tense for the vowel of *peek* than it is for the one in *pick*. Similarly, the vowel of *boat* is produced with the tongue somewhat more tense than in the production of the vowel of *book*. Tension may also be felt in the muscles behind the chin.

Before we go into our more detailed discussion of the individual sounds of our language, we might review briefly some features of vowel production. All vowels, unless intentionally whispered, are voiced, continuant sounds. When they are produced as isolated sounds, the tongue tip is usually placed behind the lower gum ridge. The vowel sounds are differentiated as a result of the activity of the blade, the middle, or the back of the tongue elevated to different positions (heights) within the mouth cavity. Some vowels are produced with muscle tension as an additional characteristic. The articulatory aspects that characterize the production of each of the vowels are now considered.

The Front Vowels

/i/ (ē) As in *See*[2]

The vowel /i/ is a high, front, tense vowel.

An examination of the front-vowel diagram (Figure 12–1) will reveal that /i/ is produced with the blade of the tongue arched high in the front of the mouth. It is produced with a considerable degree of tongue tension and a lesser degree of lip tension. When

[2] Hereafter the phonetic symbol (IPA) and the dictionary symbol are presented only at the head of each section for the individual new sound to be studied. In the exposition thereafter, only the IPA symbol is shown.

/i/ is produced as an isolated sound, the lip position approximates a tight-lipped grin. Tension should also be present in the muscle bulge behind the chin.

Muscle tension is necessary to produce a clear /i/ and to distinguish it from the vowel /ɪ/ (ĭ), which is a more relaxed sound.

The sound /i/ has many different English spellings. The most frequent include *e, ee, ea, ei, i,* and *ie,* as in *be, see, each, receipt, ski,* and *believe.*

PRACTICE MATERIALS

each	easy	eke	eerie
even	eager	equal	ego
ether	eel	eaves	Easter
east	eat	ease	edict
Eden	easel	eagle	Erie
beach	beast	appease	decent
breathe	feast	conceive	machine
breed	meat	please	crease
cheese	sweet	breeze	team
heat	yield	intrigue	achieve
beet	steel	sneeze	tease
dean	creep	reed	speed
agree	pea	tree	sea
glee	flee	ski	spree
esprit	key	bee	lea
tee	she	we	knee
fee	dee	free	quay

PHRASES

sleek fleet	sweet tea
beagle's fleas	believe and achieve
decent dean	deals and deeds
Pete is neat	steamed-up team
Oakie from Muskogee	eerie breeze
seasoned trees	gleeful tease
concealed sneeze	steel quays
believe to achieve	beets and peas
wheeze to tease	fields and trees
Eve and Eden	Steve at Eton

SENTENCES

1. The Marines seized the beach.
2. Enid said the steamy heat was a good enough reason to leap off the quay into the deep sea.
3. The chief was piqued because of his belief that the esprit of his police was not what it should be.

4. The machinist took a seat after cleaning his reamer.

5. Green peas and beans have as much protein as many pieces of beef.

6. MacNeal took a ball peen hammer and proceeded to beat the sheet of steel.

7. Anita was not pleased with Lita's teasing.

8. The sleek sneak thief beat his way up the creek.

9. Speed freaks are exceedingly heedless of their bodies' needs.

10. Jeanne, a weaver, believed in using green beads.

SELECTIONS

1. Oh, what a tangled web we weave,
   When first we practice to deceive.
   —SIR WALTER SCOTT, *Lochinvar*

2. John Ruskin believed that in a state of grief we may deceive ourselves as to our ability to reason.

3. Even the weariest river
   Winds somewhere safe to sea.
   —ALGERNON CHARLES SWINBURNE, *The Garden of Proserpine*

4. Speak roughly to your little boy,
   And beat him when he sneezes:
   He only does it to annoy,
   Because he knows it teases.
   —LEWIS CARROLL, *Alice's Adventures in Wonderland*

5. We are the music-makers,
   And we are the dreamers of dreams,
   Wandering by lone sea-breakers,
   And sitting by desolate streams;

   World-losers and world-forsakers,
   On whom the pale moon gleams;
   Yet we are the movers and shakers
   Of the world for ever, it seems.
   —ARTHUR W. O'SHAUGHNESSY, *Ode, Stanza 1*

/ɪ/ (ĭ) As in *Bit*

/ɪ/ is also a high, front vowel. /ɪ/ differs from /i/ in two respects; /ɪ/ is produced with a tongue position somewhat lower than is /i/ and *without articulatory tension.*

The lip position for /ɪ/ is approximately a relaxed smile in contrast with the tight-lipped grin for /i/. The difference in tension and lip position may be observed if you place your hand behind your chin and look in the mirror as you change from the word *heat* to *hit.*

The most frequent spelling for /ɪ/ is the letter *i* as in *sit, wit, fit,* and *lit;* other spellings include *u, ui,* and *e,* as in *busy, build,* and *English.*

Some speakers use the vowel /ɪ/ for the final *y* in words such as *busy, city,* and *petty.* Other speakers are likely to use a vowel somewhere between /i/ and /ɪ/. Still others may use a vowel closer to /i/ than to /ɪ/.

Determine your own practice by testing yourself with the following lists of words.

The words are to be read across the page. Avoid any suggestion of the vowel /i/ for the words in the third column.

greed	greedy	grid
fleet	flitty	flit
seat	city	sit
peat	pity	pit
key	kitty	kit
meat	meaty	mitt
cheese	cheesy	chit
we	weedy	wit
leak	leaky	lick
reed	reedy	rid
bead	beady	bid

PRACTICE MATERIALS

ibid	idiom	ignite	igloo
ilk	its	ingot	infer
imp	is	Italy	intake
ink	itch	indicate	ignore
Indian	inch	inn	insert
into	imply	ignorant	image
imbue	ingrate	impale	impact
build	quip	pinnacle	children
mist	list	fist	grip
business	tryst	strip	flick
differ	women	shrimp	whisk
fill	wishes	shrill	hymn
quick	drip	grill	quilt
wilt	mince	lick	think
eclipse	instill	bib	admit
addict	crib	simple	spin
insipid	insistent	timidity	willy-nilly
frantic	abyss	aphid	antic
flint	frisk	ticklish	twitch

hit and miss	frantic antics	tryst in the mist	skip the ship
twist and spin	hint of wit	skinny fists	fill the till
lick the lips	flick of the wrist	itch to be rich	Tim is slim
win and grin	grilled shrimp	busy and dizzy	pickled with dill
lift the lid	inch by inch	spilled milk	written with quill

SENTENCES

1. Unlike in Mississippi, winter sets in grimly, heavily, and insistently in Minnesota.

2. The British ships drifted into the Atlantic slip.

3. Detective Investigator Hill discovered that Phil and Elizabeth Winston, a pair of twins, had built an illegal still.

4. Will Gilston, the village pharmacist, filled the prescription with insight and skill.

5. Linda Simpson made a quick trip to Riverton.

6. Simmons, who lives in Missouri, wished to be convinced of the merits of the bill.

7. "The wit is insipid," insisted the still livid critic.

8. The transit system claimed in a writ that the citizen's petition was illegal.

9. Mick whistles "Dixie" if he wishes to seem busy.

10. The kitten was sitting pretty in the kitchen cabinet.

SELECTIONS

1. "Dear pig, are you willing to sell for one shilling
Your ring?" Said the piggy, "I will."
—EDWARD LEAR, *Nonsense Songs*

2. Walt Whitman remembered things for us, impossible but intelligible,
and which will become unintelligible at our peril.
—KARLE WILSON, *Classic Americans: Walt Whitman*

3. Cynicism is intellectual dandyism.
—GEORGE MEREDITH, *The Egoist*

4. The moving finger writes, and having writ,
Moves on. Nor all your piety nor wit
Shall lure it back to cancel half a line,
Nor all your tears wash out a word of it.
—*The Rubáiyát of Omar Khayyám* (Translated by Edward Fitzgerald)

5. As someday it may happen that a victim must be found,
I've got a little list—I've got a little list,
Of society's offenders who might well be underground,
And who never would be missed—who never would be missed,
—SIR WILLIAM S. GILBERT, *The Mikado*

/i/ (ē) and /ɪ/ (ĭ)

For persons with Spanish as a first language and others who may have difficulty in distinguishing between the front tense vowel /i/ and the relaxed /ɪ/, the following material should be of help. Place your hand behind your chin and feel the tension for the vowel in the first word of each pair. The second word, in contrast, should have a relaxed chin.

seat	sit	leak	lick
beat	bit	sheep	ship
meat	mit	sleep	slip
heat	hit	peach	pitch
greet	grit	leap	lip
cheap	chip	green	grin

peep	pip	heap	hip
fleet	flit	peak	pick
reed	rid	greed	grid
feel	fill	heel	hill
steal	still	neat	knit

In the following sentences, the first italicized word has the tense vowel [i]; the second has the relaxed vowel /ɪ/.

1. They climbed to *reach* the *rich* mine.
2. The *beans* were stored in *bins*.
3. Much *steel* is *still* imported.
4. The *team* counted on *Tim*.
5. Ten *sheep* were sent by *ship*.
6. A rod and *reel* were lost in the *rill*.
7. The *deed* he *did* took courage.
8. At *least* ten items were on the *list*.
9. His *feet* were the right size; the shoes didn't *fit*.
10. *Cheap* paint will *chip*.
11. Sue broke her *heel* when she climbed up the *hill*.
12. The *leaking* jar was good for *licking*.

/ɪ/ (ĭ) in Unstressed Syllables

The vowel /ɪ/ occurs rather frequently in the unstressed syllables of many polysyllabic words, as in add*ed*, fret*ted*, tep*id*, *in*ept, *in*stead, and *im*ply. In some instances, the speaker may use the vowel /ə/ rather than /ɪ/ in the unstressed syllable. The following word lists will provide practice with the /ɪ/ in unstressed positions.

practice	wedded	impart	plosive
merit	sterile	instead	corrosive
encrusted	junket	inept	listed
frosting	rusted	immerse	watches
bursting	tempted	intend	matches

In the following lists, the /ɪ/ may occur in either the stressed or the unstressed syllable or syllables, as well as in both syllables of the compound words. Some of the unstressed syllables may be pronounced with /ə/.

finish	filmstrip	imprinting	hissing
impending	picnic	finicky	statistics
implicit	rivet	instinctive	simplicity
inflict	impinge	misgiving	indicative
intuitive	kindling	consistent	linguistic
limpid	thicket	insipid	trivet

primitive instincts	simplistic insistence
vivid intelligence	implicit statistic
thrilling tidbit	inhibited kinship

/e/ (ā) As in *Mate*

/e/ is a midhigh, front vowel. Most Americans are more likely to produce the vowel /e/ as part of the diphthong /eɪ/ than as a pure vowel. Whether produced as part of a diphthong or as a pure sound, /e/ is a tense, front, midhigh vowel (see the front-vowel diagram, Figure 12–1).

Some speakers use the diphthongal form more or less regularly in a stressed syllable and the pure vowel form in an unstressed syllable. There are, however, no words in our language that would be distinguished in meaning from one another on the basis of the use of a pure vowel /e/ or the diphthongal form /eɪ/. We do not recommend the cultivation of either form for the sake of consistency. We do, however, recommend that excessive prolongation of the diphthong to a triphthong [eɪə] be avoided.

The vowel /e/ or the diphthong /eɪ/ is most frequently represented in spelling by the letter *a*, as in *date*, *mate*, and *hate;* other frequent spellings include *ay, ai, ey,* and *ei,* as in *say, mail, they,* and *vein.*

PRACTICE MATERIALS

ace	angel	aviary	ate
ail	April	ape	ache
age	aim	aviator	aid
apex	Asia	eighteen	aphid *louse*
base	brake	trait	braided
bait	crate	chaotic	fateful
bail	place	grate	station
deign	plate	lace	caged
date	rate	chaste	strafe
sake	flake	awake	failure
away	filet	sleigh	replay
dray	repay	dismay	relay
shay	delay	bay	ray
pay	hay	neigh	portray
day	may	betray	fray
weigh	they	play	display
native	abate	restate	ratio

Note whether you distinguish between the vowel and the diphthong forms in the following sentences. Careful listening may help you to decide that the sentence context may make a difference.

1. Peyton draped crepe paper around his place.

2. Jesse James was outraged by the railroad station's great unbreakable safe.

3. May has thirty-one days.

4. Jane was fond of angel food cake or anything else that Nathan would bake for her.

5. Casco Bay is in the state of Maine.

6. Dale won the relay race on Saturday.

7. Crane saw strange shapes riding in the gray mist.
8. Raymond gazed in dismay at stagestruck Rachel.
9. Grace watched the plane fly off into space.
10. *Arizona Ames* is a tale by Zane Grey.
11. Stacey complained of a variety of aches and pains.
12. The caged lion was enraged.

SELECTIONS

1. If I can stop one heart from breaking,
   I shall not live in vain;
   If I can ease one life the aching,
   Or cool one pain,
   Or help one fainting robin
   Unto his nest again,
   I shall not live in vain.

   —EMILY DICKINSON, *Part I, Life*

2. Dale said, ''Good day,''
   And left the fray
   And lived to play
   Another day.

3. In one of his fables, Aesop stated that it is easy to be brave from a safe and distant place.

4. Let us have faith that right makes might.

   —ABRAHAM LINCOLN, Address, *Cooper Union, 1960*

5. He left the name at which the world grew pale,
   To point a moral, or adorn a tale.

   —SAMUEL JOHNSON, *The Vanity of Human Wishes*

6. A little rule, a little sway,
   A sunbeam in a winter's day,
   Is all the proud and might have
   Between the cradle and the grave.

   —JOHN DYER, *Grongar Hill*

/ɛ/ (ĕ) As in *Help*

/ɛ/ (ĕ) is a midfront vowel. The vowel /ɛ/ (ĕ) differs from /e/ (ā) in that the former is produced with a slightly lower front tongue position and *without articulary tension*.

The most frequent spelling for the vowel /ɛ/ is the single letter *e*; other spellings include *a* as in *any*, *ay* as in *says*, *ai* as in *said*, and *ea* as in *bread*. The vowel /ɛ/ is also heard in the words *bury*, *guess*, and *leopard*.

PRACTICE MATERIALS

In the lists of words for initial and medial /ɛ/, avoid any tendency to prolong the vowel into the diphthong /ɛə/.

edit	enemy	elegant	engineer
effort	emblem	enzyme	enterprise

ebb	empty	enter	engine
end	any	energy	exit
echo	elf	elk	elder
egg	elbow	edge	effort
etch	edible	entry	extra
else	edit	ensign	empire
attend	second	tether	trend
reckon	restless	festive	gender
beckon	said	jest	center
lend	gem	wren	theft
guess	thread	deaf	health
pleasant	meant	check	pensive
self	tent	ready	settler
friend	chest	descent	weather

PHRASES

meant well	bent for hell
guess again	friend in the end
steady trend	desert weather
elfin jests	tense elders
edible eggs	pensive Frenchmen
ready guests	gentle echoes
enter and exit	thefts of gems
pleasant self	beckon the deaf
messy chest	lent the rent
bent head	spent wealth
guest for the quest	stealthy elf

SENTENCES

1. Betty sent a letter every day to her best friend, Edna Phelps.
2. Ned, although wealthy, avoided getting into debt.
3. Many men and women are deaf because they will not attend to any but themselves.
4. Jerrie sent her regrets to Heddy because she could not attend the weekend reception.
5. Stella was energetic and often restless, yet seldom ready for steady effort.
6. The leopard spends little effort in meaningless gestures.
7. Wilde held that he could resist everything except temptation.
8. Bellow's terrier was adept at picking up the scent.
9. Edna developed her method by deft and careful measurements.
10. The empty room held the breath of Beth's perfume.

SELECTIONS

1. The rest to some faint meaning make pretence,
   But Shadwell never deviates into sense.

   —JOHN DRYDEN, *Mac Flecknoe*

2. And Marlowe, Webster, Fletcher, Ben,
   Whose fire-hearts sowed our furrows when
   The world was worthy of such men.
   —ELIZABETH BARRETT BROWNING, *A Vision of Poets*

3. Were it not better to forget
   Than but remember and regret?
   —LETITIA LANDON, *Despondency*

4. I do not love thee, Doctor Fell.
   The reason why I cannot tell;
   But this alone I know full well,
   I do not love thee, Doctor Fell.
   —THOMAS BROWN, *Verses Written As a Student at Oxford*

Make certain that clear distinctions are made for the vowels in the italicized words in the sentences that follow.

1. The *pen* was placed next to the *pin*.
2. *Ed* called for *aid*.
3. *Fred* was seldom *afraid*.
4. *Ben*, where have you *been?* bɪN   Buet Bɛn
5. The *men* were mean and *lean*.
6. The singer was *ready*, but her voice was *reedy*.
7. Sue *said* that she found the *seed*.
8. *Fred* fought to be *freed*.

/æ/ (ă) As in *Bat*

/æ/ (ă) is a low, front vowel. It is almost always produced with a lax tongue; occasionally some contexts call for a slightly tense tongue, but emphatic tension should be avoided. The tongue is lower in position and the mouth wider open for /æ/ than it is for /ɛ/ (see the front-vowel diagram, Figure 12–1).

The letter *a*, as in *mash*, *pack*, *rack*, and *sack*, is the most frequent spelling representation for the vowel /æ/.

In some parts of the United States, the vowel blend /ɛə/ tends to be substituted for the vowel /æ/. In much of the United States, a vowel closer to /ɛ/ than to /æ/ is heard in words in which the vowel is followed by the sound /r/, as in *marry*, *parry*, *Harry*, and *Mary*.

PRACTICE MATERIALS

Determine your own practice for the following words in which the vowel /æ/ is an acceptable pronunciation. Doubts, if they exist, should be determined by the usage of respected speakers in your community.

bad	parrot	clan	slam
map	match	jam	tank
cap	shall	hack	bag
can	carry	fact	trapped
chance	jackal	began	begat
hag	Sally	lamb	path

asp	attic	after	ash
at	anthill	and	answer
angle	antler	act	add
apple	anchor	alkaline	aster
atom	agonize	ample	Alice
angry	abduct	annual	Alps
clash	slab	tagged	brash
crab	wrap	trapper	crash
crack	lacking	jagged	hack
stack	slapped	ragged	wax
mash	flax	flagging	hatched
pack	bagged	wrapped	satin

PHRASES

brash prank	tangled and mangled
Andy's antics	dappled band
candy and jam	ham sandwich
crack back	animal crackers
ragged and jagged crags	sagging flags
pack the bags	agonizing answer
apple mash	stand fast
wham bam	stand on hands
facts and fancies	bag of plans
sang on the strand	fantastic plans

SENTENCES

1. Frank is a crackerjack at racking and stacking packages.
2. Hank carried into the camp a bag of apples strapped to his backpack.
3. Fran was in a time jam and used Pam's notes to cram for the last exam.
4. The Swiss Alps have many jagged peaks and crags.
5. Jam and pancakes make a snack for a boy and a meal for a man.
6. Tad fancied himself a man of unflagging action.
7. Alan went to California to enhance his acting career.
8. A good match is preceded by a good catch.
9. The cab's wheels sank deep into the sand.
10. Calvin's spirits never flagged, though he was hatless and ragged.
11. A hammer rather than an ax should be used for banging a tack.
12. Sam wrapped Jan's ham sandwiches in wax sacks.

In the following sentences be careful to avoid excessive tension or nasality in the vowels of the italicized words. Keep your jaw and tongue relaxed.

1. *"Can Hank manage* the task?" asked *Nathaniel.*
2. "The *ban* on *canned ham* is dropped," announced *Pam.*

3. *Dan* and *Sam* ran a fast race on the *strand.*

4. Alfred had *random* thoughts when he *catnapped.*

5. *Frank planned* to raise *Angus* cattle.

6. *Andrew* enjoyed *active* sports *and planned matches.*

7. Sally, who was no *namby-pamby,* lived in a *narrow* house in a *narrow* alley.

SELECTIONS

1. Close to the sun in lonely lands,
   He clasps the crag with crooked hands;
   Ring'd with the azure world he stands.
   —ALFRED, LORD TENNYSON, *In Memoriam*

2. He casts off his friends, as a huntsman his pack,
   For he knew when he pleas'd he could whistle them back.
   —OLIVER GOLDSMITH, *Retaliation*

3. Daniel wanted a girl to marry:
   He loved Pam and Fran and also Sharrie;
   He asked, then prayed one would not tarry—
   She'd be the girl that he would marry.

   But Dan, because he was not chary,
   Found that his plan would soon miscarry,
   For Pam and Fran as well as Sharrie
   Would not accept Dan as one to marry.

   Now Dan, poor Dan,
   Had neither Pam
   Nor Fran
   Nor Sharrie;
   Said Dan, "I will not tarry,
   The girl for me
   Is really Carrie."

   —J. E., *Miscarried Aspiration*

/a/ (à)

/a/ (à) is a low, front, lax vowel.

We are intentionally excluding a key word for the vowel /a/ because most Americans use this sound not as a pure vowel but only as the first element of the diphthong /aɪ/, as in *I, my,* and *ice.* The pure vowel /a/ is used by a minority of American speakers, most of whom probably reside in the New England area. These speakers would use the vowel in words such as *ask, grass,* and *mask.*

In regard to tongue position, the vowel /a/ is a compromise between the front vowel /æ/ (ă) and the low, back vowel /ɑ/ (ä), as in *calm.*

There is, of course, no objection to cultivating the vowel /a/ if there is some cultural reason for doing so. We would suggest, however, if you do "cultivate" this vowel, that the practice be accompanied by some degree of consistency and that you avoid fluctuating between /a/ in *dance, craft,* and *mask* and /æ/ for *France, laugh,* and *ask.*

PRACTICE MATERIALS

Determine your practice in the use of the vowel /æ/ or /a/ for the following materials. Consistency of vowel pronunciation is recommended but not prescribed.

half	class	last	mast
ask	calf	advance	dance
grass	task	craft	demand
mask	laugh	France	bath
pass	staff	laugh	bask

SENTENCES

1. The birds took their bath in the moist grass.
2. We attended a dance wearing masks.
3. The craft took off for France.
4. The cowboy's task was to rope the calf.
5. Cass attended his last class at Harvard.
6. Claspell danced along the path when his master-of-arts degree was granted.
7. The command staff studied their plans on the top of a cask.
8. The branding of calves is a vanishing craft.
9. Half of the staff enjoyed the laugh.
10. By chance, Chancellor found the pass.
11. The advanced class had demanding tasks.
12. Laughingly, Dan took his stance as he clasped his black hat.

The Back Vowels

/a/ (ä) As in *Calm*

/a/ (ä) is a low, back, lax vowel. The back vowels, we recall, are those that are produced with the back of the tongue most active (see Figure 12–2). In changing from the low, front vowel /æ/ to the back vowel /a/, the tongue arching is moved from the front to the back of the tongue.

The vowel /a/ is produced with the tongue in about as low a position as it is likely to assume without the application of direct external pressure to the flat of the tongue. The mouth is open wide and the lips are unrounded.

In spelling, the /a/ is most frequently represented by the letters *a* and *o*. In words such as *ah, alms, charm, psalm,* and *balm,* the sound /a/ is consistently heard throughout the United States. In the words *hot, cot, cog, ox,* and *stock,* there is less consistency in pronunciation. Many speakers use the /a/ vowel, but others use a variant with lip rounding /ɒ/ (ŏ), which is absent for /a/.

Still others use the vowel /ɔ/ (ô), or one very close to it, in words such as *balm, calm,* and *psalm.*

PRACTICE MATERIALS

ah	Arnold	argyle	argosy
are	argue	arbor	ardent
alms	archer	army	Arthur
armor	artful	ark	archives
aqua	dark	harmed	father
alarm	hearten	qualify	balmy
calm	guard	sergeant	carved
cargo	bother	parked	partner

quality cargo	sergeant of the guard
calm charmer	smart partner
scarred farthing	artful archer
Arctic stars	charms of palms

SENTENCES

1. Arnold was a watchful guard.
2. Arthur wanted to live on a farm.
3. Clark was the first to see the star in the dark sky.
4. Though the weather was balmy, the army sergeant wore his parka.
5. Varnish may conceal a large amount of tarnish.
6. Martha was an ardent bargain hunter.
7. When Charles became a father, he was alarmed to realize that he was not as calm as a guardian angel.
8. Noah's ark had a well-guarded cargo.

Most speakers use the vowel /ɑ/ for the following words with *o* spellings. Others modify the sound by some lip rounding and so produce a sound that is or approximates /ɒ/ (ŏ).

Determine your tendency by looking at your mouth in a mirror as you practice with the following materials.

bog	odd	nod	pod	groggy
cod	option	cot	otter	docket
olive	cog	job	fodder	potted
Bob	Robin	knob	farthing	rotted
bomb	jog	cobweb	sodden	cognate
robin	rocky	romp	swab	motto
occupy	frog	rob	locket	socket
ox	hot	hod	respond	rocket
got	golf	pocket	stop	topper

spotted the plot	locked box
soggy frock	toss the rock
shock of fodder	hot pot
dogged golfer	frog on a log
mock bomb	rotted bog

SENTENCES

1. Jock, an old Scot, carried a frog in the pocket of his golf bag.
2. Stockwell was shocked to learn that a robber stole his stopwatch.
3. *Lox* is a term for the liquid oxygen used as a fuel for rockets.
4. Robert sat calmly on the rock despite the hot weather.
5. Alfalfa is a crop used as fodder for stock.
6. Mollie, the fishmonger, sold cod and haddock.
7. Botwell was locked up for watering stock.
8. A frog may frighten an ox.
9. Olive had to exercise an odd option.
10. We were too shocked to respond after we were robbed.
11. Bob Stockton insists that nobody knows who killed Cock Robin.
12. Lucy put her locket in her pocket to hide it from Curly Locks.

SELECTIONS

1. Hickory dickory dock,
   A frog jumped on the clock;
   The clock struck one,
   This was no fun,
   The frog preferred a log.

2. Camelot, a dot
   Of space in time,
   Begot
   By need of man
   To spot and plot
   A dream
   Of what
   Man hopes of man:
   Of Lancelot
   Tried by Guinevere,
   Of Arthur
   Tried by love and fear
   And knowing
   More than he could know.
   Camelot, a dot
   Of time that was, to be
   A spot to plot
   And prophetically, to see.
   　　　　—J. E., Suggested by T. H. White's *The Once and Future King*

3. "Who killed Cock Robin?"
   "Not I," said Rob.
   "Not I," said Bob.
   So we'll not know
   Who did this job.

/ɒ/ (ŏ)

/ɒ/ is a low, back, lax, rounded vowel.

As noted in the immediately preceding discussion, the vowel /ɒ/ is used by some Americans in words in which the vowel /ɑ/ is used by others. The vowel /ɒ/ is also used as a variant for the vowel /ɔ/ (ô), as in *dog* and *cough*.

In manner of production and in acoustic impression, /ɒ/ is somewhere between /ɔ/ and /ɑ/. The vowel /ɑ/ is low and lax and is produced with a slight rounding of the lips.

No list can be given of words for which the vowel /ɒ/ is consistently used through-out the United States, or even in any major area within the United States. Although not confined to eastern New England, the sound /ɒ/ is more likely to be heard there than elsewhere.

The vowel /ɒ/ may be heard in words in which the spelling includes the letter *o* followed by the consonants /f/, /θ/ (th), or /s/. It is not, however, limited to these spellings.

PRACTICE MATERIALS

In the practice materials that follow, determine what your pronunciation is for the key words, and compare your pronunciation with that of the respected members of your community. First, however, you may wish to review the previous word lists and sentences for the vowels /ɑ/ or /ɒ/. Do you pronounce any with the vowel /ɔ/ (ô), as in *ball?*

boss	froth	across	office
cloth	loft	along	aloft
cost	lost	glossy	choral
florid	song	moral	floral
floss	toss	mossy	wrongly
fog	crotch	Tom	porridge

PHRASES

costly crossing	frothy broth
flossy moss	odd job
lost officer	immoral choral
tossed aloft	sorry loss
soft morals	hot coffee
lot of bombast	potted hogwash

SENTENCES

1. Ross objected to the accusation that he was lost in the fog.
2. Socrates and Aristotle were ancient Greek philosophers.
3. Olga was not superstitious, but she was often seen to knock on wood.
4. Roth crossed the office to the coffeepot.
5. Bob and Rosalie scoffed at the florid Bostonian officer's morals.
6. Foster tossed glossy paint on the canvas in his loft.

7. Rose walked softly across the mossy forest sod.
8. The frosty weather made Ross cough.
9. Coffee has become a costly broth.
10. A moth should not scoff at the flame.

SELECTION

The moonlight is the softest, in Kentucky,
Summer days come oftest, in Kentucky,
Friendship is the strongest
Love's fires glow the longest
Yet a wrong is always wrongest
  In Kentucky.

—JAMES H. MULLIGAN, *In Kentucky*

Additional practice material is provided following the discussion of the vowel /ɔ/ (ô).

/ɔ/ (ô) As in *Author*

/ɔ/ (ô) is a low, back vowel produced with definite lip rounding. The tongue is slightly higher for /ɔ/ than it is for /ɑ/ and /ɒ/ (see the back-vowel diagram, Figure 12–2).

The most frequent spellings for /ɔ/ include *a* as in *ball*, *aw* as in *lawful*, *au* as in *taught*, *ou* as in *bought*, and *o* as in *horse*.

In many words, including some of those used as examples in the previous paragraph, the vowel /ɑ/, and less frequently /ɒ/, may be heard instead of /ɔ/. Some of the variations are more-or-less uniform according to geographic regions; others seem to be more individualized, according to the speaker's choice.

PRACTICE MATERIALS

If you are not certain of your own pronunciation habits, practice before a mirror will help to distinguish the /ɔ/ from the /ɑ/ pronunciation. If you wish to establish a clear distinction, make certain that your lips are rounded for /ɔ/; for /ɑ/, the lips are less rounded, and the tongue is lax.

In the list that follows, the words of the first two columns are most likely to be pronounced with the vowel /ɔ/; the words of the other columns are likely to be pronounced with /ɑ/ or /ɒ/. The vowel /ɔ/ may, however, be used for any of these words.

hall	hawk	song	frog
ball	sawing	wrong	torrid
fought	call	soft	orange
taught	chalk	lost	foreign
wall	flawless	off	porridge
August	awesome	cost	forest
auto	claws	coffin	horrible

The words in the following list are most likely to be pronounced with the vowel /ɔ/ rather than either of the other back vowels we have studied.

author	calked	orphan	stall
awkward	yawn	north	organ
tall	falter	halt	thorn
nought	ordeal	shawl	horse
horn	fourth	reform	snort
corn	born	morbid	scorned
fortune	mourning	normal	storm

PHRASES

stalking-horse	morbid author
August storm	law and order
normally warm	orphan of the storm
corn stalk	born to yawn
pause for nought	calked yawl
warm shawl	fourth brawl
orderly borders	snort in scorn
fawn at dawn	flora and fauna

SENTENCES

1. Dawson was taught to be a quarterback.

2. The cautious crew balked at manning the yawl into a squall.

3. Sawyer, a politician, called for law and order though he was appalled at the faults of the laws.

4. Augusta found it an awful ordeal to listen to the author's halting, faltering reading of his paltry lines.

5. Morbid tall stories leave some people yawning.

6. Kansas is proud to be corny in August.

7. Quarter horses don't always cost a fortune.

8. Saul's widow wore a black shawl as a token of her mourning.

9. Paul called to inform us that automobile traffic was stalled on the northbound lanes, but normal toward the south.

10. Norman, a tall adolescent, was normally awkward.

11. Any safe port is a good port to be sought in a storm.

12. Coventry Patmore held that ''Love was the sole mortal thing of worth immortal.''

SELECTIONS

1. Small showers last long, but sudden storms are short.
                                    —WILLIAM SHAKESPEARE, *Richard II*

2. Ah, distinctly I remember it was in the
        bleak December;
And each separate dying ember wrought its
        ghost upon the floor,
Eagerly I wished the morrow;—vainly
        I had sought to borrow

From my books surcease of sorrow—
    sorrow for the lost Lenore—
For the rare and radiant maiden whom
    the angels name Lenore—
Nameless *here* for evermore.

—EDGAR ALLAN POE, *The Raven*

3. The law is the true embodiment
    Of everything that's excellent.
    It has no kind of fault or flaw.
    And I, my Lords, embody the law.

—W. S. GILBERT, *Patience*

/o/ (ō) As in *Mode*

/o/ (ō) is a midhigh, rounded, back vowel. (See back-vowel diagram, Figure 12–2, p. 159.) The tongue position is higher for /o/ than for the vowel /ɔ/. The vowel /o/ is only infrequently used as a pure sound. In most contexts, this sound is likely to be lengthened into the diphthong [oʊ].

The most frequent spellings of the vowel /o/ or the diphthong /oʊ/ are the letters *o*, *oe*, *oa*, and *ow*, as in *no*, *foe*, *boat*, and *grow*.

There is no special value in working to maintain a distinction between the vowel /o/ and the diphthong variant /oʊ/. The phonetic context will generally determine whether the vowel or the diphthong will be used. There is value in avoiding an excessive prolongation so that a triphthong ending with a weak vowel /ə/ is produced, and a word such as *hold* [hold] becomes [hoʊəld].

PRACTICE MATERIALS

oh	goad	rogue	forgo
oak	ogre	Olympic	open
oath	okay	omen	opium
oboe	okra	omit	over
ochre	oleander	opal	owe
clove	stove	sew	story
abode	cone	moat	scone
bloat	float	mowing	sole
bowl	grown	roast	stone
chose	hone	rote	tome
coast	lode	soak	towel
coke	lope	sold	whole
cold	lower	soap	zone
ago	follow	Ohio	sloe
beau	glow	potato	slow
doe	hollow	roe	though
ego	Joe	row	toe
flow	low	show	woe

PHRASES

Idaho potato	yeoman host
frozen cold	approach the post
bold fellow	notorious host
strove for glory	old domain
stoic chauffeur	most thorough
bony roast	honing stone

SENTENCES

1. Yellow Hair's soldiers opened the road to the Dakota goldfields.

2. Jones had a toehold on the steep slope but still had to hold on to the rope.

3. Joe's host served a roast that was worthy of his glowing boast.

4. Low clouds drifted over the coast.

5. Some folks make their homes in geodesic domes.

6. The old tug slowly towed the showboat down the Ohio with the river's flow.

7. Smoke from burning coke and coal rose into the ozone.

8. Homer's epic poetry told of hope and sorrow.

9. Hogan's goat loped over the frozen slope.

10. O'Neal was broke, but no one would float him a loan.

SELECTIONS

1. Rattle his bones over the stones.
He's only a pauper whom nobody owns.
—THOMAS NOLL, *The Pauper's Drive*

2. Silence is no certain token
That no secret grief is there;
Sorrow which is never spoken
Is the heaviest load to bear.
—FRANCES R. HAVERGAL, *Misunderstood*

3. Death is a common friend or foe,
As different men may hold,
And at his summons each must go,
The timid and the bold.
—MICHAEL JOSEPH BARRY, *The Place Where Men Should Die*

/ʊ/ (o͝o) As in *Book* and /u/ (o͞o) As in *Pool*

/ʊ/ (o͝o) is a high, back, lip-rounded vowel. The tongue is lax and in a higher position than for the vowel /o/.

The spellings for /ʊ/ include *u* as in *pull*, *full*, and *put; oo* as in *book* and *cook; ou* as in *could* and *would;* and *o* as in *wolf.*

In many words of old English origin, especially those spelled with *oo*, practice varies as to the use of /ʊ/ or the vowel /u/ (o͞o). For comparative purposes, therefore, we need to describe the vowel /u/.

/u/ (ōō) is characterized by more lip rounding than any of the other vowels in American-English speech. /u/ is the highest of the back vowels (see back-vowel diagram, Figure 12–2, and compare /ʊ/ and /u/). The tongue is tense, in contrast with the lax tongue for /ʊ/. The most frequent spellings for /u/ are *oo* as in *school, fool, ooze,* and *choose; o* as in *do; u* as in *dupe;* and *ou* as in *coup* and *soup*.

The distinction between /ʊ/ and /u/ may be brought out by a comparison of the pronunciation of the following pairs of words.

/ʊ/	/u/	/ʊ/	/u/
book	boon	pull	pool
brook	bruise	roof	rule
crook	croon	shook	shoed
look	Luke	stood	stewed
nook	noon	wood	wooed

Determine your pronunciation of the words on the following lists. If your tongue is tense and your lips rounded, you are using the vowel phoneme /u/; if your tongue feels relaxed and your lips are not so distinctively rounded, then you are probably using the vowel phoneme /ʊ/. Do not be surprised if you are not entirely consistent in your vowel usage for the words that follow. Many Americans vary according to the individual word. Make certain, however, that your pronunciation is distinctly either /u/ or /ʊ/.

pull	pool
roof	hoop
room	hooves
broom	root
group	rule
soot	suit

PRACTICE MATERIALS

The material that follows is for practice with the vowel /ʊ/. Note its regular occurrence as a medial sound.

cushion	bullet	courier	footwear
would	bully	crooked	tourist
hook	bulwark	cuckoo	woody
boor	bushing	durable	woofer
moor	butcher	rookie	wool
booklet	bouillon	hooded	goodness
Buddhism	boulevard	took	soot
ambush	cookie	bushel	pushed

PHRASES

hooked a cookie	took the books
boorish moor	bushel of soot
good wood	wooden bookcase
rookie courier	Lynbrook Boulevard
durable bulwark	took booklets
sugary pudding	neighborhood bulletin

SENTENCES

1. Goodman took Buddy Wolfe's hand and shook it.
2. No one could say whether the butcher was an unhooded crook.
3. The cook took the cookies from the oven and put in a well-seasoned pullet.
4. Woodville did not believe that good books could be misunderstood.
5. Brooks, a bulwark in her neighborhood, read the bulletin from a wooden platform on the roof.
6. Cardinal Cooke read the papal bull from the pulpit.
7. We took the rural path across the bushy moor.
8. Hook gave Mrs. Bull a bushel of cookies.
9. Being hoodwinked means having the wool pulled over your eyes.
10. We pulled out of the woods when we saw a wolf.

/u/ (o͞o)

The following material is for practice with the vowel /u/.

hoop	cool	doom	fruit
jubilee	raccoon	dual	gooey
junior	cooper	dues	goon
roost	coulee	duel	glue
womb	coupon	duke	goose
croup	croon	dune	hoot
boob	crouton	duty	July
boon	crude	fluid	loop
boot	clue	fool	loose
bouffant	crusade	frugal	rumor

PHRASES

booted fools	June moon
crusading duke	shrewd baboon
gloomy groom	soup spoon
womb to tomb	cool fruit
loose rumors	crude glue
Lou and Sue	too soon to sue

SENTENCES

1. During July, at noon, Cooper cools off in the pool.
2. The duke led his troops in the crusade.
3. Ruth gets moody when someone croons "Blue Moon."
4. Lou said he was one who knew the plural of mongoose.
5. Fools in some groups prefer rumors to truth.
6. Newman did not choose the brew; he preferred the stew.
7. The shrew threw a soup spoon at the goose.
8. The overripe fruit oozed a sugary gooey fluid.
9. Cooper rued the day he played the buffoon.

10. June is a woman of many moods.
11. Two fools fought a duel in the dunes.
12. The crooner loved to rhyme *soon* and *moon*.

Many /u/ words are preceded by the sound /j/ (y) as in *you, youth, use,* and *hue*. In some of these words, the spelling *y* suggests the sound /j/, but in others the spelling is not a guide to the pronunciation. The following list contains some of the more frequent /ju/ words. Note the frequency of *hu* spellings.

fuse	useful	feud	hew
you	utilize	cue	accuse
youth	mule	mute	huge
usury	hue	imbue	humor
unique	pupil	review	pew
eulogy	amuse	few	humid
humus	humane	Hugh	Hugo

PHRASES

unique humor	huge pew
humane use	used a few
refused to review	fused the feud
amusing eulogy	mute accusation
accused youth	mute pupil

SENTENCES

1. Few youths enjoy humid weather.
2. Our usury laws need review.
3. The mute mule carried a huge load.
4. Eulogies are not intended to be amusing nor unduly platitudinous.
5. The unique feud began over a ewe and was resumed every Tuesday.

There is considerable regional and individual variation in the use of /ju/ (y$\overline{oo}$) or /u/ ($\overline{oo}$) for some words. Tendencies exist on historical bases and may influence local and individual pronunciations. In general, our advice is to follow the pronunciations of persons in your community whose speech is deserving of respect. Do not strain for consistency for groups of words. Instead, work for consistency in the acceptable pronunciation of individual words.

ADDITIONAL PRACTICE MATERIALS

SENTENCES

1. There was much ado resulting from loose rumors about Hughes the recluse.
2. Lucy had to choose whether to buy good boots or new books.
3. A few groupings of ever-blooming bushes grew in the humid garden.

4. The detective reviewed her clues about the stolen jewels.
5. The well-ruled troops moved through the woods.
6. Too few students utilize the knowledge they accrue.
7. Rupert spooned out raccoon stew and put croutons in the soup.
8. Duke saw a blue bull in the bushes, but refused to pursue it.
9. The youths in the pew grew gloomy when the unmoving eulogy was read from the pulpit.
10. Ruth's hat was adorned with a blue goose plume.
11. Drury was neither crude nor rude but he did enjoy a chance to brood.
12. Hooper tootled his flute and played music to suit his mood.

SELECTIONS

1. Give me the room whose every nook
Is dedicated to a book.
—FRANK DEMPSTER SHERMAN, *The Library*
2. Every new movement or manifestation of human activity, when unfamiliar to people's minds, is sure to be misrepresented and misunderstood.
—EDWARD CARPENTER, *The Drama of Love and Death*
3. Lewis was mute about an issue he considered to be moot. Rufus wanted to pursue the issue and viewed Lewis as being snooty for his mutism. When Lewis finally did choose to speak, all that he said was, "Rufus, you may choose to argue, but I don't give a hoot."
4. In his review of *Aikin's Life of Addison*, Macaulay, an astute critic, wrote, "The highest proof of virtue is to possess boundless power without abusing it."
5. W. S. Gilbert, who wrote spoofy lines to Arthur Sullivan's tunes, with good humor asked:

Wherefore waste our elocution
On impossible solution?

Surely, and astutely, he advised:

Life's a pleasant institution,
Let us take it as it comes.
—Adapted from *The Gondoliers*

Central Vowels

The *central vowels* are those that are made with the middle of the tongue arched toward the palate. The central vowels include /ɝ/ (ûr), /ɜ/ (ûr), /ɚ/ (ər), /ə/ (ə), and /ʌ/ (ŭ) (see central-vowel diagram, Figure 12–3, p. 159).

Syllable stress is often the determining factor that differentiates one central vowel from another. A second feature is the presence or absence of *r* coloring. For example, the vowels of *further* may be either /ɝ/ (ûr), or /ʌr/ (ŭr) in the stressed syllable and /ɚ/ or /ə/ in the unstressed syllable, depending on regional usage. Similar vowel differences are found in the words *curler*, *hurler*, and *purser*. In our descriptions of the central vowels, we emphasize the position of the vowel in regard to these features: syllable stress and *r* coloring.

/ɝ/ (ûr) or /ɜ/ As in *Bird, Curl,* and *World*

Most Americans use the vowel /ɝ/ in the previously indicated key words and in the accented syllable of words such as *avert, guerdon, journal,* and *unfurl*. Some phoneticians consider the /ɝ/ to be essentially a variety of the /r/ sound and suggest that the articulation of the sound can best be acquired by lengthening the initial /r/ of words such as *rose, red,* and *rim*. Such an /r/ might be produced with the tongue as a whole slightly retracted and the middle of the tongue raised toward the soft palate. We may think of the sound /ɝ/ as a vowel blended with the vowelized consonant /r/. The lips are unrounded for the production of /ɝ/.

Speakers who generally do not use the /r/ sound except when the letter *r* is immediately followed by a vowel are likely also to use /ɜ/ rather than /ɝ/ in the key words given in the preceding paragraph. The sound /ɜ/ is produced with a slightly lower tongue position, with the lips unrounded, and without the /r/ coloring of /ɝ/.

The use of /ɝ/ or /ɜ/ is largely a matter of regional practice. In the list of words that follows, most Americans would use /ɝ/. Many speakers in New England, in New York City, and in the southern coastal states, however, use /ɜ/. Individual speakers who have been influenced by British speech or who were trained for the stage with eastern or British "standard" diction might also use /ɜ/, regardless of where they live.

We may note that the spelling of words in which /ɝ/ or /ɜ/ is used usually includes the letters *ur, or, ir,* or *ear*. The word *colonel* is one of the few exceptions in which the spelling does not include the letter *r*.

Some speakers substitute the diphthongal blend /ɜɪ/ for the vowel /ɜ/. The word *bird* may then become [bɜɪd] and *girl* may become [gɜɪl]. This diphthongal variant seems acceptable to many speakers in the South.

PRACTICE MATERIALS

earl	ergot	irk	urbane
early	ermine	Irma	urchin
earn	err	Irwin	urgent
erg	erstwhile	urban	urn
birch	germ	lurk	term
birth	gird	mirth	terse
curb	gurgle	nerve	turban
curt	herb	pearl	turf
dirge	herd	purse	turn
dirt	hurt	spurn	verse
fern	jerk	surge	virtue
flirt	learn	swerve	work
aver	deter	inter	sir
blur	err	occur	spur
burr	fur	purr	stir
cur	her	refer	were
demur	infer	shir	whir

PHRASES

assert firmly	disturbed purser
curved surface	certain person
tense sermon	earnest urging
affirm and aver	unfurl with a swirl
irksome urchin	avert being hurt
determined person	swerving skirts
shirk the burden	certain purpose
worried personnel	worthy circles
burrow in the furrow	rehearse the verse

SENTENCES

1. Birds work to find worms lurking in turf.
2. The crew worked in earnest to avert collison with the iceberg.
3. Sir Bertram Burbank preferred to adjourn rather than demur.
4. Colonel Burton took his furlough in Berkeley.
5. Erwin was stirred by the fervent urge of the sermon.
6. The whirring turbine produced the urgently needed current.
7. It took courage for Curt to spur his pony into the whirling herd.
8. The customers were terse but the merchant far from taciturn.
9. A bird in the hand is worth a good deal on earth.
10. Shirley did not bestir herself to avert the falling urn.
11. Turner spurned any purse he did not earn.
12. Gilbert's captain of the *Pinafore* served a term in an attorney's firm.

SELECTIONS

1. Werther had a love for Charlotte
    Such as words could never utter;
 Would you know how first he met her?
    She was cutting bread and butter.

 Charlotte was a married lady,
    And a moral man was Werther,
 And for all the wealth of Indies,
    Would do nothing for to hurt her.
          —WILLIAM MAKEPEACE THACKERAY, *Sorrows of Werther*

2. The flowers appear on the earth; the time of the singing of birds is come, and the voice of the turtle is heard in our land.
          —*Ecclesiastes*, 10–12

3. In his essay *The World*, the Earl of Chesterton wrote: "I assisted at the birth of that most significant word 'flirtation' which dropped from the most beautiful mouth in the world."

4. There once was a girl named Myrtle
    Whose mind was earnest and fertile;
 She trained Burton, her purple pet
    turtle
 A thirty foot fence to hurtle.
    Poor Myrtle,

Poor turtle!
Had Myrtle trained Burton to skirtle
Or spurn what he could not hurtle
Myrtle would still have her turtle
As well as a mind that was earnest
and fertile.

—J. E., *Dirge for a Purple Turtle*

/ɚ/ /ər/ (ər) and /ə/ (ə) As in Unstressed Syllables of *Ever* and *Other; About* and *Sofa*

The vowel /ɚ/ is the unstressed "equivalent" of /ɝ/. In words such as *earner* and *murmur*, the first syllable vowels are stressed and so are pronounced as /ɝ/ by most American speakers. The second, unstressed, syllable is pronounced /ɚ/ by the same speakers—the majority of Americans who habitually pronounce medial or final *r*'s whenever the letter occurs in the spelling of the word.

/ɚ/ is a lax, unrounded midvowel. It has a lower tongue position than /ɝ/. Because of its occurrence in the unstressed position, /ɚ/ is less intense and shorter in duration than its stressed counterpart.

/ə/ is a midvowel produced with a lax tongue and unrounded lips in a position slightly lower than /ɜ/.

/ə/, the vowel *schwa* (a weak or neutral vowel), is probably the most frequently used vowel in our language for the following reasons:

1. It is the most frequently used vowel in unstressed syllables regardless of the spelling of the vowel. Some examples of the varied spellings are indicated in the italicized letters of: *a*lone, sof*a*, foc*u*s, lab*e*l, and prec*iou*s.

2. In addition to its occurrence in unstressed syllables of polysyllabic words, /ə/ is also the most frequently used vowel when prepositions, articles, conjunctions, and auxiliary verbs are unstressed in sentence context. For example, in the sentence, "I of*ten* find it difficult *to* believe *the* man," each italicized word or syllable may appropriately be pronounced with the vowel /ə/.

3. The vowel /ə/ also replaces /r/ in words such as *hear, dare,* and *cure* for those speakers who do not pronounce final *r*'s or *r*'s in general unless they are immediately followed by vowels. These, of course, are the same speakers from New England, New York City, and parts of the South who use /ɜ/ rather than /ɝ/ in stressed syllables.

PRACTICE MATERIALS

Check the pronunciation in your community and decide whether you prefer /ɚ/ or /ə/ for the unstressed syllables of the following words and phrases.

amber	cluster	hatter	otter
after	collar	hunter	other
alter	dollar	junior	ponder
answer	drummer	learner	rather
baker	either	leisure	settler
center	further	matter	tether
cleaner	greater	nadir	whether

PHRASES

bother for mother	other brother
fender bender	proper neighbor
leather cleaner	roller coaster
letter opener	summer weather
modern actor	tender murmurs
blunder and wonder	under and over

SENTENCES

1. Ivan's letter deserved a longer and better answer.

2. Basketball players are taller than most other professional athletes.

3. Diller's neighbors sent her flowers and hoped that she would soon be over her illness.

4. After they squandered their treasure, Baker and Peters left the poker table.

5. Anson, a reporter and editor, believed that a newspaper should be accountable to its readers.

6. Palmer could not decide whether he enjoyed seeing himself reflected more in a mirror or in the behavior of his children.

Note the occurrence of the "weak" vowel /ə/ in the unstressed syllables of the words, the phrases, and the sentences that follow.

above	annoy	tuba	American
about	agree	soda	urban
grammar	coma	parade	murmur
oppose	offense	opinion	parade
allow	anoint	data	surgeon
appoint	Texas	Canada	precious
avoid	assist	circus	stirrup
amiss	asunder	opera	typical

PHRASES

around and about	alone in Texas
azaleas and petunias	Alberta in Canada
agree and disagree	Emma and Stella

SENTENCES

1. The speaker spoke with a typical Texas drawl.

2. A tuba may be annoying to hear alone.

3. Canada is north or above the United States of America.

4. Vienna is the capital city of Austria.

5. Sir Francis Bacon, the famous philosopher, was one of Queen Elizabeth I's most intelligent advisers.

6. Edna liked bananas with her breakfast cereal.

7. The Russians opposed every agenda item approved by the Americans.

8. The baritone agreed to sing the aria when he learned that he would be accompanied by the Philadelphia Opera Orchestra.

9. Ella advised Eva that she always avoid annoying gorillas who appeared to be asleep.

10. Matilda Dillon was appointed professor of urban studies at the Metropolitan Junior College in Idaho.

11. Selma, a vegetarian, had an okra salad for luncheon and cucumbers for dinner.

12. Emma was fond of flowers and especially of azaleas and petunias.

/ʌ/ (ŭ) As in *Cup*

/ʌ/ is produced with a relatively relaxed tongue arched a little bit toward the middle or the back of the palate. If it is produced with the middle of the tongue arching, it is a midvowel. Many persons, however, produce the sound with the back tongue arching as for a back vowel rather than a midvowel. Either way, the mouth is open fairly wide *without* lip rounding. The tongue should be arched higher for /ʌ/ than for /ɑ/, so that a clear distinction is made between these vowels and between words such as *sup* and *sop*, *suck* and *sock*, and *nut* and *not*.

The vowel /ʌ/ is represented by several letters in spelling, including *u* as in *cup*, *ou* as in *double*, and *o* as in *done*.

Except for the tendency of some speakers to produce an /ɑ/ instead of /ʌ/, the vowel causes little difficulty. For those persons who may be inclined to make the /ɑ/ substitution, it might be of help to know that /ʌ/ is the vowel that we are alleged to make when we supposedly grunt, "Ugh."

PRACTICE MATERIALS

The first set of exercises should help to establish the distinction between /ʌ/ and /ɑ/. Be certain to raise your tongue slightly higher for /ʌ/ than for /ɑ/. The mouth is somewhat more open for /ɑ/ than for /ʌ/. Note that /ʌ/ appears only in stressed syllables.

/ʌ/	/ɑ/	/ʌ/	/ɑ/
come	calm	gut	got
done	don	color	collar
sup	sop	chuck	cock
cut	cop	hut	hot
muck	mock	fund	fond
dull	doll	bubble	bobble
ruck	rock	bum	bomb
shut	shot	lug	log
slug	slog	buddy	body
nut	not	rump	romp

In the sentences that follow, the first italicized word contains the vowel [ʌ], the second the vowel [ɑ].

1. Do *come* and *calm* down.
2. A job well *done* is what *Don* liked.
3. The *pup* was frightened by the loud *pop*.
4. It was poor *luck* to lose the key to the *lock*.
5. The bear *cub* was fond of corn on the *cob*.
6. The *duck* hunter fired from the *dock*.
7. The *hut* was exposed to the *hot* sun.
8. She *wondered* where he *wandered*.

SELECTIONS

1. By gum and by golly,
   Fun is not folly;
   By golly by gum,
   Folly's not fun.

2. Asked Bumpers of Lumpers,
   "Will you carve this big cod?"
   Replied Lumpers to Bumpers"
   "I will, if you prod."

ADDITIONAL PRACTICE MATERIALS FOR /ʌ/

ulna	umbrage	umpire	unctious
up	other	udder	upward
under	onion	utter	ulcer
us	ugly	uncle	Ulster
upper	usher	oven	ultimate
hustle	bustle	numb	dumb
blubber	chunk	cucumber	discussion
blood	lunge	asunder	mud
blunder	mumble	assumption	much
brother	mutton	begun	rugged
bud	once	benumb	stuck
cub	rubber	instruct	tuck
club	supper	lump	won
done	punish	hungry	thunder
cuff	rough	enough	thumb
love	monkey	honey	funny
buck	bubble	trouble	rubble
buckle	double	thrust	rebuttal

PHRASES

lucky hunch	hungry for money
rugged brother	month of Sundays
supper club	country cousin

double trouble	something for mother
munch for lunch	muddy lump
blunt instruction	rough monkey

SENTENCES

1. Buddy wanted to hunt for another buck in the upland country.

2. Uncle Chuck likes onions and mustard with his mutton.

3. "If that's your assumption," the judge instructed, "you are making an utterly foolish blunder."

4. Dudley hadn't had so good a supper in a month of Sundays.

5. Buckley had muddled her way out of dozens of troubles.

6. Duncan's uncle has ulcers.

7. The umpire raised his thumb and sent one of the benumbed players to the clubhouse.

8. Rough, troubled seas can make landlubbers blubber.

9. Father sewed another button on his young son's cuff.

10. General "Blood and Guts" Patton was considered a blunt, rugged officer.

SELECTIONS

1. It's a song of a merryman, moping mum,
Whose soul was sad, and whose glance was glum,
Who sipped no sup, and who craved no crumb,
As he sighed for the love of a ladye.
　　　　　　　　—W. S. GILBERT, *The Yeoman of the Guard*

2. Life's a pudding full of plums;
Care's a canker that benumbs.
　　　　　　　　—W. S. GILBERT, *The Gondoliers*

3. Not a face below the sun
But is precious—unto one.
　　　　　　　　—SIR EDWIN ARNOLD, *Facies Non Omnibus Una*

4. Double, double, toil and trouble;
Fire burn and cauldron bubble.
　　　　　　　　—WILLIAM SHAKESPEARE, *Macbeth*

5. The camel's hump is an ugly lump
Which well you may see at the Zoo;
But uglier yet is the Hump we get
From having too little to do.
　　　　　　　　—RUDYARD KIPLING, *How the Camel Got His Hump*

6. Love in a hut, with water and a crust,
Is—Love, forgive us! cinders, ashes, dust.
　　　　　　　　—JOHN KEATS, *Poems, Lamia*

7. Wonders are many, and none is more wonderful than man.
　　　　　　　　—SOPHOCLES, *Antigone*

13

Diphthongs

Diphthongs are vocalic glides (a blend of two vowels) that are uttered on a single breath impulse within a single syllable. A superficial analysis of the diphthong as well as a literal interpretation of the term suggests that a diphthong is a combination of two sounds. Ladefoged took exception to the notion that a diphthong is a blend of two vowels:

> Each of these sounds involves a change in quality within the one vowel. As a matter of convenience, they can be described as movements from one vowel to another. The first part of the diphthong is usually more prominent than the last. In fact, the last part is often so brief and transitory that it is difficult to determine its exact quality. Furthermore, contrary to the traditional transcriptions, the diphthongs often do not begin and end with any of the sounds that occur in simple vowels.[1]

Actually, a diphthong is the product of a continuous change of articulatory movement, and so of sound, beginning with the initial vowel of the blend and culminating in the second vowel. The first phonetic symbol of a diphthong really represents the *approximate initial position* of the articulators, and so of the first component sound. The second symbol represents the *approximate final sound*. Thus, the diphthong /ɔɪ/ (oi) is initiated with the sound /ɔ/ (o). The organs of articulation are then modified to produce a continuous change of sound until the diphthong is completed with what approximates the vowel /ɪ/ (ĭ).

First, we will consider three American-English phonemic diphthongs. Each represents a distinctive sound unit, and each serves as a basis by which we distinguish between spoken words not otherwise determined by context. The phonemic diphthongs are /aɪ/ (ī) as in *I* and *my;* /ɔɪ/ (oi) as in *boy* and *toy;* and /ɑʊ/ (ou) as in *house* and *out.*

[1] P. Ladefoged, *A Course in Phonetics* (New York: Harcourt Brace Jovanovich, 1975), p. 69.

Earlier, in our study of the individual vowel sounds, nonphonemic variants of the vowels /e/ (ā) and /o/ (ō) were considered.[2] Another group of sounds that might be considered diphthongal variants are the sound combinations of persons who do not pronounce final *r*'s. This group of sounds includes /ɪə/, /ʊə/, /ɔə/, and /ɛə/ as pronunciations for words such as *dear*, *poor*, *core*, and *care*.

/aɪ/ (ī) As in *Ice* and *Nice; Arrive* and *Reply*

The diphthong /aɪ/ is initiated with a raising of the tongue in the front part of the mouth. It ends, as indicated, with the vowel /ɪ/.

The most frequent spellings for /aɪ/ are *i* at the beginning and in the middle of the words and *y* as the final letter of words, as in *ice*, *spice*, *entice*, *my*, and *cry*.

PRACTICE MATERIALS

I	fine	bright	fired	apply
iambic	pipe	China	fight	astride
icicle	viaduct	cider	fly	beguiling
I'd	abide	citation	high	deny
Idaho	alive	cry	hind	espy
ideal	arrive	dice	mine	pantomime
identity	archive	dine	quite	remind
iodine	bias	dire	side	reply
ion	Bible	devise	pyre	required
ire	biceps	entire	strive	unsightly
ivy	by	file	style	untiring
slice	fried	blight	dive	shine

PHRASES

dry ice	spicy dining
type style	butterfly light
bright smile	ironic hindsight
iron biceps	refined designs
right height	rhyming iambs
sly guile	dire signs
drive by night	slice of pie
light eyes	admire kindness
frightful crime	iodine ions
highly spiced	quite nice
sly and snide	inspiring sight
wise foresight	feisty feline

---

[2] The reference is to the use of /eɪ/ in words such as *ace, ale, tame,* and *base* and the use of /oʊ/ in words such as *oaf, node,* and *pole.* The meanings of these words would not change whether the vowel /e/ or the nonphonemic diphthong /eɪ/ is used for the first series of examples or the vowel /o/ or the diphthong /oʊ/ for the second series.

SENTENCES

1. On Fridays, Myra and Dinah liked to eat fried rice at the Chinese diner.

2. McBride invited Lyons to look at the diagram of his device for exercising his biceps.

3. The night riders were frightened of a daylight flight.

4. Ty Cobb's spikes produced fright when he decided to slide sideways into base.

5. Writers need to be reminded that the use of irony is often as unwise as it is unkind.

6. A tiger without stripes is a dire sight.

7. The guide reminded us of the time our shiny canoe quietly glided beside the island.

8. By midnight Giles still had to drive another ninety-five miles to the dike.

9. We may aspire to pie in the sky, but it is neither a spicy nor a satisfying diet.

10. Bribery and riot are high crimes.

11. The Lord High Executioner aspired to an object sublime, to make each punishment fit the crime.

12. Ida was delighted that her citation would be filed in the Iowa archives.

SELECTIONS

1. There is a smile of love,
And there is a smile of deceit,
And there is a smile of smiles
In which these two smiles meet.

—WILLIAM BLAKE, *The Smile*

2. Tiger! Tiger! burning bright
In the forests of the night,
What immortal hand or eye
Could frame thy fearful symmetry?

—WILLIAM BLAKE, *The Tiger*

3. My object all sublime
I shall achieve in time—
To make the punishment fit the crime.

—W. S. GILBERT, *The Mikado*

4. A silence in thy life when, through the night,
The bell strikes, or the sun, with sinking light,
Smites all the empty windows.

—EDWARD ROBERT BULWER-LYTTON, *The Wanderer in Holland*

5. When I was five
My father was the wisest man alive;
At ten and five
I wondered he had wits enough to thrive;

At five and twenty
He had acquired new brains a-plenty.

—J. E., Intellectual Evolution

6. Virtue itself turns vice, being misapplied;
   And vice sometime's by action dignified.

—WILLIAM SHAKESPEARE, Romeo and Juliet

7. Light seeking light doth light of light beguile.

—WILLIAM SHAKESPEARE, Love's Labour's Lost

8. When your Imp of Blind Desire
   Bids you set the Thames afire,
   You'll remember men have done so—in the Files.

—RUDYARD KIPLING, The Files

9. Though in silence, with blighted affection
   I pine,
   Yet the lips that touch liquor must never
   touch mine!

—GEORGE W. YOUNG, The Lips That Touch Liquor

10. She walks in beauty, like the night
    Of cloudless climes and starry skies;
    And all that's best of dark and bright
    Meet in her aspect and her eyes;
    Thus mellow'd to that tender light
    Which Heaven to gaudy day denies.

—GEORGE GORDON, LORD BYRON, Hebrew Melodies

/aʊ/ (ou) /ɑʊ/ As in *Now* and *How*

Whether the speaker produces /aʊ/ or /ɑʊ/ in the indicated key word depends phonetically on whether the front or the back of the tongue is elevated in the first part of the diphthong. It is likely that this articulatory habit is determined by what one hears in his or her community. Both pronunciations are used by cultured and educated speakers throughout the United States.

The tendency to substitute the vowel /æ/ (ă) for the first element of the diphthong is one we recommend avoiding or correcting. We also recommend avoiding or correcting the triple vowel combinations [æaʊ] or [æɑʊ] for either /aʊ/ or /ɑʊ/.

The most frequent spellings for the diphthong are *ou* as in *out, house,* and *mouse,* and *ow* as in *cow, how,* and *brow.*

PRACTICE MATERIALS

ouch	cloud	douse	gout	anyhow
ours	clown	dowel	house	announce
hours	clout	down	howl	rebound
oust	couch	drought	jowl	allowance
outer	council	drown	mound	endow
blouse	county	flounder	mount	impound
bough	coward	flour	mouse	disavow
bounce	cowl	foul	mouth	uncrowded

bound	crouch	flower	plow	redoubtable
bower	crown	gouge	powder	astounding

PHRASES

powdery flour	carouse and shout
mound of flowers	crowd of thousands
hound's jowl	astounding rebound
drowning flounder	about to announce
stout plowman	tower of power
towering cloud	scowling mouth
fouled out	mounted the bough
powerful clout	county council

SENTENCES

1. The ball bounded off the tower and rebounded out of bounds as a foul.

2. Lowry was proud to announce that the crowd numbered about a thousand.

3. Astounded by a mouse, the hound aroused us with his howls.

4. Parts of the Southwest suffer from drought and powder-dry soil.

5. The count, who announced that he represented the crown, flouted his power before the stout councillors.

6. McCloud frowned at the scoundrel lounging on her couch.

7. When asked, ''How now,'' the brown cow did not know how to take a bow.

8. The hour-long shower drowned the flowers.

9. Bowers denied that he was the glowering coward who shot Mr. Howard.

SELECTIONS

1. While from a proud tower in the town
Death looks gigantically down.
—EDGAR ALLAN POE, *The City in the Sea*

2. Ye rigid Plowmen. Bear in mind
Your labor is for future hours.
Advance! Spare not! nor look behind!
Plow deep and straight with all your powers!
—RICHARD HENRY HORNE, *The Plow*

3. He who doubts from what he sees,
Will ne'er believe, do what you please,
If the Sun and Moon should doubt,
They'd immediately go out.
—WILLIAM BLAKE, *Auguries of Innocence*

4. Time writes no wrinkle on thine azure brow—
Such as creation's dawn beheld, thou rollest now.
—GEORGE GORDON, LORD BYRON, *Childe Harold's Pilgrimage*

5. The strongest castle, tower and town,
The golden bullet beats it down.
—WILLIAM SHAKESPEARE, *Sonnets to Sundry Notes of Music*, IV
6. Lord Howard wanted out—
Of this there was no doubt—
But he shouted, "I am no coward."
And so fought on Lord Thomas Howard.
—J. E., Suggested by Tennyson's *Flower in the Crannied Wall*

/ɔɪ/ (oi) As in *Boy*, *Soil*, and *Noise*

The diphthong /ɔɪ/ is appropriately produced by beginning with the back, rounded vowel /ɔ/ and ending with the front vowel /ɪ/. The most frequent spellings include *oi* and *oy*, as in *oil*, *boil*, *toy*, and *boy*.

Some speakers tend to substitute /ɝ/ (ûr) for /ɔɪ/. This tendency is generally considered nonstandard, and we recommend that it be avoided or corrected. Another tendency to be avoided is the substitution of /oɪ/ for /ɔɪ/.

PRACTICE MATERIALS

boiler	hoist	noisy	anoint
boisterous	hoyden	oily	annoy
boycott	join	ointment	despoil
cloister	joist	point	embroil
coin	loin	quoits	employ
coy	loiter	roister	recoil
foible	moist	royal	exploit
goiter	loyal	soy	rejoice

PHRASES

boisterous roisterers	soiled coin
loyal to royalty	poisoned oyster
soybeans and poi	toy boycott
noisy boys	annoying foibles
broiled loin	exploited loyalty
moist ointment	joyful noise

SENTENCES

1. McCoy ran a noisy, boisterous joint.
2. Roy exploited the oil that lay beneath his soil.
3. Doyle's voice sounded as if he were poised, but his words were annoyingly poignant.
4. Royal heads were anointed with oil.
5. Lloyd joined the floorboards to the joists.
6. She may look coy when embroidering doilies but she is often a roisterous hoyden.
7. Spoiled oysters are poisonous.

8. The little boy avoided stepping on the toys in the foyer.

9. Few enjoy being employed as decoys or foils.

10. Joy spoiled Croydon's ploy to purloin the royal coins.

11. Floyd was loyal to his boisterous friends, who were frequently embroiled in annoying exploits.

12. Boyle would never boycott a choice, broiled loin chop.

SELECTIONS

1. She was a hoyden,
   Yet could play coy
   As a cloistered maiden
   Or a boisterous boy.

—J. E. *Tried and Untrue*

2. The long guns poised,
   Exploded and recoiled
   From fire and burst of noise
   And what they had despoiled.

—J. E. *Annoying Toys*

/ɛə/ (âə) As in *There*

The diphthong /ɛə/ is used instead of the more frequently heard /ɛr/ or /ɛɚ/ by persons who omit *r*'s in their pronunciation except immediately before vowels in the same syllable. It is heard in such words as *air, their, fair, care, dare, chair,* and *pear*.

/ɛə/ is also heard as a not entirely approved substitution for the vowels /æ/ or /a/ in words such as *ask, last, class,* and *bath*.

Speakers who generally pronounce their *r*'s when the letter *r* occurs in the spelling are likely to use the combination /ɛr/ or /ɛɚ/ rather than /ɛə/ in the words that follow:

PRACTICE MATERIALS

air	lair	compare	repair
bear	fair	declare	unaware
care	their	chair	heirloom
dare	wear	forbear	heiress
flair	affair	prepare	impair
hair	beware	welfare	despair
spare	scarce	square	scared

PHRASES

air fare	undeclared warfare
scared hare	their welfare
scarce hair	dared to forbear
pared pears	bears and mares
their chair	cared and despaired

SENTENCES

1. Few dare to impair a bear's welfare.
2. Mary carried the heirloom chair upstairs.
3. Claire rode her mare to the dairy fair.
4. "Beware! This is not your affair," Blair said with a cold stare.
5. The daring are often scared, despite their devil-may-care airs.
6. Fairlington insisted that because it was not his affair he would not take the dare.
7. The pair changed their wares for an heirloom that needed repair.
8. Adair declared that he was unaware of his impaired love affair.

SELECTIONS

1. Fair tresses man's imperial race ensnare,
And beauty draws us with a single hair.
—ALEXANDER POPE, *The Rape of the Lock*

2. Said Dairlington to Fairlington,
"However various,
You're reliably nefarious."

Said Fairlington to Dairlington,
"Were you not undarious,
You too might be nefarious."

—J. E., *Point Counter Point*

/ɔə/ (ôə) **and** /oə/ (ōə)

The diphthongs /ɔə/ and /oə/ are used by persons who are inclined to omit the /r/ from their pronunciations except before vowels. Practice in regard to /ɔə/ and /ɔr/ or /oə/ and /or/ varies along the following lines. (The transcriptions [ɔɚ] and [oɚ] are alternatives for [ɔə] and [or].)

In words such as *horse, lord, accord,* and *north,* usage is fairly uniform throughout the United States. The pronunciation is /ɔr/ for most Americans and /ɔə/ in the "*r*-dropping" sections of the country.

Usage varies between /o/ and /ɔ/ pronunciations for the words *board, mourning, course,* and *more.* These words are pronounced with either /o/ or /or/ by most American speakers. In the New York City area, these words are pronounced with /ɔ/ by "native" speakers. Thus, except for the New York City area, most Americans make distinctions between the words *horse* and *hoarse, for* and *four,* and *cord* and *cored.* The sound /ɔ/ is more likely to be used for the first word of these pairs and the /o/ for the second.

PRACTICE MATERIALS

Determine your own practice by comparing the pronunciation of the following pairs of words.

aural	oral
border	boarder

horse	hoarse
morning	mourning
war	wore
coarse	course
four	fore

born to mourn	north of the border
explored the fort	forty horses

Formosan export

SENTENCES

1. Guns were stored in the fort.

2. Each pull on his oars brought McCord closer to the shore.

3. Four hours of riding on her horse brought her to the border.

4. The lion roared itself hoarse because it wanted more food.

5. The owner of the resort inn was noted for being in accord with forty different points of view.

6. Dora explored the piano for a lost chord.

7. More and more, Nora found sweeping the porch to be a chore.

8. The matador saw the roaring bull burst through the door.

SELECTIONS

1. Cruel Remorse! where Youth and Pleasure sport,
And thoughtless Folly keeps her court—
                    —ANNA L. BARABAULD, *Ode to Remorse*

2. Come in the evening, or come in the morning,
Come when you're looked for, or come without warning,
Kisses and welcome you'll find here before you,
And the oftener you come here the more I'll adore you.
                    —THOMAS O. DAVIS, *The Welcome*

3. He will hold thee when his passion shall have spent its novel force,
Something better than his dog, a little dearer than his horse.
                    —ALFRED, LORD TENNYSON, *Locksley Hall*

4. Three poets, in three distant ages born,
Greece, Italy, and England did adorn.
                    —JOHN DRYDEN, *Under Mr. Milton's Picture*

5. Society is now one polish'd horde,
Formed of two mighty tribes, the *Bores* and *Bored.*
                    —GEORGE GORDON, LORD BYRON, *Don Juan, Canto XIII*

6. Said Hawthorne to Portia:

"Though I was born
A unicorn,
I would dearly adore
A second horn."

Replied Portia to Hawthorne:

"I will not scorn
But I love you as you were born.
Because you are unique
With a single horn."

—J. E., *From Lines That Could Be Verse*

/ɪə/ (ĭə) As in *Dear* and *Year*

The diphthong /ɪə/ (ĭə), as noted earlier, is used by persons who omit medial and final /r/ sounds from the pronunciation of such words as *dear, fear, hear, beard, cheerful,* and *earful*. Throughout most of the United States, all of these words are more frequently pronounced with the combinations [ɪr] or [ɪɚ] rather than with the diphthong /ɪə/.

PRACTICE MATERIALS

Determine your own pronunciation of the following words and compare them with the pronunciation of respected speakers in your community.

beard	pier	gear	piercing	earwig
beer	cheer	queer	seared	nearly
dear	arrear	cheerful	fierce	sincere
fear	mere	earful	spear	tearful
hear	drear	fearful	bier	Shakespeare
merely	clear	we're	year	hearsay

PHRASES

fearfully dear	steer clear
eerie bier	year's arrears
we're here	tearful earful
queer gear	fiercely pierced
near and dear	appeared sincere
sincerely cheerful	dreary pier

SENTENCES

1. Geary's beard appeared to be seared.
2. The hunter's gear included a fearful-looking spear.
3. The trees looked dreary because of the sere leaves.
4. A fierce fire destroyed the pier.
5. Beardsley was not considered a cheerful person because of his habit of crying in his beer.

SELECTIONS

1. The skies they were ashen and sober;
 The leaves they were crisped and sere—
 The leaves they were withering and sere;

It was night in the lonesome October
Of my most immemorial year.

—EDGAR ALLAN POE, Ulalume

2. Damn with faint praise, assent with civil leer,
And without sneering, teach the rest to sneer.

—ALEXANDER POPE, Prologue to Satires

/ʊə/ (o͝oə) As in *Poor*

The diphthong /ʊə/ is likely to be used by speakers who are inclined to pronounce /r/ only in contexts in which the letter *r* is immediately followed by a vowel. These speakers would probably use /ʊə/ rather than [ʊr] or [ʊɚ] in words such as *poor, sure,* and *tour.* Others may use /ʊ/ in all of these words.

PRACTICE MATERIALS

Determine your own pronunciation of the words and phrases that follow and compare each with what is current in your community.

poor	allure	assure	fury
sure	moor	jury	endure
tour	boor	ensure	touring

toured on the moor   poor but demure
boorish jurist   ensure the jury

SENTENCES

1. Be he rich or poor, there is little that is alluring about a boor.
2. What we cannot cure we must learn to endure.
3. If you're surely poor, you can hardly afford to tour among the Moors.
4. The jury had to control their fury to ensure a fair and enduring verdict.
5. Though Moore was a poor woman, she felt socially secure.
6. The cat's nine lives were no insurance against curiosity.
7. The sailors were glad to have their ship securely moored after enduring the fury of the storm.
8. As the touring boorish actor sawed the air in fury, the director told the producer, "Rest assured, this ham will never be cured."

SELECTIONS

1. "I'll be judge, I'll be jury," said cunning old Fury.

—LEWIS CARROLL, Alice's Adventures in Wonderland

2. I'll make assurance doubly sure,
And take a bond of fate.

—WILLIAM SHAKESPEARE, Macbeth

3. How small of all that human hearts endure
That part which laws or kings can cause or cure.

—SAMUEL JOHNSON, Lines Added to Goldsmith's Traveller

/eɪ/ (ā) As in *Gale*

Earlier, we discussed /eɪ/ as a nonphonemic variant of the vowel /e/. At this point, we merely present additional practice materials that include words that may be appropriately pronounced with the diphthong /eɪ/.

PRACTICE MATERIALS

aid	blade	nail	wane
ale	blaze	pace	weight
aim	braise	skate	await
bail	cape	tame	detain
bait	hail	taint	dismay
bane	mail	trait	waiver
Dane	fame	drain	refrain

SENTENCES

1. After his zany escapade, Ray was detained in jail without bail.

2. Brady labored at the mason's trade.

3. Erica Blaine told her famous friend Dave Dane that fate was about to play a painful hand.

4. Blaine asked whether Major had to take the late plane to Spain.

5. The stranger paid the bill that the waiter had placed on the table and went on his way.

6. Gail could not refrain from weighing mail on the postal scale.

7. Crayton did not hesitate to use the radio-telephone to relay each day's weighty news.

8. Kate waved to Sadie as they made their way through the shady dale.

9. Lady Jane Grey had a quaint way of betraying her famous status.

10. Rain came with daybreak, as if nature did not want the croquet game to be played on the graded field.

SELECTIONS

1. Said Grayson to Payson,
   "By the way that you behave
   I cannot help but assay you
   As primate trained to shave."

   Said Payson to Grayson,
   "The way in which you rave
   Makes primates seem ascendant,
   However you behave."

   —J. E., *Evolution*

2. All human things are subject to decay,
   And, when fate summons, monarchs must obey.

   —JOHN DRYDEN, *Mac Flecknoe*

3. What of the faith and fire within us
   Men who march away
   Ere the barn-cocks say
   Night is growing gay?

—THOMAS HARDY, *Men Who March Away*

/oʊ/ (ō) as in *Bone* and *Prone*

Earlier we discussed /oʊ/ as a nonphonemic variant of the midhigh, rounded, back vowel /o/. We now present some additional practice materials in which /oʊ/ may be appropriately used. We should have in mind, however, that words such as *bone, home,* and *grow* do not change in meaning whether they are pronounced with the vowel /o/ or the diphthong /oʊ/.

Speakers for whom Spanish is a first and dominant language are likely to use the vowel /o/ rather than the diphthong /oʊ/. Those who do will not distinguish between the vowel in the salutation ''Como esta'' and the usual American-English diphthong pronunciation in the name of the popular singer *Perry Como* or in the words of the list that follows.

PRACTICE MATERIALS

boast	slope	focus	notice
bone	goal	alone	acetone
bonus	hold	although	bestow
bowl	knoll	cyclone	regrow
cone	loan	Dover	resole
drone	moan	below	unknown
ghost	prone	enroll	homely
crocus	broach	postal	romance

SENTENCES

1. Joan made her home in the adobe hut on the knoll.
2. The troll was prone to fall into the old moat.
3. Although he kept his hold on the controls, the captain broke his nose when the ship almost rolled over.
4. Greta Garbo boldly chose to lead her own life over the moans of nosy reporters.
5. The rogue stole the brooch and the old robe from Toni's home.
6. The old rover warmed his hands over the coals glowing in his host's golden bowl.
7. The wind blows and moans across the road to Nome.
8. Rose told Mona that she preferred older and homely men because they were supposedly easier to control.

SELECTIONS

1. I know a bank wheron the wild thyme blows,
   Where oxslips and the nodding violet grows.

—WILLIAM SHAKESPEARE, *A Midsummer Night's Dream*

2. I'm growing frugal of my gold;
I'm growing wise, I'm growing—yes—
   I'm growing old.
                    —JOHN GODFREY SAXE, *I'm Growing Old*

3. Avenge, O Lord, thy slaughtered saints whose bones
Lie scattered in the Alpine mountains cold;
Ev'n them who kept thy truth so pure of old
When all our fathers worshiped stocks and stones.
                    —JOHN MILTON, *On the Late Massacre in Piedmont*

4. I know his name, I know his note,
That so with rapture takes my soul;
Like flame the gold beneath his throat
His glossy cape is black as coal.
                    —WILLIAM DEAN HOWELLS, *The Song the Oriole Sings*

14

Consonants: The Lip (Bilabial) Sounds

Consonants, we recall, are speech sounds produced as a result of the modification of the outgoing breath stream by the organs of articulation. The form of modification produces the characteristics (features) peculiar to the various consonants. Unlike vowels, which are all voiced sounds, unless the speaker is intentionally whispering, some consonants are appropriately voiced and others are appropriately voiceless.

The description and manner of production of each of the consonant sounds are considered individually. Precautions to be observed and the pitfalls to be avoided are indicated for those sounds that some American-English–speaking adults find difficult.

The Favored Articulatory Contact

Many languages seem to have a favored place of articulatory contact. In French, Spanish, and Italian, many sounds are produced by contact between the tongue tip and the upper teeth. In German, the point of contact is a bit lower. In American English, the favored contact area is the upper gum ridge. At this point, by contact with the tongue tip, the sounds /t/, /d/, /l/, and /n/ are articulated. A fraction of an inch behind the gum ridge, articulatory placements are made for the sounds /s/, /z/, /ʃ/ (sh), /ʒ/ (zh), /tʃ/ (ch), /dʒ/ (j), and one of the varieties of /r/.

Because of the proximity of articulatory positions of American-English sounds and those much like them in Spanish, French, Italian, and German, the tendency to carry over foreign-language speech habits is understandable. We should also be able to appreciate the need for special precautions and considerable practice to overcome these foreign-language influences. A good beginning in correcting such influences, and in establishing an awareness of the favored place of American-English articulation, is to study the diagram of Figure 14–1.

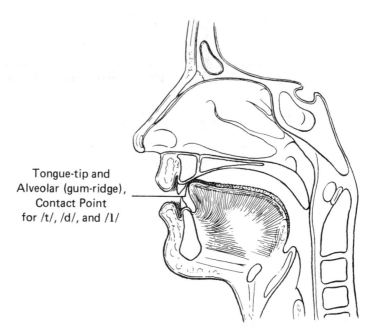

Tongue-tip and
Alveolar (gum-ridge),
Contact Point
for /t/, /d/, and /1/

FIGURE 14-1   Diagram indicating the "favored contact area"
for American-English consonants. The upper gum ridge is the
contact point for /t/, /d/, and /1/. Essentially the same tongue-
tip and gum-ridge contact is made for /n/.

The consonant sounds are presented approximately according to the place of major
articulatory activity, proceeding from the front to the back of the mouth (see Table 14–
1). This order of presentation is not to be interpreted as necessarily the most desirable
or the prescribed one to be followed. We believe that the specific order of consonant
study should be determined by the instructional needs of the students or the philosophy
of the teacher. An individual student, aware of his or her own limitations in diction,
or striving for improvement in a given direction, might well begin with the sound, or
one of the sounds, requiring attention. An instructor might determine the order of consonant study based on a screening of the group of students. The sound most in need of
improvement for the largest number of students in the class may then be selected as
the one with which to begin. If the instructor believes that it is better to teach a relatively difficult sound by contrasting it with another, easier sound for the student, then
this may become the proper initial sound to be studied. An instructor who has many
students coming from a given speech region and who, on the basis of experience, is
able to anticipate frequent consonant difficulties may choose to begin the improvement
program in the light of these anticipations. The instructor will soon learn whether the
students are living up to expectations or whether his or her own program for this particular group of students is in need of modification. Such an approach will afford the
individual student and the class as a whole the greatest amount of instructional time
and the opportunity for work on common problems and for frequent review during the
course of a term.

An alternate rationale for the order of presentation of the consonants is one based

Table 14–1. Classification of the Consonants of American-English Speech

Manner of Articulation	Lips (Bilabial)	Lip-teeth (Labio-dental)	Tongue-teeth (Lingua-dental)	Tongue-Gum-ridge (Alveolar)	Tongue-Hard-palate (Post-alveolar)	Tongue-Blade-palate (Palatal)	Tongue-velum (Velar)	Larynx (Glottal)
Voiceless stops	p			t			k	ʔ
Voiced stops	b			d			g	
Voiceless fricatives	ʍ (hw)	f	θ (th)	s	ʃ (sh)			h
Voiced fricatives		v	ð (ŧħ)	z	ʒ (zh)			
Nasals (voiced)	m			n			ŋ (ng)	
Lateral				l				
Glides (vowel-like) (consonants)	w				r*	r j (y)		
Voiceless affricate					tʃ (ch)			
Voiced affricate					dʒ (j)			

*In our discussion of the /r/ phoneme, the variable characteristics of /r/ are considered.

on a knowledge of normal speech-sound acquisition in children. This approach would call for approximately the following order:

1. /m/, /p/, /b/
2. /n/, /f/, /h/, /ŋ/ (ng)
3. /w/, /j/ (y)
4. /k/, /g/
5. /t/, /d/, /l/, /r/
6. /s/, /z/, /ʃ/ (sh), /tʃ/ (ch)
7. /θ/ (th), /ð/ (th), /v/
8. /ʒ/ (zh), /dʒ/ (dz), /hw/

The Bilabial Sounds

/p/ As in *Pea, Soap, Separate,* and *Spy*

/p/ and /b/ are bilabial, closed-lip, stop consonants. These sounds are produced as a result of a lip-closing action that momentarily stops the flow of breath. Both of these sounds require a raised palate so that after the lip action, the sound produced is emitted orally rather than nasally, as indicated in Figure 14-2.

All but three American-English sounds are normally produced with an elevated soft palate. Except for the three nasal consonants /n/, /m/, and /ŋ/ (ng), the reader should assume that the directions for the production of a sound include the one to *elevate the soft palate*.

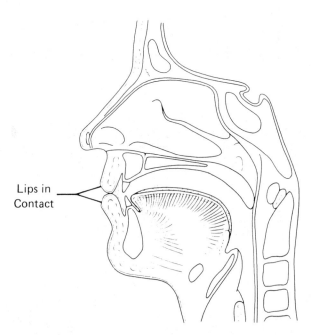

Lips in Contact

FIGURE 14–2 Articulatory positions for /p/ and /b/. The lips are tightly compressed and the soft palate is raised.

The sound /p/ in initial or stressed positions, as in *pea* and *plate*, requires considerable breath pressure. The lips must be tightly compressed to permit the production of a vigorous /p/. In unstressed positions there is considerably less breath pressure and less vigorous lip action. In all positions, /p/ is a voiceless sound. When /p/ is followed by a vowel, a distinct puff of breath (plosion or aspiration) should accompany the completion of the sound. In final positions, /p/ may not be "exploded."

PRACTICE MATERIALS

pea	pool	person	pound
peat	pull	pert	pout
peel	poor	purse	powder
pill	poke	pun	power
pit	pole	put	peace
paid	paltry	pike	pitch
pay	paw	pile	peg
pen	park	pine	patch
pat	pond	point	pack
path	pot	poise	poem

When a medial /p/ is followed by a stressed vowel, a distinct puff of air should accompany the completion of the /p/. In combinations preceded by an /s/, however, the aspirate quality is considerably reduced.

MEDIAL (STRESSED POSITIONS)

appeal	rapport	apart	rupee
appease	repair	repay	turnpike
repeat	repartee	upon	repugnant
repeal	impact	apology	umpire
unpin	report	deport	suppose
repaid	repatriate	despair	epistle
repent	repose	support	inspire
repel	oppose	superior	inspect
repast	appoint	superb	respite

For a medial /p/ in unstressed positions, the lip activity is less vigorous, and there is less accompanying breath puff in anticipation of the sound following the /p/.

MEDIAL (UNSTRESSED POSITIONS)

deepen	stupor	rapier	napping
happy	sweeping	steeple	chopping
carpet	champion	taper	clapped
typify	grapple	stepping	flippant
tipped	hoping	clipping	wrapper
depot	vapid	reaper	slipper
tepid	gaping	taping	rapid

[p] *IN FINAL POSITION—WEAKLY ASPIRATED*

keep	hoop	nap	leap
hip	hope	nape	reap
cape	cup	mop	hope
map	cop	mope	wipe

[pl] *AND* [pr] *BLENDS—REDUCED ASPIRATION FOR THE* [p]

plea	plume	plight	place
please	Pluto	pliant	play
plenty	plot	plow	pleasure
plate	plum	applaud	plural
plain	plug	aplomb	plunder
plan	pluck	plausible	plunge
preen	prune	price	spread
pray	reprove	pride	sprite
prick	proof	proud	sprawl
press	prawn	prow	sprain
prank	prod	praise	spree
prattle	prolix	approve	prized

[p] *FOLLOWED BY* [t]—*LITTLE OR NO ASPIRATE QUALITY FOR THE* [p]

aped	escaped	hoped	rapped
apt	gaped	lapped	reaped
capped	gapped	leaped	roped
caped	heaped	loped	soaped
draped	hipped	mapped	yapped

[p] *FOLLOWED BY* [s]—*LITTLE OR NO ASPIRATE QUALITY FOR THE* [p]

apes	flaps	jumps	pops
beeps	flips	lapse	pups
capes	gaps	loops	raps
cops	hopes	mops	ropes
dips	hops	napes	tapes

SENTENCES

1. The respected Ping-Pong players napped before they played.
2. Pickled jalapeno peppers were too potent for Peter Piper.
3. Paul put a pippin apple into the piglet's mouth.
4. Peterson produced a sample of a productive paint that was presumed not to chip.

5. Some companies employ Pinkerton operatives to prevent predators from plundering their premises.

6. Springer polished the pistons of his "chopper."

7. "Spot" is not an appropriate appellation for springer spaniels, poodles, or Pekingese; it is perfect for plain, dappled pups.

8. Deliah wrapped the snappers she caught in a piece of clean newspaper.

9. Some people are pleased to see ships pulling out of port to the open sea.

10. With practice, in his prime, Plunkett could put his powerful passes precisely where he pleased.

11. The proud prince placed too low a price on the approval of the people.

12. "Pippa Passes" is a poem by Robert Browning.

SELECTIONS

1. "I fly from pleasure," said the prince, "because pleasure has ceased
   to please."   —SAMUEL JOHNSON, *Rasselas*

2. When the hounds of spring are on winter's traces,
   The mother of months in meadow or plain
   Fills the shadows and windy places
   With lisp of leaves and ripple of rain.
                    —ALGERNON CHARLES SWINBURNE, *Atalanta in Calydon*

3. Now when a doctor's patients are perplexed,
   A consultation comes in order next—
   You know what that is? In a certain place
   Meet certain doctors to discuss a case
   And other matters, such as weather, crops,
   Potatoes, pumpkins, lager-beer, and hops.
                         —OLIVER WENDELL HOLMES, *Rip Van Winkle, M.D.*

4. By heaven, methinks it were an easy leap
   To pluck bright honour from the palefaced moon,
   Or dive into the bottom of the deep,
   Where fathom-line could never touch the ground,
   And pluck up drowned honour by the locks.
                                 —WILLIAM SHAKESPEARE, *Henry IV*

PRACTICE DIALOGUE FOR /p/

"No soy rico, soy pico"

Parish Priest. Parishioners repent! A few paltry pennies for the paupers is pathetic. When I pass the plate this Palm Sunday please, I implore you, plunge into your pockets! The pope can pray for prosperity, but you must provide for the impoverished—or they will perish!

Parishioner. Padre, we are not penurious cheapskates, just prudent. The plant on Carps Parkway employed us to program, repair, pack, and ship Pippin Computers. When the plant was wiped out, paychecks to employees stopped. Your appeal is simply impossible. Our pockets and purses are empty. We are the poor people! But we still aspire to help the impoverished. Please, padre, I, Pepito, can tell you, "No soy rico, soy pico."

/b/ As in *Bean, Rabid,* and *Robe*

/b/ is a voiced, lip-stop, unaspirated consonant produced with less lip and breath pressure than /p/. Lip activity should be precise so that there is a clear-cut stop and release action for the /b/, even though it is less vigorous than for the /p/.

By way of review, /b/ is articulated with (1) a firm closing of the lips; (2) a compression of air behind the lips; and (3) a sudden parting of the lips to release the *vocalized sound.* Final /b/ may be articulated without the explosive or release phase.

PRACTICE MATERIALS

Make certain that you show a clear distinction between /p/ and /b/ in the following words, phrases, and sentences.

peak	beak	prick	brick
pay	bay	peen	bean
pane	bane	punk	bunk
paste	baste	plank	blank
pare	bare	planned	bland
paid	bade	pass	bass
pace	base	pat	bat
hup	hub	mop	mob
cup	cub	cop	cob
rip	rib	lope	lobe
fop	fob	rope	robe

staple	stable
ample	amble
rapid	rabid
napped	nabbed
nipped	nibbed

PHRASES

pass the bass   cup for a cub
barely paired   planned to be bland
peaked beak   patted the baseball bat
          complain without blame

SENTENCES

1. Pete Brady bastes his roast beef with tomato paste.
2. Paula bailed the boat with a pail.

3. The punted ball bounced against the goalpost.
4. Buck packed his bags and paid his bill.
5. Better peach pies are baked without pits.
6. The belt was made of leather pelt.
7. Bertha begged Pat to hang his coat on a peg.
8. Piper bowed nobly and jumped from the parapet.

ADDITIONAL PRACTICE MATERIALS

INITIAL

bean	boon	burn	broom
bill	bull	bud	bruise
bale	boor	breach	brought
beg	boat	bring	brain
back	ball	bread	brine
bask	bog	brass	brown
busy	bulk	bleed	bloom
bunch	burrow	blink	blue
base	bird	black	block
blame	burst	breath	blurt

MEDIAL

about	table	somebody	disturbing
abate	feeble	habit	rubber
abbey	stable	noble	ribbon
abet	number	tumble	tribute
abhor	lumber	fumble	robust
Abner	obtain	trombone	thimble

FINAL

rib	tube	disturb	curb
crab	nub	cube	jibe
web	rub	hob	daub
stab	robe	sob	cob
dab	lobe	rob	mob

PHRASES

fumbled and mumbled	everybody is somebody
borrowed robe	numbered crabs
pale banner	about to bloom
rupees for rubies	ambled in the bog
habitual busybody	broken bower
Beulah	beaned by a
Babette	baseball

SENTENCES

1. Bill is fond of brown berries and broiled bass.
2. Ben abhorred boasting but liked to be busy.
3. Bacon and beans were a habit with Bess and Bob.
4. Benton played a brass tuba in the Boys Band.
5. Somebody permitted the black horse to break out of the barn.
6. Few buds bloom in February to attract bees.
7. The stable was swept with a bulky, brown broom.
8. Lobsters and crabs were brought in on the old, flat-bottomed boat.
9. Bricks and boards are basic building materials.
10. Brad slammed the ball for a three-base hit.

SELECTIONS

1. But far on the deep there are billows
   That never shall break on the beach.
   —A. J. RYAN, *Song of the Mystic*
2. This truth within thy mind rehearse,
   That in a boundless universe
   Is boundless better, boundless worse.
   —ALFRED, LORD TENNYSON, *The Two Voices*
3. I am weary of days and hours,
   Blown buds of barren flowers,
   Desires and dreams and powers
      And everything but sleep.
   —ALGERNON SWINBURNE, *The Garden of Prosperine*
4. Beauty can pierce one like a pain.
   —THOMAS MANN, *Buddenbrooks*

In your practice on the word list and other material that follows, pay special attention to the items that have [bl] and [br] blends to avoid any suggestion of a /w/ sound following the [b]. Additional practice materials for these blends follow:

bleep	block	breeze	bride
blip	bluff	brim	broad
blade	bloody	brake	brow
blank	blow	brand	brute

PHRASES

brutish brow	brought brunch
broad bluff	broken brooch
brown blade	embroidered blanket
brought to the brink	blurb of blarney
brainy bride	blameless blip
bland blend	blocked the blow
blithely blundered	bluebells in bloom

SENTENCES

1. Bryan called Brandon's bluff.
2. Blanch invited Blivan to brunch.
3. The wind blew brine over the broad deck of Brandon's boat.
4. Blake was no blue-eyed brute.
5. Brenda and Bryce were blissful buddies.

PRACTICE DIALOGUE FOR /b/

Breakfast at Bubba's Bakery

Boyd. Mr. Bubba, bag me six buttermilk biscuits, a bran roll, a blueberry muffin, and a buttery hot-cross bun. Because you have no tables, I'll grab a bite of breakfast on my bicycle.

Mr. Bubba. Buddy, for breakfast at Mr. B's you get bagels. Everybody buys boxes of them—nobody bugs me for biscuits!

Boyd. But . . . what's a bagel?

Mr. Bubba. It's a humble, chubby ball of bread with a hole like a dough-nut. I boil then bake it until it's lightly browned. For breakfast, you break it in half, brush on a bit of butter, then eat it with a glob of blueberry jam. It's beautiful to your taste buds! Please, be my guest—take a jumbo bite!

Boyd. Mr. Bubba, I don't want to bruise your feelings, but a bite of your beloved rubbery bagel brought on heartburn. Maybe I'll break my habit and skip breakfast today.

Mr. Bubba. Boy, you've got a feeble belly, but you're no namby-pamby. You boldly braved the unknown and took a bite of my bagel. So I'm going to bend the rules and bring you a piece of my best, freshly baked banana bread. We'll just call it brunch, not breakfast. Boyd, it's bliss-ful!

/m/ As in *Me, Summer,* and *Plum*

/m/ is one of the three nasal, continuant consonants. As such, it is produced with a lowered soft palate, nasal cavity reinforcement, and nasal emission. /m/ is articulated with the lips in relaxed contact and the teeth slightly parted. Vocal fold vibration is a necessary accompaniment for the /m/, as well as for the other two nasal sounds. As indicated in Figure 14–3, the tongue usually lies at the bottom of the mouth in the production of the /m/.

The sound /m/ is usually represented by the single letter *m*. Occasionally, the *m* is followed or preceded by a "silent" letter, as in *lamb* and *dumb*, *psalm* and *calm*. The sound is found in initial, medial, and final positions. Unless hurried, slurred, or pro-duced with the lips too tight, the /m/ is a relatively easy sound to produce. As sug-gested in our discussion on nasal reinforcement (see pages 97–98), the /m/ lends full-ness and roundness to the voice. The material and exercises for /m/ in the section on the voice should now be reviewed (see pages 98–99).

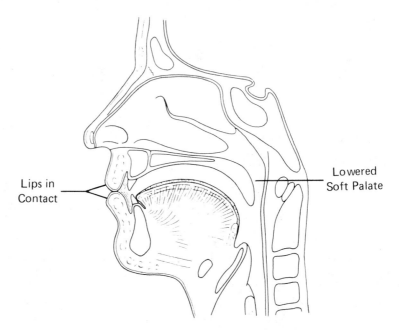

FIGURE 14–3   Articulatory positions for /m/. Note the lip contact and the lowered soft palate.

PRACTICE MATERIALS

me	main	most	mirth
meek	mend	mode	murky
meal	met	mote	murder
mean	mess	motive	mud
meat	man	motor	moist
middle	map	mourn	mouth
milk	mash	mortar	mount
mist	mask	mauve	mouse
make	mass	mock	my
mate	match	month	might
mail	mood	mob	mine
made	moon	monk	mile

MEDIAL

demean	ember	foaming	human
seemly	emanate	reformed	humor
seamstress	embank	informing	grimy
dreaming	embassy	armor	slimy
remit	embattle	termed	omit
permit	cement	termite	remind
simple	amnesty	terminal	remedy

Amy	remove	grumble	remark
emblem	emote	stumble	almond
empty	bemoan	umbrella	lament

FINAL

beam	game	groom	worm
seem	gem	tomb	term
team	stem	tome	drum
theme	phlegm	comb	hum
dream	lamb	dome	I'm
dim	ham	home	dime
trim	tam	form	climb
slim	sham	dorm	grime
aim	slam	calm	crime
same	doom	farm	prime
tame	room	alarm	column
blame	broom	bomb	autumn

In a final, unstressed position, the final /m/ may sometimes have syllabic value. What is your pronunciation of the words that follow?

chasm	schism	spasm	bedlam
bottom	rhythm	theism	bosom
prism	atom	truism	column

Is your pronunciation the same for the words in the following phrases?

bottom of the chasm	columns of prisms
schism in theism	rhythm of spasms

In the following material, work for a light, sustained /m/. At first, exaggerate the length of the /m/ and avoid carrying over the nasal quality to proximate nonnasal sounds.

SENTENCES

1. Moss covered the bottom of the maples in the Maine forest.
2. Miniver mourned for memories that might have been.
3. Termites undermined the dismal mansion near Miami.
4. Mamie grumbled because she stumbled over Mike's umbrella.
5. Mason was phlegmatic about matters that make most ill-humored persons storm in anger.
6. Mending and making neat seams were Amanda's prime ways of staying calm.
7. The monk remained in good humor as he informed his mourning friends about the grimy tomb.
8. Mortar, a material employed for masonry, is made by mixing lime or cement with sand.
9. Humanity maintains continuity by making much of memories.
10. Emily, broom in hand, was in no mood to be stymied by a mouse in either animal or human form.

11. Men and women are mighty in their ability to transform molehills into mountains by mentation, emendation, or imagination.

12. Morton dreamed that no mound was too high for him to climb nor any chasm too wide for him to jump.

13. Emerson held that each mind has its own method.

14. Neither men nor women with empires in their minds can long remain humble or calm.

15. Many monuments to human beings in time need their own memorials.

16. The moon may look on many men and women, but each has but one moon.

17. Remembrance, and repentance, often come together in the morning.

18. Lamb and ham make fine mincemeat.

19. Simmons climbed up from the bottom of the chasm.

20. Rhyme and rhythm do not necessarily produce a truism.

SELECTIONS

1. In *Man and Superman*, George Bernard Shaw made these observations:

> **a.** "The more things a man is ashamed of, the more respectable he is."
>
> **b.** "An Englishman thinks he is moral when he is only uncomfortable."
>
> **c.** "Marriage is popular because it combines the maximum of temptation with the maximum of opportunity."

2. Neil Armstrong, on landing on the moon, summed up his thinking and his mood with the statement: "One small step for man, one giant leap for mankind."

3. Terence manifested his understanding of humanity and his insight into himself when he noted that "Nothing which is common to mankind is foreign to me."

4. I have thought some of Nature's journeymen had made men and not made them well, they imitated humanity so abominably.

—WILLIAM SHAKESPEARE, *Hamlet*

5. Go! You may call it madness, folly;
You shall not chase my gloom away!
There's such a charm in melancholy,
I would not, if I could, be gay.

—SAMUEL ROGERS, *To———*

6. In his *Maxims*, Nietzsche remarked, "Many a man fails to become a thinker for the sole reason that his memory is too good."

7. On their own merits modest men are dumb.

—GEORGE COLMAN, *The Heir-at-Law*

8. Many loves of many a mood and many a kind
Fill the life of man, and mould the secret mind.

—ALGERNON SWINBURNE, *Erechtheus*

PRACTICE DIALOGUE FOR /m/

Football and the Married Man

Marvin.   Tampa Bay meets Miami in Tampa's home stadium today. After the monsoon, the summer air is humid and moist, and the field is a muddy swamp. Remember, Emma, the Rams from Anaheim creamed Tampa Monday, so they've got murder on their minds. It might be a smashing game!

Emma.   Those men can't maneuver in that grimy slime. They stumble and tumble and get mired in the muck. What a mess.

Marvin.   Emma, watch the TV! Tampa fumbled and the team's found themselves stymied at the midfield marker. Those dumb bums! Now Miami's man crams the ball under his arm, slams through the columns of his enemies, making a run for it. They meet like two embattled armies. That's drama, Em!

Emma.   Marvin, it's bedlam! The game was made up by moral and mental amputees. The team members remind me of lumbering mammoths, animals mashing each other into mincemeat. They merely imitate human emotions.

Marvin.   Woman, you misunderstand! Football imitates modern dance. It has theme, form, rhythm, and meaning. The moves are diagrammed. It's a mass rhumba or samba—quite harmless.

Emma.   You mean a rumble, not a rhumba. Miami's man was bashed, rammed, and mangled on that marshy field. He's crumpled, his helmet is mashed, and he limps to the ambulance. That's some mean samba, Marv! The game is plumb dumb. Mayhem for money—that's criminal!

Marvin.   Emma, lamb, I am dim. But you, like a beam of light or a flaming ember, illumine my mind. Football is competitive, combative, remorseless, and embittered. A man can compare it only to a mismanaged marriage!

The Bilabial Glide Consonants: /ʍ/ or /hw/ (hw) As in *What* and *When*, and /w/ As in *Will* and *Wit*

The consonants /ʍ/ or /hw/ and /w/ are *glide sounds*. Such sounds are produced with the organs of articulation in movement from an initial, determinate position to a final position determined by the sound that immediately follows. The sound /ʍ/ or /hw/ is voiceless; /w/ is voiced. Both are initiated with the lips rounded in a close, pursed position as for the vowel /u/. The tongue is raised in back toward the soft palate. Study Figure 14–4 for the initial position for the lip glide sounds. Note that the lips do not touch the teeth, as they necessarily do for the sounds /f/ and /v/. The palate is raised for the bilabial glide sounds, and the sounds are emitted orally.

/ʍ/ (hw) occurs in words spelled with *wh* initially or medially. Many speakers,

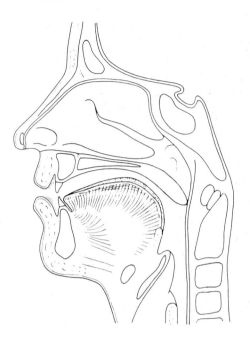

FIGURE 14–4   Initial articulatory position for glide sounds /ʍ/ and /w/. Note that the back of the tongue is raised.

however, use the voiced /w/ rather than the /ʍ/ in words such as *why, what,* and *when.* The /ʍ/ also occurs in contexts following a /t/, /s/, or /k/ as in *twine, swim,* and *quit.*

PRACTICE MATERIALS

To determine whether you use a /hw/ or /w/, place your hand in front of your mouth for the trial words *what* and *where.* The /hw/ should begin with a definite stream of unvocalized breath. In contrast, /w/ is vocalized and there is no obvious stream of breath. The word pairs that follow should help to make the distinction between the two sounds.

/hw/	/w/	/hw/	/w/
whither	wither	while	wile
where	wear	white	wight
wheel	weal	whether	weather
whet	wet	whacks	wax
what	watt	whirled	world
which	witch	whine	wine
when	wen	Whig	wig
whirred	word	whish	wish
whale	wail	whist	wist
whey	way	whoa	woe

INITIAL /hw/

wheat	whistle	wharf	whiting
wheedle	whelp	whimper	whittle
wheeze	whence	whimsy	whipsaw

whiff	whirl	whiskey	whang
whim	whistling	whiffle	wheal
whip	whop	whinny	whetstone
whisper	whorl	whisker	whelp

MEDIAL /hw/

pinwheel	somewhat	meanwhile	unwholesome
anywhere	awhile	bobwhite	buckwheat
nowhere	somewhere	freewheeling	erstwhile
elsewhere	bullwhip	flywheel	everywhere

PHRASES

where and when	wet weather
which way	whet your whistle
wore a watch	whispered wishes
whimsical words	witch or wight
wild wormwood	winding byway

SENTENCES FOR /hw/ AND /w/ CONTRAST

1. Do you prefer the song of the bobwhite or of the whippoorwill?

2. What was Wilson's whispering about?

3. Walt Whitman was somewhat wordy.

4. The Whig thought it whimsical to wash the Tory's wig in whiskey.

5. Wallace yelled "whoa" and whistled, but his horse went for the wheat.

6. The *White Witch*'s engines whirred as the steamer went off on the whaling voyage that would take her around the world.

7. The bewhiskered old man whet his knife and whittled away on a piece of wax.

8. Management was whipsawed, with the white-collar workers on one side and labor on the other, and there was no way in which either could win or persuade the other.

9. Winton wished to go back to Wichita and hear the wind wail through the Western Union wires.

10. Wiggins whispered that he was ready to go somewhere, anywhere, away from where he was.

ADDITIONAL PRACTICE MATERIALS FOR /w/

wad	walk	web	wide
wade	wall	we'd	wield
wafer	wan	wed	wife
waffle	wander	week	will
wager	want	weigh	window
waif	ward	weird	wing
wail	wash	weld	woman

wait	wean	wen	won't
waive	wear	wet	wood
wake	weave	wick	worst

MEDIAL /w/ (note that the spelling may be u *and* o *as well as* w*)*

biweekly	await	inward	unworthy
unwieldy	reweigh	unwavering	rewed
bewitch	away	awoke	earthworm
unwitting	awake	unworn	reworked
unwary	bewail	rewarned	anyone
unwept	byway	onward	everyone
unwelcome	unwilling	reweave	everyway
unwise	unworldly	reward	inquire
bewilder	unwanted	unwind	liquid
unwell	unwonted	reweb	require

SENTENCES

1. Wales has many rewarding and wonderful sights.
2. Kingsley wrote that "men must work, and women must weep."
3. Wilton walked west through the quagmire to earn one reward.
4. New York's Broadway, once a cowpath, is now known as the Great White Way.
5. Woodrow Wilson was president when the United States entered World War I, "the war to end all wars."
6. During World War II, General Dwight Eisenhower once was reputed to have wept while reviewing his troops.
7. Willy walked away into the woods, unaware that wolves and quagmires lay that way.
8. In weaving, the woof thread goes between the warps to form a web.
9. Watson wondered whether the equation would work out.
10. The lawyer winked unwisely at the bewildered witness.
11. The westerner wasted his wages on unwise wagers.
12. Whiskey is a liquid that can bewilder one in the worst way.
13. Welch wound up and swatted the wasp on the window.
14. Wanda tripped over a wet twig and twisted her ankle.
15. The once-bright flame waxed and waned and withered into nothingness.

SELECTIONS

1. Fame talks about the where and when
   While folly asks the why and wherefore.
   —WINTHROP PRAED, *Epitaph*

2. The Whence and Whither give no rest,
   The Wherefore is a hopeless quest.
   —SIR WILLIAM WATSON, *An Epistle to N. A.*

3. Those who have wealth must be watchful and wary.
   —THOMAS BAYLY, *I'd Be a Butterfly*

4. I want what I want when I want it.
—HENRY BLOSSOM, *Mlle. Modiste*

5. The world is a wheel, and it will all come round right.
—BENJAMIN DISRAELI, *Endymion*

6. A wail in the wind is all I hear;
A voice of woe for a lover's loss.
—W. C. CHANNING, *Lament for Thoreau*

7. Oscar Wilde and James Whistler were members of a group of wonted wits. Wilde admired Whistler, who was quick-witted in social repartee, whereas Wilde's wit was more apparent in his writing. One day, according to Ingelsby, the biographer of Wilde, Whistler said something that was extraordinarily witty, even for him. Wilde, overwhelmed with admiration, said, ''Oh Mr. Whistler, I wish I had said that.''

Whistler, in turn, replied, ''Don't worry, Wilde; you will, you surely will.''

PRACTICE DIALOGUE FOR /hw/ *AND* /w/ *CONTRASTS*

The Whispering Wind

Wendy Willard.   My story, *The Whispering Wind*, is about Edweena, a wacky whiffet, who is whisked away from her squalid life by Ward, the son of a wealthy whiskey merchant. He woos Edweena, twirling her through the social whirl in Wichita. Everyone whispers that she's unworthy, but Ward worships her. Their love is almost quashed when Ward's whaling boat is whipped by the waves of a winter storm, and lost in a whirlwind. Woebegone, Edweena watches the water from the wharf, wailing over the lost whaling boat, awaiting word of Ward's whereabouts. Meanwhile Ward, washed ashore in the West Indies, whiles away the hours whittling a white water canoe and waits for Edweena. His unwavering faith is rewarded when Edweena sails a sea-worthy vessel through an estuary and finds him, swimming while he whittles wood. They wed and have a wonderful life, full of unwieldy wealth. Well, Professor Winchell?

Professor Winchell.   Wendy, this is not the work I required. I wanted you to work on self-awareness. To acquire the wherewithal to create, you must look inward.

Wendy Willard.   I wonder whether you can understand, Professor Winchell. Edweena *is* Wendy Willard—or what I wish I were. I'm from Whittier, California. I've never quivered or wasted away in the heat of a wicked passion nor waltzed across Wichita. I won't whine in my wine, but I could win awards for warming and rewarming bottles, diaper washing, and nose wiping.

Professor Winchell.   I don't want to whipsaw you, Wendy, but nowhere do you write how you feel about your withering existence.

Wendy Willard.   Within weary housewives everywhere lives an Edweena. She is a freewheeling wanderer, wise yet bewildered. She never whimpers or bewails her fate. She says ''Whoa!'' to her woes and hides her weariness. When will you see she is as real a woman as Wendy Willard?

Professor Winchell. Edweena, as woman to woman, I will ask you just where and how did you get your window on the world? Well, you have a weird wit, but it is not unwelcome. You win! Don't waste your time reworking the whimsical *Whispering Wind!* We can't all be as witty as Mark Twain, or as sophisticated if not as wise, as Oscar Wilde or Dorothy Parker. Try to be the best possible Edweena Willard and learn to write with gentle wit. Let Elinor Wylie be your model.

/w/ and /v/

Some persons, probably because of foreign-language influence, tend to confuse the bilabial /w/ with the labiodental (lip-teeth) /v/. The following word pairs should help to establish the distinction between these two sounds. Observe the lip action in a mirror, and make certain that there is no contact of the teeth and lips for the /w/.[1]

PRACTICE MATERIALS

wane	vein	wend	vend
wary	vary	worse	verse
west	vest	wine	vine
weld	veld	wiper	viper
wiser	visor	wow	vow
went	vent	wile	vile
wet	vet	wail	veil

SENTENCES

1. It is wise not to get caught in a vise.
2. Wine is made from the fruit of the vine.
3. Wilma West was fond of her velvet vest.
4. As the vain writer grew older, his ability was on the wane and his verse became obviously worse.
5. To vend his various wares he had to wend his weary way and be wary of wily customers along the wayside.
6. The knight looked wiser behind his visor.
7. We were puzzled at the witch's vow never more to use her wiles for vile purposes.

SELECTIONS

1. There is not in the wide world a
   Valley so sweet

---

[1] See subsequent discussion of /v/ in Chapter 15.

As that vale in whose bosom
The bright waters meet.

—THOMAS MOORE, *The Meeting of the Waters*

2. No longer mourn for me when I am dead
   Than you shall hear the surly sullen bell
   Give warning to the world that I am fled
   From this vile world, with vilest worms to dwell.

—WILLIAM SHAKESPEARE, *Sonnet 71*

PRACTICE DIALOGUE FOR /w/ *AND* /v/ *CONTRASTS*

Vending Wedgewood Valley Wines

Vintner. Vernon, I'm very wary of wordy verses that veil the truth. Wedgewood Valley varietal wines are good values, and our vintage wines are wonderful. I'm warning you, it's wise to stay away from vulgarity.

Vernon the Advertiser. Very well. "I vow you'll go 'wow' when you wise up with Wedgewood Valley Wines! They are virtually the best in the west!"

Vintner. That's vulgar in the worst way! I can't vie with your wit, but your verse couldn't be worse. "Wedgewood Valley vintage wine goes well with veal and vegetables." Now, my words have vim and vigor!

Vernon the Advertiser. What about, "Don't waste your wages on vinegary wines. Win a victory with Wedgewood Valley!"?

Vintner. Vern, your wit is withering on the vine. Go visit the Wedgewood Valley Winery for a week. Wend your way through the vast woods, and wander with your wife through the wet vineyards. Witness the vaults, where the wine in vats is like washed velvet. Water your wit with visions of verdant woods and velvety wines. Then you'll find the words to vend my wares.

Vernon the Advertiser. Sir, I'm weary of your wordy verbiage and vain ways. Your vision of the world is veiled in the worst way. We vend your wines with vulgar words because the wines you vend are vile!

15

The Lip–Teeth Sounds

The lip–teeth (labiodental) consonants /f/ and /v/ present little or no difficulty for native English speakers. Persons for whom Spanish is a first language may carry over a tendency from their native tongue and use the sounds /b/ and /v/ interchangeably. Another tendency of these speakers is to substitute a sound intermediate between /b/ and /v/.

Speakers with a Germanic background may confuse /v/ and /w/ because the letter *w* is pronounced /v/ in German. Fortunately, the pronunciation of the letter *v* as /v/ is consistent in English, so that spelling serves as a reliable guide. Speakers whose language is German may also need to overcome their inclination to pronounce the letter *f* as /v/.

/f/ As in *Feel, Fun, Afraid,* and *Enough*

/f/ is a voiceless, fricative, lip–teeth (labiodental) consonant. It is made by pressing the lower lip against the upper teeth and forcing a stream of breath between the narrow spaces of the upper teeth or between the lower lip and the upper teeth. The soft palate is raised to prevent nasal emission of breath. (See Figure 15-1.)

In spelling, the sound is most frequently represented by the letter *f*. Other spellings include *ph* as in *phrase* and *gh* as in *rough*. The sound occurs in initial, medial, and final positions.

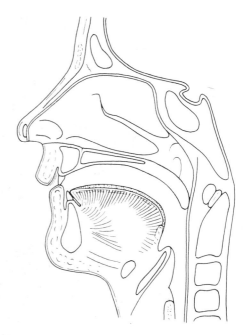

FIGURE 15–1 Articulatory position for /f/ and /v/. Note lower lip contact with upper incisor.

PRACTICE MATERIALS

feed	fad	fob	fire
feel	fan	fog	fowl
fib	food	fox	foible
fin	fool	firm	foil
fit	full	first	foist
fail	phobia	fudge	feud
fame	photo	fuss	fume
fed	falter	fight	fuse
felt	fork	file	future
fence	fought	find	few
coffee	defeat	afford	afar
enfeeble	after	effort	stuffing
effete	aft	soften	rifle
sphere	raft	affirm	trifle
efficient	raffle	refurbish	stifle
sphinx	laughed	unfurl	sapphire
swift	refuse	roughen	refute
chafed	effuse	shuffle	prophet
effect	careful	sofa	reference
defend	barefoot	loafer	breakfast
beef	skiff	chafe	half
chief	cliff	deaf	staff
reef	whiff	chef	graph

belief	stiff	chaff	enough
thief	strafe	laugh	tough
tiff	safe	calf	golf

[fl]

flee	fluke	flirt	flutter
fleet	flute	flourish	flight
flip	flood	flurry	fly
flame	flaw	flub	flounder
flu	floral	flunk	flour
float	Florence	flush	flout

[fr]

free	fret	frozen	afraid
frill	frank	fraught	affray
fray	France	frolic	affricate
freight	frugal	front	affront
freckle	fro	fry	infringe
frisk	frame	Fred	effrontery

PHRASES

coffee at four	flight of fancy
fit as a fiddle	defective fuse
fraught with fear	fluttery flower
flow of traffic	fickle finger of fate
fancy-free	frozen flounder
defuse the feud	frenetic flight
refuted the prophet	cheerful earful
graphic offer	laughter from afar

SENTENCES

1. Despite Fred's fickleness, he gave no obvious offense to Freya or to any of her friends.

2. Phil Philbrick was frankly considered a diamond in the rough.

3. After the fog lifted, the fast planes took off for foreign lands.

4. Coffee, although not a food, is a favorite breakfast drink for many of us.

5. Frank and his father are very fond of golf and fishing but not of stuffing themselves with fudge.

6. Florence and Phineas, who were born in France, made a swift but efficient visit to a fishing village in Finland.

7. Fran went to her physician because of her frequent sniffles.

8. The chef served the roast pheasant on a fancy chafing dish.

9. The thief came to grief over the theft of the sapphire.

10. Farnum had a phobia of fire even in a fireplace.

SELECTIONS

1. Careless of censure, nor too fond of fame,
Still pleased to praise, yet not afraid to blame,
Averse alike to flatter or offend,
Not free from faults, nor yet too vain to mend.
—ALEXANDER POPE, *Essay on Criticism*

2. Time stoops to no man's lure;
And love, grown faint and fretful,
With lips but half regretful
Sighs, and with eyes forgetful
Weeps that no loves endure.
—ALGERNON CHARLES SWINBURNE, *The Garden of Proserpine*

3. A faithful friend is a strong defence: and he that hath found such an one hath found a treasure.
—*Ecclesiasticus*, 6:14

4. Fare thee well! And if forever,
Still forever, fare thee well.
—GEORGE GORDON, LORD BYRON, *Fare Thee Well*

5. When tillage begins, other arts follow. The farmers therefore are the founders of civilization.
—DANIEL WEBSTER, *Remarks on Agriculture*

PRACTICE DIALOGUE FOR /f/

Famous and Forty

Freelance Journalist. Fame is fickle and fleeting, but you refuse to fade! At forty, you are a full-fledged film star. Your faithful fans want to know if the fight for fame and fortune is rough and frustrating.

Film Star. I did not fly, swift and unfettered, into my elevated sphere. I floundered and faltered and fell time after time. But I was tough enough to laugh at the foibles of fate, and deaf to the prophets of doom. I was careful to feel my feet firmly on the ground as I forged ahead. Frankly, because of my belief in the future, I refused to be fazed by the frustrations of fate, and my life flourished.

Freelance Journalist. Father Time is a thief. But at forty, you are a phenomenon! Fit as a fiddle, your sapphire eyes shine forth from a face that is firm and flawless. Did you fly to France to have fun and frolic?

Film Star. I took a flight to France to breakfast in my favorite café and to flit barefoot among the flowers. I can afford to fly to France for a refreshing little frolic, and fun will outfox Father Time.

Freelance Journalist. Does fame infringe on your family life?

Film Star. Fortunately, my family is deaf to foolish gossip. Frannie, my daughter, is freckled and effusive and laughs at my folly. My boy,

Raphael, is not afraid to offend any oaf who tries to fuel the fires of discord with foul lies. Finally, we don't flaunt our fortune, but financial freedom keeps my family cheerful and safe from strife.

Freelance Journalist.   Are you having an affair with an old flame? A famous fellow who frets because you're forgetful?

Film Star.   If you are referring to Phantom Phil, we are now fast friends. I prefer to forget we had a tiff.

Freelance Journalist.   What free-floating thoughts do you have for females who want to follow in your footsteps? Feel free to pontificate.

Film Star.   It's a stiff climb up a rough cliff to fame and fortune. If you have the stuff to tough it out, don't freeze out of fear. Laugh, stay cheerful, and never loaf. Finally, don't be afraid to fail! Fear of failure can stifle your finest efforts!

/v/ As in *Vie, Provoke,* and *Live*

/v/ is the voiced cognate of /f/. It is, of course, produced like the /f/, except that the /v/ is voiced and requires less breath pressure than the /f/.

Except for the *f* of *of,* /v/ is spelled as it is sounded.

The sound /v/ causes little or no difficulty for American-English speakers. As we have noted, some foreign-born speakers may have difficulty because they confuse the /v/ and the /w/. (See discussion and practice material for /v/ and /w/, pages 224-225.)

In context, when it is immediately followed by a voiceless consonant, as in ''I've ten cents'' or ''Give Tom the book,'' the /v/ is normally produced with partial devoicing. It is also partially devoiced when it occurs at the end of a phrase or a sentence such as in ''I had five'' or ''We enjoyed the drive.''

PRACTICE MATERIALS

Venus	valley	vault	visit
veal	van	vaunt	vile
venal	value	varnish	vine
veer	vend	varlet	vital
vigor	very	verse	vulgar
vim	vary	virtue	vulture
victor	voodoo	vernal	volume
vein	vogue	voice	volunteer
viper	verb	verify	verge
vale	vote	void	Volga
vapor	voracious	vice	vowel
evening	paved	proven	reverse
Eva	shaved	grooved	nervous
even	revel	hooves	convert
believing	event	roving	jovial
given	prevent	clover	revile
livid	having	Dover	trivial

evil	gavel	marvel	avoid
devil	travel	carving	invite
raving	ravel	starving	lover
staved	avid	avert	cover
deceive	delve	mauve	dive
receive	shelve	starve	strive
heave	have	carve	alive
sleeve	salve	nerve	hive
give	move	curve	naive
live	groove	swerve	resolve
gave	prove	glove	revolve
knave	rove	above	twelve
slave	stove	shove	love
stave	strove	dove	trove

PHRASES

vile varlet	village on the Volga
vaunted virtue	nervous in the service
varied voices	swerved at the curve
jovial rival	carving of veal
avid knave	twelve drivers
vigorous and vital	violin virtuoso
vain victories	marvelous maneuvers
vernal voice	vital visit
clover from Dover	beloved trivia

SENTENCES

1. Victor, for fear of becoming a victim, would not volunteer to test the voodoo.

2. Eve, an avid traveler, began her voyage from Dover to the Everglades.

3. The devil, for his evil purposes, can be a scrivener and a versifier, as well as a quoter of scriptures.

4. It is naive to approach a beehive without a veil for covering.

5. Jovial conversation accompanied Vera's carving of the turkey.

6. Some have tried to improve the figure of Venus with drapes, but very few have tried gloves.

7. Twelve Javanese were found roving through the river valley.

8. Valentine banged his gavel to put a stop to the verbalization at the convention.

9. The thieves found it of value to cultivate a Harvard accent.

10. Vinson resolved to give up his vain ways and to live a life of value.

SELECTIONS FOR /f/ AND /v/

1. Ever let the Fancy roam,
Pleasure never is at home!

—JOHN KEATS, *Fancy*

2. At thirty, man suspects himself a fool;
   Knows it at forty, and reforms his plan;
   At fifty chides his infamous delay,
   Pushes his prudent purpose to resolve;
   In all the magnanimity of thought
   Resolves, and re-solves; then dies the same.

   —EDWARD YOUNG, *Night Thoughts*

3. Nothing is given so profusely as advice.

   —FRANÇOIS, DUC DE LA ROCHEFOUCAULD, *Maxim 110*

4. All civilization has from time to time become a thin crust over a volcano of revolution.

   —HAVELOCK ELLIS, *Little Essays of Love and Virtue*

5. All is ephemeral—fame and the famous as well.

   —MARCUS AURELIUS, *Meditations*

PRACTICE DIALOGUE FOR /v/

Relative Values

Evelyn.   Above all, value is relative. If you believe virtuous living is the best revenge against civilization, you will revile all trivial striving. You will find a village home off an unpaved gravel road near a river to be a treasure trove. A person who values nature would love to spend an evening watching the mauve sky, listening to the clever voice of an unshaven lover echo in the private void. Just reveling in the naive pleasures of being alive makes life worth living!

Victor.   But a man who is a slave to his voracious appetite would starve at that river. His life revolves around a meal of marvelous veal. No matter how heavy, he never volunteers to diet. Above all, he loves invitations to the much-vaunted events at restaurants that are in vogue. Jovial and gentle as a dove when the food is good and the service invincible, he is livid when prevented from eating his victuals!

Evelyn.   A man of vain victories must live above the law and give less than he receives. He will ravish varlets and invest in movies simply to prove his unswerving nerve. He loves to move in the groove with venal men who vanquish their more virtuous rivals. He is driven and reveals himself in vigorous activity. He must believe that nothing can prevent his victories, but he is not easily deceived. He invests and reinvests in proven ventures. To spend an evening watching a vale of fog slowly cover an unwavering river would make him very nervous.

Victor.   I've talked to avid travelers who live to visit every spot on earth. They move from a village on the Volga to the cliffs of Dover. They venture into casinos in venal Las Vegas, then drive through the vernal Everglades in a Rover.

Evelyn.   Victor, I revel in our conversations. We delve into what it means to be alive. But I need a reprieve from this clever unraveling. Please, Vic, let's drive to the movie on Vincent Avenue.

16

The Tongue–Teeth Sounds

The tongue–teeth consonants /θ/ (th) and /ð/ (th) present some difficulties for native speakers of English as well as for persons with foreign-language backgrounds. The causes of these difficulties and exercises for overcoming them are presented in individual considerations of these sounds.

/θ/ (th) As in *Thin, Thank,* and *Theory; Anything* and *Truthful; Faith* and *Earth*

The /θ/ is a voiceless fricative. It is produced by placing the tip of the tongue lightly against the back of the upper teeth or slightly between the teeth. Air is forced through the place of contact to produce the characteristic fricative quality. In spelling, the sound is represented by the letters *th*. The sound /θ/ may occur initially, medially, or finally.

/θ/ tends to be a somewhat troublesome sound for many speakers. Native-born Americans exposed to substandard or dialectal speech influences may substitute a /t/ for the initial /θ/, so that words such as *thin* and *three* are pronounced as though they were *tin* and *tree.* Foreign-born speakers who do not have the /θ/ in their native language tend to substitute their nearest approximation for it. Frequent substitutions include a dentalized /s/ and a dentalized /t/. A comparison of Figures 16–1 and 17–1 for the /θ/ and /t/ and practice with the material that immediately follows should help to establish the distinctions between /θ/ and /t/ and between /θ/ and /s/.

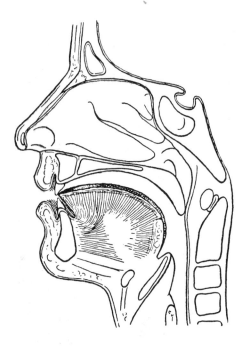

FIGURE 16–1 Representative articulatory positions for /θ/ (th) and /ð/ (t͟h) as postdental sounds. Note the contact of the tongue tip with the upper teeth.

PRACTICE MATERIALS

Distinguish between /θ/ and /t/.

thank	tank	theme	team
thin	tin	thought	taught
through	true	deaths	debts
thread	tread	ether	eater
thrill	trill	sheaths	sheets
thick	tick	forth	fort
thrips	trips	bath	bat
thorn	torn	oath	oat
wrath	rat	hearth	heart
wraith	rate	Gertha	Gerta
faithful	fateful	ruthless	rootless
myths	mitts	booth	boot

Distinguish between /θ/ and /s/.

theme	seem	thought	sought
think	sink	thumb	sum
thick	sick	thigh	sigh
thing	sing	thin	sin
thank	sank	kith	kiss
thaw	saw	myth	miss
thong	song	thane	sane
faith	face	moth	moss

truth	truce	bath	bass
mouth	mouse	math	mass
worth	worse	fourth	force
north	Norse	path	pass

SENTENCES FOR /θ/, /t/, AND /s/ CONTRAST

1. We felt a thrill in hearing the trill of the thrush.
2. Theodore was regarded as being a man true blue, all through.
3. The tick was found in the thick woods.
4. Ted, a good student, thought that he had been well taught.
5. Thelma heard the story through and thankfully believed it to be true.
6. Catherine could sing about almost anything.
7. The ache in Matthew's thigh brought forth a deep sigh.
8. The thick, acrid smoke made Thaddeus feel sick.
9. Ms. Thornton declared the story to be a myth.
10. Few traces are left of what was once the region of Thrace.

Some black English dialect speakers substitute an /f/ for the /θ/ in the final position in words such as *bath*, *mouth*, and *both*. Speakers who do this and who wish to change their pronunciation of final /θ/ words may use the practice materials that follow. They should make certain that the final articulatory position is postdental, and not labiodental.

breath	math	forth
cloth	path	wreath
faith	north	uncouth
growth	south	truth
health	teeth	Ruth
mirth	both	dearth
pith	broth	Beth

The following sentences provide the opportunity for establishing final /θ/ and /f/ sounds.

1. The truth was that Muff had little faith in Beth.
2. The rough road went north and south.
3. Both Biff and Jeff wore their cloth coats.
4. Though it may be hard, it is usually worthwhile to study math.
5. The sleuth caught the uncouth thief.

ADDITIONAL PRACTICE MATERIALS FOR /θ/

three	through	thud	thousand
theme	throe	thunder	thymus
thesis	throat	thump	theory
thimble	throne	third	threat
thicken	thrall	Thursday	throttle
theft	thought	thirst	thrust
thalamus	thwart	thirteen	thicket

thank	thaw	thigh	theology
thread	thrash	thrush	thyroid
thrips	thrive	thrum	Thrace

ether	pathos	enthusiasm	lengthen
breathy	pathetic	author	strengthen
anything	bathtub	orthodox	earthy
nothing	wrathful	orthopod	forthright
healthy	ruthless	slothful	toothless
wealthy	truthful	mirthful	atheist
stealthy	ethyl	toothache	method
rethread	birthday	mythical	lethargy
deathly	earthquake	synthetic	panther
youthful	hawthorn	arithmetic	Cathay

frothy	fifths[1]	sixths[1]	months[1]
wreath	booth	month	hearth
beneath	uncouth	mouth	sleuth
myth	both	warmth	troth
pith	oath	south	froth
kith	fourth	growth	length
faith	north	eighth	fifth
death	moth	ninth	breath
zenith	cloth	path	truth
wrath	dearth	mammoth	Ruth
stealth	earth	worth	Beth

PHRASES

faithful youth	thankless theory
wrathful truth	third Thursday
warmth of the south	enthralled with the myth
north of Cathay	thwarted atheist
fifth birthday	ruthless threat
oath unto death	zenith of growth
south of Fourth	youthful stealth
thick as thieves	mammoth toothache

CONTRAST IN /θ/, /t/, AND /s/

Theme for Thanksgiving

Ms. Matthews.   Today's theme for our diet team is "It's no sin to be thin—think before you sink a tooth into that chocolate mousse." Face the fact that it will be hard to keep the faith over Thanksgiving. You big eaters might need ether. It's a myth that you must miss the whole meal. Just don't kiss your kith for baking cakes. Learn to sigh and fuss over

---

[1] Speakers should guard against a tendency to substitute a /t/ or omit the /θ/ in these words.

Gran's turkey thigh. It's no myth that you have to keep your mitts off the pie to get thin as a tin pin.

Gertha. Ms. Matthews, the theme here seems to be that you deserve a wrathful fate if you thrill to eat cake. But I saw you thaw a torte and cut a slice so thick it made me sick. How can you thumb your nose at the sum of those calories?

Ms. Matthews. Gertha, I thought I taught you that I sought eternal youth—and found it! You must make a truce with the truth. I'm a wraith half your size who rates a size six dress. Now, it's not worth a worse deprivation than dieting to get thin. Don't miss Thanksgiving altogether. But until then, take an oath to eat nothing but cooked oats! That's what Theodore and I have done. Truthfully, I suspect that Theodore may be cheating.

SENTENCES

1. Arithmetic is thought to be the most elementary form of mathematics.

2. *Thank you*'s are better than threats in strengthening associations.

3. Matthew learned how to be thoughtful rather than ruthless in telling the truth.

4. The warmth of the day made Theodore lethargic.

5. Thelma, unlike her brother Thaddeus, enjoyed birthdays with kith and kin.

6. The famous author Shaw thought that youth is wasted on the youthful, but neither Thalia nor Thea thought that this was so.

7. Ruth considered the eighth day of the month her thoroughly lucky one.

8. Beth spotted the panther creeping stealthily through the thicket.

9. There was no dearth of growth from the fertile soil of the South.

10. Thursday is the fifth day of the week.

SELECTIONS

1. The youthful Keats was the author of many famous lines. Among the best known are the following from *Endymion* and *Ode on a Grecian Urn:*

A thing of beauty is a joy forever:
Its loveliness increases; it will never
Pass into nothingness.

''Beauty is truth, truth beauty''—that is all
Ye know on earth, and all ye need to know.

2. In *My Lost Youth,* Henry Wadsworth Longfellow, often called the poet of the hearth, wrote:

A boy's will is the wind's will,
And the thoughts of youth are long, long thoughts.

3. On the thirty-second day of the thirteenth month of the
    eighth day of the week,
  On the twenty-fifth hour and the sixty-first minute, we'll
    find all things that we seek.

  —SAM W. FOSS, *The Eighth Day of the Week*

4. Said Bertha to Gertha,
  "You seem full of mirth;
  Does your ungentle laughter
  Endanger your girth?"

  Said Gertha to Bertha,
  "I am full of mirth,
  And my broad, healthy laughter
  Is good for my girth."

  —J. E.

5. For wrath killeth the foolish man, and envy slayeth the silly one.

  —*Job,* 5:2

PRACTICE DIALOGUE FOR /θ/

Youthful Enthusiasm

Atherton. Our orthodox theology class was enthralling on Thursday. We
studied Hegel, a sleuth who ruthlessly searched for the truth. His di-
alectical method, where synthesis is created through thesis and antith-
esis, is a thumping thrill! At the end of his pithy speech, Mr. Wings-
worth pointed out that to lengthen a theory does not give it strength.
Where were you this Thursday? Were you held in thrall of your mam-
moth atheist southern authors?

Theodore. Atherton, I thirst for a more earthy truth. Thursday, as stealthy
as a thief, I threaded my way up the path that leads through the thick
hawthorns to the mouth of the northern lake. There I saw a panther
thrashing about in the thicket, caught in the throes of a rage. I held
my breath and faced the threat of death from this beast with the frothy
mouth. But as he was about to throttle me, the earth beneath my feet
quaked, and the panther lost his teeth!

Atherton. Theodore, it's the ninth time this month that you missed theology. Your lethargy is both slothful and pathetic. This birthday you'll
be thirty. You do nothing to justify your youthful existence, nor to
acquire wisdom and wealth.

Theodore. Atherton, sloth is therapy for my soul. Your youthful enthusi-
asm for theory is fine, but I do not thrive on myth or the teachings of
the faithful. Thursday I took a bath in the lake and baked in the warmth
of the southern sun. Sitting by the hearth for months and studying theories will threaten your health. Take my path to the northern lake,
listen to the thrush, and watch the fog thicken. Don't throw away your
youth!

Atherton.   I'll spend my youth in thought, thank you. The zenith of growth
is to know truth from myth—something thoroughly worth all my en-
thusiasm!

/ð/ (th) As in *That* and *Those; Either* and *Weather;*
Bathe and *Breathe*

/ð/ (~~th~~) is the voiced cognate of /θ/. It is represented by the letters *th* and may occur
initially, medially, or finally, as in *these, bathing,* and *wreathe.* The /ð/ is produced
with light tongue-tip contact either behind the upper teeth or between the cutting edges
of the teeth. Air is forced through the place of contact while the vocal folds are in
vibration.

There is no certain way of determining whether a particular word should be pronounced with a /θ/ or a /ð/. We may note a tendency—in initial positions, at least—
for words that are stressed and significant in a sentence, such as nouns, verbs, and
adjectives, to be pronounced with the voiceless /θ/. Pronouns, articles, and conjunctions, which are more likely to be unstressed and weak in sentence context, tend to be
pronounced with a /ð/. As a result, the /ð/ tends to occur more often than the /θ/ in
our speech.

Persons who are inclined to substitute a /t/ for a /θ/ are also likely to substitute a /d/
for a /ð/. The first set of practice materials should help to establish a clear distinction
between the /d/ and the /ð/. (See page 250–251 for a description of /d/.)

PRACTICE MATERIALS

Distinguish between /ð/ and /d/.

thee	dee	their	dare
they	day	thence	dense
then	den	lather	ladder
than	Dan	lathe	laid
though	dough	loathe	load
those	doze	seethe	seed
thy	dye	other	udder
thine	dine	worthy	wordy

PHRASES

loathed the load	wordy but worthy
their foolish dare	writhed on their ride
then to the den	the other udder

SENTENCES FOR /ð/ AND /d/

1. Dan was taller than his brother.
2. Most of us loathe a heavy load.
3. There are few children who can resist a dare.
4. They devoted the day to thinking worthy thoughts but did few worthy
deeds.

5. Ted thought that even though he could not help make the dough, he could enjoy breathing the aroma of the baking bread.

6. They went thence into the dense forest.

7. Though they had coffee with their doughnuts, they nevertheless dozed off.

8. They rode all day to dine with their wordy but worthy brother.

ADDITIONAL PRACTICE MATERIALS

these	than	the	thine
this	those	thus	them
then	though	thy	therefore
they	there	that	therein
either	weather	although	mother
neither	feather	loathing	bother
heathen	lather	brother	logarithm
leather	rather	father	further
breathe	soothe	scythe	swathe
bathe	scathe	writhe	teethe
wreathe	blithe	tithe	with

SENTENCES

1. Although she was loathe to speak her mind, mother thought that she knew best.

2. Neither mother nor brother enjoyed foggy weather.

3. The word *thine* is the possessive form of *thou.*

4. *This* and *that* are demonstrative pronouns.

5. Mother is fond of feathered creatures.

6. The ghosts gathered among the other blithe spirits.

7. Leather is being replaced by plastic in the making of clothing.

8. The heather withered in the field.

9. The heathen considered it a bother to bathe.

10. Although the birds were of a feather, they preferred not to flock together.

SELECTIONS FOR /θ/ AND /ð/

1. Let us crown ourselves with rosebuds before they be withered.

—*Wisdom of Solomon*, 2:8

2. At the door of life, by the gate of breath,
There are worse things waiting for me than death.

—ALGERNON CHARLES SWINBURNE, *The Triumph of Time*

3. But he who loveliness within
  Hath found, all outward loathes,
For he who colour loves, and skin,
  Loves but their oldest clothes.

—JOHN DONNE, *The Undertaking*

4. Fame sometimes hath created something of nothing.
—THOMAS FULLER, *Of Marriage*

5. Rather than love, than money, than fame, give me truth.
—HENRY DAVID THOREAU, *Conclusion*

6. Those who would be successful in counterintelligence must be thorough in their projections and be able to think out what others may think that they think. Somehow, they must be able to think ahead of their opposite numbers. Those who fail so to think are not likely to think that they think for very long.

PRACTICE DIALOGUE FOR /ð/ AND /d/ CONTRAST

Wordy Questions and Worthy Deeds

Dan the Farmer. I will answer any worthy questions as long as they're not wordy, Dave.

Dave. Why did those workers doze off at dinner?

Dan the Farmer. They started their day at dawn. They laid that heavy drain pipe, after using the lathe to cut it. Then they replanted seed that was scattered by the seething winds. Then they went into the dense woods to clear a road.

Dave. Why will no one dare ride that dark horse over there?

Dan the Farmer. If you writhe when you ride a horse of that breed, you may never breathe again!

Dave. Why don't you milk that other cow, the one with the heavy udder? It must loathe its milky load!

Dan the Farmer. Dave, rather than asking these wordy questions, do a worthy deed. Though you're small, you can knead dough for Dee. Or climb the ladder for the soap and lather the leather saddle. Then meet me in the den. Just remember, your mother bade you bathe before you dine with your father.

17

The Tongue-Tip to Gum-Ridge and the Postdental Sounds

A glance at the consonant chart will reveal that the tongue-tip to gum-ridge (lingua-alveolar) and the postalveolar sounds include a third of the American-English consonants. The lingua-alveolar and the postalveolar articulatory positions are distinctive in our language. For this reason, the sounds in these groups are given detailed consideration.

The Tongue-Tip to Gum-Ridge Sounds

The Phoneme /t/

We begin our study of the tongue-tip to gum-ridge consonants with the [t] as in *tea*, *ton*, and *too*. If the contact point and manner of articulation for this [t] are mastered, the speaker will have an excellent point of reference for the production of other American-English alveolar speech sounds.

In this section, devoted to the phoneme /t/, we present separate materials for several of the allophones of /t/. In keeping with phonetic practice, the allophones are indicated in brackets [ ]. Allophones, we recall, are variants of phonemes and are the actual sounds that we produce in contextual speech. Allophones may be "defined" as the nondistinctive features of phonemes, the features that do not result in differences in our perception of words and their meanings.

[t] As in *Ton, Until,* and *Utopia*. To produce the [t] as in *ton* or as an isolated sound, the tongue is raised so that the tongue tip comes into contact with the upper gum ridge (see Figure 17–1). The soft palate is raised to prevent nasal emission of breath. The sides of the tongue near the tip are in contact with the upper molars. The tongue, tense

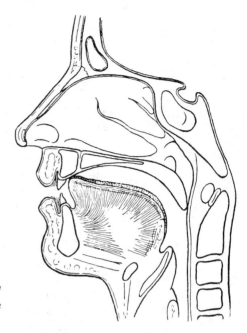

FIGURE 17–1   Articulatory position for /t/ and /d/. Note the contact between the tongue tip and the alveolar (gum) ridge.

and extended, is held in this position for a fraction of a second. Then, quickly, and as completely as possible, the tongue is retracted, with a resultant slight "explosion" of air at the tongue tip. This should be felt as a puff of breath if you hold your hand in front of your mouth.

The [t] as just described occurs whenever the sound appears in a stressed syllable and is immediately followed by a vowel. The [t] in such contexts is a lingua-alveolar (gum-ridge), stop-plosive consonant. In producing this [t], observe the following cautions:

1. Make certain that the tongue tip is in contact with the gum ridge and *not the upper teeth*. The contact, when broken, should be quick and complete.

2. Do not permit the tongue to slide so that contact is made between the front surface of the tongue and the gum. If this happens, a [ts] blend is likely to be produced.

PRACTICE MATERIALS

Establish the contact position for the stressed [t] by practice with the material that follows. Repeat each of the words in the lists at least three times.

INITIAL

tea	take	too	tole
tee	ten	tube	talk
tip	tell	took	taught
tell	tag	tomb	tog
tape	tap	toe	top
turn	type	town	tone
Turk	time	tower	team

tub	tide	toy	teach
ton	tile	toil	tease
tie	tire	towel	tool

MEDIAL *(followed by a vowel)*

attend	intern	Utopia	partake
atone	iterate	Utah	pitied
attack	deter	intake	rotate
attempt	detect	eternal	entire
attach	until	retool	historical
attain	utensil	retook	intone
entire	intense	return	intend

PHRASES

talented team	ton of tin
take your time	talk and tell
tip to top	took the tea
ten and ten	ten times ten
twenty and two	turn the tape
tap the top	take a turn
the town tower	tie the tag

SENTENCES

1. Tom played a tuba to tease Ted.
2. Ted's toe was taped but it still hurt.
3. Tell Tillie the time when it is 2:00 P.M.
4. Tea was served privately for the two who wanted to be entirely alone.
5. The tower was attacked and attained.
6. Time and tide are eternal verities.
7. Tuesday was made tag day in town.
8. Utah is named for the Ute Indians.
9. The intern detected a contagious tic.
10. Tom turned detective to test his attainments at detection.

Final [t]. A final [t] is exploded (aspirated) when it is followed by a vowel in the next word within the same phrase, as in *the cat is here.* Most persons either do not aspirate the final [t] at the end of a sentence, as in *I'll come at eight,* or produce this [t] with little aspiration (a slight puff of breath). The same tendencies hold for final [t] at the end of a phrase within a sentence, as in *it might be right.*

PRACTICE MATERIALS

ant	fate	late	effete
bait	fat	dote	but
eat	bat	note	cut
it	boot	bought	hut

ate	emit	blot	hurt
might	foot	right	naught
out	flout	night	suit
quoit	incite	sought	root
sight	blight	fort	shoot
sweet	discreet	elite	defeat

SENTENCES

1. We will eat at eight.
2. Is football or basketball the favorite American sport?
3. Nat was hurt by the split bat.
4. Mint and fruit juice make for a pleasant drink.
5. The boat was lost in the mist late at night.
6. Naught could induce Chet to emit a sound.
7. Most adolescents like to eat things that are sweet.
8. The note was brought by a servant who wore a blue suit.
9. The quoit contest was won by the Ute.
10. A well-fitted boot will not hurt the foot.

[t] As in *Safety*.   The sound [t] in an unstressed syllable followed by a vowel is produced in a less vigorous manner than when it occurs in a stressed syllable. The contact between tongue tip and gum ridge is not held as long as for a stressed [t], and there is less of a breath puff following the breaking of the contact. Avoid assimilating the unstressed [t] in the direction of either substituting a [d] for it or omitting the sound entirely.

PRACTICE MATERIALS

The words that follow provide practice for the unstressed [t].

pity	hatter	hefty	jetty
city	latter	utter	tempted
plenty	faulty	bitter	twenty
better	mountain	fifty	written
letter	scatter	thirty	litter
kitty	witty	fretted	patted

Practice in discriminating between the unstressed [t] and [d] in the following pairs of words.

latter	ladder	wetting	wedding
betting	bedding	written	ridden
heated	heeded	butting	budding
bitter	bidder	tenting	tending
rating	raiding	contented	contended
shutter	shudder	writer	rider

The following words provide practice for [t] followed by a vowel and/or in the final position.

tell	waste	fateful	bit	tat
ten	last	inter	flat	tent
till	quite	contain	flute	taste
time	after	rotary	hoot	tight
told	comet	twine	root	taught
tab	lout	twist	tote	toot
tangle	between	twig	wart	tort
toll	return	palliate	what	twist
at	continue	unite	flirt	twit
boat	atone	beet	wheat	tossed

SENTENCES

1. Ten and ten and two count up to twenty-two if counted correctly.

2. Tom Tucker will have to be told to wait for tomorrow.

3. Ted, please put the cat and the light out before you take off.

4. The tidings of the times portended that temptation was to be avoided at all cost.

5. On his trip to Utah, Thomas sat next to a taciturn gentleman from eastern Texas.

6. The stars twinkled brightly in the Oriental sky.

7. Tess taught that it was easier to start than to stop a fight.

8. Thomson could not take being twitted, although he was expert at taunting others not quite his size.

9. Stuart and Tonia were upset because they had to wait for twenty minutes between the acts.

10. Too few learn in time that it is for them for whom the bell tolls.

SELECTIONS

1. Temptation can be many different things to different people. It has been a time-honored subject for the poet, the moralist, the dramatist, and the philosopher. Some views of temptation are presented in the quotations that follow.

    a. "I can resist everything except temptation," Oscar Wilde had one of his characters protest.

    b. In contrast, the ever-optimistic Robert Browning asserted in his *Ring and the Book:*

> Why comes temptation but for man to meet
> And master and make crouch beneath his foot,
> And so be pedestaled in triumph?

    c. Finally, for the moment at least, we have the terse statement of the British humorist and poet Douglas Jerrold, who in his *Catspaw* contended: "Honest bread is very well—it's the butter that makes the temptation."

2. Take hands and part with laughter;
    Touch lips and part with tears;

Once more and no more after,
   Whatever comes with years.

   —ALGERNON CHARLES SWINBURNE, *Rococo*

3.   O, it is excellent
   To have a giant's strength; but it is tyrannous
   To use it like a giant.

   —WILLIAM SHAKESPEARE, *Measure for Measure*

4. The great physicist Albert Einstein, with a note of sadness, once revealed that fate, in order to inflict a penalty on him for his contempt of authority, had imposed a state of authority on him.

[t] As a Final, Morphemic Sound As in *Chased* and *Lunched*. Note its consistent representation in spelling by the letters *ed*.

based	diced	spiced	polished
raced	placed	creased	pounced
chased	branched	lunched	grossed
faced	lanced	munched	crossed
graced	bunched	tossed	nursed
laced	hunched	bossed	trooped

SENTENCES

1. Tina munched as she lunched on the spiced meat.
2. Tom hunched in pain when his finger was lanced.
3. They trooped to the right of the triple-branched route.
4. Tom placed third when he raced in a leased car.
5. The haunched tiger pounced on its timid prey.

Other Varieties of /t/

As indicated earlier, the consonant /t/ varies somewhat in its manner of production and the acoustic end result according to speech context. Some of the more frequent variations are now considered.

[t] Followed by /θ/ (th) or /ð/ (th) As in *Right Things* and *At The*. In combinations such as *at the, hit that, light things,* and *eighth,* the [t] is produced by contact between the tongue tip and the upper teeth rather than at the gum ridge. The dentalized [t] in these combinations is produced as a result of the assimilative influence of the next sound, /θ/ or /ð/, which is articulated dentally.

This variety of /t/ is least likely to be produced defectively by persons with foreign-language backgrounds. It is the variety most likely to be produced habitually by speakers whose English speech is influenced by French, Spanish, Italian, or German.

PRACTICE MATERIALS

wet thaw	fat Thane
eighth time	sweet thoughts

hit the ball	right thinking
swat the fly	bright theorist
light the lamp	light theme
stout thump	correct theory
went there	hurt thumb
at third	meet at the tank
not at three	promised thanks

SENTENCES

1. Bright theories by intelligent theorists result in right thoughts.
2. Tom struck out the eighth and the last time at bat.
3. Tess could not bear to swat the fly.
4. The poet thought in slight themes and tiny stanzas.
5. Ted liked to light the lamp no later then eight at night.
6. Shelley wrote that our sweetest themes for songs are those that tell of saddest thoughts.
7. Burt thanked Thelma for her right thinking.
8. Nat thanked Theodore for not thwarting him in developing his complete thesis.
9. After the first thaw, the wet thatched roof leaked.
10. The pert theorem was based on correct theory.

[t] Followed by /l/ or /n/ As in *Little* and *Button*. When the [t] sound is immediately followed by an /l/ or an /n/, it is not necessary to remove the tongue tip from the gum ridge to complete the sound. Instead, the sides of the front part of the tongue break contact with the side teeth to permit a *lateral* escape or explosion of breath. When the [t] is followed by [l], as in *little, battle, settle, kettle,* and *mortal,* the breath of the explosion is emitted laterally.

In words in which [t] is followed by /n/, as in *written, button, cotton,* and *rotten,* the tongue position is maintained in going from the [t] to the /n/. When the velum is lowered for the /n/, a nasal rather than an oral explosion takes place. If you place your hand just below the nostrils, you should be able to feel a nasally emitted puff of air.

There is a marked tendency to substitute a throat or glottal (laryngeal) click sound for the [t] when it is followed by /l/ or /n/. This substitution, in American speech, is generally considered substandard. You may check your tendency toward glottal substitution by placing your hand at your larynx while speaking the lists of words and sentences that follow. If you feel a click, it is likely that you are using a glottal (laryngeal) "catch" sound instead of the [t]. To avoid this tendency, pay special attention to the prescribed manner of articulation for the [t] in [tl] and [tn] combinations.

PRACTICE MATERIALS

cattle	fettle	fatten	wanton
beetle	mortal	bitten	rotten
battle	glottal	button	fountain
metal	bottle	cotton	written
whittle	scuttle	gotten	fatten

settle	rattle	mountain	mutton
mental	spittle	subtle	mitten

SENTENCES

1. Myrtle was in fine fettle as she filled the kettle and anticipated the toast.

2. The mutton chops were too tough to be eaten.

3. The ill-gotten gains were hidden in the mountain.

4. Little by little, Benton analyzed the contents of the bottle.

5. The buttons were whittled out of wood.

6. The kitten played with the cotton mitten.

7. Skelton hoped to become immortal by well-written words.

8. A metal figure of Triton dominated the fountain.

9. Martin found it difficult to fatten his mutton.

10. On his climb up the mountain, Fenton stopped to fill his metal bottle.

[t] Followed by /s/ and Preceded and Followed by /s/ As in *Pets* and *Posts*. In contexts in which the [t] is immediately followed by an /s/, the tip of the tongue is permitted to slide forward in anticipation of the /s/. Care should be taken not to omit the [t] entirely, especially in combinations in which the [t] is medial between two /s/ sounds. The fine articulatory movements required for the [sts] combination increase the tendency to omit the [t].

PRACTICE MATERIALS

Practice with the words, phrases, and sentences that follow should help to focus attention on the precise articulation that is required for [ts] and [sts].

baits	eats	roasts	toasts
pets	pots	insists	pests
lots	flights	breasts	ghosts
gates	paints	posts	resists
facts	mists	rests	persists
lasts	jests	masts	tests

PHRASES

eats sweets	first sights
nuts and bolts	bats and ghosts
paints the posts	resists the pests
posts at gates	persists and insists
lots of facts	flights of bats

SENTENCES

1. The last acts of plays should be the playwright's best.

2. Painted pots were placed next to the fence posts along the streets.

3. Gray mists stopped the planes' flights from the airports.

4. The hard facts of life may interfere with the attainments of the heart's desires.

5. Birds' nests were found in the nets hanging from the masts.

6. Stone persists in presenting lists of facts at times when jests or stories of ghosts are more to listeners' tastes.

SELECTIONS

1. Hope springs eternal in the human breast:
Man never is, but always to be, blest.

—ALEXANDER POPE, *Essay on Man*

2. Now cracks a noble heart. Good night, sweet prince,
And flights of angels sing thee to thy rest.

—WILLIAM SHAKESPEARE, *Hamlet*

3. Even with the utterly lost, to whom life and death are equally jests, there are matters of which no jest can be made.

—EDGAR ALLAN POE, *The Masque of the Red Death*

4. He leaves for America's history and biography, so far, not only its most dramatic reminiscence—he leaves, in my opinion, the greatest, best, most characteristic, artistic, moral personality.

—WALT WHITMAN, *Death of President Lincoln*

PRACTICE DIALOGUE FOR VARIETIES OF /t/

Burt the Baseball Star

Sports Announcer. Burt, that ball you batted is still in flight. It's the eighth time you hit the ball and landed a man at third. Is it right thinking that busts those bats?

Burt the Star. I had gotten fat on mutton and had to whittle down. I got thin as I ate the leanest little roasts and turkey breasts. That is cause for lots of toasts!

Sports Announcer. There's a lot of rotten tripe written about you. What they say is that your wanton drinking persists.

Burt the Star. Those pests should button up about my battle with the bottle until they get the facts straight. If I was drunk, I could not hit that mosquito right there with a kettle. Write the facts and scuttle the rumors. My busted bats prove I'm in fine fettle!

/d/ As in *Done, Ado,* and *Glad*

The consonant /d/ in *done* is articulated in essentially the same manner at the /t/ in *ton,* except that the /d/ is voiced. The /d/, like the /t/, is a variable sound. The varieties of /d/ parallel those of /t/. Faults in the articulation of /d/ also parallel those for /t/, the chief one being the tendency toward dental articulation. A second tendency to be avoided is the substitution of a /t/ for a /d/ in words in which the final /d/ should be voiced. This fault may be especially noted in the speech of German-born persons or of persons for whom German was and perhaps continues to be a strong influence. The probable reason is that the final /d/ does not occur in German.

PRACTICE MATERIALS

The first set of materials should help establish a clear distinction between /t/ and /d/. Make certain that the /t/ is voiceless and the /d/ is voiced.

Distinguish between initial [t] and [d].

tame	dame	tuck	duck
teem	deem	tune	dune
tip	dip	tomb	doom
tense	dense	toll	dole
tamp	damp	tummy	dummy
tail	dale	toe	doe
ten	den	taunt	daunt
tan	Dan	tot	dot
time	dime	town	down
too	do	touch	Dutch

Distinguish between medial [t] and [d].[1]

kitty	kiddy	writing	riding
fated	faded	wetted	wedded
knotted	nodded	butted	budded
utter	udder	grated	graded

SENTENCES

1. The kitty delighted the kiddy.

2. A rose is fated to become faded.

3. Dan contended and seemed contented to come second in the duel race with Tania.

4. Dotty heeded the advice to keep her den heated.

Distinguish between final [t] and [d].

seat	seed	brute	brood
bit	bid	note	node
ate	aid	naught	gnawed
late	laid	not	nod
mat	mad	coat	code
let	led	writ	rid
bat	bad	cart	card
set	said	stunt	stunned
cat	cad	hurt	heard
beat	bead	curt	curd

---

[1] See pages 245, 253–254 for additional practice materials to distinguish between [t] and [d] in medial, unstressed positions.

SENTENCES FOR FINAL [t] *AND* [d] *DISTINCTIONS*

1. Dot said, "I'm set."
2. The elderly patient ate without aid.
3. The lawyer could not get rid of the writ.
4. Dick was heard to shout, "I'm hurt."

PRACTICE MATERIALS FOR /d/ IN VARIOUS POSITIONS

INITIAL

deal	daze	dart	dire
deep	duel	dark	dear
din	dough	dirt	dean
day	dote	dearth	dream
debt	dawn	dub	drip
dance	dock	dike	drain
dew	dog	doubt	draw
dale	damp	dull	does

PHRASES

deep in dew	dull and damp
dance till dawn	daily dozen
day by day	duel in the dew
dark and dreary	due date
din at daybreak	dull ditty
dry desert	denizen of the deep
dog at the dock	delicate dough
dearth of dough	dire dream
dime a deal	doubtful Dan
down the drain	deep in daisies

MEDIAL

adder	adduce	bedding	grander
admit	fading	bedlam	hinder
ardent	hidden	candor	needed
oddly	eddy	splendor	indoor
edict	adverse	random	odious

FINAL

add	amid	said	spade
crowd	old	lead	code
rude	bald	heed	abode
hoard	fraud	reed	node
heed	curd	rod	aloud
ode	brood	toad	cloud
mode	druid	mood	mold

SENTENCES

1. Undaunted by earlier failures, Diane and Ted led a dozen determined ladies to begin a ten-day diet.

2. Dan claimed that frequently he could not distinguish between Dick's candor and his rudeness.

3. As the day was dying, a deep-red cloud rested on the mountaintop.

4. The dog's barking at dawn warned Daniel and helped him to undo a dastardly plot.

5. Duncan brooded over the fraud that deprived him of his gold and his abode.

6. Daybreak is considered the correct if not the good time for undertaking duels.

7. The crowd did not heed the warning to disperse.

8. London is reputed to be a city of dense fog and bright-minded traders.

9. The drug made Dick's head droop as he dropped off to sleep.

10. Matilda married her doting admiral, who wrote an ode to his bride.

11. David took heed of every detail as he decoded the note.

12. Druidism is a religion that was once prevalent in the lands that are now England and Ireland.

[dz]

adds	cards	reeds	fords
beads	fades	steeds	raised
beds	heads	rides	hazed
aides	hides	reeds	meads
brides	minds	lads	nodes
buds	roads	girds	rods

[d] *FOLLOWED BY* **[θ] (th)** *OR* **[ð] (th)**

had that	herd the cattle	ride through
hid the ball	sad thoughts	width and breadth
heard the call	rid the land	ford the stream
amid the crowd	hoarded things	heed the leader

SELECTIONS FOR /t/ *AND* /d/

1. But when I tell him he hates flatterers,
He says he does, being then most flattered.
—WILLIAM SHAKESPEARE, *Julius Caesar*

2. Cowards die many times before their death;
The valiant never taste of death but once.
—WILLIAM SHAKESPEARE, *Julius Caesar*

3. When Adam was created,
He dwelt in Eden's shade,
As Moses has related,
Before a bride was made;
Ten thousand times ten thousand
Things wheeled all around,

Before a bride was formed
Or yet a mate was found.

—GEORGE PULLEN JACKSON, *Wedlock*

4. No living man can send me to the shades
Before my time; no man of woman born,
Coward or brave, can shun his destiny.

—HOMER, *Iliad*

5. Said Trixon to Dixon,
"You look full of thought;
I'll offer you tuppence
Though it may be worth nought."

Said Dixon to Trixon,
"Your offer's quite tempty
But not for ten tuppence,
Would my mind for you empty."

—J. E., *A Thought's a Thought for All That*

6. According to Mark Twain, Adam was the only person who could know for certain that when he said a good or witty thing nobody could have said it at any time before him.

7. Mark Twain also advised that we try to get out of an experience only the insight and wisdom that is in it and stop there. He cautioned us not to be like the cat that, after sitting down on a hot stovelid, never again sits down on a hot lid. That is all to the good unless the cat also decides never again to sit on any lid, hot or cold.

/t/ AND /d/ REVIEW (including contrasts between /t/ and /d/)

Dialogue for a Saturday Night

Tilden.   You know football is my favorite sport. Saturday night I want to attend an out-of-town game in Utah. I bought tickets on the twenty-yard line. Our talented University team, with its budding players, could get hurt butting heads with Utah. But in our entire history we have not been defeated on a Saturday night. We'll beat those ten-ton trucks that consider themselves hot-shot athletes.

Edweena.   But what about the women's tennis tournament tonight? Last Saturday we attended the football game, where overgrown adolescents tackled, attacked, pounded, and punched each other. Tomorrow night I want to root for our tennis team. Our team placed in the top ten. I took Tina to tryout, and even when she chased a ball, she graced the court with beauty. In tennis, the competition is intense but seldom does one get badly hurt.

Tilden.   Once most women seemed content to be volunteers, to give freely of their time. Now they are setting things to right. They compete in bidding for hefty salaries along with the male stars. Of course, if we like to watch tennis, we pay at the gate. Tomorrow, let's take the tube downtown and watch the track meet, just for a change.

Edweena.   It's a pity to stay in the city and waste the last night of August. Let's wash the boat from top to toe, retool, and take it out on the water. We can suit up at night and tread water in the moonlight. We will have tea for two, listen to the flute concert at the jetty, and flirt. The night will take a fateful twist as we are tossed about on the tide. We'll return Tuesday and continue to teach the delights of poetry to the elite.

Tilden.   Edweena, dear, instead, why don't we mountain-climb outside of town and partake of Utopia away from the city litter. We can pitch a tent on a flat rock and quote from letters that poets have written to their loved ones.

Edweena.   Tilden, that's a delightful idea! We can blot out all thoughts and talk of nothing. There's no sight as sweet as the scattered clouds above the city.

/s/ As in *Sea, Asleep, Icy, Best,* and *Less*

The consonant /s/ is a high-frequency, voiceless, tongue-tip fricative that requires careful and precise articulatory action for its production. The adjustments involve the following:

1. The tongue is raised so that the sides are pressed firmly against the inner surfaces of the upper molars.

2. The tongue is slightly grooved along the midline. Air is forced down along this groove.

3. The tip of the tongue is placed about a quarter of an inch behind the upper teeth. The tongue tip is almost in position for a /t/. (Persons not able to attain this adjustment will probably find it easier to place the tongue tip close to the lower gum ridge.)

4. The teeth are brought in line, with a very narrow space between the rows of teeth.

5. The breath stream is directed along the groove of the tongue toward the cutting edges of the teeth.

6. The soft palate is raised to prevent nasal emission of the sound.

Use a mirror to see the articulatory adjustments for the /s/. The recommended articulatory position is represented in Figure 17–2.

In producing the /s/, exercise special care to avoid having the tongue tip touch either the upper teeth or the gum ridge. Neither should you permit the tongue tip to slide down so as to protrude between the rows of teeth. The first articulatory error will result in the production of a [ts] blend or in a lateral sound resembling a voiceless [l]. The second fault will result in the production of an infantile lisp resembling a [θ] (th).

Persons who habitually produce /t/ and /d/ sounds with dental rather than gum-ridge contacts are likely to lower the tongue tip for the production of /s/. The result, in most instances, is the production of a dull, low-pitched sibilant.

In some instances, the articulatory adjustments just described do not help to produce the desired result of a high-frequency, sibilant sound. Occasionally, the person, possibly because of an unusual mouth structure, must make individual adjustments to arrive at the same acoustic end result. With some articulatory adjustments, a low-pitched

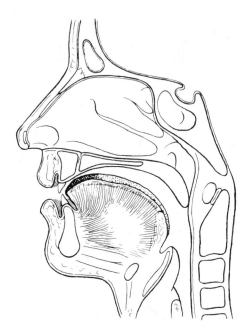

FIGURE 17–2 **Articulatory adjustments for /s/ and /z/. Note that the tip of the tongue is slightly retracted from the upper gum ridge.**

sound may be the best that the individual can achieve. Most persons, however, regardless of their articulatory mechanism, can learn to produce an /s/ that acoustically resembles the high-pitched fricative just described.

Apart from the manner of articulation, the sound /s/ in American-English speech may present some difficulty for the foreign-born speaker because of the varied spelling representations of the sound. The most frequent representation is the letter *s;* other representations include *ss* as in *less, sc* as in *scene, c* as in *race,* and *x* as in *hoax.*[2] The foreign-born speaker of English may be forgiven her or his failure to know when to produce the sound /s/ if we realize the many ways in which the letter *s* may be pronounced. In addition to the /s/, we have /ʒ/ (zh) as in *treasure,* /ʃ/ (sh) as in *sure,* and /z/ as in *his.* To add to the consternation of the foreign-born speaker, we also have the "silent" *s* as in *island* and *aisle.*

PRACTICE MATERIALS

Because of the frequency of the /s/ in American-English speech, we recommend that a considerable amount of attention be given to this sound. Practice first to produce the sound in isolation until a clear, high-frequency sibilant can be articulated at will. Then, incorporate the sound into nonsense syllables. The advantage of nonsense-syllable practice in the early stages of establishing or correcting a sound lies in the avoidance of habits of articulation that may be faulty. Suggested nonsense-syllable combinations precede the word lists.

---

[2] Actually, the *x* in *hoax, fox, six,* and *tax* represents the sound blend [ks], as in the words *kicks, licks,* and *peaks.* The [s] in these words is the second component of the sound blend [ks].

seef	sif	sef	saf	sek
sah	sof	soo	sook	sawp
sut	sug	sul	sool	sipe

ahsah	ahsaw	eesaw	aysaw
ohso	ohsoo	ooso	oosoo
eensay	unsaw	akso	amsoo

INITIAL[3]

see	sew	suck	circuit
seat	soak	seal	cease
say	saw	sale	citric
sane	sought	ceiling	cinch
sin	sog	sigh	scenic
sit	sop	cite	scent
set	song	civil	scepter
sell	sock	cider	science
sat	sir	cigar	scion
sag	certain	cinder	screen
sue	soil	cipher	screw
soot	sun	circle	scratch

MEDIAL

aster	insist	aspect	pursue
asset	insert	lessen	insignia
asleep	boost	essay	tracing
mist	rooster	icy	trousseau
hasten	boast	pressing	bracer
pest	bossy	blessing	hoist
last	twosome	history	peaceful

FINAL

bless	remiss	peace	rehearse
crease	loops	choice	loss
leaps	loose	voice	dross
miss	dose	terse	hiss
kiss	horse	verse	hex
pace	Norse	curse	fix
race	bus	fuss	tricks
bets	truss	mouse	cheeks
debts	puss	house	plates
pass	worse	dress	waits
caps	hearse	niece	fleets

---

[3] Additional word lists are provided for [s] blends. Some of the words of the early lists may be used again when the frequent [s] blends are presented.

| farce | entice | boss | keeps |
| nervous | goodness | famous | purpose |

[s] *PRECEDED AND FOLLOWED BY A VOWEL*

deceive	casing	assume	gusset
acetic	assay	twosome	russet
precede	resale	isobar	assign
acid	assemble	isolate	nicety
assimilate	assent	isotype	oscillate
asymmetry	asset	assault	ossify
aseptic	brassy	assort	ascend
essay	glassy	asunder	assail
lacing	messy	assert	asylum
assonant	Bessemer	basic	mason

PHRASES

safe and sane	list of assets	Norse horse
civil suit	peacefully asleep	rehearse the verse
sagging sales	prestigious essay	dress nicely
science series	boastful insignia	acetic acid
soggy soil	passive resistance	terse essay
sad scene	swift pace	sweet syrup

SENTENCES

1. Six swift horses started in the historic race at Seaside.
2. Sue, a suave, slim lass, wore a silk dress.
3. Simon Sweet fussed about the small, squeaking mouse.
4. Selma insisted that clever verse must be terse but not assonant.
5. Simson had a steady fondness for sweet cider and salted nuts.
6. The storm-tossed sloop sank beneath the spray off Salem.
7. Stevenson was a scientist who liked to be certain of his evidence and facts.
8. Stella was enticed by the high ceilings of the house.
9. "Puss in Boots" is a story for small children who like to listen.
10. Some historians say that there is no such thing as a bad peace.

If the /s/ sound cannot be mastered directly, it may be of help to begin with a /t/ and to work initially for a [ts] blend. This is especially helpful for persons who have no difficulty with the /t/ but who do have some with the /s/. The words that follow should be useful for this approach.

cleats	meats	fats	kites
heats	mats	yachts	riots
beats	cats	divots	blunts
bits	hoots	blots	nights
gets	notes	ruts	blights

debts	floats	hurts	weights
hits	thoughts	flights	quoits
fights	lights	nuts	rates

PHRASES

bits of sweets	gets into fights
notes the beats	stunts in flights
hits the lights	heats the meats
ruts and divots	cheats at quoits
nuts and bolts	pats the pets

SENTENCES

1. Betsy's debts were incurred because of high interest rates.
2. Patsy enjoyed lifting weights.
3. The nets were thrown from the yachts.
4. He who gets into fights must expect hurts.
5. Rivets and nuts and bolts of various weights were used to install the posts.

PRACTICE DIALOGUE FOR /s/ *(emphasizing* ci *and* ce *spellings)*

Talking in Circles

Lucille.   Let's describe life in terms of circles, using simple sentences.

Vincent.   That's a cinch. The tents in a circus sit in a circle balancing on cinder blocks.

Lucille.   My niece speaks in circles when she tries to be civil.

Vincent.   You can race around the ice-skating rink because it is round rather than hexagonal.

Lucille.   I'm certain your voice will sound twice as loud in a round room with a high ceiling as it does outdoors.

Vincent.   Orange juice is a choice drink made from round citrus fruit.

Lucille.   The round band that encircles a cigar costs less than a cent and has a nice tobacco scent.

Vincent.   My sister is at the center of her circle of friends, and they surround her like a cement fence.

Lucille.   Constance deceives herself that she is well-rounded in the art of romance.

Vincent.   I could cite more examples, but let's cease playing this silly game and step into the manse.

Lucille.   That's an enticing offer if it includes a nice glass of icy apple cider!

/θ/ (th) and /s/

Some speakers must exercise caution not to confuse the voiceless /θ/ (th) with the /s/. The /θ/ is properly produced with the tip of the tongue in contact with the back of the upper teeth or slightly protruded between the teeth (see Figure 16–1, p. 234). This contact is to be avoided for the /s/.

PRACTICE MATERIALS

The following pairs of words should help to establish the difference between articulatory positions and acoustic results.

thin	sin	think	sink
theme	seem	thaw	saw
thick	sick	thuds	suds
thank	sank	thought	sought
thigh	sigh	thong	song
thumb	sum	third	surd
thane	sane	thunder	sunder
path	pass	worth	worse
bath	bass	kith	kiss
truth	truce	myth	miss
math	mass	Beth	Bess
faith	face	wraith	race

Make certain that the distinction between the /θ/ and the /s/ is made clear in the following material.

PHRASES

truce with truth	sought a thought
faith saved face	saw the ice thaw
kiss for kith	a sane thane
math for the masses	sang bass in the bath

SENTENCES

1. In counting the sum, the boy used his fingers and his thumb.
2. The thick smoke made us feel sick.
3. The lightning that tore the sky asunder was followed by thunder.
4. Because the cook did not think, he clogged the sink.
5. No thinking person can win a race with a wraith.
6. Though not a sin, it is a thin faith that is limited to saving face.
7. Although Sam did not catch the bass, he enjoyed a bath in the sunny stream.
8. The thane sanely took the path that led over the mountain pass.
9. Bess Ross and Beth Roth are kissing kith and kin.
10. Theodore did not seem to be able to find a theme or think of a thing to say or sing to Thelma.

FREQUENT [s] BLENDS AND CLUSTERS

INITIAL [sk]

scheme	scalp	score	sky
skiff	scab	scorch	scare
skin	scan	scorn	scallop
skill	scandal	skirt	scamp
skip	scant	scar	skewer
skit	scatter	Scot	sketch
schedule	school	skull	skeptic
scale	schooner	skunk	squire

MEDIAL [sk]

risking	discount	Alaska	Ruskin
discuss	ensconce	basket	landscape
asking	Muskogee	escape	musket

FINAL [sk]

brisk	whisk	bask	task
disk	desk	flask	tusk
frisk	musk	mask	rusk

INITIAL [st]

steam	stay	sterile	stark
steel	stain	stirrup	start
steep	station	stew	starve
steer	stealth	stole	style
stiff	step	stone	store
still	stem	stove	stork
stick	stigma	stack	stock
sting	stool	stamp	stop
stint	stout	stub	storm
steady	stoop	stunt	story

MEDIAL [st]

Easter	roster	wasteful	basting
feasting	mastiff	coaster	toasted
blister	tasty	costly	castor
master	blasted	frosted	castaway
monster	aster	musty	punster
boasting	oyster	pasted	hoisted

FINAL [st]

beast	mist	past	host
east	best	roast	cost
least	rest	post	frost

priest	pest	roost	lost
yeast	guest	just	first
fist	cast	rust	nursed
list	last	toast	oust
kissed	mast	most	Faust

INITIAL [skr]

scream	script	scrap	scrawl
screech	scrutiny	scramble	scrub
screen	scribble	scroll	scribe
scrivener	scrape	scruple	scrabble
scrimp	scrod	scruff	scrawny

MEDIAL [skr]

discredit	miscreant	descry	unscrew
discreet	proscribe	describe	prescribe
discriminate	discretion	enscribe	inscrutable

INITIAL [str][4]

streak	strain	straw	strut
stream	strength	strong	stripe
strip	strap	strop	strive
stricken	strew	struck	strident
string	stroke	struggle	striate
stray	stroll	strike	structure

MEDIAL [str]

restrict	instruct	upstream	distrust
construe	restraint	district	distress
constrain	unstrung	destroy	dystrophy
constrict	hamstring	distraught	frustrate
construct	restrengthen	distract	prostrate

INITIAL [sm]

smear	smack	smart	smug
smithy	smooth	smolder	smudge
smitten	smote	smother	smile
smell	small	smirk	smite
smelter	smock	Smyrna	smirch

INITIAL [sw]

Sweden	swing	swoon	swan
sweep	sway	swoop	swamp
sweet	sweat	swollen	swallow

[4]There is a tendency for the [s] in the [str] blends to approximate or actually to become an /ʃ/ (sh). Avoid this tendency, which may have been given some status by American "he-man" screen actors.

swig	swelter	swarm	swine
swim	swear	swirl	swipe
swivel	swag	swap	swindle

INITIAL [sn]

sneak	snap	snare	snatch
sneer	snoop	snort	snipe
sniff	snow	snub	snicker
snip	snob	snuff	snug
snail	snarl	snake	snore

FINAL [ns]

wince	fence	glance	romance
pence	quince	lance	prance
hence	mince	manse	enhance

MEDIAL [ns]

answer	balancing	instead	punster
dancer	instant	install	bouncing
Frances	instill	ensnare	winsome
Anselm	Dunstan	Winston	density

INITIAL [sp]

speed	span	spore	spun
speak	sparrow	sparse	spunk
spill	spat	spark	spy
spin	spew	spare	spike
speck	spool	Sparta	spine
spell	spook	spirit	spout
spade	spoof	spur	spoke
Spain	Spode	spurt	spoil
spent	spawn	sponge	spider
spaniel	spinal	sporadic	spiel

FINAL AND MEDIAL [sp]

lisp	crisp	despondent	despoil
asp	grasp	despair	despot
hasp	rasp	desperate	respect
clasp	cusp	aspire	respond
wasp	grasping	despise	respite
wisp	resplendent	bicuspid	perspire

[spl]

split	splendid	splurge	splotch
spleen	splice	splutter	splendor
splay	splint	splash	splat

[spr]

sprain	sprinkle	sprout	sprung
sprig	sprint	spruce	sprocket
spread	sprite	spry	spring

PRACTICE MATERIALS FOR BLENDS

SENTENCES

1. The sponge is the internal skeleton of a sea animal.
2. A scallop is a bivalve mollusk.
3. Scones are thin cakes made skillfully by the Scots.
4. Skelton swung his ax skillfully to split the stack of spruce logs.
5. The squid is a species of cuttlefish.
6. The northwest coastal area of the United States is sprayed by steady moist winds called *chinooks*.
7. Stewart Scranton, and six stalwart hunters set out to obtain scarce elephant tusks.
8. The swift schooner brought in a catch of sea horses and starfish.
9. Prescott always felt like strutting when he squired his sweet Stella.
10. Scribbled and scrawled manuscripts are likely to receive scanty attention from schoolmasters.
11. The old scow was covered with scale from stem to stern.
12. The sudden squall upset the skiff in the swift, swirling waters.
13. Spring rains may come in sprinkles.
14. The sprite was a spry spirit.
15. Smith was smitten by a small girl in a smock.
16. Sperry was smart but did not suggest being smug.
17. Stacy's voice demonstrated frequent strident tones except when he sang bass.
18. Snead was famous, or perhaps infamous, for his stentorous snoring.
19. Struggle, if it is not fruitless, helps to make the struggler strong.
20. The scribe scrutinized his efforts on his manuscript and seemed to be satisfied with the results.

[sts] and [sks]

The combinations [sts] and [sks] are somewhat difficult because of the quick and precise tongue action needed in their production. Avoid a tendency to omit the first *s* in these clusters.

PRACTICE MATERIALS

The following word lists, phrases, and sentences should be useful as practice materials.

beasts	pests	boasts	toasts
feasts	rests	coasts	bursts

fists	casts	posts	firsts
lists	lasts	roasts	jousts
pastes	boosts	ghosts	musts
waists	roosts	hosts	rusts
discs	asks	tasks	whisks
risks	basks	husks	flasks
frisks	masks	tusks	casks

PHRASES

roasts for feasts	discs of tusks
musks for hosts	asks for risks
flasks for toasts	unmasks the boasts
lists of tests	hosts for ghosts

SENTENCES

1. Stella expressed her regrets that the insect pests spoiled the outdoor feasts for her guests.

2. Two blasts signaled that the jousts were about to begin as tests for the knights.

3. Ghosts do not bother with boasts.

4. Six gun blasts were fired at the animal pests.

5. Good hosts demonstrate an air of unconcern about costs.

6. Risks must be assumed in many tasks.

7. Large oaken casks were used as tops for desks.

8. Wister beat his fists against the posts to scare the beasts from their roosts.

[skw]

Avoid approximating or substituting an /ʃ/ (sh) in [skw] blends. Note the spelling of *squ* in the words:

squab	squamous	squeak	squirm
squad	square	squeal	squire
squalid	squat	squib	squirt
squall	squander	squint	squiggle
squalor	squeamish	squirrel	squaw

INITIAL [s] AND FINAL [ʃ] (sh)

Be sure to distinguish between the initial [s] and the final [ʃ] in the following words.

sash	squash	swash
smash	swish	squeamish
stash	squish	Swedish
splash	squarish	slash

INITIAL AND FINAL [s]

sacks	status	socks	sequence
sauce	source	slips	smacks
sense	seats	slants	streets

since	souse	spots	sinks
saints	sites	spurts	stunts
sweets	saps	speaks	squeaks
swaps	surfs	spouts	scuffs
sass	stoops	smokes	skirts

ADDITIONAL PRACTICE MATERIALS FOR /s/ IN VARIOUS CONTEXTS

SENTENCES

1. Genius without a sensible striving for work may be a waste of superior intelligence, at least, so Sylvia insisted.

2. Signs on the highways offer sage advice to passing motorists.

3. Simonson's satire was frequently indistinguishable from his attempts at farce; both efforts were fierce but seldom humorous.

4. Charles Dickens opens his *Tale of Two Cities* with the words: "It was the best of times. It was the worst of times."

5. Susan was pleasant and almost always easy to please. Sam was surly and almost impossible to tease.

6. Unseasonal scarcity of rains as well as inconsistent distributions have resulted in producing America's dust bowls.

7. Stanley observed that disease frequently attracts more attention than a healthy state of affairs, whether it be in persons or in nations.

8. Sooner's sullen silences spoke eloquently for his negativistic status.

9. Jurists are supposed to listen to all aspects of arguments and decide on issues presented to them.

10. The ascending moon cast a silvery light over the serene sea.

SELECTIONS

1. However erroneous, the assumption that genius is somehow associated with some signs of madness has a long history. Seneca, citing Aristotle, asserted that "There is no great genius without some sign of madness." Dryden, in the seventeenth century, stated, "Great wits are sure to madness near allied." In his preface to *The Man of Genius,* Lombroso, a nineteenth-century philosopher, said, "Good sense travels on the well worn paths; genius, never." And so, according to Lombroso, most of us who consider ourselves sensible persons do not understand the deviancies of genius and consider the superior and outstanding intellects as insane, at best harmlessly insane. Mark Twain, in his essay on *Genius,* described the state of genius as "A supreme capacity for getting its possessor into trouble of all kinds." Edward Young, in his essay on *Night Thoughts,* written in the eighteenth century, may have anticipated and summed up our beliefs in associating genius with insanity in these lines:

> Ah, how unjust to Nature and himself
> Is thoughtless, thankless, inconsistent man!

2. H. L. Mencken, the so-called sage of Baltimore, enjoyed having people think of him as an acidic and outrageous person. He sometimes earned this right by sentences such as ''Philosophy consists very largely of one philosopher arguing that all others are jackasses.''

3. The rest to some faint meaning make pretence,
> But Shadwell never deviates into sense.
>
> —JOHN DRYDEN, *Mac Flecknoe*

4. A nap . . . is a brief period of sleep which overtakes superannuated persons when they endeavor to entertain unwelcome visitors or to listen to scientific lectures.

> —GEORGE BERNARD SHAW, *Tragedy of an Elderly Gentleman*

5. How *Homo sapiens* arrived at speech is lost in prehistory. Speaking humans speculate about the onset of speech and through speech conjecture and rationalize, and, according to their needs, present interests, prejudices, and inclinations. The mystery and beginning of speech may be repeated in the cycle of infant development, but the infant forgets how it acquired speech as soon as it becomes a speaking child. Once again, adults speculate about the onset of speech in children and about their prelingual stages of development. This is history, fascinating speculative history, with testimony abstracted from those who speak without telling us how or why. The task of learning to speak is immense. The immensity of the task, fortunately, is unconsciously and unwittingly assumed by the child. Before he or she knows the size or significance of the responsibilities to be assumed, the normal child has accepted and practiced the verbal habits—the ways of speaking— of her or his special culture and thus becomes a transmitter of the verbal habits of those with whom she or he lives. Speech is considered by most linguists a human species-specific function.   —J. E.

PRACTICE DIALOGUE FOR FREQUENT [s] BLENDS AND CLUSTERS

Restaurant Blues

Customer. I want to splurge tonight to impress Frances my fiancé.

Waitress. It's not hard to squander a fortune in a costly restaurant like Sparrow's.

Customer. For my first course, I want pasta with steamed clams. Frances will start with your splendid watercress soup.

Waitress. On Sunday, we serve only a spinach salad, which I can sprinkle with bean sprouts.

Customer. Then let's skip right to the second course. I'm squeamish about squid, so I'll settle for scallops broiled on a skewer. Frances has discriminating taste, so bring her a rare skirt steak that is smothered in crisp onions. Don't forget the bread sticks.

Waitress.　The best I can do is beef stew or scrambled eggs with squash.

Customer.　This restaurant boasts the highest prices in town! We came here to celebrate with a feast, not to eat kitchen scraps!

Waitress.　I can serve you a sticky baked Alaska with a thick sweet sauce. If you prefer a sponge cake, we have one left over from Easter.

Customer.　I'm no snob, but I could not resist the status of Sparrow's. Now the lack of style in this scandalous place has ruined our celebration.

Waitress.　Why don't you just take a brisk, swift stroll on the east side of the street to the Punster. It is a small and respectable place with simple food. Sparrow's is fancier, but at the Punster, you won't be swindled. Frances will admire your style.

/z/ As in *Zoo, Cousin, Azalea,* and *Buzz*

Except for the accompanying vocalization of the /z/, the sound is produced like the /s/. /z/ may be described as a lingua-alveolar, voiced fricative. Generally, it is produced with somewhat less tongue-muscle tension than is necessary for the /s/.

The spellings for /z/ are varied and include *z* as in *zero, s* as in *rose* and *nasal,* and *zz* as in *buzz.*

Persons who have difficulty with the articulation of the /s/ are also likely to find the /z/ troublesome. Vocalization, however, may conceal some of the acoustic faults that become apparent when an /s/ is defectively produced. If your best /s/ is articulated with the tongue tip behind the lower teeth rather than behind the upper gum ridge, the same adjustment should be made for the production of /z/.

PRACTICE MATERIALS

INITIAL

zebra	zest	zircon	zeal
zee	zephyr	Zouave	Zeno
Zeeland	Zachary	Zurich	zone
zinc	zoo	zither	zip
zinnia	Zeus	zyme	zoology
zany	zoom	zealous	zounds
zenith	zodiac	Zion	zygote

MEDIAL

teasing	spasm	designate	design
pleasing	plasma	nozzle	desire
blizzard	music	cousin	enzyme
lazy	using	dozen	raising
daisy	dozing	used	noisy

pleasant	causing	desert	reason
resin	buzzer	deserve	appeasing
hazard	poser	preserve	resign

FINAL

ease	whose	because	toys
please	choose	repose	annoys
tease	doze	crows	boys
his	woes	yearns	ties
fizz	hose	spurns	replies
raise	grows	burns	dyes
maize	goads	buzz	rhymes
days	claws	eaves	wise
has	flaws	cows	surmise
lads	calls	browse	symbols

Morphemic /z/

A morpheme, we recall, is a minimal unit of meaning in a language. A morpheme may be a single word or a part of a word. *Buds* is a two-morpheme word: *bud* plus *s* to indicate plural.

The list for the final /z/ included several examples in which the sound had morphemic significance as a plural marker and/or as an indicator of grammatical tense. These examples include the words *claws, calls,* and *toys.* The following list is of words in which the final *s,* pronounced /z/, is part of a separate, final syllable. Many of the words may serve either as nouns or verbs.

PRACTICE MATERIALS

aces	doses	exposures	lunches
bunches	dozes	hunches	plunges
buzzes	eases	hunters	raises
chooses	entices	inducers	reposes
advises	bridges	praises	splices
masters	plunders	plasters	stencils

SENTENCES

1. Zebras are animals found in most zoos.

2. The museum was open eight hours a day in all seasons.

3. Zoë wisely dozed off when others fell victim to their desires and yearnings.

4. Symbols are human beings' way of preserving and communicating the values, dreams, and ideas of their cultures.

5. Zachary was not able to afford diamonds and so presented zircons to his best girls.

6. Snows make the mountains near Zurich ever-pleasant views to beholders.

7. The Mormons converted the desert into green pastures.

8. Girls and boys soon learn that some words can tease and others can please or appease.

9. Zinnias bloom late in the summer season, but daisies are early flowers.

10. The blizzard caused the travelers hours of delay in their journeys.

11. Zymes are disease germs that cause zymotic diseases.

12. Maize grows in many farms and fields.

[dz]

Persons who have difficulty with the articulatory position for /z/ might find it helpful to begin with /d/ and to "move" from /d/ to /z/. Be sure that you start with a tongue-tip to gum-ridge contact for the /d/ and then retract the tongue tip slightly for the /z/. Practice with the following.

adds	fads	fades	woods
weeds	cads	chords	cards
beads	lads	fords	rods
lids	moods	hoards	brides
bids	foods	birds	chides
maids	toads	herds	tides
raids	loads	builds	grounds

Additional /z/ Blends

Many of the words of the practice lists for medial and final /z/ contain blends of /z/ with a preceding /m/, /b/, /v/, /n/, /l/, or /d/. The word lists and materials that follow feature these combinations.

PRACTICE MATERIALS

FINAL **[mz]**

beams	gems	brooms	alms
creams	frames	combs	calms
reams	names	domes	charms
teams	crams	homes	harms
rims	lambs	storms	qualms
whims	booms	forms	alarms
hems	tombs	norms	farms
stems	chums	climbs	germs
clams	crumbs	chimes	firms
hams	numbs	dimes	terms

FINAL **[bz]**

Thebes	webs	dabs	tubes
cribs	ebbs	stabs	absorbs

fibs	jabs	tabs	cobs
nibs	cabs	cubes	nobs
robs	lobes	hubs	disturbs
swabs	jobs	nubs	herbs
squabs	robes	stubs	verbs

FINAL [vz]

believes	delves	wharves	shoves
deceives	shelves	carves	drives
eaves	elves	starves	hives
thieves	calves	curves	knives
gives	halves	nerves	strives
lives	grooves	serves	thrives
braves	moves	swerves	wives
knaves	proves	doves	leaves
staves	roves	gloves	weaves
waves	stoves	loves	saves

FINAL [nz]

beans	stains	ruins	darns
screens	remains	fawns	burns
bins	dens	mourns	turns
fins	glens	dawns	spurns
grins	bans	groans	guns
brains	clans	owns	runs
trains	loons	stones	tons
lanes	boons	barns	gowns
refrains	tunes	earns	clowns
mines	signs	coins	joins

FINAL [lz]

deals	gales	coals	boils
keels	jails	coles	coils
wheels	nails	foals	spoils
hills	bales	moles	tiles
tills	duels	goals	miles
frills	fools	falls	wiles
mills	spools	appalls	jowls
stills	tools	stalls	cowls
gills	pulls	lolls	towels
wills	bulls	hobbles	owls

FINAL [dz] (additional words)

heeds	heads	goads	reminds
bleeds	weds	loads	herds
reeds	dads	frauds	curds

deeds	lads	swords	words
weeds	goods	towards	abides
bids	hoods	hods	hides
rids	foods	nods	glides
aids	moods	pods	abounds
fades	broods	floods	hounds
wades	intrudes	buds	rounds

SENTENCES /z/

1. Jones had qualms about touching coins because they might be covered with germs.

2. Ben's wife believed that homes are kept clean by new brooms and zealous sweepings by husbands who take turns with wives.

3. Zale, a business executive, ordered frames for his wife's glasses that were encrusted with diamonds and other gems.

4. Zach Grimes had whims that resulted in his telling many zany fibs.

5. Hundreds of corncobs were stored in cribs on farms.

6. The thieves wore gloves when they stole the wares from the wharves.

7. Human brains are able to deal with symbols and signs.

8. The young of horses and asses are called foals.

9. Trains still carry goods to and from farms, as do planes and buses.

10. The storm's fury left many of the town's homes in ruins.

11. Sandra's dreams always were to write her country's refrains.

12. Ted's moods led him to take long walks down country lanes, and he seldom used roads.

/z/ and /s/

Some persons with foreign-language backgrounds have difficulty in distinguishing between the /z/ and the /s/. If the element of voice is not distinctive, then both phonetic and semantic differences may be broken down in word pairs such as *price* and *prize*, *race* and *raise*, and *zoo* and *sue*.

PRACTICE MATERIALS

Practice with the word pairs, phrases, and sentences that follow to make certain that the /z/ is clearly voiced and that the /s/ is voiceless.

zee	see	lose	loose
zeal	seal	prize	price
zip	sip	doze	dose
zinc	sink	pads	pats
zoo	sue	sends	cents
zone	sown	bids	bits
peas	peace	codes	coats
rays	race	kids	kits
maize	mace	beds	bets
his	hiss	knees	niece

pays	pace	fuzz	fuss
bays	base	rise	rice

PHRASES

lose what is loose	sown in a zone
price of the prize	sip with zip
kits for kids	a dose to doze
notes of nodes	bids for bits
plays first base	prize for a price

SENTENCES

1. A seal eats fish with considerable zeal.
2. The bids ran high for the bits of gems.
3. The prize was won at a sizable price.
4. Selma and Zelda went to see the Zuyder Zee.
5. Zinc was used to line the rusty sink.
6. Cousin Sue enjoyed her trip to the zoo.
7. The lost codes were found in the pockets of the coats.
8. The maize was pounded with a mace.
9. Grace and her husband, Zeke, disliked seeing their cattle graze in rented fields.
10. The racer was given a razor as a prize.
11. Simpson, although not a psychologist, astutely observed that the things persons say to themselves constitute the basis for deciding what they will say to those who supposedly are listening to them.
12. When Susan sighed, there was little need to explain her sighs by spoken words.
13. Sylvia was statuesque and stately, and yet blissfully unconscious of these signal attributes.
14. The twins insisted that all the tales to which they listened be twice-told tales.
15. The American Psychological Association includes a division called the Society for the Psychological Study of Social Issues.

SELECTIONS FOR /s/ AND /z/

1. In his *Unsocial Socialist,* George Bernard Shaw argued that "a day's work is a day's work, neither more nor less, and the man who does it needs a day's sustenance, a night's repose, and due leisure whether he be a painter or a ploughman."

2. *Sneer words* are defined by William Safire, a columnist for *The New York Times,* as "adjectives that put some distance between the speaker and the subject by saying 'I'm using the next word under protest.' " Safire gives several examples of sneer words, such as *self-proclaimed, self-styled,* and the much-used *so-called.* It seems that feelings of displeasure and disdain now have their own punctuation, mostly featuring the use of hyphenated words and quotation marks.

3. In some societies, sloth is considered the deadliest of sins.

4. Most sociologists assess social class on the basis of a person's years of education, his or her vocation or profession, and his or her place of residence.

5. The cosmologist Rees has observed that the absence of evidence does not constitute evidence of absence.

6. The world is still engaged in a massive armaments race designed to insure continuing equivalent strength among potential adversaries. We pledge perseverance and wisdom in our efforts to limit the world's armaments to those necessary for each nation's own domestic safety, and we will move this year a step toward our ultimate goal—the elimination of all nuclear weapons from this earth.

—PRESIDENT JIMMY CARTER, Inaugural Address, 1977

7. For our bad neighbor makes us early stirrers,
Which is both healthful and good husbandry.
Besides, they are our outward consciences,
And preachers to us all, admonishing
That we should dress us fairly for our end.
Thus may we gather honey from the weed,
And make a moral of the devil himself.

—WILLIAM SHAKESPEARE, *Henry V*

8. There is a silence where hath been no sound,
There is a silence where no sound may be,
In the cold grave—under the deep, deep sea,
Or in wide desert where no life is found,
Which hath been mute, and still must sleep profound.

—THOMAS HOOD, *Silence*

9. Terms ill defined, and forms misunderstood,
And customs, where their reasons are unknown,
Have stirred up many zealous souls
To fight against imaginary giants.

—MARTIN F. TUPPER, *Of Tolerance*

10. Good laws lead to the making of better ones; bad ones bring about worse. As soon as any man says of the affairs of the State, "What does it matter to me?" the State may be given up for lost.

—JEAN JACQUES ROUSSEAU, *The Social Contract*

11. In this best of all possible worlds, the Baron's castle was the most magnificent of castles, and his lady the best of all possible Baronesses.

—VOLTAIRE, *Candide*

12. It is indeed a desirable thing to be well descended, but the glory belongs to our ancestors.

—PLUTARCH, *Of the Training of Children*

13. Of all the causes which conspire to blind
Man's erring judgment, and misguide the mind,
What the weak head with strongest bias rules,
Is pride, the never-failing vice of fools.

—ALEXANDER POPE, *An Essay on Criticism*

14. At least a quarter of a century ago, the British scientist Launcelot Hogben wrote an essay suggesting choices and procedures for intrastellar communication. The essay, "Astroglossa or First Steps in Celestial Syntax," proposes that the signals—the units of the language, or glossa—be based on concepts of numbers. This suggestion derives from the assumption that numerals are the most universal of all symbols. So humans who wish to establish intrastellar correspondence must do so through numerals, serving as signals, with these properties: (1) by sequence or order, the signals become symbols; (2) by rules of usage, the signals constitute a syntax.

15. While running for the presidency of these United States, Adlai Stevenson advised his San Francisco listeners that wise persons do not try to hurry history.

16. There was neither time nor season
When Summers could reason;
To him, logic was treason,
A state of mind
Esoteric, unkind
To which all his perceptions
Were stoically blind.

—J. E., *Retrospective Appreciation*

PRACTICE DIALOGUE FOR CONTRASTING /z/ AND /s/

Silly Sue at the Zoo

Zane. I took Sue to the zoo today. I was afraid I would lose her if I let her run loose.

Melissa. The zoo is so much fun! Just to stand and gaze at the prize gorillas is worth the price of admission.

Zane. First, I took Suzie to see the zebras. The mother zebra fends off threats to her young by keeping them away from the fence. The babies just zip around and sip water all day, gazing at the spectators.

Melissa. Did Sue burst out laughing when she saw the birds with the bizarre feathers?

Zane. Your niece fell to her knees and tried to squeeze an ostrich! I raised her to her feet, and we raced over to the seals before the zookeeper had us arrested.

Melissa. When you take Sue to a place like the zoo, she plays hard.

Zane. Sue fed the seals with lots of zeal because it was illegal.

Melissa. The only thing that will faze Suzie is coming face to face with a tiger. She's scared he will lose his temper and hiss at her. Zane, Suzie is fast asleep now, so we can eat our steak and peas in peace.

Zane. After a dose of your crazed niece on Sunday, all I want to do is doze until Tuesday!

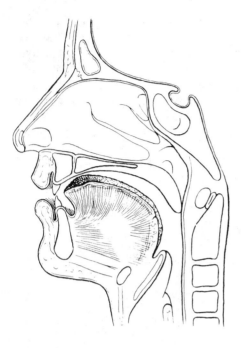

FIGURE 17–3 Articulatory adjustments for /ʃ/ (sh) and /ʒ/ (zh). Note that the tongue tip is retracted more than it is for /s/ and /z/. Compare with Figure 17–2 (page 256).

The Postalveolar Sounds /ʃ/ (sh) and /ʒ/ (zh)

/ʃ/ (sh) As in *She, Ashore,* and *Ash*

With the consonant /s/ as a basis for comparison, the /ʃ/ (sh) should be easy to master. The sound is produced with the entire tongue drawn a little further back than for the /s/. The groove of the tongue is larger and the tongue as a whole is broader. The stream of breath is forced through the large groove of the tongue and emitted between the rows of teeth. /ʃ/ is usually produced with slight lip rounding. Acoustically, the principal concentration of energy is in a lower frequency band than that of /s/. Phonetically, /ʃ/ may be described as a voiceless, orally emitted, blade-tongue, postalveolar, fricative sound (see Figure 17-3).

/ʃ/ has several spellings. The most frequent is the combination *sh,* as in *she.* Other frequent spellings include *ti* as in *nation, si* as in *tension, ci* as in *precious, ch* as in *machine, s* as in *sure,* and *c* as in *ocean.*

For some speakers with foreign-language backgrounds and for some who may have high-frequency hearing losses, the similarities in spelling and in manner of articulation may cause confusion between the /ʃ/ and the /s/. Emphasis on lip rounding and on the more retracted and relatively larger-grooved tongue for the /ʃ/ should help to contrast it with and distinguish it from the /s/.

PRACTICE MATERIALS

Practice before a mirror with the word pairs that follow should be helpful.

she	sea	shoe	sue
sheik	seek	shoot	suit

sheep	seep	show	sew
shield	sealed	shawl	Saul
ship	sip	shore	sore
shin	sin	shop	sop
shay	say	shot	sot
shake	sake	shock	sock
shad	sad	shy	sigh
shall	sal	shed	said
brash	brass	gash	gas
clash	class	plush	plus
mesh	mess	rushed	rust
leash	lease	fashion	fasten
mash	mass	crash	crass

Maintain the difference between the /ʃ/ and /s/ in the following phrases and sentences.

Shad looked sad	clash in class
a sealed shield	she went to see
shipped to be sipped	no shoe for Sue

1. Sue held that it was no longer in fashion to use buttons to fasten shoes or shirts.

2. The brass instruments clashed with a sound that was brash.

3. The mess of mash was shipped by sea.

4. Sam enjoyed steamed shad that he bought in a shop near the seashore.

5. Was it Celia or Sheilagh who sold sea shells along the Bayshore near Ocean Shores?

ADDITIONAL PRACTICE MATERIALS FOR /ʃ/

she	shoe	shirt	shriek
sheen	shoot	shirk	shrimp
ship	should	shut	shred
shin	shook	shun	shrewd
shay	shone	shout	shrub
shame	show	shower	shrine
shell	shawl	shine	shroud
shed	shore	shy	shrank
shall	shop	sugar	shrink
shaggy	shock	shark	shrug
leashing	lashes	pressure	fission
wishing	passion	quashed	hushing
ashamed	fashion	machine	Flushing
glacier	pushing	pension	national
nation	cushion	delicious	fractious
patient	lotion	conscience	crashed

precious	ocean	anxious	rushing
dashes	caution	mission	washed
leash	hash	hush	Danish
wish	crash	harsh	blemish
fish	bush	marsh	English
dish	push	rush	garnish
mesh	burnish	tarnish	Flemish
flesh	furnish	varnish	brandish
flash	punish	Amish	gnash
cash	blush	vanish	lush

PHRASES

Flush with cash	Danish dishes
shrank in shame	passion for fashion
ship to shore	shocking crash
burnished dishes	showered good wishes
shouted impatiently	Flemish shrine
shunned the shay	tarnished machine
motion of the ocean	delicious portion

SENTENCES

1. Ocean fishing furnishes a livelihood for many British fishers.

2. The shaggy Prussian brandished his tarnished sword.

3. Hamlet had an anxious and disturbed conscience.

4. Shaw was not ashamed to be fractious.

5. The chef earned a pension for his well-garnished dishes.

6. ''Pshaw,'' said Sheila, as she shrugged her shoulders and added two portions of sugar to her milk shake.

7. The motion of the ship on the ocean made a patient of the man from Flushing.

8. A flash flood transformed the shrubless field into a marsh.

9. Some nations have a passion for peace; others seem to have a passion for aggression.

10. Ship-to-shore communication is available for most of our nation.

11. Do you anticipate a clash among the boys in the class?

12. Sam Sherman shunned the sun even when smeared with squash sun lotion.

SELECTIONS

1. I think that, as life is action and passion, it is required of a man that he should share the passion and action of his time at peril of being judged not to have lived.

    —JUSTICE OLIVER WENDELL HOLMES, Memorial Day Address, 1884

2. For he might have been a Roosian,
    A French, or Turk, or Proosian,
    Or perhaps Itali-an!

But in spite of all temptations
To belong to other nations,
He remains an Englishman!

—W. S. GILBERT, *H. M. S. Pinafore*

3. Friendship is a sheltering tree;
Oh the joys that came down shower-like,
Of friendship, love, and liberty, . . .

—SAMUEL TAYLOR COLERIDGE, *Youth and Age*

4. Daniel Shays was a captain of the militia during our Revolution against the British. Later, during the period of the Confederation and in a time of financial depression, Shays led an armed insurrection against the Massachusetts government. The insurrectionists were made up substantially of farmers. They protested that the salaries of public officials were too high. In addition, they petitioned against the imposition of high taxes. Shays's petitions, protestations, general dissensions, and finally his insurrection are believed to have hastened the ratification of the Federal Constitution by Massachusetts.

5. They shall beat their swords into plowshares, and their spears into pruning hooks; nation shall not lift up sword against nation, neither shall they learn war any more.   —*Isaiah, I, 4*

PRACTICE DIALOGUE FOR /ʃ/ (*emphasizing contrast between* /ʃ/ *and* /s/)

Ship to Shore

Sheila the Salesperson.   That's no shoe for an ocean voyage, Sue. The plush insoles are a plus, and many women have rushed in to buy the rust-colored pair. But there is no rubber sole to cushion your step and take the pressure off your shins. It would be a shame if your feet got sore the minute you stepped ashore to go sight-seeing.

Sue.   The open mesh toe would be a mess the first time I was caught in a harsh rain shower. Still I want a shoe with some flash to wear to sip champagne with the ship's captain.

Sheila the Salesperson.   Why don't you buy this pretty silk shirt? You can hand-wash it and it won't shrink. It's all the fashion to fasten your blouse with tarnished buttons made of brass.

Sue.   Sheila, you know I have a passion for shiny silks, especially if they show up my shoulders. But I'm not flush with cash and I still have to buy a warm shawl from Mr. Saul, just down the street. I wish that you could show me how to sew.

Sheila the Salesperson.   Sue, if I showed you how to sew, I would be short on sales. Suppose I sell you the silk blouse at a discount. You would then save enough to buy this swanky swimsuit. It's modest enough for a shy suitor who tends to be on the serious side.

Sue.   Sheila, you're a savvy salesperson. It's a swift sale. But be sure our settlements include the discounts.

/ʒ/ (zh) As in *Azure, Treasure, Rouge,* and *Decision*

The sound /ʒ/ (zh) is a voiced, postalveolar fricative. It is produced in the same way as the /ʃ/, with accompanying vocal fold vibration.

/ʒ/ occurs medially or finally in English words. The most frequent spellings for this sound are *z* as in *seizure, s* as in *treasure, si* as in *vision,* and *ge* as in *rouge.* The word *genre,* of French derivation, begins with /ʒ/.

PRACTICE MATERIALS

azure	intrusion	vision	persuasion
casual	measure	regime	incision
confusion	pleasure	glazier	derision
contusion	seizure	delusion	precision
decision	treasure	implosion	exposure
explosion	usual	erosion	illusion
conclusion	version	lesion	occasion
beige	corsage	garage	persiflage
camouflage	entourage	ménage	rouge

PHRASES

usual confusion   adhesion from a lesion
azure illusion   measure of pleasure
casual decision   seizure of a treasure
occasion for persuasion   visual delusion

SENTENCES

1. The Eurasian found nothing more pleasurable than an azure sky.

2. The collision was a result of one driver's poor vision and another's poor decision.

3. The physician had to make an incision to cut through the adhesion.

4. A mirage is a visual delusion causing mental confusion.

5. Because Borgia was given to persiflage, his decisions always seemed unusually casual.

6. The invasion by an infantry division was preceded by an explosion of the camouflaged airfield.

7. The glazier won prestige by the precision of her work.

8. Confusion resulted in numerous contusions among members of the treasure-hunting entourage.

9. The intrusion of the police prevented the seizure of the gold.

10. Persuasion brought about legislation to prevent soil erosion.

SELECTIONS

1. He weaves, and is clothed with derision;
    Sows, and he shall not reap;

His life is a watch or a vision
   Between a sleep and a sleep.
                    —ALGERNON CHARLES SWINBURNE, *Atlanta in Calydon*

2. Rich the treasure,
   Sweet the pleasure,
   Sweet is pleasure after pain.

                         —JOHN DRYDEN, *Alexander's Feast*

3. Frazier, an expert glazier, was given to visual illusions and to occasional delusions. Unfortunately, he also acted in the light of these visionary aberrations. Frazier's demise was a result of this inclination. On the final and fatal occasion, Frazier was confronted with an escaped tiger that had hidden in his garage. Because of a visual illusion, Frazier insisted that the tiger was his cat, *Felis domestica,* a member of his own ménage. In the light of this decision, he began to pat the animal. The beast, not sharing the illusion and having no delusions about itself as a domestic treasure, attacked and devoured Frazier. The job was done with dispatch and precision. Thus, poor Frazier was consumed, a victim of a visual illusion and of delusionary behavior. Frazier was a culinary pleasure but no measure for this member of the genre *Panthera tigris.*

4. When a man's busy, why, leisure
   Strikes him as wonderful pleasure:
   'Faith, and at leisure once is he?
   Straightway he wants to be busy.

                          —ROBERT BROWNING, *The Glove*

5. Coleridge, a visionary poet, on frequent occasions welcomed illusions. He wrote of pleasure-domes and of rivers that casually wound their way "through caverns measureless to man."

PRACTICE DIALOGUE FOR /ʒ/ (zh)

The Measure of a Man

Woman.   It's unusual to find you in this much confusion over the measure of a man.

Woman Friend.   I treasure the pleasure of John's company and enjoy gazing into his azure eyes. But on occasion, his version of the truth does camouflage reality.

Woman.   You mean that his persiflage is filled with casual lies.

Woman Friend.   His vision is clouded with delusions of his own worth. He demands that we travel with an entourage to establish his prestige. If I suggest that his friends are an intrusion, I invite derision. No form of persuasion will change him.

Woman.   It sounds to me as if you've already come to a conclusion and made a decision.

Woman Friend.   The more exposure I have to John, the greater is my disillusionment. The goodness I see reflected in his azure eyes is merely a mirage. I have come to a conclusion and no new version or persuasion will change my vision or alter my conclusion.

/tʃ/ (ch) As in *Chest, Orchard,* and *Match*

The sound /tʃ/ (ch) is a blend of /t/ and an immediately following /ʃ/ (sh). It may occur initially, medially, or finally. The blend, a combination of a stop and a voiceless fricative sound, is classified phonetically as an *affricate.* This voiceless affricate is regularly represented by the letters *ch* in spelling.

The sound may be troublesome for speakers for whom English is not a first language and in whose native language the /tʃ/ does not occur. For example, it may be troublesome to native French speakers because it does not occur in French. For such persons, the most frequent tendency is to substitute the second element, [ʃ], for the blend /tʃ/.

PRACTICE MATERIALS

The exercises that follow should be of help in differentiating between /tʃ/ and /ʃ/.

cheer	sheer	hatch	hash
cheat	sheet	latch	lash
choose	shoes	march	marsh
chairs	shares	match	mash
chin	shin	much	mush
catch	cash	witch	wish
crutch	crush	watching	washing
ditch	dish	catching	cashing
leech	leash	hutch	hush
batch	bash	charred	shard

PHRASES

too much mush	choose new shoes
shares the chairs	wish of a witch
march in the marsh	slashed chin and shin
chores at the shores	cash for the catch

SENTENCES

1. The sailors had to chip the charred paint from the ship.
2. Fido, a shaggy dog, liked to chew on an old shoe.
3. The sheik had a scar on his cheek.
4. On chosen occasions, it may be pleasant to share a chair.
5. Cheryl bruised her chin and her shin.
6. Charles insisted that one spoonful of mush is much too much.
7. The cheerless marine went on a march through the marsh.
8. Lady Macbeth hoped that the witch would help her realize her cherished wish.

9. After a tennis match, Cheryl enjoyed a dish of pistachio ice cream with mashed cherries.

10. The fishermen had a good fish catch that they sold for spot cash.

ADDITIONAL PRACTICE MATERIALS FOR /tʃ/

cheese	chance	churn	chore
chief	chant	chug	change
chill	chewed	chum	Charles
chimp	choose	chunk	chirp
chain	choke	chowder	choice
chafe	chose	chide	chat
check	chalk	China	chicken
chess	chuck	chive	chin
channel	chop	chime	Chester
champ	char	child	chap
reaching	brooches	marching	bachelor
beeches	broaching	urchin	batches
pitcher	coached	birches	paunches
kitchen	encroaching	lurching	parched
exchange	orchard	searching	righteous
hatchet	launched	bunched	preaching
each	match	staunch	couch
teach	dispatch	porch	slouch
speech	blotch	scorch	pouch
ditch	watch	torch	touch
witch	pooch	lurch	clutch
fetch	encroach	birch	such
wrench	coach	bunch	research
detach	reproach	hunch	squelch

PHRASES

charred chops	staunch bachelor
righteous preaching	watchful pooch
squelching speech	enriching research
branches of birch	churning in the channel
chess champion	unlatched the kitchen

SENTENCES

1. Charles was taught by those he coached to observe the difference between teaching and preaching.

2. After searching in the orchard, Chester found the chart under the beech tree.

3. Chuck liked cheese and chives as well as chutney with his sandwiches.

4. The church supper featured chicken and chowder.

5. The child was chided for chewing her chalk.

6. Chambers had a hunch that the peaches in his orchard needed watching from poachers.

7. In a close match, the Chilean champion won the chess contest.

8. Some choose to eat their steak charred, but Charles and Charity chose marinated chunks.

9. Birches are a climbing challenge for many children.

10. Chilton was partial to choice, slightly scorched chops.

SELECTIONS

1. When I was a child, I spake as a child, I understood as a child, I thought as a child; but when I became a man, I put away childish things.

—*I Corinthians* 13:11

2. In his essay, *Time and Change: The Gospel of Nature,* John Burroughs stated, ''Nature teaches more than she preaches.''

3. I'm not a chicken, I have seen
Full many a chill September.

—OLIVER WENDELL HOLMES, *The September Gale*

4. Said Chester to Chase,
''You chew as you race;
Though chewing's a chore,
A choice chop's not a bore.''

Said Chase to friend Chester,
''As a child it was best, sir,
To chomp as I'm able
Or I'd have no choice at table.''

—J. E., *The Race Is to the Quick*

PRACTICE DIALOGUE FOR /tʃ/ **(ch)** [*including material contrasting* /tʃ/ **(ch)** *and* /ʃ/ **(sh)**]

The Staunch Bachelor

Rachel.   Why does a charming chap like yourself remain a staunch bachelor?

Charles.   I choose to remain unattached because I am my own perfect match. There's too much mush written about the richness of marriage. I don't need someone to choose my shoes or chide me when I grow a paunch. I don't want to see my hutch filled with bone China or be reproached for the way I chugalug a pitcher of beer.

Rachel.   How do you stay free of those who would latch onto you? Your cash makes you a good catch.

Charles.   I check my dates carefully and watch out for fortune hunters.

Rachel.   Do you know that most of the men I've researched sit in a chair and watch TV on Sunday rather than share the chores with their wives?

Charles. Exchanging chitchat with the wife while watching the washing machine choke on batches of dirty laundry is not my idea of an enriching afternoon.

Rachel. Would a woman's touch in the kitchen encroach on your lifestyle?

Charles. I can chop a bunch of chuck meat and turn it into cheeseburgers myself. I can also charboil chops, and my chilled cucumber chowder achieves perfection.

Rachel. Is there a chance that a fetching wench can change your single status?

Charles. Rachel, not much chance. Why is it that righteous people like you are are always preaching about choice, then chastise me because I choose to be alone?

/dʒ/ (j) As in *Age, Adjust,* and *Budge*

/dʒ/ (j) is the voiced cognate of /tʃ/. This voiced sound blend may occur initially, medially, or finally. In *judge* and *George*, it occurs both initially and finally. In *agent* and *engine*, the affricate /dʒ/ occurs medially. The most frequent spellings for /dʒ/ are *g*, *j*, and *dg*, as in *wage*, *jam*, and *ridge*.

Many American and English speakers tend to unvoice /dʒ/ when the blend occurs in final positions. French, Spanish, and German speakers may have difficulty with the voiced affricate because the sound does not occur in their native languages.

Speakers who have difficulty in deciding whether a given word calls for /dʒ/ or /tʃ/ should be helped by the relative frequency of the *ch* spelling for the unvoiced sound and the inclusion of the letter *j* or *g* for the voiced affricate.

PRACTICE MATERIALS

The purpose of the first set of exercise material is to establish the distinction between the two affricates.

gin	chin	jigger	chigger
jar	char	jug	chug
jeer	cheer	bridges	screeches
jest	chest	badge	batch
jump	chump	ridge	rich
jeep	cheap	surge	search
joke	choke	liege	leech
Jane	chain	singe	cinch
Madge	match	purge	perch

PHRASES

chug of the jug	chump to jump
batch of badges	a match for Madge
jeers not cheers	change of range
chili for Jill	lunge for lunch

SENTENCES

1. The region was rich in majestic visions.
2. Charles and Marge marched over the bridge.
3. Jim found a batch of badges in the gem-studded chest.
4. The orange-painted carriage carried Jim and Jane to their marriage.
5. Gene's dog, Jigger, was full of itches because he had been a host to chiggers.
6. The judge would not budge from his injudicious judgments.

ADDITIONAL PRACTICE MATERIALS

jeans	jewel	germ	junior
jib	June	jar	jury
giraffe	judicial	journey	just
gipsy	joke	jowl	jute
jig	jovial	jug	jade
jail	Jonah	jump	jilt
jay	jaunt	giant	general
jet	jaw	jibe	germane
gem	job	joint	genius
jack	jog	join	gentle
besieged	agent	adjust	larger
regent	changed	ajourn	margin
imagine	ranging	surgeon	region
regenerate	major	urgent	disjoint
hedging	stranger	merger	enjoin
wedged	ajar	legion	lounging
ledger	rajah	soldier	gouging
badger	plunged	budget	rejoin
liege	huge	nudge	sponge
siege	sledge	grudge	bilge
ridge	forge	oblige	discharge
bridge	engorge	gouge	dirge
rage	barge	singe	grange
stage	large	fringe	strange
edge	urge	surge	derange
pledge	merge	emerge	average
carriage	bulge	orange	peerage
marriage	fudge	revenge	steerage

PHRASES

besieged agent	marriage merger
huge sledge	gentle genius
just jurist	large stranger
plunged over the ridge	avenged a grudge
jibes and jeers	enraged rajah
hedge on the ridge	ledger for a budget

SENTENCES

1. After landing on the ridge, a legion of soldiers was discharged from the giant jet planes.

2. Janice Jones, an imaginative lawyer, jovially engaged the judge and with germane arguments, urged both judge and jury to be judicious.

3. Dr. James, a diligent surgeon, adjusted Joe's disarranged jaw.

4. Jonah had a strange journey in a giant whale.

5. Gerald, a gentleman of the peerage, once traveled by steerage.

6. Justice cannot always be determined by jurists.

7. Jargon is a strange form of language usage enjoyed by children.

8. June was in a rage because she was rudely nudged by Julian, who generally was considered near genius.

9. Jane was both just and gentle in making germane judgments.

10. Sturgeon is a major Russian item exported in jars and small jugs.

11. The hedge under the bridge was edged with gentian violets and geraniums.

12. Even though it was a semiprecious gem, Joyce enjoyed the jade.

13. Julie thought it a joke for James to adhere rigidly to his budget.

14. Jenny and Jed searched for sponges along the rock ledges under the huge bridge.

15. Marge and Jane joined a jaunty group for a trip on a barge.

The sentences that follow should be practiced with a view toward maintaining vocalization for the final /dʒ/. Make certain that vocalization continues so that there is no substitution of /tʃ/ for the voiced affricate.

1. The judge enjoined George and Marge from marriage.

2. Madge would not budge from her strange position.

3. John stood at the edge of the ridge but did not jump.

4. Jones yielded to his urge and ate a large orange.

5. At two years of age, the average child can speak her or his language.

6. A large suspension bridge was built over the huge gorge.

7. The grange was the scene of a battle of revenge.

8. The stage was set for a strange play.

In the following sentences, make certain that you distinguish between the /dʒ/ and the /ʒ/. The first italicized word(s) will include the blend /dʒ/; the second will have the voiced fricative /ʒ/.

1. A *general* commands a *division*.

2. Charles *pledged* himself to a life of *pleasure*.

3. A *jury* found Wilson guilty of *usury*.

4. *Agile* Peter climbed a hill to admire the *azure* sky.

5. *Drudgery,* in *measure,* is part of living.

6. Ben *rejected* attempts at *collusion*.

7. *Judge Johnson* carefully announced her *decision*.

8. Charles liked to *imagine* finding rich *treasure*.

9. Chet *enjoyed* his *ménage*.

10. *Jill* drove her car into the *garage*.

SELECTIONS FOR /dʒ/

1. Casey Jones was a railroad engineer and a figure legendary for his courage. Casey had a predecessor, an engineer named Jimmie Jones, for whom the following verses were written:

On a Sunday mornin' it began to rain,
'Round the curve sped a passenger train,
On the pilot lay poor Jimmie Jones,
He's a good old porter, but he's dead and gone.

This verse for Casey Jones varies somewhat:

On a Sunday morning it begins to rain,
'Round the curve sped a passenger train,
Under the cab lay poor Casey Jones,
He's a good engineer, but he's dead and gone—

Casey, born John Luther Jones, for all the legend built about him, was a real engineer who worked for the Illinois Central Railroad. When he had his fatal collision, Jones headed engine Number 638 out of the Memphis yards. The switchmen "knew by the engine's moans that the man at the throttle was Casey Jones." Casey, cannonballing through the rain, knew that he was about to pile up into a freight train on the siding. He ordered his fireman to jump, and Casey himself died an engineer's death, one hand on the brakes and the other on the whistle cord.

—JOHN A. LOMAX and ALAN LOMAX (Eds.), Adapted from "The Legend of Casey Jones," *American Ballads and Folk Songs*

2. And what's a life?—a weary pilgrimage,
Whose glory in one day doth fill the stage
With childhood, manhood, and decrepit age.

—FRANCES QUARLES, *What Is Life?*

3. George Jenson generalized that judgments are geneally made most judiciously when the judger does not jump too hastily to conclusions. This generalization, Jenson acknowledged, was a subjective judgment, but one about which he could feel objective because it had germinated slowly after genuine and judicious study.

4. Although psychology had its genesis in philosophy, many psychologists as well as sociologists are urging that psychology emerge as a genuine science. Through technology and research, the general public may be the large gainers from the marriage of technology with scientific psychology.

5. In *Antigone,* Sophocles held that it is both dreadful and unjust "when the right judge judges wrong."

PRACTICE DIALOGUE FOR /dʒ/ [j]

To Stage a Merger

Jud the Stage Producer. Do you think the average Joe can relate to your imaginative stage play, *Junior's Revenge?*

Reginald the Writer. The audience is generally just. Junior is jilted by his financée Jade and becomes a jewel thief who forges checks. It's a story of rage, revenge, and regeneration.

Jud the Stage Producer. But Junior is a strange and deranged joker who somehow manages to stay out of jail.

Reginald the Writer. He hides the gems in a barge and journeys down the mountain in disguise, doing odd jobs.

Jud the Stage Producer. It's a huge budget for a regional play set in the Blue Ridge Mountains of West Virginia. There's a giant cast with major roles for largely overpaid stars. We need to adjust the scope of the project so there is a larger margin for failure.

Reginald the Writer. My agent is besieged with urgent offers for this play. He wants me to jump a jet and join him in California. There are legions of producers who want to arrange a deal with me.

Jud the Stage Producer. Reggie, that's bilge. This play's too regional and disjointed to generate a surge of interest. I want to oblige you because you are a genius and I genuinely like your play.

Reginald the Writer. I guess the bulging budget demands a joint venture. Let's join my agent Jack in California and make a merger with a person who is outrageously rich. Only don't ask me to take a knife to my pages like a surgeon just to adjust the budget!

The Lingua-Alveolar Nasal

/n/ As in *No, Any,* and *Again*

/n/ is a voiced, nasal, tongue-tip to upper-gum-ridge sound. In common with the other nasal consonants, /n/ requires nasal reinforcement and is emitted nasally. /n/ is a continuant sound.

To produce the /n/, the tongue should be elevated and the entire tongue tip should be in contact with the upper gum (alveolar) ridge. The soft palate is relaxed (see Figure 17–4).

In spelling, /n/ is represented by the letter *n*. In some words, a silent letter precedes the *n*, as in *know, gnat,* and *pneumatic.*

The sound /n/ presents little difficulty except that it may be slurred or replaced by a nasalized vowel in medial positions, especially in unstressed syllables, as in *contact, infer,* and *inform.* The /n/ is likely to be treated with greater articulatory respect in initial and final positions. Because of the high frequency of occurrence of the sound in American-English speech, careful articulation of the /n/ is strongly recommended.

PRACTICE MATERIALS

/m/, we recall, is produced with the lips in gentle contact and, like [n], with the soft palate lowered. For /m/, the tongue usually lies relaxed at the floor of the mouth. You may increase your awareness of the difference between the /n/ and the /m/ by practice with the word pairs that follow.

knit	mitt	knock	mock
knee	me	knob	mob
need	mead	note	mote

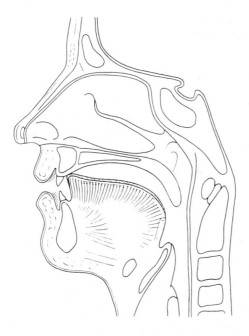

FIGURE 17–4 Articulatory adjustments for /n/. Note the relaxed (lowered) soft palate as well as the contact of tongue tip and the gum ridge.

nock	mock	null	mull
nude	mood	neat	meat
nail	mail	night	might
net	met	nice	mice
name	main	Norse	Morse
Nile	mile	new	mew

PRACTICE MATERIALS FOR /n/ IN VARIOUS POSITIONS AND CONTEXTS

INITIAL

knee	natal	node	nut
niece	knell	notary	knuckle
neat	neck	gnome	number
kneel	nebula	gnaw	knife
near	knack	naughty	nice
knit	gnash	nautical	noise
nip	narrow	knob	now
nimble	natural	nocturn	notch
nape	nasty	nurse	pneumonia
name	nook	nerve	knew
nail	noose	nurture	knoll
nasal	nose	nub	knowledge

PHRASES

noise in the night   near the nook
gnawing note   now or never

nice number	narrow notch
nimble gnome	nape of the neck

Make certain that an articulatory contact is made between your tongue tip and your upper gum ridge for the medial and final /n/. Failure to make this contact will result in the substitution of a nasalized vowel for the nasal consonant. Prolong the contact in the lists and phrases that follow.

MEDIAL /n/

anneal	grinning	plaintive	fender
menial	spinet	fainting	rented
screening	sinful	feigned	banded
dinner	hinted	fence	handed
sinner	tainted	fend	landing
thinner	saintly	defense	standing
blandish	demanded	intoned	spondee
vanish	cannibal	morning	respond
candy	stoned	dawning	despondent
dandy	telephoned	bonfire	fonder
bundle	bind	joining	pinch
trundle	kindly	connect	bench
cunning	miner	intact	branch
hunted	finer	instead	launch
gunner	ground	confer	munch
burning	hound	consume	lynch
turned	pound	confess	binge
furnace	frowning	definite	strange
burnish	lounge	inflect	lounge
furnish	coined	infest	sponge

PHRASES

Andy Dandy	fender bender
ineffective defense	feigned a faint
plaintive sound	intoned the lines
pounded the ground	turned around
sounds of a hound	fond of munching
intact connection	turned cunningly

FINAL

bean	amen	cone	spurns
lean	main	hone	stern
scene	lane	drone	burn
dean	grain	moan	run
mean	can	roan	done
sin	fan	brawn	stun
win	plan	faun	fine

tin	began	scorn	dine
hen	span	barn	down
ten	spoon	darn	frown
again	loon	gone	crown
when	dune	turn	brown

The consonant /n/, like /m/, can sometimes have syllable value without the "help" of a vowel. /n/ is or may be pronounced as a syllabic sound when it occurs in a final unstressed position. This is the case in the words that follow.

button	kitten	mutton	seven
cotton	leaden	open	sudden
deaden	maiden	oven	token
heaven	mitten	rotten	leaven
reason	ribbon	poison	fatten

ADDITIONAL PRACTICE MATERIALS

main avenue	mutton dinner
strange scene	cunning hunter
dine at seven	fine and dandy
eleven turns	morning news
again and again	tin horn
barn dance	change of plan
munch lunch	cotton mittens
ground sirloin	pound of beans
intuition and knowledge	nine tokens

SENTENCES

1. Diana and Dan were fond of meandering in the garden.
2. Nathaniel wondered why his friend Ron, the owner of a ninety-foot launch, could ever find reason to frown.
3. The missionary endeavored to teach the cannibal the difference between having a friend for dinner and having dinner with a friend.
4. Nona, as a sign of affection for her husband, began baking in her oven set at seven in the morning.
5. Frances looked stunning in her ten-pointed crown.
6. Minton confessed that he was inclined to strange hunches.
7. Nine sloops were anchored at Blanding's Landing.
8. Nettleton insisted that today's apparently insane notions may be the next day's brilliant insights.
9. Spencer and his son used a bundle of branches for their bonfire.
10. Every morning Nadine intoned nine plaintive tunes.
11. A neologism is a new, or invented, word.
12. The new highway connected nine old towns.
13. Mauldin was smitten by the antics of the kitten.

14. Cotton was inserted between the partitions to deaden the sound.

15. Nell knitted mittens for her friend Newton.

SELECTIONS

1. The true test of civilization is not the census, nor the size of cities, nor the crops—no, but the kind of man the country turns out.

—RALPH WALDO EMERSON, *Society and Solitude*

2. John Henry, Cardinal Newman, in his *Idea of a University* said that "it is almost a definition of a gentleman to say he is one who never inflicts pain."

3. There were gentlemen and there were seamen in the navy of Charles II. But the seamen were not gentlemen, and the gentlemen were not seamen.   —THOMAS BABINGTON MACAULAY, *History of England*

4. In *Design Science,* Buckminster Fuller cautioned us, "Change the environment; do not try to change man."

5. Beginnings and endings

    a. In the beginning was the word.

—*The Gospel According to John,* I,1

    b. Saint Augustine maintained that "Man was created in order that a beginning might be made."

    c. The beginnings and endings of all human undertakings are untidy, the building of a house, the writing of a novel, the demolition of a bridge, and, eminently, the finish of a voyage.

—JOHN GALSWORTHY, *Over the River*

    d. The time to stop a revolution is at the beginning, not the end.

—ADLAI STEVENSON, Speech, San Francisco, September 9, 1952

    e. More than an end to war, we want an end to the beginnings of all wars.

—FRANKLIN D. ROOSEVELT, Address written for Jefferson Day Dinners broadcast, April 13, 1945 (Roosevelt died April 12, 1945)

6. Samuel Johnson, the eminent eighteenth-century English writer, cynic, and brilliant conversationalist insisted that most persons' minds are persistently involved in avoiding the present. In Johnson's own language, "No mind is much employed upon the present; recollection and anticipation fill up almost all our moments."

Johnson "edited" a dictionary with many entries that were expressions of his own sentiments. For example, he defined *oats* as "A grain, which in England is generally given to horses, but in Scotland supports the people."

7. No man can justly censure or condemn another, because no man truly knows another. . . . Further, no man can judge another, because no man knows himself.   —THOMAS BROWNE, *Religio Medici*

8. When Dan was young and had no sense,
He bought a horn for eighteen pence,
But the only tune that Dan could learn
Was "High on a Hill and Around a Turn."

—J. E., Adapted from an old English ballad

PRACTICE DIALOGUE FOR /n/

Donna and the Children

Mrs. Nelson. Donna, I'm annoyed that you telephoned me at Anna's dinner party to complain about the antics of my children. Another night, it might not matter, but Anna served a main course that I enjoy. On the phone, you hinted that Cain, Melanie, and Nigel were naughty. Now kindly explain.

Donna. Mrs. Nelson, you know I never moan or groan unless I am nearly despondent. This morning Cain and I painted the fence green. Nigel made notches in the newly painted fence with his knife, and nailed the mailbox shut. Meanwhile, Melanie pretended to down the can of thinner. I nearly went insane. I bundled her up, ready to trundle her off to the emergency room. Then she confessed she was only pretending.

Mrs. Nelson. That's only a minor inconvenience and no reason to interrupt my dinner. I never hinted that my children were saintly.

Donna. I'm not finished. When I demanded that they munch some lunch at eleven, the children vanished. I found Melanie and Cain in the garden consuming a pound of candy.

Mrs. Nelson. It's rotten to binge on fattening candy, but it need not concern you.

Donna. After lunch, Nigel tried to poison the kitten with rancid food. He tied it up with a ribbon and built a bonfire with a bunch of branches. I managed to untie the kitten in the nick of time.

Mrs. Nelson. I confess Nigel has a strange imagination. But he never intended to injure the kitten.

Donna. I heard a noise earlier tonight and found Nigel standing next to the station wagon. He had driven the car and knocked down the fence. When I asked your fourteen-year-old son about the bent fender he had no defense.

Mrs. Nelson. Never mind, the car was rented. Donna, you have reason to want to punish the children, but give them another chance! Next week I want to go to the barn dance in Newtown.

Donna. Change that plan, Mrs. Nelson. I'll never tend your nasty children again—not for all the money in the universe!

The Lingua-Alveolar Lateral

/l/ As in *Late, Alone,* and *Bell*

/l/ is a lingua-alveolar, voiced, lateral sound. This vowel-like consonant may occur initially, medially, or finally. As may be noted from the spellings of several of the

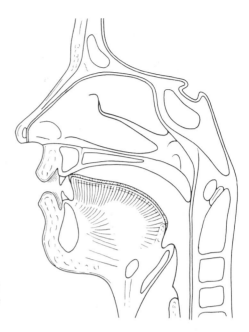

FIGURE 17–5 Most frequent articulatory adjustments for /l/. Note the tip-of-the-tongue contact with the upper gum (alveolar) ridge.

words in the first two sentences of this paragraph, /l/ is represented in spelling by the letter *l* or the letters *ll*.

/l/, like /t/ and /d/, is usually produced with the tongue tip in contact with the upper gum ridge. Unlike the stops /t/ and /d/, the /l/ has a continuant and vowel-like quality. To achieve this quality, the blade of the tongue (the portion just behind the tongue tip) is lowered to permit vocalized breath to escape over the sides. The soft palate is raised to prevent nasal emission of sound. Vocal-fold vibration regularly accompanies the articulatory action for the /l/. (See Figure 17-5.) The /l/ is designated by some phoneticians as a *liquid* sound.

PRACTICE MATERIALS

In producing the sound /l/, make certain that the *tip* and *not the blade* of your tongue is in contact with the gum ridge. Avoid contact between the tongue tip and the teeth.

INITIAL

lean	loose	lock	lace
leap	lute	learn	lake
lip	loom	lug	lower
late	load	lie	lapse
let	lawn	like	lane
lack	lot	low	linger
laugh	lost	lout	loin

In some contexts, before consonants and in final positions, a variant of the /l/ sound may be produced with a quality referred to as *dark*. This results from a slight elevation of the back of the tongue. It may be heard in many of the words that follow.

MEDIAL

callous	gallop	elevate	elect
heels	pooled	alike	allow
hills	pulse	align	pallid
hailed	cold	sleep	palace
held	stalled	ballad	tailor
gals	gold	elope	tilted
bells	enfold	alter	build

FINAL

deal	zeal	jail	kale
keel	tool	earl	gale
till	full	gull	ball
pale	foal	foil	guile
fell	hall	tile	eel
pal	doll	cowl	pearl
dale	roll	broil	hurl

INITIAL AND MEDIAL

lability	lollipop	literally
lively	listless	lifelong
lonely	lullaby	likely
lowly	Lillian	leaflet
lately	lilting	liability

INITIAL AND FINAL

legal	lawful	Lionel
labile	lentil	loll
lethal	labial	lisle
libel	liberal	logical
loyal	lonely	lightly

PHRASES

likely tale	lordly labor
light laughter	tile floor
lie low	cold lair
learn a lot	clanging bells
linger longer	build a wall
let live	gold and pearls
lovely lullaby	hill and dale
sleep well	mail a letter
dull tool	lower the load

held Hal	dill pickles
languish alone	pallid lady
lethal leap	logical conclusion
lonely flyer	lilting lyric

SENTENCES

1. Lillian Lawton, a lawyer known for her cold logic, specialized in libel suits.

2. Lila sang a lilting lullaby to her infant child.

3. Lou and Lisa picked flowers on the hill, close to the landfill.

4. Helen liked lentil soup, especially when prepared by Lionel.

Most of the /l/ sounds in the preceding practice material may be characterized as "light" and are produced, as indicated in the description of the sound, by tip-of-the-tongue to gum-ridge contact. Most final /l/ sounds are similarly produced but have a "darker" quality. A different kind of [l], essentially a palatalized variety, occurs when the [l] is followed immediately by a /j/ (y) sound, as in *million, billion,* and *value,* and *ball yard, Bill yearns,* and *will you.*

Initially, the same tongue-alveolar contact is made for this allophone of /l/ as for the "light" sound. However, unlike in the production of the "light" [l], the tongue blade rises toward the palatal portion of the roof of the mouth in order to produce a /j/ (y) sound.

The following sentences incorporate a palatalized [l] sound as well as the "light" and "dark" varieties.

1. William regretted his failure to make a million.

2. A billion is a thousand times a million.

3. The large lot was converted to a ball yard.

4. Leslie asked, "Bill, will you join me in billiards after you mail your letter?"

5. Although Malvina was normally a lighthearted lady, she occasionally played the role of a hellion.

/l/ Preceded by /p/ or /b/

Some persons produce an "infantile" sound in contexts in which the /l/ is immediately preceded by a /p/ or /b/. This effect is frequently a result of failure to make the tongue-tip to gum-ridge contact for /l/. A /w/-like sound is produced as a carry-over of the lip movement of the /p/ or /b/.

PRACTICE MATERIALS

For the following practice materials, avoid lip movement for the [l]. Make certain that there is a definite tongue-tip to gum-ridge contact for the sound.

| please | plume | bleed | blue |
| Pliocene | pluck | blame | blood |

pleasant	plausible	blink	bloat
play	plot	blend	bluff
plan	plunder	bland	blot
pledge	plight	black	blind

The following word pairs and sentences should help to establish a clear distinction between /l/ and /w/.

weep	leap	wade	laid
wack	lack	wit	lit
wag	lag	way	lay
wax	lacks	wear	lair
went	lent	wet	let
wick	lick	wane	lane
wad	lad	wean	lean
weak	leak	wife	life
Will	Lill	wink	link

SENTENCES

1. Bill firmly believed that some children are lacking a timely whacking.
2. A candle that lacks wax will not burn.
3. Bell joined a lay-away plan for the leap year.
4. Lona saw the moon wane when she strolled down the lane.
5. Blaine and Wayne let themselves become all wet when they strolled in the rain.

ADDITIONAL PRACTICE MATERIALS FOR /l/ IN VARIOUS CONTEXTS

lean	loom	glide	claw
lip	law	glaze	clue
lace	lock	glower	club
left	log	glimpse	cloy
lance	learn	glue	clan
glance	lunch	glutton	climb
loot	lion	clean	clutter
lose	glow	class	cluster
glen	glare	blip	blunt

PHRASES

lean and lanky	leg of lamb
grind the glass	stolen loot
clean but cluttered	claws of a lion
fell off a log	lying glances
blighted plight	lawful plot

SENTENCES

1. Lola rarely listened to her lover's lilting lyrics.
2. The melodramatic play had an implausible plot.
3. Lila dreamed of a knight with a plume and a lance.
4. Lyman hoped to lead Linda to the altar.
5. William built a pool in the middle of his lawn.
6. The gulls flew over Great Salt Lake.
7. Hal and Lou were childhood pals.
8. The politician was long on verbiage but short on lucid explanations.
9. Light laughter may be eloquent if well timed.
10. Gold was found in the hills of California.
11. Deliah planned to pilot her own plane.
12. The ballad related an unlikely tale.
13. Lillian was scolded for falling asleep in her Latin class.
14. A gold locket was lost on the lawn near the lodge.
15. Wilson was slow at leaping—especially to misleading conclusions.

SELECTIONS

1. In his *Popular Fallacies,* Charles Lamb held, "A pun is a pistol let off at the ear; not a feather to tickle the intellect."
2. The cruellest lies are often told in silence.

         —ROBERT LOUIS STEVENSON, *Virginibus Puerisque*

3. Old and young, we are all on our last journey.

         —ROBERT LOUIS STEVENSON, *Crabbed Age and Youth*

4. Glory be to God for dappled things—
For skies as couple-colored as a brindled cow;
For rose-moles all in stipple upon trout that swim.

         —GERARD MANLEY HOPKINS, *Pied Beauty*

5. I do not love thee, Doctor Fell,
The reason why I cannot tell,
But this alone I know full well;
I do not love thee, Doctor Fell.

         —THOMAS BROWN (Paraphrase of Martial)

6. Political democracy, as it exists and practically works in America, with all its threatening evils, supplies a training school for making first class men. It is life's gymnasium, not of good only, but of all.

         —WALT WHITMAN, *Democratic Vistas*

7. Charles Lamb, a prolific letter writer and essayist, was versatile and eclectic in his interests. In his *Essays of Elia,* he lamented, "The red-letter days, now become, to all intents and purposes, dead-letter days." In a letter to poet-laureate Robert Southey, Lamb acknowledged, "Anything awful makes me laugh. I misbehaved once at a funeral."

Lamb had a low opinion of people who borrowed books. He held them to be "mutilators of collections, spoilers of the symmetry of shelves, and creators of odd volumes."

Recalling his childhood days, Lamb wrote sentimentally:

I have had playmates, I have had companions,
In my days of childhood, in my joyful school days.
All, all are gone, the old familiar faces.

8. Claude Lucas, a loner but not a lonely man, held it to be folly to believe any statement with political implications until it is firmly denied. It is doubly so, Claude lamented, when the denial comes from a diplomat or a politician in a diplomat's clothing.

9. The world is a difficult world, indeed,
And people are hard to suit,
And the man who plays on the violin
Is a bore to the man with the flute.

—WALTER LEARNED, *Consolation*

10. When the lion fawns upon the lamb,
The lamb will never cease to follow him.

—WILLIAM SHAKESPEARE, *King Henry VI,* Part III

11. A light year is the distance light travels in a single solar year. Translated into meters, a light year is 5.87 million million miles.

In an address, the astronomer Frank Drake told his listeners that electrical bargains are still available. For the price of about a dime's worth of electricity, it is possible to send a ten-word telegram a full one hundred light years beyond our earth.

12. Most persons, astronomists and extraterrestrial experts included, like others to think well of them. Scientists concerned with establishing extraterrestrial communication are confronted with a dilemma. If it does become possible to confirm that there are civilizations at least as intelligent as ours in outer space, we would want to impress our extraterrestrial neighbors with the quality of our intellects, to impress them so that they would think well of our thinking. This, however, may not be possible and perhaps may even prove to be embarrassing. If we consider the intellectual trash produced daily by our radio and television commercials and by the news media, it is altogether likely that the extraterrestrial civilizations already have a discouragingly realistic picture of civilization on planet Earth; extraterrestrialists have arrived at their own conclusions about the level and quality of our intellectual life. However bleak the thought, this may explain why we have failed to receive any identifiable responses to our signals.

—[Adapted from *How Real is Real?* by Paul Watzlawick
(Vintage Books, 1977, p. 178)]

13. Since time immemorial, and probably before recorded time, pictorial representation has been the means employed to communicate in the absence of a common oral or verbal language system. Manual signing is an extension and an elaboration of pictorial representation. Interestingly, manual signing has also proved to be successful in our efforts to communicate with high-level primates, such as selected chimpanzees.

14. The Order of the Dolphins is composed of persons whose scientific interests are in extraterrestrial communications. The name of the order was chosen out of respect for dolphins and the scientists' wholesome appreciation of their intelligence and gentleness, rather than as an indication of a high level of interest in dolphin "language."

15. All human behavior is the result of the way on which one nerve cell relates to another cell in the complex circuitry of the globular, alluring, cellular mass of billions of nerve cells we refer to as the brain. This oatmeal-colored mass of multibillion cells is the last and most highly developed part of the neurological mechanism.

PRACTICE DIALOGUE FOR /l/ IN VARIOUS CONTEXTS

William's Blues

David.   William, you are a lousy lout for leaving a lovely lady like Daisy at the altar. What made you lose your zeal and cool your heels?

William.   I'm so lost and feel so blue I can't even sleep. My pledge to make Daisy my lawful wife was a heartfelt goal. Now all I have left of my pearl of a girl is a gold lock of her hair.

David.   Did you get cold feet when you saw the bridal lace and heard the wedding bells toll?

William.   Please believe me, I am not to blame! It was her blue-blooded family that foiled our plans. They are a clannish lot and thought me a social climber. They did not allow that our love was legitimate because I could not build her a palace. Daisy and I plotted to elope, but she foundered. Then I got a letter in the mail that pleaded with me to lie low for a while. I watch her play on her lawn a lot and listen to her laugh, but I know she is lost to me.

David.   Daisy is really one in a million, but her family is lethal. I apologize for blaming you. Don't languish here alone any longer, old pal. Hurl the lock of hair into the cold, still lake. Then let's fill up on cool ale. With luck, you will forget the lovely lady!

18

The Vowel-like Sound /r/

There is considerable variation in the production and pronunciation of /r/ according to context and regional practice. In regard to the latter, as we indicated earlier, some persons in the areas of eastern New England, eastern Canada, New York City, and the southern coastal states pronounce an /r/ only when it is immediately followed by a vowel, as in *reach, rise, grows, boring,* and *Marion,* and omit /r/ in other contexts. Most Americans, however, pronounce an /r/ sound whenever the letter *r* appears in the spelling of a word, regardless of whether the immediate next sound is a vowel or a consonant. The general tendency for most Americans is to produce an /r/ in words such as *cart, bargain,* and *turn* as well as in contexts such as *around, through,* and *pour it.*

We consider three varieties of /r/. Two of these call for the production of the *r* as a semivowel or vowel-like consonant. The third is a fricative and, more characteristically, a consonant sound.

Allophones of /r/ are presented in brackets [ ].

[r] As in *Rise, Rose,* and *Around*

There are two ways of producing an [r] when the sound is immediately followed by a vowel in a stressed syllable. The first method is to raise the tongue tip toward the roof of the mouth. The tongue tip may be brought close to the gum ridge, but actual contact with the gum ridge should be avoided. The tongue tip may also be flexed slightly toward the back of the mouth. Compare Figure 18–1, demonstrating production of this type of [r], with Figure 14–1, illustrating the /t/, /d/, and /l/ sounds.

The second method of articulating an [r] before a vowel in a stressed syllable more nearly approximates the production of a vowel sound. The tip of the tongue is lowered and the central portion of the tongue is raised toward the roof of the mouth about where

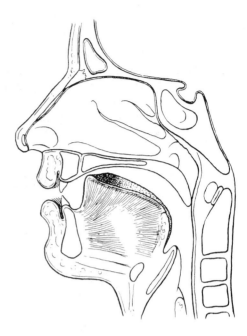

FIGURE 18–1   Articulatory adjustments for retroflex [r]. Note that the tongue tip is slightly flexed toward the back of the mouth.

the hard palate ends and the soft palate begins. This position is illustrated in Figure 18–2. For both of these varieties of [r], the sound is produced with accompanying vocal-fold vibration.

If you have no difficulty with either variety of [r], there is no need for concern or consistency about manner of production. If you have difficulty with the sound, however, and tend to produce this [r] so that the effect is much like that of /w/, then you

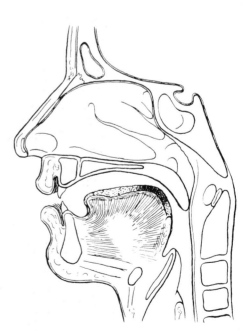

FIGURE 18–2   Articulatory adjustments for central [r]. Note the lowered front portion of the tongue and the raised central and back portions.

should analyze your efforts for tongue-tip and central [r] and try consistently to produce your best [r] sound. Experience suggests that persons who tend to confuse /w/ and /r/ usually improve by establishing and regularly using a tongue-tip [r]. Persons who tend to confuse /l/ and /r/ may do better by establishing and consistently producing a central-position [r], a variety usual in combinations or blends when the preceding sound is /k/ or /g/, as in *crease* or *great*. Whichever variety you produce, do not prolong the sound excessively and do not convert the [r] into a distorted vowel.

PRACTICE MATERIALS FOR [r] FOLLOWED BY A VOWEL

INITIAL

read	rail	room	roll
reach	rage	rude	rope
ream	red	rule	raw
rid	rest	rook	wrought
rim	rack	roof	rock
rate	rap	rote	rod
rug	rice	royal	wren
rough	rise	roam	wreck
run	rhyme	roost	roast
rout	ripe	raucous	wrangle
round	real	road	wrestle

MEDIAL (followed by a vowel)

around	erase	harangue	harass
arid	error	bearing	erode
Arabic	berate	bereave	surrogate
arable	barometer	beret	baron
arrange	barium	boron	theory
bureau	borough	oral	oracle
orange	bury	weary	thorough
orator	Orion	Byron	moron
marry	tarry	surely	purely
tarot	tearing	wiring	thereon
moral	thereabout	correct	morose

PHRASES

barium ore	Byronic oration
berate the baron	arid arroya
Arabic oracle	correct the error
orange beret	moribund bureaucrat
Oriental arrangement	eroded borough
raw rope	enraged parent
royal road	rhythmic run
raucous wrangle	rain rinse

rough rider	rudely raging
rote memory	really rugged
wrought iron	rim of brine
roam forests	run around
rice recipes	wretched aroma
rise and run	wrecked lorry
ripe berries	arose in peril

For the medial [r] followed by a consonant, check your practice and pronunciation with what is current in your community. Do you include or omit this [r]?

MEDIAL (followed by a consonant)

pierce	art	smart	mourn
fierce	part	dart	dormitory
beard	warm	swarm	wired
seared	warn	forlorn	tired
chart	farm	orphan	hired
charm	unharmed	scarf	Martha
storm	absorb	dwarf	Marvin
alarm	fork	north	York
harm	pork	forth	inform
ark	hard	ward	torn
corn	adorn	Norman	Berlin
perform	torque	armor	scorned

PHRASES

northern storm	target for darts
partly warm	pierce the pork
horse and cart	started to arm
tired and forlorn	inform the partner
orphan of the storm	harmful warts
absorbing art	charming in parts
bearded dwarf	chart the course
fierce farmer	alarmed York

For the final [r], is your practice in the omission or the inclusion of the final [r] consistent with that for medial [r] followed by a consonant? It is, for most speakers.

FINAL

dear	are	four	bother
hear	bar	more	mother
fear	car	lore	ignore
near	far	core	father
care	mar	soar	sister
dare	star	ire	tower
fair	boor	dire	shower

mare	moor	sire	paper
their	cure	sour	plumber
lair	tour	flower	summer

PHRASES

pare the pear	winter shower
hear sister	ignore brother
near the bar	tour the moor
their paper	lair for the bear
dire cure	summer flower
dear mother	four to a car

For special medial [r] words, review the discussion of the /ɜ/ (ûr) and /ɝ/ vowels (see pages 184–185).

SPECIAL MEDIAL WORDS

earn	surf	verve	surly
birth	stern	turf	curl
mirth	burn	shirt	curtain
terse	girl	girth	certain
first	whirl	nerve	lurch
nurse	heard	serve	churl
purse	hurl	spurn	yearn

PHRASES

first thirst	churned and hurled
terse girl	burned earth
curved turn	swerve with verve
earn the purse	heard in church
lurch and whirl	burst with mirth
serve the nurse	uncertain person
first spurned	hurled to the turf

Distinction Between /r/ and /w/

Persons who tend to produce /r/ so that it resembles /w/ should work to establish a clear acoustic difference between these sounds. The /r/ should be produced without lip activity and, preferably, with the tongue tip raised toward the gum ridge. The /w/ should be produced with lip movement and without front-of-the-tongue activity.

PRACTICE MATERIALS

The following materials should help to establish the distinction. Use a mirror to see what you do, and listen carefully to hear what happens with and without lip movement.

Distinguish between /r/ and /w/ in the following word pairs.

rack	wack	rill	will
reap	weep	roof	woof
read	weed	run	won
reek	week	ring	wing
red	wed	rue	woo
wren	wen	room	womb
rest	west	row	woe
rag	wag	ride	wide
rage	wage	rise	wise
rate	wait	rare	wear
rain	wane	rile	wile

Difficult [r] Combinations

Words beginning with [p] and [b] followed by [r], as in *prize* and *breeze,* may be troublesome because of the lip activity required for the first sounds. The fault is similar to the one in our previous discussion of the [l] preceded by [p] or [b].

PRACTICE MATERIALS

Avoid lip movement for the [r] as you practice with the materials that follow.

preach	praise	prude	sprawl
preen	press	prove	proud
prince	precious	probe	prow
print	prank	prone	pride
pray	prattle	prawn	price
pretty	prudent	spry	spring
breech	braise	brood	brought
breeze	breast	brew	broad
brick	break	broke	brow
bring	brain	broth	bride
bray	brash	brawn	brine
brass	abrasion	brief	upbringing

PHRASES

preen with pride	pressed for proof
preach prudence	princely prank
proved by the probe	prone to pride
praised by the press	pretty print
profound and prolific	proof of promise
broken brick	brain and brawn
brewed a broth	abrupt and brash
abrasively brief	bruised brow
bread for brunch	brother of the bride
brief brawl	brutal breach

SENTENCES

1. Brooks declared that it is easier to preach than to practice, but more productive to practice than to preach.

2. Kurt Lewin presented psychologists with the provocative assertion that there is nothing as practical as a really good theory.

3. It was frequently difficult to determine whether Brown was erudite or broadly abstruse.

4. Preston's behavior seemed to be crisp and abrupt, but his friends protested that it was probably pretense.

5. Pritchard's manners made it apparent that his abruptness was nurtured by underlying prevalent rudeness.

6. Brian Brice, who was first among referees, avoided cries of outrage among the players by presenting them with the practicing ground rules in clear writing.

7. Many laboratories for testing hearing provide sound-treated rooms for audiometric evaluations.

8. Brenda's bright laughter brought warmth to mornings that would otherwise have been gray and dreary.

9. The crude bridge crumbled under the burden of the overloaded truck.

10. Priscilla, a soprano virtuoso, performed brilliantly in a program of original lyrics.

[gr] and [kr] Blends

Some persons find the combinations [gr] and [kr], as in *green* and *cream*, somewhat difficult. If you are one of those, we suggest that you establish a central tongue [r], the second of the [r] sounds described, for the [gr] and [kr] combinations (see Figure 18–2).

PRACTICE MATERIALS FOR [gr] AND [kr]

The following materials should be of help.

cream	crest	crew	crock
creek	crept	crude	crowd
crib	cram	crow	crown
crayon	crash	croak	crime
cradle	craft	crawl	scribe
green	grew	grind	grist
greet	group	grape	grief
grin	grope	grime	grace
grit	grow	groom	grade
grate	gross	gruel	grant
grain	groan	groove	graze
grenadine	grog	grand	growl
grass	grotto	grunt	grudge
grapple	grub	grasp	gruff

PHRASES

green grass	grand grin
grind grain	prone to prattle
grunt and groan	pride in upbringing
greet Grace	crash the craft
ground grain	Cripple Creek
craved a crumb	grew grapes
green grub	greasy crock
griped about the gravy	overgrown grain

SENTENCES

1. Granger ground the organically grown grain for breakfast bread.

2. Great pride may bring greater grief.

3. The gray horse was well groomed by Bruce.

4. The green car crashed into the gray cart on Bryant Road.

5. Grayson, a practical man, came to grips with his bristly problem.

6. More than grain may be grist for a mill.

7. Brian poured the grog out of the cracked crock.

8. The wrestlers grunted and groaned as if they carried a truly mutual grudge.

9. The proud groom grinned at his prudent bride.

10. Graceful Greta pruned the blue-green grape vine.

[fr]

Another combination that causes some difficulty is [r] preceded by [f]. Practice with the following words and sentences.

frame	frappé	French	fringe
friar	freckle	fruit	from
freeze	fresh	frugal	frock
frigid	friend	fro	front
frail	fragile	froze	fry
freight	frank	frog	fraught
fraud	freedom	fritter	frown

SENTENCES

1. Freya enjoyed fresh fruit and cream frappés.

2. Fred and his French friend, François, enjoyed frogs' legs and crumbled crackers.

3. The fragile frame was shipped by air freight from France to Great Britain.

4. Freedom will survive only if it is nurtured and shared by those who are free.

5. The frantic general avoided the dangers of exposure at the front.

6. Friar Tuck was proud to be a friend of Robin Hood.

7. Frugality is no insurance against fraud.

8. The frigid weather kept everything in a deep, prolonged freeze.

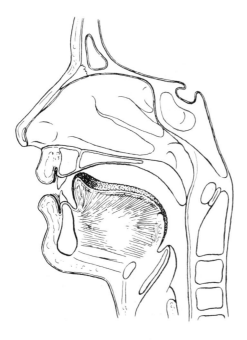

FIGURE 18–3   Tongue position for fricative [r]. Note the tongue position close to but not in contact with the upper gum ridge and the lowered position of the middle and back portions. This [r] is a postdental fricative.

[r] As in *True, Through,* and *Dry*

A third variety of [r] approximates a fricative sound in manner of production. It is articulated by placing the tip of the tongue close to but not quite touching the gum ridge. When air is forced over the tongue tip, a fricative [r] is produced (see Figure 18–3). When this variety of [r] occurs in the initial position, the sound is vocalized. When it occurs after a voiceless sound, as in *three* and *tree,* the [r] may be completely or partly unvoiced. This [r] is not as frequently produced by American speakers as the other varieties considered earlier.

This allophone of [r] is described as a postdental fricative. It is most likely to be-produced after tongue-tip consonants such as [t], [d], and [θ] (th).

PRACTICE MATERIALS

Practice with the material that follows.

treat	tread	true	trot
tree	track	troop	trouble
trip	trap	truce	trunk
trigger	trash	trout	tripe
train	tram	trophy	try
trade	transit	tropic	trowel
three	thrash	throttle	throng
thrift	through	thrush	Thrace
thrill	throne	thrall	threaten
thresh	throw	thrive	throat
thread	throb	thrombus	thrust

dream	draft	droop	dry
dread	dram	drum	drub
dray	drape	drop	drudge
dragon	Andrew	drawn	druid

PHRASES

droopy dragon	dreadful dream
drawn drapes	dreary drudge
thrifty trade	enthralled throng
three trout	trouble in transit
thrilled by the treat	thrush in the tree
thrived on tripe	tricky throttle
trips by train	dreamy trio

SENTENCES

1. The weary troops arranged a morning truce.
2. Trenton enjoyed his train trips but tried to avoid street trams.
3. The fast-running stream was noted for its trout.
4. The triple-threat athlete won several trophies.
5. Dumas observed that truth is great because fire cannot burn nor water drown it.
6. Travis and Drake declared a brief truce in their recurrent quarrels and went fishing for trout.
7. The throng cheered as the trotters raced around the track.
8. Throttle in hand, the engineer sped the train through the night.
9. A thrush built a nest in the branch of the tree.
10. Trash should not be thrown from moving trams.
11. The drum major drained every drop from the dram of cordial.
12. Andrea dreamed that her dear friend, Andrew, would become her dragon killer.
13. Druids were priests in ancient Britain.
14. The drover carried his trunk on an old dray.
15. The secret draft contained a dangerous drug.

Linking [r] and Intrusive [r]

Earlier, we discussed the regional tendencies in producing and pronouncing words in which the letter *r* is final in the spelling. The [r] in contexts such as *far away, near us, for it, for old,* and *bear it* is usually heard as a linking sound between vowels. If you listen closely to the production of the linking [r], you will note that it is produced with less vigor and is of shorter duration than the initial [r] or the medial [r] in stressed positions. Acoustically, the sound is much like the [r] in unstressed syllables, as in the words *berry, marry, carry,* and *ferry*.

Occasionally, an [r] sound is intruded where the spelling of the word does not include the letter *r*. It is most likely to be intruded in combinations such as *law and order, idea of, America, is,* and *vanilla ice*. It is apparently easier to maintain speech fluency by inserting an [r] between words when one ends and the next begins with a vowel than to produce two vowels in succession. The intrusive [r] is generally considered substandard, and its use is therefore not recommended.

PRACTICE MATERIALS

Practice with the following phrases and sentences. Read each slowly and avoid the intrusive [r].

PHRASES

law of a country	saw a sight
idea of it	Irma and Emma
Nebraska and Nevada	Stella, always Stella
Victoria is regal	China is breakable
Martha arrived	Rosa is eager

SENTENCES

1. North America and South America are in the Western Hemisphere.
2. I saw Edna order a vanilla ice cream soda.
3. Peterson liked his job as a law officer.
4. Barbara is fond of sliced banana in her breakfast cereal.
5. The idea of an essay should be apparent to an intelligent reader.
6. Grandma almost always enjoyed reading stories to her grandchildren.
7. We saw a three-act drama at the Astor Theater.
8. Nora enjoyed resting on the sofa at noon.
9. Sheriff Truman helped to establish law and order in the area of Nevada and California.
10. Rhoda always had bright ideas, but Ira avoided them.

/l/ and /r/ Contrast

Some speakers for whom English is a second language seem to have difficulty in making clear distinctions between /l/ and /r/. The phoneme /l/ is not present in some Asiatic languages, and the phoneme /r/ is absent in others. The following pairs of contrast words and phrases should help to establish the distinction between the phonemes.

PRACTICE MATERIALS

leap	reap	look	rook
leaf	reef	law	raw
lend	rend	load	road
lid	rid	lock	rock
lip	rip	lot	rot
laid	raid	low	row
lap	rap	lie	rye
lack	rack	lies	rise
lug	rug	light	right

PHRASES

lacked a rack	late for the rate
lot of rot	look for the rook
right sheds light	a load on the road
lie in the rye	a lack of a rack
a leaf of the reef	a wrap for the lap

ADDITIONAL PRACTICE MATERIALS FOR /r/ IN VARIOUS POSITIONS AND CONTEXTS

SENTENCES

1. Brown showed no gratitude when the state provided him with free room and board for four years, and he broke out of the brig.

2. O'Brien took every possible opportunity to proclaim his Irish breeding and his proud name.

3. Random thoughts are the products of free reveries.

4. The mixture we breathe called air contains approximately four parts of nitrogen to one part of oxygen.

5. The timorous groom was afraid to carry his bride across the threshold into their new and very own three-room apartment.

6. Crisp and crackly leaves inform us of summer's end.

7. Contemporary weather forecasters are much more accurate than were their predecessors a generation ago.

8. Rabies are transmitted by animals that have contracted hydrophobia.

9. Vandenburg Air Force Base has rocket-firing apparatus.

10. Thoreau for long periods lived as a recluse.

11. The crafty real-estate broker appropriated the poor widow's property when she could not meet the mortgage requirements.

12. Theories should be supported by relevant data and proved by experience.

13. In *Prue and I,* George Curtis remarked, "The pride of ancestry increases in the ratio of distance."

14. Three officers of the law arrested thirteen disturbers of the peace.

15. The right to freedom of expression is a cherished part of the American heritage.

16. Aesop warned that most persons would be sorry if their wishes were gratified.

17. In a letter to an editor, Abraham Lincoln wrote, "I go for all sharing the privileges of the government who assist in sharing its burdens."

18. Contrary to Shakespeare's view of King Richard III, some historians reveal that the brief reign of Richard was remarkable for legislation that tried to safeguard the rights of poor persons against abusive barons.

19. According to Pindar, "The best of healers is good cheer."

20. In *Oedipus Rex,* Sophocles wrote, "the greatest griefs are those we cause ourselves."

SELECTIONS

1. *Hubris* is a word derived from the Greek meaning arrogance arising from overbearing pride or from uncontrolled feelings. The term *hubris* is used to imply that it is a supercilious, graceless state of wanton arrogance that properly precedes a person's fall.

2. In his writing *Of the Training of Children*, Plutarch clearly observed that though it is certainly desirable to be well descended, the glory really belongs to our ancestors.

3. Cryptography is the study of constructing and breaking codes. When cryptography is applied to code breaking rather than code creating, it provides an example of the human search for bringing order out of an apparently random occurrence of events.

4. How was the Devil dressed?
O, he was in his Sunday's best;
His coat was red, and his breeches were blue,
And there was a hole where his tail
    Came through.

           —ROBERT SOUTHEY, *The Devil's Walk*

5. I was angry with my friend:
I told my wrath, my wrath did end.
I was angry with my foe:
I told it not, my wrath did grow.

           —WILLIAM BLAKE, *A Poison Tree*

6. Richard Rumbold's last words, according to the historian Macaulay, were "I never could believe that Providence had sent a few men into the world, ready booted and spurred to ride, and millions ready saddled and bridled to be ridden."

           —THOMAS BABINGTON MACAULAY, *History of England*

7. Omar Khayyám, expressed the poet's wish to be freed from the trials and tribulations of yesterdays and tomorrows. The poet's lines are:

Ah, my beloved, fill the cup
that clears today of past regrets
and future fears.

A more realistic versifier, without being cynical, might reply:

There is no drug, no cup, no wine
That will rid this day, this hour of time
Of yesterdays regrets, nor provide a better tomorrow
Free of its own measure, its burden of sorrow.

8. Robert Pryor was chronically perplexed with a perennial problem concerning his recalcitrant memory. "Frankly," he informed his dearest friend, Terence Bradfield, "I don't really know which is the greater of my problems: trying to remember what I forget, or trying to forget what my cerebral resources are able to remember."

Bradfield, who had a well earned reputation for practical realism, replied, "Don't worry, Richard. There is really very little that you forget that is worth your while remembering. If you learn to put your cortical cells to rest for brief periods, you will almost certainly recall what it is urgent for you not to forget.''

Pryor was not certain that he truly understood his friend's serious advice. However, Bradfield's words had such a profound ring to them that he did not inquire further about their meaning. In fact, he forgot what the problem was that he had presented to Terence Bradfield. But Robert Pryor felt better, more comfortable, almost serene, and, for reasons that he did not try to understand, considerably more secure about his tricky memory.

9. In his essay ''Masters: Portraits of Great Teachers,'' Alfred North Whitehead observed, ''There is danger in clarity—the danger of overlooking the subtleties of truth.''

10. In *The Prophet* Kahlil Gibran wrote, ''Remembrance is a form of meeting.'' Gibran also wrote, ''Forgetting is a form of freedom.''

PRACTICE DIALOGUE FOR /l/ AND /r/ CONTRAST

A Raw Deal

Buyer. Look, you tried to rook me when you sold me this throw rug. You led me to believe it was red, but in the right light, it's a wretched orange.

Rug Salesperson. That is a lot of rot. You must have a wry sense of humor to say I lied. It's clearly red.

Buyer. Buddy, I had to lug this rug on a bike that lacked a rack. I rode with it wrapped in my lap. It was a heavy load to carry up this steep road!

Rug Salesperson. I'm sorry, but you returned this rug too late to rate a refund.

Buyer. Your lies make my temper rise. There must be a law against such a raw deal!

Rug Salesperson. I won't sink so low as to row with you. Leap into a lawsuit, and we will see who reaps the rewards.

DISTINCTION BETWEEN /r/ AND /w/

The Tomblike Room

Edweena. I rue the day I let you woo me into taking this trip. This hotel room is the size of a small tomb, and I heard something woof on the roof!

Marvin. I'll ring for the clerk and ask for a room in the other wing.

Edweena. The rest of the rooms in the West End Motel are full. Let's rest a while before we become too riled.

Marvin. If the rain would wane a bit we could pack the car rack and take a whack at another motel.

Edweena. At this rate we could wait forever. This room reeks as if the window has been shut for weeks!

Marvin. It's rare for you to wear a frown while we are on an adventure. You usually bear up no matter how rare and ridiculous the circumstances.

Edweena. It is wise to rise to the occasion when you travel. The wage you pay for frustrated rage is a sleepless night.

Marvin. Tomorrow the storm will surely dry up, and we will go down to the rill and read poetry.

Edweena. All right. But tonight I will reap the rewards of rightful anger before I will myself to sleep.

19

The Velar and Palatal Sounds and the Laryngeal Fricative

The Velar Palatal Sounds /k/ and /g/

/k/ As in *Key*, *Because*, and *Luck*

/k/ is a voiceless, velar, stop sound. It is produced by raising the back of the tongue to the elevated soft palate so that a firm contact is made between these articulators (see Figure 19–1). In contexts in which the [k] is followed immediately by a vowel, air is impounded at the place of contact and suddenly and completely released when the contact is broken. The sound is then said to be aspirated.

The sound of /k/ has several representations in spelling. The most frequent include *k* as in *key*, *c* as in *cat*, *ch* as in *chasm*, *qu* as in *quick*, and one element of the sound blend (ks) represented by the letter *x* as in *fix* and *six*.

The /k/ sound must be produced with energetic action of the articulators. Persons with normal control of their articulatory organs should find the /k/ sound an easy one to make, regardless of contextual position.

Persons with weak palates and those with cleft palate, often even after repair, may have nasal emission when the /k/ is produced.

PRACTICE MATERIALS

cape	kale	come	coat
keep	could	came	cough

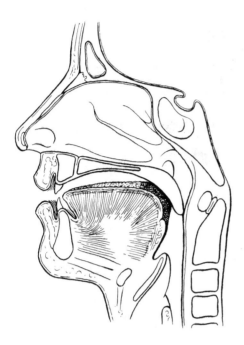

FIGURE 19–1 Articulatory adjustments for /k/ and /g/. Note the contact of the back of the tongue with the elevated soft palate.

key	coach	cap	cod
queen	cope	calf	chord
chemical	chorus	character	quash
ken	caught	cool	curb
kit	call	coop	curt
bacon	became	token	minks
beacon	because	blacken	Manx
weaken	recourse	reckon	thanks
bicker	require	booked	attacking
wicked	requite	looking	blocked
checker	enquire	turkey	boxed
ache	stake	rake	fork
beak	stork	lake	forsook
meek	talk	take	mistook
sick	Turk	back	stock
tick	spike	rack	dike
fake	amuck	hook	like
cake	cock	chaotic	kapok
kick	quack	kirk	coke
kink	cook	quirk	comic
quick	cosmic	konk	cork
coca	cockle	cocker	cackle
cockney	coconut	cocoon	cockcrow
conclude	concourse	connect	coccyx
consequence	concave	Quaker	quackery

PHRASES

keen conclusion	Manx cat
keep clam	honking turkey
keen kitten	basket of biscuits
camp cook	murky liquid
calm cow	mocked uncle
queer cat	quick kick
quaint chorus	cock crow
quiz kid	sick calf
call Kate	cook book
six knocks	thank Carl

BLENDS: **[kl]** *AND* **[kr]**

clean	class	clot	climb
cleat	clue	clergy	cloud
click	close	clerk	clown
clip	claw	club	cloister
cleanse	clod	clump	Klondike
clash	clog	clutch	clause

cream	credit	crew	crust
crease	credulous	crude	crouch
creed	crest	crow	crowd
creek	crane	crawl	crown
crib	crag	crop	crime
crisp	crack	cross	cry

PHRASES

critical crowd	clean cloth
crusty crown	clumsy clown
crude crystal	clatter and clash
crossed crop	cloistered clergy
Kris Kringle	clever clue
crackle and crunch	clippety clop
creep and crawl	cluttered closet

[ks]

leaks	rocks	makes
peaks	socks	talks
wax	bucks	mosque
attacks	fakes	extra
packs	folks	bakes

PHRASES

leaks in the dikes	picks and packs
lax folks	peaks and rocks
racks of socks	wicks and wax

SENTENCES

1. The hawks alighted on the high peaks.
2. Folks who are lax may fall into cracks.
3. Clara Burks, an architect, presented the specs for the new mosque.
4. The hikers packed extra socks into their packs.
5. Max, who lives in Bucks County, had no use for fakes or quacks.

[kt]

Note the frequent *ed* spelling as a past-tense indicator.

act	pact	cooked
peaked	snacked	hooked
racked	snaked	liked

PHRASES

mocked the pact	smoked and joked
lacked tact	cooked and stoked
whacked and decked	provoked and smacked

SENTENCES

1. At his peak, Pluncket could kick the ball wherever he liked.
2. Kathy was peaked because Kevin snacked as she worked.
3. Cranston broke the pact with Krissy when he hooked the cookies.

SENTENCES: [k] *IN VARIOUS PHONETIC CONTEXTS*

1. Much to her dislike, Katherine had to keep her collie in a kennel.
2. Kate was calmed by the ticktock of the clock.
3. The drunkard was lachrymose because his crock contained no quart of alcohol.
4. Quartz is a common mineral that occurs in crystals and is a frequent component of many rocks.
5. Carl found it calming to bask in the sun on the flat rocks.
6. The schooner carried a cargo of crackers, cookies, and kindred cakes for tykes.
7. Connie liked percolated coffee and scones for breakfast; Carl elected bacon and eggs.
8. The choir sang quaint songs in the Scottish kirk.
9. Kitson was the captain of the cruiser that carried a cargo of Turkish goods to the Congo.
10. The blackhearted cook was caught in the crowd with his basket of biscuits and a cooked turkey.

SELECTIONS

1. Themistocles, being asked whether he would rather be Achilles or Homer, said, ''Which would you rather be—a conqueror in the Olympic Games, or the crier that proclaims who are conquerors?''

—PLUTARCH, *Themistocles*

2. Nor all that heralds rake from coffin'd clay,
Nor florid prose, nor honied lies of rhyme,
Can blazon evil deeds, or consecrate a crime.
—GEORGE GORDON, LORD BYRON, *Childe Harold's Pilgrimage*

3. By the pricking of my thumbs,
Something wicked this way comes.
Open, locks,
Whoever knocks!
—WILLIAM SHAKESPEARE, *Macbeth,* Act IV

4. Harlequin without his mask is known to present a very sober countenance, and was himself, the story goes, the melancholy patient whom the Doctor advised to go and see Harlequin.
—WILLIAM MAKEPEACE THACKERAY, *The English Humorists*

5. I know the Kings of England, and I quote the fights historical,
From Marathon to Waterloo, in order categorical.
—W. S. GILBERT, *The Pirates of Penzance*

6. Edgar A. Robinson described Lincoln as a man uniquely capable of meeting rancor with laconic and cryptic humor.

7. Jack was nimble,
Jack was quick,
Yet came a cropper
Over a candlestick.

PRACTICE DIALOGUE FOR /k/

Clark the Critic

Clark the Critic. I did quite like your quirkish play *Junior's Revenge*. It crackled with crisp comic wit. The unrequited love between the key characters has a nice tragic quality.

Regina the Writer. Thanks, Clark. My agent Jack deserves the credit for the musical chorus and the cosmic conclusion.

Clark the Critic. My only critical comment is that the chaotic plot ran amuck, which weakened the story.

Regina the Writer. We booked the play in Cape Cod so we could quickly work out the kinks before taking it to Broadway.

Clark the Critic. Would it crush you if the crowd were to mock Junior and conclude that the play was a fake?

Regina the Writer. If this college crowd were to attack the play, I could cope.

Clark the Critic. How do you keep cool when your career as a playwright is at stake?

Regina the Writer. I walk down by the creek because it calms me. I try to keep my perspective, but talking like this makes my head ache. Let's walk across town to the lake, where the clean air will clear my mind. You can continue your inquiry and probe my weaknesses while I catch some haddock for dinner.

/g/ As in *Go, Forget, Aghast, Egg,* and *Rogue*

/g/, the voiced cognate of /k/, is a velar, stop sound. It is produced in the same way as the /k/, except that a less vigorous contact is required for the /g/.

/g/ is usually represented by the letter *g* or the letters *gg* in spelling; less frequently, it is represented by *gh*. The sound is also part of the consonant blend represented by the letter *x* in words such as *examine* and *exact*. The sound may occur initially, medially, or finally.

PRACTICE MATERIALS

gear	gale	gherkin	gird
geese	gape	goat	girth
gift	gaff	gall	gull
give	gap	gauze	goiter
guilt	ghoul	got	gown
guest	ghetto	guard	guide
meager	vaguely	embargo	beguile
begin	began	regard	disguise
digging	aghast	engulf	misguided
signal	again	laggard	tiger
forget	lagoon	beggar	bogus
regale	regulate	haggard	dugout
league	Hague	rogue	bug
fatigue	plague	morgue	snug
intrigue	vague	hog	shrug
dig	hag	log	dug
rig	snag	iceberg	flog
egg	fugue	erg	vogue

[g] *BLENDS:* [gl] *AND* [gr]

glean	glad	glob	mingle
glib	gland	glum	single
glisten	glass	glut	haggle
glitter	gloom	glide	tingle
glaze	gloat	glower	tangle
glen	globe	eagle	struggle
greed	grand	grope	grind
green	grass	groan	gripe
grid	grew	grow	egress
grip	groom	gross	angry
grade	group	growl	engrave
grain	groove	ground	ingrate

PHRASES

grape grower	great engraving
grin grimly	growl and gripe

glitter and glisten	grind grain
angry ingrate	glum glower
glad groom	global struggle
green grass	engrossed group
grim greeting	graph diagram
begrudging growl	grumble and grunt

[gz] IN MEDIAL
AND FINAL POSITION
(often as a plural marker −s)

leagues	nags
legs	togs
rigs	rugs
wigs	begs
rags	snags
lags	flags
lugs	exact
twigs	examine
ergs	example

PHRASES

lugs the rugs	exalted rigs
examined the rags	exert ergs of energy
exact examination	exotic wigs

Contrasting /k/ and /g/

There are two elements of contrast in the /k/ and the /g/. The first is the readily apparent element of voice that is present in the /g/ and absent in the /k/. The second is the less obvious aspect of vigor of articulation that characterizes the /k/ more than the /g/.

PRACTICE MATERIALS

cam	gam	pick	pig
cat	gat	rack	rag
kill	gill	hack	hag
cap	gap	peck	peg
coat	goat	tack	tag
coast	ghost	sack	sag
cool	ghoul	buck	bug
cull	gull	tuck	tug
cut	gut	chuck	chug
came	game	stack	stag

PHRASES

coat of goatskin	nagging backache
bagged a buck	pecked at the packed pig
calm ghost	bags on their backs

SENTENCES

1. Chuck and Kathy liked to hear the chug-chug of locomotives.
2. The half-empty sack was inclined to sag.
3. An old ghost haunted the Gold Coast.
4. Goatskin makes a crude but warm coat.
5. A tack was used to hang the rag tag on the rack.
6. A gull can cull food along a seacoast.
7. When Buck was tucked into his sleeping bag, he felt as snug as the proverbial bug in the rug.

ADDITIONAL PRACTICE MATERIALS

SENTENCES

1. Morgan, a good cook, gained a reputation for his baked goose.
2. Margo, a gourmand, was glad to be married to Morgan.
3. An embargo was placed on the cargo of sugar.
4. Greta was aghast when, in an unguarded moment, she forgot to stop for a traffic signal.
5. Gordon's luggage had an engraved name tag.
6. Despite his name, Goodfellow was a rogue whose beguiling smile ensnared the misguided.
7. Despite his hunger, the beggar would eat nothing but frogs legs.
8. The fog lingered on and grounded the planes in Gander.
9. Peg and Gilda were eager to get to the football game.
10. The gargoyle appeared to have a vague grin.

SELECTIONS

1. Here Skugg lies snug
   As a bug in a rug.

   —BEN FRANKLIN, *Letter to a Friend*

2. Algernon Charles Swinburne argued that a poet who begins no bigger than a tadpole cannot grow into anything bigger than a frog.
3. The gift of gaiety may itself be the greatest good fortune.

   —IRWIN EDMAN, in *The Bookman*

4. "All that glitters (glisters) is not gold" is a line that most English-speaking boys and girls regard as Shakespeare's. Yet, a bit of digging reveals that the "gold glitter or glisten or glister" theme is repeated in English as well as in non-English literature. Cervantes wrote, "All is not gold that glisters." From Chaucer, in his *Canterbury Tales,* we gather that "But al thyng which that shineth as the gold, Nis nat gold." Spenser in his *Fa-*

erie Queen also regretfully recalled that "Gold all is not that doth golden seem."

—Based on notes from JOHN BARTLETT, *Familiar Quotations*, 13th ed., p. 77

PRACTICE DIALOGUE FOR /g/

The Major League Game

Grant the Sportscaster. Meg, you're a great slugger! You gripped that bat and hit a ground ball that gave your team the game! Congratulations!

Meg. I just guided that grounder toward the gate and ran myself ragged. I don't mean to be glib, but what a hit.

Grant the Sportscaster. Was it a grueling struggle to achieve your goal of playing in major league baseball? Did the other guys on the team grumble and glower at you in the dugout?

Meg. At first the guys were angry that I had the gall to dig in my heels and grapple with the game. There was a lot of griping, and I got a grim greeting from them. They begrudged me every grand homer I hit and greeted my gaffs with glee. But now they're glad I hung in there and made the grade.

Grant the Sportscaster. How did your intriguing career begin?

Meg. I grew up in the ghetto, where I was grateful for a meager egg for breakfast. I was single-minded and disguised myself as a guy to make little league. I was so good that when they got a glimpse of me as a girl, they forgot the regulations and let me in the group.

Grant the Sportscaster. What advice would you give a woman who is gifted and eager to grab a little glory in the major leagues?

Meg. Don't let the growling and grunting of the players plague you. Gird up, ignore fatigue, and give it all you've got!

The Velar Nasal /ŋ/

/ŋ/ (ng) As in *Wing* and *Singer*

/ŋ/ is a velar nasal sound. It is produced, as indicated in Figure 19–2, by raising the back of the tongue so that it is in contact with the lowered soft palate while the vocal folds are in vibration. /ŋ/ is a continuant sound that is reinforced and emitted nasally. In American-English speech, the /ŋ/ occurs either medially or finally, but never initially.

The /ŋ/ is represented by the letter *n* or the letters *ng*. The sound usually occurs in words in which the letter *n* is followed by either a *k* or a *g* in the same syllable. /ŋ/ is generally not heard in standard speech in combinations where the *n* and the *g* that follows are in different syllables, as in *ingrate, congratulate,* and *engross.*

Except for possible confusion between the /n/ and the /ŋ/, there is seldom any dif-

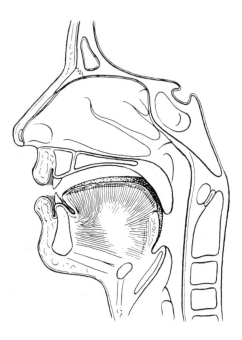

FIGURE 19–2 **Articulatory adjustments for /ŋ/ (ng). Note the relaxed (lowered) soft palate and the lowered front portion of the tongue. The back of the tongue is in contact with the soft palate.**

ficulty in the actual articulation of the velar nasal sound. There is some tendency, however, for some speakers to add either a /g/ or a /k/ following the /ŋ/, so that all words containing the velar nasal sound are pronounced either [ŋg] or [ŋk]. (In context, a [g] or [k] regularly follows an [ŋ]). This tendency may frequently be traced to the influence of a foreign dialect. A second influence may be attributed to the speaker's failure to remember the pronunciation of the particular word relative to the omission or the inclusion of the /g/ or the /k/. A third influence is a direct result of the manner of articulating the /ŋ/. If the soft palate is raised before the contact between the tongue and the palate is broken, a /k/ or a /g/ sound is produced. To avoid adding either of these sounds when only the velar nasal is required, the speaker must watch her or his articulatory timing. Specifically she or he must make certain that the back of the tongue is moved away from the soft palate before raising the soft palate to block off the entrance to the nasal passage.

To know how to produce an /ŋ/ is not enough. We must also know whether the velar nasal is to be followed by a velar stop /k/ or /g/, or by some other sound. There is, of course, only one reliable way to learn the pronunciation of a word with velar nasal consonants. The reliable way is to study each word individually, using an up-to-date, large dictionary as a pronunciation guide. A second approach of general help is to learn the so-called rules for the use of the velar consonants in English speech:

1. When a word ends with the letters *ng* or *ngue*, the pronunciation calls for the /ŋ/. Examples include *wing, rang, tongue,* and *meringue.*

2. Usually, when a suffix is added to a root word that is pronounced with the /ŋ/, the pronunciation calls for the /ŋ/. Examples include *swings, rings, singer, longing,* and *stinging.* The exceptions to this general rule include the comparative and superlative forms of the adjectives *long, young,* and *strong: longer, longest; younger, youngest;* and *stronger, strongest.* These are pronounced with [ŋg].

3. Where the letters *ng* are medial in a root word, as in *finger, tingle, hunger, an-*

gle, extinguish, and *single,* standard pronunciation calls for the use of [ŋg]. An exception is the pronunciation of *gingham* as [giŋəm].

4. In combinations in which the letter *n* is immediately followed by *k, c,* or *x* in the same syllable, the [ŋk] is used. Examples include *link, hank, bunk, distinct, anxious,* and *larynx.*

Note that not all words that include the letters *ng* in their spelling call for /ŋ/ in their pronunciation. For example, words such as *range, binge, singe, tinge,* and *longevity* are pronounced with the combination [ndʒ] rather than with either the /ŋ/ or the [ŋg].

Apply these rules to the list of words that follow.

[ŋ]	[ŋg]	[ŋk]
wing	single	link
rang	spangle	anchor
young	younger	wink
harangue	elongate	sank
evening	anger	bunk
ringing	bungalow	trinket
longing	longest	sphynx
swings	tingle	length[1]
strong	stronger	strength[1]
singing	longest	larynx

Practice to Establish a Final /ŋ/ (ng)

Speakers who tend to add a /g/ or a /k/ to words that should properly end with the /ŋ/ should be helped by contrasting the stops /g/ and /k/ with the nasal continuant /ŋ/. The stop sounds call for an abrupt stopping of the breath and frequently for the emission of a puff of air. The /ŋ/ should be produced so that the nasally emitted sound dies away gradually. At the outset, exaggerate the length of the sound so that it is prolonged to two or three times what it might be in normal conversational speech.

PRACTICE MATERIALS

In your practice with the material that follows, establish your timing and control. Prolong the /ŋ/ and continue, without stopping, to complete the phrase.

holding it	speaking up
hang on	reaching it
young once	during an evening
giving up	baking apples
swing it	exciting acts
going on	being able
teaching all	altering everything
cooking oil	telling a truth
trying on	tongue exercise
staying away	exciting events

[1] The words *length* and *strength* are acceptably pronounced with or without a [k] before the final sound.

running on	cutting up
standing up	cruising around
doing all	taking a break
letting it	sailing away

SENTENCES

1. Browning occasionally failed to see the distinction between teaching and preaching.

2. Cumming's loving husband was fond of baking and cooking.

3. Blanding explained his behavior by reminding all who observed his fooling that one can be young only once.

4. Maturing is often more painful than growing older and growing up while so doing.

5. During his childhood, young Bennington learned that telling a truth may solve as many problems as running away.

6. Waring always longed for things that past hoping did not give him.

7. A waiting throng assembled at the Long Island train station.

8. ''Long ago'' is a fond and indefinite time for recalling and reliving old dreams.

9. Young Arthur, the future king, did not know the source of his strength for pulling out the sword from the stone.

10. Baring unfortunately learned that to be smiling and beguiling is not easy for one lacking in aptitude for acting.

11. Passive observing is not satisfying for those who have a yearning for participating and acting.

12. Springer was better at haranguing others than at correcting errors of his own making.

FINAL /ŋ/

Practice the following final /ŋ/ words and then incorporate them into phrases in which each word is followed by one beginning with a vowel (e.g. *among us*).

ambling	laughing	trying	staying
among	morning	asking	rang
bang	owning	boring	swing
bring	pacing	chanting	tong
doing	putting	fading	yearning
everything	sing	gasping	zooming
fling	sting	handing	daring
hang	throng	humming	darling
king	wrong	landing	fang
long	young	moaning	amazing
mining	looming	nothing	being
seeing	yelling	flying	pretending

MEDIAL /ŋ/

The words that follow conform to Rule 2: a suffix is added to a word ending in the letters *ng*.

bearings	longs	borings	clanged
beings	mornings	fangs	endings
bringing	paintings	gaspings	firings
darlings	pronged	hanged	gangster
evenings	questionings	longing	drawings
flinging	songbird	throngs	strongly
hangmen	tracings	twangy	tongueless
kingly	wrongly	youngster	winged

SENTENCES FOR MEDIAL AND FINAL /ŋ/

1. ''Shooting the stars'' enables navigators to get their bearings when sailing.

2. Young Loring banged on the door because there was no response to his shouting and ringing.

3. Many Swiss youngsters belong to bellringer societies.

4. The mockingbird can imitate the songs of other songbirds but has no identifying song of its own.

5. The king's minstrel sang a song portending exciting events in Nottingham.

6. Billings, in a complaining but not a whining voice, asked her husband to stop rearranging the furniture without first warning her of what he was intending.

7. As a youngster, Sterling learned that telling the truth was more than a tongue exercise.

8. Topping specialized in raising longhorn cattle.

9. Ingrid Corning enjoyed teaching all she knew to her young students.

10. Livingston Channing thought his children to be darlings whenever they listened to his singing.

FINAL [n] *AND* [ŋ]

In easygoing, informal speech, many speakers use an [n] rather than [ŋ] as the last sound in words that end with *ng* in their spelling, as in *going, running, speaking,* and *eating.*[2] The same tendency holds for many southern and black-English dialect speakers in both formal and informal speech. However, most American-English speakers do make distinctions in their pronunciations of words such as *bin* and *bing, sin* and *sing,* and *run* and *rung.* The following material should help to establish the distinction between final [n] and final [ŋ] for speakers who wish to accept our recommendation to observe the difference.

---

[2] It may be of interest to note that in Elizabethan English, words spelled with final *ng* were pronounced with [n] rather than [ŋ].

ban	bang
fan	fang
kin	king
tan	tang
pan	pang
sin	sing
run	rung
stun	stung
bun	bung
win	wing
clan	clang

SENTENCES TO ESTABLISH [n] VERSUS [ŋ] DISTINCTIONS

1. Sterling rang the bell as he ran along the road.
2. Fan removed the fang from the snake.
3. Lord Baring was kin to the king.
4. Golding was the first to run up each rung of the ladder.
5. The tan fluid had no tang.
6. Starling, a fledgling stunt pilot who was determined to win, took to wing with a prayer.

[ŋg]

When the letters *ng* occur within the root of a word, the pronunciation includes [ŋg], as in *angle*.

PRACTICE MATERIALS

anger	fungus	languish	tangle
Anglican	ganglion	languor	tingle
anguish	gangly	mangle	wrangle
Bangor	hunger	mingle	distinguish
bungle	ingot	Mongol	Rangoon
Congo	jangle	mongrel	sanguine
dangle	jingle	penguin	singular
dungaree	jungle	shingle	triangle
England	kangaroo	single	linger
finger	language	spangle	elongate

The following suffix words are pronounced [ŋg] and are exceptions to the *ng* rule.

longer	stronger	younger	prolongate
longest	strongest	youngest	diphthongal

[ŋk]

The following words are pronounced with [ŋ] followed by [k].

anchor	dank	Manx	slink
ankle	drink	mink	spunk

banker	dunk	monk	tank
bankrupt	flunk	monkey	trunk
blank	frank	pink	twinkle
brink	hanker	plank	uncle
Bronx	ink	rank	lynx
bunker	jinx	rink	larynx
clink	junk	sank	pharynx
crank	lanky	sink	conquer

PRACTICE MATERIALS FOR [ŋg] AND [ŋk]

English language	Uncle Frank
singular Anglican	trunk of junk
anger and anguish	ranking banker
elongated wrangle	dunk in the tank
hungry mongrel	blink and wink
single spangle	Bronx conqueror
Congo jungle	pink mink
linger longer	larynx and pharynx
dangling dungarees	lanky Yank
mangled ganglion	slinking lynx

Although rules have been suggested for determining the pronunciation of words spelled with *ng* and *nk,* there are many words that do not conform to the rules and have current pronunciations that are a result of assimilative influences or of the influences of analogy. Thus, a word such as *hangar* is now likely to be pronounced no differently from the word *hanger* (influence of analogy); *income* is likely to be pronounced with a velar adjustment /ŋ/ rather than the alveolar /n/ (influence of assimilation). In the final analysis, if you are not certain of the pronunciation of an *ng* or *nk* word, you should check the pronunciations either by listening to other respected speakers or by consulting an "authoritative" current dictionary. It is suggested that you check the following words if you are at all uncertain about the pronunciations.

banquet	fishmonger	rancor
Binghamton	gingham	tranquil
congress	inquest	wrangler

SENTENCES FOR [ŋg] AND [ŋk]

1. Although Waring was the youngest sibling, he was more daring than Hank, the oldest and strongest brother.

2. Franklin irritated his larynx and pharynx by making throaty, angry noises.

3. Despite their natural carrying cases, it seems unlikely that kangaroos will replace donkeys for bearing our burdens.

4. Fielding wanted to become a distinguished linguist.

5. If vowels are elongated, they tend to become diphthongized.

6. Blandings had cause for agonizing while overseeing the building of his dream house.

7. Golding, a lanky New England Yankee, became an outstanding wrangler.

8. Sterling's young wife could not decide whether the trimming for her coat should be of lynx or mink.

9. Browning enjoyed dunking doughnuts and eating languidly, thinking of every meal as a banquet.

10. Bingham, emulating Lincoln, wanted to be considered a tranquil person who held no rancor.

ADDITIONAL PRACTICE MATERIALS FOR [ŋ] IN VARIOUS CONTEXTS

SENTENCES

1. The competing youngsters enjoyed singing "The Daring Young Man on the Flying Trapeze."

2. Movements of the tongue modify breath from the lungs in creating articulate speech.

3. Wilding learned that listening for longer periods than speaking was earning him a reputation for conversing.

4. After long years of waiting and striving, Browning's yearnings were rewarded by his Uncle Frank.

5. Planes flying at ever-increasing speeds are making small ponds of our oceans.

6. All morning the angry waves pounded the New England shore.

7. The word *wrangler* has distinctly different meanings in England and in the United States.

8. Loring was no stranger to angling in swift-running waters.

9. Although she was dressed in gingham, the maid from Birmingham caught the eye of the young king.

10. The bellringer needed all his strength to keep the bells clanging.

11. Many banquets are spoiled by long harangues.

12. Bob enjoyed filling his lungs with the fresh morning air before undertaking the day's chores.

SELECTIONS

1. He's a wonderful talker, who has the art of telling you nothing in a great harangue.   —MOLIÈRE, *Le Misanthrope*

2. Sad was the ending of Mike O'Day,
Who died maintaining his right of way.
His right was clear, his will was strong,
But he's just as dead as if he'd been wrong.
                    —ANONYMOUS, Epitaph (twentieth century)

3. "Nothing, so it seems to me," said the stranger, "is more beautiful than the love that has weathered the storms of life. . . . The love of the young for the young, that is the beginning of life. But the love of the old for the old, that is the beginning of—of things longer.

—JEROME K. JEROME, *The Passing of the Third Floor Back*

4. On deck beneath the awning,
    I dozing lay and yawning;
    It was the grey of dawning,
        Ere yet the sun arose;
    And above the funnel's roaring,
    And the fitful wind's deploring,
    I heard the cabin snoring
        With universal noise.

—WILLIAM MAKEPEACE THACKERAY, *The White Squall*

5. Deep into that darkness peering, long
    I stood there, wondering, fearing,
    Doubting, dreaming dreams no mortal
    Ever dared to dream before.

—EDGAR ALLAN POE, *The Raven*

6. As I went out one morning to breathe the morning air,
    I heard a dear old mother saying, "O my daughter fair,
    You better go wash them dishes and hush that flattering
        tongue,
    You know you want to marry and that you are too
        young."

—Adapted from *Lolly-Too-Dum*, American Ballad

7. A little learning is a dangerous thing;
    Drink deep, or taste not the Pierian spring.

—ALEXANDER POPE, *An Essay on Criticism*

8. A very merry, dancing, drinking,
    Laughing, quaffing, and unthinking time.

—JOHN DRYDEN, *Alexander's Feast*

9. Human beings have many reasons for feasting and eating, most having little or nothing to do with hunger or the body's continuing need for being fed.

10. A man—I let the truth out—
    Who's had almost every tooth out,
    Cannot sing as once he sung,
    When he was young as you are young,
    When he was young and lutes were strung,
    And love-lamps in the casement hung.

—WILLIAM MAKEPEACE THACKERAY, *Mrs. Katherine's Lantern*

PRACTICE DIALOGUE FOR /ŋ/

Teaching Geniuses

Painting Teacher. The young geniuses among us think nothing of staying up all evening and working on drawings or paintings. You find them going on and seldom, if ever, giving up. They are the ones you find laughing in the morning at the exhausting amount of effort it takes for their ongoing endeavors. Their yearning to see their own drawings and paintings hang in the wing of a gallery is all-consuming. Nothing will stop these young artists from attaining their goals.

Young Hopeful. Are you telling us that we never have fears of failing? All artists are given to self-questioning and entertain doubts about their talents. I have a hard time believing that a genius never fails or never feels like cutting up a drawing and flinging it into the nearest spring. There are mornings when doing a sketch and reaching for glory are frustrating when not outright boring!

Painting Teacher. Despite what I seem to be hearing, my general finding is that these amazing youngsters find painting to be an exciting art. They do spend long hours in the evening asking me if they are wrong, and often they are actively doubting everything in their thinking and attempts at creating art. But in the dawning of a new and shining morning, their negative feelings fade away. As long as the songbirds sing their hopeful songs, these young geniuses will be found working to bring us a kingdom of things that are beautiful. Teaching these youngsters is demanding, but it is also satisfying and thrilling.

PRACTICE DIALOGUE FOR [ŋg] AND [ŋk]

Tales of Uncle Frank

Uncle Frank. In the Congo jungle, I learned to play the bongos and monkeyed around in dungarees with the kangaroos.

Dinky. How did you distinguish yourself in England, Uncle Frank?

Uncle Frank. In the dank fog I tangled with a hungry lynx who hankered after the junk food in my trunk. With a single shot, I sank him.

Dinky. In Anchorage, where they speak the English language, you did more than attend banquets.

Uncle Frank. I drank until I was tranquil and watched the spunky penguins mingle in a freshwater tank. I wrangled with a fishmonger for the slinky birds and gave them to the Bronx Zoo.

Dinky. Why didn't you linger longer in Anchorage?

Uncle Frank. I'm a ranking banker who would go bankrupt if I stayed away from Bangor too long. I admit it's angering to languish away in a bank all day, ankle deep in paper and ink. Here my only challenge is to conquer the anguish of boredom.

The Palatal Glide

/j/ (y) As in *Year, Unite, Humid,* and *Argue*

/j/ (y) is a vocalized, palatal glide sound. In acoustic effect, it is vowel-like in quality because it is an unobstructed and continuant sound. /j/ glides or moves from the initial position of the vowel /i/ to a final position determined by the sound that immediately follows it. The initial articulatory position calls for the tongue to be arched toward the front of the hard palate and for the lips to be parted and retracted as though for a smile. The soft palate is raised and the vocal folds are in vibration throughout the production of the sound.

When the /j/ sound is represented by a single letter in spelling, it is by the letter *y*. In medial positions, /j/ may be represented in spelling by the letters *io, ie,* and *ia.* Frequently, however, in both initial and medial positions, there is no spelling representation for the /j/. The sound often becomes part of vowel blends, as in *unite* and *unify.*

PRACTICE MATERIALS

yield	yak	yoho	Europe
yeast	Yankee	yacht	young
yearly	you	yonder	yowl
yes	youth	yard	yucca
yen	York	yule	yesterday
yet	yawn	yearn	usual[3]
yellow	yawl	use[3]	usurp[3]
yank	yoke	unit[3]	eulogy[3]

Check your pronunciation of [hj] in the following words.

huge	humid	humility	Hugo
human	humidor	humor	humus
humane	hue	humanoid	hubris
Hubert	Hughes	hews	humerus

MEDIAL [j]

Daniel	companion	accuse	volume
genial	familiar	refuse	collier
genius	billiard	confuse	review
senior	canyon	amuse	stallion
vineyard	million	onion	beauty
lanyard	abuse	bunion	opinion
Communion	galleon	beyond	bemused

[j] (y) Preceded by an Initial Consonant

The inclusion of a /j/ after an initial consonant varies according to context and regional practice. It is optional in words such as *Tuesday, tune,* and *new* and in many other words that begin with the sounds /t/, /d/, or /n/. If there are no special influences to direct your choice, regional usage should be followed.

PRACTICE MATERIALS

/j/ is regularly included after the first consonant in the word list that immediately follows. It is optional in the second word list.

---

[3] In these words, the /j/ may be considered part of the diphthong /ju/. Other words of this type include *unite, union, Ural,* and *euphony.*

I

pure	fuel	cute	music
pupil	few	future	futile
beauty	feud	huge	fusion
muse	humane	view	mule
mute	humorous	cupid	puny

II

Tuesday	due	knew	nuisance
new	tube	nuclear	nude
tune	numerous	duke	Nubian
tuba	duty	tumult	newt
constitute	reduce	institute	gratuity
destitute	annuity	plume	restitute
induce	platitude	acumen	enduring

PHRASES

inhuman abuse	pure and beautiful
fueled the feud	view of the future
refused to be amused	humorous muse
musical tune	puny tuba player
due on Tuesday	huge institute
familiar opinions	destitute seniors

SENTENCES

1. The feud began on Tuesday over a puny gratuity.
2. Daniel's attitude indicated that he had no use for platitudes.
3. The dude took a dim view of his own future.
4. A united Europe has not yet been achieved.
5. The youth yearned for baked yams.
6. Cupid sometimes seems amused by those he seems to confuse.
7. The pack mule carried a huge load through the canyon.
8. William, a Yale student, enjoyed yesteryear's music.
9. Newton, a Yankee, enjoyed sailing his yawl.
10. Eugene, a Yorkshire millionaire, was fond of playing billiards.
11. Was Yarnell astute in refusing to believe that no news was good news?
12. The yet-to-be-completed institute was mute evidence that many were taking refuge from their duty.

SELECTIONS

1. Hugo, while still a youth, realized that it is futile to yearn for yesteryear or to take emotional or intellectual refuge in the past. All our yesteryears are continuous with the years ahead; all yesterdays constitute a prologue to the future tomorrows.

2. Yates, though not a genius, argued that in his view of the nature of things, it is the peculiar duty of human beings to endure what, individually or collectively, they cannot at a given moment cure.

3. The captain of the *Pinafore* refused to yield to the temptation to use bad or abusive language.

4. Beauty is its own excuse for being.

—RALPH WALDO EMERSON, *The Rhodora*

PRACTICE DIALOGUE FOR /j/ (y)

Beautiful Music

Danielle. How do you view your future companion?

Hugo. I yearn for a pure and beautiful muse who is unusually genial. She must be a pupil of life who approaches each new day with amusement. And you?

Danielle. I have no yen for yachts or huge annuities, but I'd love to see Europe while I'm young. I want no mute with few opinions for a companion but our arguments must not turn into feuds. I want Cupid to bring me a human being with a sense of humor and humility.

Hugo. I want someone who approaches her numerous duties cheerfully and is useful in her youth.

Danielle. I want a genius who never speaks in familiar platitudes.

Hugo. My wife's voice should be soft in volume and sound like flute music. I want someone with business acumen to invest wisely so that our yearly yield will take us to Europe annually.

Danielle. I want to be united in a love that will endure a million years!

Hugo. Would it amuse you to join me in the tumultuous institution of marriage, Danielle?

Danielle. Yes, Hugo, I yearn to assume this joyous responsibility. Will Tuesday be too late?

The Laryngeal (Glottal) Fricative

/h/ As in *He* and *Who*

The sound /h/ lacks fixed or distinctive articulatory position. The sound that immediately follows the /h/ determines the position assumed by the lips and the tongue for this usually voiceless fricative.

/h/ consists of a stream of breath made discernible by the degree of contraction and vocal-fold vibration in the larynx.

Few persons are likely to have difficulty in the actual production of the /h/. The most likely basis for difficulty is that of determining whether, despite or because of the spelling of the word, an /h/ is to be produced or omitted in the pronunciation. It may be of help to know that in American-English speech the /h/ is appropriately included chiefly before vowels in stressed syllables such as *he, hot,* and *hate.* Some speakers also include the sound in words that begin with a *wh,* as in *which* and *whale.* /h/ is usually not pronounced in medial, unstressed syllables.

In words such as *human, humid, huge,* and *humor,* some speakers blend or merge the initial [h] with the immediately following [j], so that a "new" and distinctive voiceless palatal fricative sound is produced that may be represented by the symbol [ç]. If the blending is not complete, the result may be represented by the symbols [hj], as in [hjudʒ] for *huge.* We shall accept C. K. Thomas's suggestion that "Since . . . no change in meaning is effected by the shift from [hj] to [ç], most students will prefer not to bother with the extra symbol /ç/."[4]

In words in which the [h] occurs between vowels, as in *reheat, behave,* and *behead,* the [h] may be produced with partial voicing. The IPA symbol is [ɦ].

Again, because there is no change in word meaning whether or not there is partial voicing in words such as those indicated above, we shall use the symbol /h/.

PRACTICE MATERIALS

INITIAL

he	help	hoof	harm
heed	ham	home	harsh
hit	hatch	hope	her
hilt	hoot	haughty	hurl
haste	who	halt	hurt
hate	whom	hog	heard
head	hood	hot	heart
hull	height	house	humid
hump	hide	howl	huge
hungry	hoyden	human	humor

MEDIAL (note the position in stressed syllables before vowels)

unheeded	behind	unharmed	coherent
reheat	behold	unheard	dehydrate
inhabit	inhuman	rehearse	inherit
inhale	overhaul	uphold	upheaval
behave	rehash	rehouse	prehistoric
behead	cohort	somehow	enhance
reheard	perhaps	prohibit	apprehend

The following word list should help to create awareness of the [h] for persons inclined to drop the sound in the initial position. The [h] should *not* be heard in the second member of the word pairs.

hair	air	heart	art	heal	eel
hit	it	hear	ear	hike	Ike
heal	eel	her	err	hold	old
home	ohm	haul	all	hoe	owe
hire	ire	hurl	earl	hailed	ailed

[4] *An Introduction to the Phonetics of American English,* 2nd ed. (New York: The Ronald Press Company, 1958, p. 138.)

SENTENCES

1. Henry paid little heed to heights.
2. Hazel was so hungry that she enjoyed Harry's reheated hamburger.
3. Horton and Helen enjoyed living in high mountain areas that had low humidity.
4. The hen was heard to cackle and looked haughty after she hatched her egg.
5. Hate can be inherited if it is not inhibited.
6. The hog who had a habit of entering the new house was cured as a ham.
7. Hiram's heart and his sense of humor were humane.
8. The hyena held up her head and howled to the heavens.
9. Harriet's uninhibited behavior won her a reputation as a hoyden.
10. The rehearsals for *Hamlet* were held in a house held to be haunted.
11. Arthur Schopenhauer held that hatred comes from the heart and contempt from the head.
12. Hildred happily announced that Hope had found a home in her new house.

SELECTION

Harry Helton, who lived in Soho, came from a part of London where human beings were somewhat variable about their *h*'s. Harry himself was a harried husband because he could not always make it clear whether ham was something he *ate* or something he preferred to *hate*. When you heard Harry, you could not be sure whether *honey* was what he *had* or what he would like to *add* to his butterhorns. The result was that Harry often went hungry. Unhappily, Helen, his wife, was somehow never sure whether it was time to heed Harry or to humor him. One might say, "Poor Harry, poor Helen." Yet, despite it all, they had a happy home and enjoyed their habits.

PRACTICE DIALOGUE FOR /h/

Selling Houses the Hard Way

Harry the Realtor. I hate to help people like the haughty Harpers find a house. They act as if I'm a prehistoric hunter who inhabits a cave!

Hope. Mr. Harper was hot to do a hasty overhaul of his interior so the selling price of his house would be higher. When I told him he could not hope for more, he hurled the harshest insults at me that I ever heard.

Harry the Realtor. Had I heard his harangue, I would have had his head!

Hope. I told him there was an art to putting your heart in a house and making it a home. He told me that with his money he would enhance his house to the hilt. He's a horrible human being!

Harry the Realtor. Heed my advice and don't humor him. Rehearse hard-hitting retorts and hurl them back at him. I wish I could somehow prohibit those who behave inhumanly from owning homes in Henderson Heights.

Hope. Let's not rehash our humorless day. Perhaps you would join your hungry companion for a ham sandwich. How about Hugo's? Let's be hale and hearty!

epilogue

The opening chapter presented the premise that this book is concerned with the effective use of voice and diction and therefore, in a broad sense, with enhancing oral (speech) communication. Another assumption implicit in the materials presented in each chapter is that knowledge should precede action. Accordingly, as an author, I felt obligated to share information about our language—American English—and about the mechanisms for speaking, as well as some basic content about the sound system of our language. In keeping with the assumptions, standards of speech and dialectic differences were pointed out to the student readers. I do not think that there is any doubt about my "nonprescriptive" preference for the use of an acceptable standard of speech, at least in formal situations.

Also implicit in this text is the assumption that its users were motivated to improve voice and diction and so to become in these respects effective communicators. I hope that this implicit assumption has been realized in explicit results.

Now, if the readers will consider Chapters 1 through 19 a prologue, the epilogue will be brief and in the form of a few pointed quotations.

> Mend your speech a little
> Lest you mar your fortunes.
> —WILLIAM SHAKESPEARE, *King Lear*

> Speech finely framed delighteth the ears.
> —2 Maccabees 15:39

> When you meet your friend on the roadside or in the market place, let the spirit in you move your lips and direct your tongue.
> Let the voice within your voice speak to the ear of his ear.
> —KAHLIL GIBRAN, *The Prophet*

> The music that can deepest reach,
> And cure an ill, is cordial speech.
> —RALPH WALDO EMERSON, *Merlin's Song*

Voice Improvement
Checklist

Before working on the ''Voice Improvement Checklist,'' review the section on ''Objective Self-listening'' (pages 5–7).

Breathing

  1. Is your amount of air intake adequate for your speech effort? _____

  2. Is your breathing controlled and synchronized with your speech effort? _____

  3. Is your flow of breath sustained for proper phrasing? _____

  4. Is your breath expelled between phrases? _____

  5. Is your muscular action basically abdominal-thoracic? _____ Clavicular? _____

  6. Is there any evidence of excessive tension in the larynx or throat? _____

Pitch

  1. Is your range narrow? _____ Wide? _____ Patterned (monotonous)? _____

  2. Are your changes consonant with your meanings? _____ Feelings? _____

  3. Is your habitual pitch the same or close to your optimum pitch? _____

  4. Does the major part of your speech effort occur within the optimal range? _____

5. Are your individual inflectional changes appropriate to the meanings and feelings that you intended to communicate? _____

6. Is your overall intonation suggestive of a foreign pattern? _____

Loudness

1. Is the loudness of your voice adequate for the size of your group of listeners? _____

2. Do any of your listeners have to strain to hear you? _____

3. May your voice be characterized as full? _____Thin or weak? _____ Overloud? _____ Sufficiently varied and appropriate for meanings? _____

4. Are your changes independent of your variations in pitch? _____

5. Are the changes related to the meanings you wish to emphasize? _____

Quality

1. Is your voice hypernasal? _____ Denasal? _____ Breathy? _____ Husky? _____ Guttural? _____ Hard or metallic? _____

2. Is your voice reinforced only within part of the pitch range? _____

3. Is your voice varied according to the nature of the content? _____

Rate

1. Is your overall rate too slow? _____ Too rapid? _____ Unchanging? _____ Does your rate vary according to the relative importance of the units of your message? _____

2. Is your rate too rapid for effective articulation? _____ Does your overall rate include pauses between major units of meaning to permit your listeners to "digest" your meaning? _____

Personality

1. Is the overall effect of your voice pleasing? _____

2. Does your voice reflect the person you think you are? _____ Want to be? _____

=== appendix B ===

Pronunciation and Articulation Checklist

Pronunciation

1. In your overall pronunciation, are you aware of any individual variations of vowels or diphthongs from those current in your community? _____

2. Are these variations ones you wish to maintain or modify? _____

3. Do you follow regional practices with regard to /r/? _____

4. Are you aware of any dialectal pronunciations? _____ Do you wish to maintain them? _____

Articulation

1. What sounds or sound blends need improvement:
    a. Consonants? _____
    b. Vowels? _____
    c. Diphthongs? _____

2. Do you have any tendency to slur or to overassimilate? _____

3. Are your medial nasal consonants given full value? _____

4. Do you tend to give excessive nasal "coloring" to vowels or diphthongs that are in close proximity to nasal consonants? _____

5. Do you tend to unvoice final sounds such as /z/, /ʒ/, and /dʒ/? _____

6. Is your speech in general as intelligible as you would like it to be? _____ As intelligible as that of a speaker you admire? _____

appendix C

Glossary of Terms

Abdominal breathing Breathing characterized by controlled action of the abdominal muscles.

Abduction In laryngeal action, the vocal bands (folds) pulling away from the midline.

Adduction In laryngeal action, the vocal bands drawing toward the midline for vocalization.

Affricate The blend of a stop and a fricative sound. The phonemes /tʃ/ (ch) and /dʒ/ (j) are affricates.

Allophones Members or varieties of sounds within a phoneme; the sounds that are classified as belonging to a phoneme in a given linguistic system (see *Phoneme*).

Alveolar ridge The upper gun ridge.

Amplitude Extent of range. In vocalization, the greater the amplitude of the vocal bands, the louder the voice.

Articulation The modification of the breath stream by the organs of the mouth (the lips, tongue, and palate) and the laryngeal mechanism to produce identifiable speech sounds (phonemes).

Arytenoid cartilage A pyramidshaped cartilage situated in the posterior portion of the larynx. There are two arytenoid cartilages in the larynx to which the vocal bands are attached. The movements of the arytenoids influence the position and the state of tension of the vocal bands.

Aspirate quality Breathiness that accompanies vocalization or articulation.

Assimilation The phonetic changes that take place in connected speech when one speech sound is modified as the result of a neighboring sound or sounds.

Back vowels The vowel sounds produced as a result of the action (position) of the back of the tongue.

Bilabial consonants The consonants that are produced as a result of lip-closing action that stops or diverts the flow of breath.

345

Breathiness An excess of breath that may accompany vocalization.
Buccal cavity The oral or mouth cavity.

Cavity reinforcement The building up of selected vocal tones resulting from the size and shape of the individual cavity; cavity resonance.

Central nervous system (CNS) The parts of the nervous mechanism that include the cerebrum, the cerebellum, the medulla, and the spinal cord. The CNS is responsible for the coordination, control, and regulation of responses to stimuli and thus for the establishment of patterns of behavior.

Central vowels Vowel sounds produced as a result of the action (position) of the central portion or midportion of the tongue.

Cerebellum The "little brain," a part of the Central Nervous System, situated posteriorly and under the cerebrum. The cerebellum is importantly involved in the coordination of the motor activity needed for speech production.

Cerebral cortex The gray outer covering of the cerebrum. The cortex contains billions of nerve cells. Some portions of the cortex have special functions that are significant in the understanding and the production of speech.

Clavicular breathing Breathing characterized by action of the upper part of the rib cage and the shoulders.

Cognate sounds Phonemes that are produced in the same place and with the same manner of articulation and that are differentiated by the presence or the absence of vocal-band vibration; /p/ and /b/, /t/ and /d/ are cognate sounds.

Consonants Speech sounds produced as a result of either a partial or a complete (temporary) obstruction or modification of the breath stream by the organs of articulation.

Continuant consonant A consonant sound that has duration and that is produced with the articulator in a fixed position (such as /s/ and /l/), in contrast to stop consonants that are short and that result from the interruption of the breath (such as /p/ and /g/).

Contour The pitch pattern of a unit (phrase) in speech; the intonation pattern of identifiable pitch changes from the beginning to the end of a phrase.

Cricoid cartilage The ring-shaped cartilage in the lower and back portion of the larynx. The posterior part of the cricoid serves as a base for the arytenoid cartilages.

Diacritical symbols (marks) A system of alphabet letters and a number of markings used by dictionaries to indicate phonetic values.

Dialect Variations in pronunciation, word meaning, or grammar within a language system that are identified with a geographic region or a social group. Despite variations, speakers of different dialects of a language are able to understand one another. When differences become too great for mutual intelligibility, we then have different languages derived from a common language.

Diaphragm The double, dome-shaped muscle of respiration situated between the chest and abdominal cavities.

Diction The production of speech sounds in a given linguistic code; also the selection of words within a linguistic system.

Diphthongs Vocalic glides of two vowels uttered on a single breath impulse within one syllable. The phonetic symbols of the diphthong represent the approximate initial and final sounds of the glide.

Fricative A consonant produced by forcing the stream of breath between the articulators with a resultant "noisy" sound.

Front vowels The vowels produced as a result of the action (position) of the front, or blade, of the tongue.

Fundamental pitch The pitch resulting from the frequency of vibration of the body as a whole; the lowest tone in a complex tone.

Glide sounds Sounds produced as a result of the continuous movement of the articulators. The initial position of the articulators in the production of a glide is stable. The final position of the articulators is determined by the sound that immediately follows.

Glottal Referring to sounds produced as a result of laryngeal tension and action, as by a sudden stoppage and release of breath by the vocal bands.

Glottis The opening between the vocal bands.

Habitual pitch The pitch level at which an individual most frequently initiates vocalization.

Idiolect A speaker's individual variation of a dialect. Each of us speaks in an idiolect of one or more dialects of a language.

Inflection Pitch changes that occur without interruption of phonation during the production of a syllable or word. Inflectional changes may be *downward, upward,* or *circumflex* (downward and upward or upward and downward).

International Phonetic Alphabet (IPA) A system of representing the distinctive sounds (phonemes) of a linguistic code through special visual symbols.

Intonation The pattern or contour of pitch changes for a spoken phrase or sentence (see *Contour*).

Labiodental sounds Consonants produced as a result of activity of the lip (lower) and teeth (upper); lip–teeth sounds.

Laryngeal fricative The sound /h/ made discernible as a result of laryngeal tension and vocal-fold activity.

Laryngopharynx The portion of the pharynx nearest to the larynx.

Larynx The uppermost part of the trachea; the structure that includes the vocal bands; the voice box.

Lateral consonant The sound /l/ produced as a result of the emission of vocalized breath at both sides of the tongue with the tongue tip at the gum ridge.

Lingua-alveolar consonants The consonants produced as a result of contact between the tongue tip and the gum (alveolar) ridge.

Midvowels   See *Central vowels.*
Morpheme   The most elementary semantically functional unit of a language. This may be a one-morpheme word, an affix (prefix or suffix), or a root.

Nasal cavities   The cavities in the head directly above the roof of the mouth. ✓
Nasal consonants   The speech sounds produced with nasal reinforcement. In American English these are /m/, /n/, and /ŋ/.
Nasality   The quality of voice resulting from reinforcement in the nasal cavities. ✓
Nasopharynx   The portion of the pharynx nearest the entrance to the nasal cavities; the uppermost portion of the pharynx.

Optimum pitch   The pitch level at which one can usually achieve the best vocal quality and the necessary loudness with the least expenditure of energy; the pitch level at which one can initiate the voice with the greatest ease and effectiveness.
Oral cavity   The cavity of the mouth; the buccal cavity.
Oral resonance   The reinforcement of vocal tones by the oral cavity. ✓
Oropharynx   That portion of the pharynx nearest the oral cavity; the middle portion of the pharynx.

Palatal sounds   The sounds produced as a result of activity of the middle of the tongue or the back of the tongue and the palate.
Pharynx   The cavity between the esophagus and the entrance to the nasal cavity; the throat.
Phonation   The production of voice; the vibratory activity of the vocal bands in the larynx.
Phone   A speech sound (see *Phoneme*).
Phoneme   The basic unit or sound family within a linguistic system; a group or family of closely related sounds that share distinctive acoustic characteristics; the distinctive phonetic or sound ''elements'' of a word. Phonemic differences permit us to distinguish between spoken words.
Phonetic alphabet   See *International Phonetic Alphabet.*
Pitch   The attribute of sound resulting from the frequency of vibration of the vibrating body; the attribute of auditory sensation in terms of which sounds may be ordered on a scale from high to low; our subjective reaction to frequency changes or differences.
Plosive sounds   The consonants produced by a stoppage and release of the breath stream.
Postdental sounds   The consonants produced as a result of contact between an anterior portion of the tongue and the area of the mouth behind the dental ridge.
Pronunciation   The articulation of meaningful units of speech; the combining of phonemes in meaningful contextual utterance; the utterance of appropriate sounds and the placement of stress in the production of contextual speech.

Resonance   The strengthening or building up of sound either through cavity reinforcement or through the sympathetic vibration of a body in close proximity to the source of the sound (the vibrating body); the vibratory response of a body or a cavity to a sound frequency imposed on it.

Resonators   Structures so shaped that they can reinforce selected pitch ranges of sound. The principal human resonators are the cavities of the mouth, the throat, the nose, and the larynx.

Respiration   The act of breathing. Controlled breath is the motor force for speech. Normally, we speak on controlled exhaled (expired) breath.

Stop sounds   Sounds produced by a complete closing of the breath channel.

Stress   The degree of emphasis given to a morpheme or a word by the speaker's varying the loudness, the pitch, and/or the duration within a larger utterance.

Thoracic cavity   The chest or thorax.

Thyroid cartilage   The large, shieldlike fused cartilage of the larynx.

Trachea   The cartilaginous tubelike structure between the pharynx and the bronchi; the windpipe.

Velar sounds   Sounds produced as a result of articulatory activity between the soft palate and the back of the tongue.

Velum   The soft palate.

Vocal attributes   The characteristics by which we distinguish vocal efforts: pitch, loudness, duration, and quality.

Vocal bands   Two small, tough bands, or folds, of connective, or ligamentous, tissue situated in the larynx. The vocal bands are continuous with folds of muscle tissue and are connected to cartilages in the larynx. Pulsations of the vocal bands give rise to the voice.

Vocal cords   See *Vocal bands.*

Vocal folds   See *Vocal bands.*

Voice   Tones produced as a result of action of the vocal bands and reinforced by the resonating cavities.

Voice box   See *Larynx.*

Vowels   Sounds produced as a result of articulatory action without obstruction or interference of breath; unobstructed sounds produced by changes in the size and the shape of the oral cavity and by differences in the elevation of portions of the tongue.

Windpipe   See *Trachea.*

index